GEORGE ELIOT was born Mary Ann Evans on 22 November 1819 near Nuneaton, Warwickshire, on the Arbury estate of the Newdegate family, of which her father was agent. At the age of 9 she was imbued with an intense Evangelicalism that dominated her life until she was 22. Removing to Coventry with her father in 1841, she became acquainted with the family of Charles Bray, a free-thinker, and was persuaded to translate Strauss's *The Life of Jesus* (3 vols., 1846). After her father's death in 1849, she spent six months in Geneva, reading widely. On her return she lived in London in the house of the publisher John Chapman, editing the *Westminster Review*. At the focus of many radical ideas here she met George Henry Lewes, a versatile journalist, whose marriage was irretrievably ruined but for whom divorce was impossible. In 1854 she went to Germany with him, and for twenty-four years lived openly with him as his wife. Through his encouragement at the age of 37 she began to write fiction. *Scenes of Clerical Life*, serialized in *Blackwood's Magazine*, and reprinted (1858) under the *nom de plume* George Eliot, was an instant success. *Adam Bede* (1859) became a best seller; *The Times* declared that 'its author takes rank at once among the masters of the art'. In *The Mill on the Floss* (1860), and the five novels that followed, George Eliot, with increasing skill, continued the subtle probing of human motive that leads many modern critics to regard her as the greatest novelist of the nineteenth century. Lewes's death in 1878 was a devastating blow that ended her writing career. On 6 May 1880 she married John Walter Cross, a banker twenty years her junior, and on 22 December died at 4 Cheyne Walk, London.

ROSEMARY ASHTON is Professor of English at University College London, and author of *The German Idea: Four English Writers and the Reception of German Thought 1800–1860*, *Little Germany: Exile and Asylum in Victorian England* (Oxford paperbacks) and *G. H. Lewes: A Life* (Oxford: Clarendon Press).

THE WORLD'S CLASSICS

GEORGE ELIOT

Selected Critical Writings

Edited by
ROSEMARY ASHTON

Oxford New York
OXFORD UNIVERSITY PRESS
1992

Oxford University Press, Walton Street, Oxford OX2 6DP

Oxford New York Toronto
Delhi Bombay Calcutta Madras Karachi
Petaling Jaya Singapore Hong Kong Tokyo
Nairobi Dar es Salaam Cape Town
Melbourne Auckland
and associated companies in
Berlin Ibadan

Oxford is a trade mark of Oxford University Press

Introduction, Select Bibliography. Note on the Text and Explanatory Notes
© Rosemary Ashton 1992

Chronology and Biographical Paragraph on George Eliot
© Gordon S. Haight 1981
First published as a World's Classics paperback 1992

British Library Cataloguing in Publication Data
Data available

Library of Congress Cataloging in Publication Data
Eliot, George, 1819–1880.
[Selections. 1992]
Selected critical writings / George Eliot: edited by Rosemary Ashton.
p.   cm.—(The World's classics)
Includes bibliographical references (p.   )
I. Ashton, Rosemary, 1947–   . II. Title. III. Series.
PR4653.A88   1992   824'.8—dc20   91–47169
ISBN 0-19-282886-X

Typeset by Pure Tech Corporation, Pondicherry (India)
Printed in Great Britain by
BPCC Hazells Ltd.
Aylesbury, Bucks

CONTENTS

INTRODUCTION

'SEPTEMBER 1856 made a new era in my life, for it was then I began to write Fiction.' So wrote Marian Evans in her journal on 6 December 1857 under the heading 'How I Came to Write Fiction'. The man with whom she was living, George Henry Lewes, sent the first fruits of her efforts, a story entitled 'The Sad Fortunes of the Reverend Amos Barton', to the Edinburgh publisher John Blackwood on 6 November 1856. Lewes told Blackwood that the story was 'by a friend who desired my good offices with you'.[1] Marian soon adopted the pseudonym George Eliot, but she did not reveal her identity to Blackwood until February 1858, by which time her first three stories had been published as *Scenes of Clerical Life* and she had begun her first novel, *Adam Bede*, which was to make her famous and admired overnight.

The reasons for keeping her incognito as long as possible are worth recording here because of their bearing on the emergence of George Eliot, novelist, from the translator, editor, and critic Marian Evans with whom this volume is largely concerned. First, there was the relationship with Lewes. Momentous for her personally and professionally—she more than once declared that but for his enthusiastic support she would not have gained courage to write fiction—it was a true marriage of hearts and minds, but one which did not enjoy legal or social recognition. Lewes had lived according to radical Shelleyan principles, encouraging his wife Agnes in her relationship with his friend and fellow journalist, Thornton Hunt, by whom she had four children between 1850 and 1857. When Lewes became intimate with Marian in 1853, he was already living apart from Agnes but was debarred from seeking a divorce. Lewes—no hypo-

[1] G. H. Lewes to John Blackwood, 6 Nov. 1856, *The George Eliot Letters*, ed. Gordon S. Haight, 9 vols. (New Haven, Conn., 1954–5, 1978), ii. 269. This edition is subsequently referred to in the notes as *GEL*.

crite—accepted the situation, continuing to support Agnes and all her children, Hunt's four as well as his own three, for the rest of his life.[2] But he and Marian, especially Marian, were shunned by their more conventional acquaintances, and she suffered greatly from the disapproval of old friends and particularly her brother and sisters, who broke off relations with her on hearing of the liaison. She hated her notoriety, and meant to avoid increasing it if she could.

Her second reason for using a pseudonym was not unconnected to the first. Marian Evans was extremely sensitive to praise and blame. Early on Lewes described his 'friend' to Blackwood as having a 'shy, shrinking, ambitious nature'.[3] Long after she had become famous, accepted once more by a society which gradually came to terms with the puzzling fact that its greatest 'moral' novelist was the woman living 'in sin' with Lewes, she still allowed Lewes to sift through her mail and pre-read her reviews, so that he could hide from her all nasty gossip and adverse criticism. In 'How I Came to Write Fiction', reprinted here, she reveals not only Lewes's cautious but encouraging role in her emergence as George Eliot, but also her own quick inclination to give up altogether if criticized.

Yet in September 1856 this woman, proud, diffident, and painfully sensitive to her social position, had already enjoyed for several years an independent career in literary journalism. The writer who was so tentative about beginning to write fiction first picked up her pen to do so only ten days after putting it down at the end of an essay for the *Westminister Review*, on, of all subjects, 'Silly Novels by Lady Novelists'. In this witty, aggressive, 'masculine' attack on weak novels by untalented women there is no sign of uncertainty. The writing is assured, even magisterial, in its dissection of its unfortunate victims. Take the following reflection on lady novelists of what she calls the '*oracular* species':

[2] See Rosemary Ashton, *G. H. Lewes: A Life* (Oxford, 1991).
[3] Lewes to Blackwood, 22 Nov. 1856, *GEL*, ii. 276–7.

To judge from their writings, there are certain ladies who think that an amazing ignorance, both of science and of life, is the best possible qualification for forming an opinion on the knottiest moral and speculative questions. Apparently, their recipe for solving all such difficulties is something like this: Take a woman's head, stuff it with a smattering of philosophy and literature chopped small, and with false notions of society baked hard, let it hang over a desk a few hours every day, and serve up hot in feeble English, when not required.

The author of *Adam Bede* and *Middlemarch* was herself just the opposite of such a woman. Though she was the first to insist that knowledge 'of science and of life' does not in itself qualify a woman for novel-writing—for that are needed also 'genuine observation, humour, and passion', as she notes in the same essay—she certainly had more of such knowledge than many of her contemporaries, male or female. Generally agreed to be the most intellectual of Victorian novelists, she was first the most intellectual of Victorian critics. Her knowledge covered the range of contemporary concerns in literature, art, music, philosophy, religion, science, and politics. Dealing with all these topics, her critical writings up to 1856 can be seen as direct forerunners, in style and to a remarkable degree also in content, of the novels of George Eliot.

The fame of the novels has, of course, overshadowed that of the essays and translations. But if Marian Evans had never found the courage (and the husbandly encouragement) to write novels, she would have deserved our attention as a thinker and critic of importance. The writings collected here are representative of her extraordinary mind in all its strengths: power of reasoning, knowledge of facts, European range, severity, tolerance, wit, and, above all, that quality so striking also in the novels, the power of analogy. The passage quoted above from 'Silly Novels' contains a good example of her analogical power in the discussion of the silly woman's head. Another occurs in perhaps the very best of her attacking essays, 'Evangelical Teaching: Dr Cumming' (1855):

Like the Catholic preacher who, after throwing down his cap and
apostrophizing it as Luther, turned to his audience and said, 'You
see this heretical fellow has not a word to say for himself', Dr
Cumming, having drawn his ugly portrait of the infidel, and put
arguments of a convenient quality into his mouth, finds a 'short
and easy method' of confounding this 'croaking frog'.

Such readiness to compare, to draw on her wide knowledge in order to give us a lively sense of human motives
and interactions, is the very hallmark of the novels. Mrs
Tulliver in *The Mill on the Floss* is likened, in a metaphor
characteristically drawn from the world of scientific observation, to 'a patriarchal goldfish' forever trying to swim 'in
a straight line beyond the encircling glass' in her propensity
to drive her obstinate husband to do the opposite of what
she wishes him to do.[4] Lydgate's idea of remaining unen-
gaged during his early years in Middlemarch is shown being
overborne by Rosamond's opposite idea of getting him to
propose to her, for Rosamond's idea is active, whereas
Lydgate's lies 'blind and unconcerned as a jelly-fish which
gets melted without knowing it'.[5]

For the woman who wrote the novels it was second nature
to employ her wide-ranging intellect, as well as her sharp
observation (and, as the 'dialect' novels from *Adam Bede* to
Silas Marner show, her ear for speech), humour, and passion, in evoking a fictional world. Her work as a journalist
during the decade before *Scenes of Clerical Life* prepared the
ground for the particular kind of novels she was to write.

Born Mary Ann Evans in Warwickshire in 1819, she was
brought up by her father, an estates manager, after the death
of her mother in 1836. Though Robert Evans was proud of
his clever daughter, allowing her to have lessons in German
and Italian with a tutor, he had no thoughts of her following
a career. The family belonged to the pious Evangelical wing
of the Church of England, but Mary Ann became friendly
with the family of Charles Bray, a wealthy and philanthropic
ribbon manufacturer in Coventry who professed 'modern'
views in philosophy and religion. In due course Mary Ann

[4] *The Mill on the Floss* (1860), bk i, ch. 8.
[5] *Middlemarch* (1871–2), ch. 27.

shocked her father when, under the free-thinking influence of the Brays', she refused to go to church with him. For the next seven years, until his death in 1849, she and her father lived in a state of uneasy truce. During this time her interest in the historical criticism of biblical texts led her to take over from the Brays' sister-in-law, Rufa Hennell, the task of translating David Friedrich Strauss's three-volume *Das Leben Jesu* (*The Life of Jesus*) for the radical London publisher John Chapman.

Following work done by such German scholars of the late eighteenth century as Reimarus and Eichhorn, who had subjected the Scriptures to scrutiny and in many cases rejected the supernatural elements in favour of a rationalist or naturalistic explanation of the events recorded there, Strauss took his study a step further. As Kant had applied his critical method to philosophy, finding both Descartes's idealism and Hume's scepticism unsatisfactory as systems of knowledge, so Strauss applied the critical method to biblical exegesis. The events related in the Gospels are to be read, according to Strauss, not as truly miraculous, nor as natural events which have been subsequently glossed as supernatural, but as fiction or myth. The shock of his analysis to orthodox Christians is somewhat softened by his reasonable, scholarly, painstaking method and tone:

It is not by any means that the whole history of Jesus is to be represented as mythical, but only that every part of it is to be subjected to a critical examination, to ascertain whether it have not some admixture of the mythical. The exegesis of the ancient church set out from the double presupposition: first, that the gospels contained a history, and secondly, that this history was a supernatural one. Rationalism rejected the latter of these presuppositions, but only to cling the more tenaciously to the former, maintaining that these books present unadulterated, though only natural, history. Science cannot rest satisfied with this half-measure: the other presupposition also must be relinquished, and the inquiry must first be made whether in fact, and to what extent, the ground on which we stand in the gospels is historical.[6]

[6] David Friedrich Strauss, *The Life of Jesus*, trans. Mary Ann Evans, 3 vols. (London, 1846), vol. i, ix–x (Preface to First German Edition). For George Eliot and Strauss, see E. S. Shaffer, '*Kubla Khan' and The Fall of*

Strauss takes each event of Christ's life recorded in the
Gospels, examining it from the supernatural, the natural,
and the mythical point of view, in order to demonstrate the
superiority of the mythical interpretation. The extract published here of this—George Eliot's first published work—is
taken from the Introduction and is illustrative of Strauss's
method throughout the book.

The labour of translating three volumes of such detailed
critical writing was immense, but Mary Ann completed her
unsung (and virtually unpaid) task with only a little grum-
bling. Her letters to Mrs Bray's sister Sara Hennell show
how seriously she studied the subject and how concerned
she was to translate correctly, in spite of there being 'not
even the devil's wages for a translator—profit and fame'.[7]

A letter to Charles Bray of October 1846, shortly after
the translation was published anonymously by Chapman,
shows that, serious and scholarly young woman though she
was, she already commanded wit and narrative talent. It is
a spoof account, reprinted here, of a visit from a German
professor seeking as a wife a person who will translate his
five-volume commentary on the Book of Tobit and other
great philosophical works. With humorous self-deprecation
she describes how the professor, desiring that his wife
should also be decidedly ugly, has naturally fixed his attention on her. An uncanny forecast of her own later life and
writing occurs when she tells Bray that she has accepted
this forerunner of Dorothea's Mr Casaubon, and will 'on
Wednesday next' become 'the Professorin and wend my way
with my tocher [dowry] and my husband to Germany'.[8]

Mary Ann's next pieces of work were, like the Strauss, a
direct result of her friendship with Bray. In June 1846 he

*Jerusalem: The Mythological School in Biblical Criticism and Secular Literature
1770–1880* (Cambridge, 1975) and Rosemary Ashton, *The German Idea:
Four English Writers and the Reception of German Thought 1800–1860* (Cambridge, 1980).

[7] George Eliot to Sara Hennell, Apr. 1846, *GEL*, i, 215. She was paid
£20 for the translation, see Gordon S. Haight, *George Eliot: A Biography*
(Oxford, 1969), 59 (subsequently referred to in the notes as *GE*).

[8] George Eliot to Charles Bray, 21 Oct. 1846, *GEL*, viii. 14–15.

became owner of the weekly *Coventry Herald and Observer*, for which she wrote her first brief essays and reviews. The most interesting of these is her article on J. A. Froude's novel about a clergyman's loss of faith, *The Nemesis of Faith* (1849). Though short, the review merits attention for the intellectual fellow-feeling shown towards Froude, who resigned his fellowship at Exeter College, Oxford, when the novel—obviously autobiographical—was published.[9] Some of Mary Ann's turns of phrase in this essay are noticeably Carlylean—'Much there is in the work of a questionable character', for example—as indeed also is much in Froude's novel itself. For Carlyle was a kind of secular guru for those young people, of whom Froude and Mary Ann Evans were but two, who had become sceptical of church dogma. In her short essay on Carlyle (1855), also included in this volume, she declares that there is 'hardly a superior or active mind of this generation that has not been modified by Carlyle's writings', particularly *Sartor Resartus* with its charting of a mind's voyage from scepticism ('The Everlasting No'), via indifference to 'The Everlasting Yea', an assertion of belief in what Carlyle calls 'natural supernaturalism'.

In her joke letter to Bray Mary Ann had called herself a 'strong-minded woman'. After her father's death, having recuperated briefly in Geneva, she became just that. Rather than return to Warwickshire to live alone or with one of her married siblings, she took the brave decision to pursue an independent career in London. Her father had left her a small annuity, but it needed supplementing. Now calling herself Marian Evans, she found lodgings with John Chapman, the friend of Bray and publisher of her Strauss translation, at 142 Strand, where he had his business and also his home. She soon became his assistant and, probably, for a short time his mistress as well. (Chapman had a wife and live-in mistress who joined forces in attacking the

[9] See J. A. Froude, *The Nemesis of Faith* (London, 1849; reprinted by Libris Press with an introduction by Rosemary Ashton, 1988).

newcomer in 1851.[10]) A fellow lodger, William Hale White, remembered this remarkable woman, 'not a this or a that or the other',[11] not, in fact, at all classifiable in the usual way:

She was one of the most sceptical, unusual creatures I ever knew . . . I can see her now, with her hair over her shoulders, the easy chair half sideways to the fire, her feet over the arms, and a proof in her hands, in that dark room at the back of No. 142... [12]

The first work she got through Chapman on arrival in London in 1851 was an article for the *Westminster Review* on R. W. Mackay's *The Progress of the Intellect, as Exemplified in the Religious Development of the Greeks and Hebrews* (1850). Well equipped by her reading and experience as translator of Strauss, with whose views Mackay agreed, Marian produced a careful, largely favourable review of Mackay's account of the history of religion and its roots in myth. In this essay, her first full-length article and her first of many distinguished contributions to the *Westminster Review*, she airs her belief in the moral and physical laws governing 'the education of the race'. She draws an analogy with geology: 'A correct generalization gives significance to the smallest detail, just as the great inductions of geology demonstrate in every pebble the working of laws by which the earth has become adapted for the habitation of men.' The article shows her acquaintance with the influential work of Sir Charles Lyell, *Principles of Geology* (1830–3), which favours uniformity in natural processes in opposition to the more widely held view of catastrophic changes as an explanation for the present state of the earth's crust. In this essay, too, she first alludes to the positivist philosopher Auguste Comte, who analysed human society and the branches of human knowledge in terms of a process involving

[10] For accounts of Chapman's household and George Eliot's place in it, see *GE*, 81–8, and Gordon S. Haight, *George Eliot and John Chapman* (New Haven, Conn., 1940).
[11] William Hale White, *The Autobiography of Mark Rutherford* (London, 1881; reprinted by Libris Press with an introduction by Don Cupitt, 1988), 110.
[12] *Athenaeum*, No. 3031 (28 Nov. 1885), 702.

three historical stages: the theological, the metaphysical, and the modern 'scientific' stage, which Comte called the positive.[13]

In 1851 the *Westminster Review* was owned by William Hickson, but during the course of the year Chapman bought it, hoping to make it once again the great organ of radical, reforming opinion it had been when Jeremy Bentham and James Mill founded it in 1824 in opposition to the Whig *Edinburgh Review* and the Tory *Quarterly Review*. Thanks mainly to Marian Evans, who edited the *Review* for Chapman in return for board and lodging, that is exactly what happened. During the 1850s the *Westminster* carried authoritative essays by liberal writers on all the important subjects of the day. The social philosopher Herbert Spencer (a kind of English Comte) was a contributor, as was his friend Lewes, who wrote on English and European literature. T. H. Huxley was the chief reviewer of scientific works. And Marian Evans was responsible for keeping Chapman— careless and liable to alienate the writers he sought to attract—under control.

From 1852 Marian wrote no more review essays for the *Westminster* until after she and Lewes (to whom she was introduced by Chapman in October 1851) had gone to Germany in 1854. She was too busy persuading Chapman's other reviewers, and cutting and correcting their work when it came into the editorial office, to do more than one or two short reviews herself during these two years. The behind-the-scenes editorial work suited her admirably. She was at the centre of free-thinking, radical, London journalism, often the only woman at Chapman's meetings and parties, yet she was able to work anonymously and so avoid notoriety.

The unusualness of Marian Evans's social position in the early 1850s can scarcely be exaggerated. When in May 1852 Chapman held a meeting of authors to attack price-fixing by the Booksellers' Association, everyone was there:

[13] For George Eliot and Comte, see W. M. Simon, *European Positivism in the Nineteenth Century* (Ithaca, NY, 1963) and T. R. Wright, *The Religion of Humanity: The Impact of Comtean Positivism on Victorian Britain* (Cambridge, 1986).

·Spencer, Lewes, Dickens, Wilkie Collins, F. W. Newman, Richard Owen, the inventor Charles Babbage—and Marian Evans. Bessie Rayner Parkes, daughter of the radical MP Joseph Parkes (who had paid the costs of Marian's translation of Strauss) recalled a dinner party held at her parents' London house at this time. Marian Evans 'used to wear black velvet, then seldom adopted by unmarried ladies . . . I can see her descending the great staircase of our house in Savile Row . . . on my father's arm, the only lady, except for my mother, among the group of remarkable men, politicians, and authors of the first literary rank.'[14] The figure she cut in London's radical circles was thus characteristically at once prominent and retiring.

Everything she had written to date—the Strauss, her reviews for Bray, her work on the *Westminster Review*—had been anonymous. Oddly, the one work to be published with her own name on the title-page was the translation of Ludwig Feuerbach's *Das Wesen des Christenthums* (*The Essence of Christianity*), which appeared at the very moment she became Lewes's 'wife', taking for herself the name Marian Evans Lewes.

The translation, for which Marian was promised £30 by Chapman, but which in the end she wrote for nothing in consideration of his dire financial troubles in 1853–4,[15] was much less onerous than the Strauss. Feuerbach's work, in one volume, is written in a lively, at times even rhapsodic, style. Though based on scholarship and research in the school of Strauss, it is not in the least forbidding or arcane. Marian sometimes objected to Feuerbach's phraseology, but she told Sara Hennell that she agreed entirely with his ideas.[16]

Feuerbach's contribution to the history of religion was to discuss religious belief in terms of men's psychological need

[14] See George Eliot to Charles and Cara Bray, 5 May 1852, *GEL*, ii. 23–5, and Bessie Rayner Parkes Belloc, *In a Walled Garden* (London, 1895; reprinted 1900), 17.

[15] See George Eliot to Sara Hennell, 25 Nov. 1853, and to John Chapman, 2 Dec. 1853, *GEL*, ii. 127–8, 130–1.

[16] George Eliot to Sara Hennell, 29 Apr. 1854, ibid. 153.

to posit perfection and then worship it under the name God. Taking religion boldly into the realms of anthropology and psychology, he reads Christianity as an essentially human phenomenon: 'The essence of Christianity is the essence of human feeling'; 'Man, by means of the imagination, involuntarily contemplates his inner nature; he represents it as out of himself'; 'the consciousness of God is nothing else than the consciousness of the species'; '*Homo homini Deus est*'.[17] Such ideas fitted absolutely with Marian Evans's; together with Carlyle's and Comte's writings, they seemed to solve the problem of belief. Those who had given up believing in a transcendent God and in Christian dogma could retain their sense of moral equilibrium, and even something of the enthusiasm and wonder which accompanies religious faith, by adopting a belief in the 'religion of humanity'.

In her devastating essay on Dr Cumming's narrow Evangelicalism, with its emphasis on faith and its intolerance of those outside its ranks, Marian Evans echoes Feuerbach:

The idea of God is really moral in its influence—it really cherishes all that is best and loveliest in man—only when God is contemplated as sympathizing with the pure elements of human feeling, as possessing infinitely all those attributes which we recognize to be moral in humanity.

Let people continue to believe in God, if they wish; but let them believe in a God who sets them an example to follow in their relations with their fellow human beings. George Eliot's novels are full of cases where one person helps another out of purely human sympathy; that some of these are clergymen—Mr Tryan in 'Janet's Repentance', Dr Kenn in *The Mill on the Floss*, or Mr Farebrother in *Middlemarch*—only serves to underline her views, for their help is described in human, not specifically religious, terms.

Indeed, *Scenes of Clerical Life*, despite its title, is imbued with Feuerbachian language. Here George Eliot took up the

[17] Ludwig Feuerbach, *The Essence of Christianity*, trans. Marian Evans (London, 1854; reprinted by Harper Torch with an introduction by Karl Barth, New York, 1957), 140, 153, 208, 270, 271.

challenge she had herself thrown down in 'Silly Novels'—to represent life among Evangelical Christians in its real, human aspect. The narrator of the third story, 'Janet's Repentance', sounds uncannily like Feuerbach: 'The first condition of human goodness is something to love; the second, something to reverence'; 'Blessed influence of one true loving soul on another!'[18] In her subsequent fiction George Eliot's method is more sophisticated and aesthetically persuasive; she lets such views emerge through the action and conversations of her characters themselves. But everywhere, from her first to her last book, she demonstrates the drama of human lives in Feuerbachian terms.

For one who was planning in 1853–4 to court social ostracism by living with Lewes, Feuerbach also offered timely moral support. In the 'Concluding Application' of his work, the greater part of which is reproduced here, he describes marriage as 'the free bond of love', as 'sacred in itself, by the very nature of the union which is therein effected', regardless of the laws of Church and State. Marian set off for Germany with her 'husband' (but no dowry), leaving behind a society agog with the news of the liaison between 'blackguard Lewes' and the 'strong-minded woman' of the *Westminster Review*,[19] but conscious of no intellectual or moral reason why she should not take this momentous step.

During her eight months in Weimar and Berlin, Marian helped Lewes with his research for the *Life of Goethe* and translated another philosophical work, the *Ethics* of Spinoza. Unfortunately, this translation remained unpublished in her lifetime, as Lewes argued with the publisher Bohn, with whom he thought he had an agreement for a translation (which Lewes originally intended to do himself), and could not find another publisher willing to take it on.[20]

---

[18] *Scenes of Clerical Life* (1858), chs. 10, 19.
[19] See *GE*, 160.
[20] Ibid. 199–200. For George Eliot and Spinoza, see Rosemary Ashton, *The German Idea*, 155–9. George Eliot's translation has recently been published (in the series Salzburg Studies in English Literature), ed. Thomas Deegan (Salzburg, 1981).

Spinoza was at least as strong an influence on her thinking as Feuerbach, of whom he was an eminent predecessor. In a series of axioms and propositions built up in strictly logical sequence, the seventeenth-century thinker seeks to define ethics in terms of the individual's attempts to control his passions by applying reasoning to them: 'An emotion which is a passion, ceases to be a passion, as soon as we form a clear and distinct idea of it'. Self-interest is accepted as man's motive force; but equally important is his sense of fellow-feeling, his ability to sympathize with another human being and thus to render his self-love truly social. Egotism is inevitable, but altruism is possible and desirable. This Spinozistic view (also influential on Comte) permeates George Eliot's novels.

The Spinozan language of 'clear ideas', of sympathy with one's fellows because of their shared humanity, however erring and unattractive they may be, is particularly evident in *Middlemarch*. There Dorothea struggles through her mistakes to a clarity of vision in her relations with her disappointing husband; and the narrator himself asks the reader to extend his/her sympathy to the dry, egotistical Casaubon, on the grounds that even he 'had an intense consciousness within him, and was spiritually a-hungered like the rest of us'.[21] A brief extract from the final part of the *Ethics* translation is reprinted in this volume.

The first journalistic work Marian undertook on her arrival in Weimar in August 1854 was an article for Chapman on 'Woman in France'. It is not her best essay, being often rather lofty in tone and containing long extracts from the work ostensibly under review, Victor Cousin's study of French women in the seventeenth century, particularly Madame de Sablé. But even here she occasionally shows her propensity to range, to view history through a wide-angled lens. The following passage has the peculiar mixture of tolerance and sharpness which distinguishes the novels:

No wise person, we imagine, wishes to restore the social condition of France in the seventeenth century, or considers the ideal

[21] *Middlemarch*, ch. 29.

programme of woman's life to be a *mariage de convenance* at fifteen, a career of gallantry from twenty to eight-and-thirty, and penitence and piety for the rest of her days. Nevertheless, that social condition had its good results, as much as the madly-superstitious Crusades had theirs.

The essay is interesting, too, as an expression of her views on the position of women, a subject which has been much commented on by recent feminist critics, most of whom either claim her rather sweepingly for the feminist cause or chide her for her timidity in not taking up the cause whole-heartedly.[22] George Eliot's views are certainly complex and sometimes contradictory, yet they are at the same time utterly consistent with what we have already observed about her attitudes and behaviour.

Having taken the strong-minded woman's course by openly living with Lewes—and so adding to those other rebellious actions of her life, displeasing her father by giving up religion and confounding convention by moving to London to live by her pen—Marian had laid herself open to charges of complete unorthodoxy. Yet, as she often insisted, and as emerges clearly from a reading of her essays and novels, her mind was of a conservative, or at least a conserving, tendency. Writing to Clifford Allbutt in 1868 about her desire to help her readers to a 'clearer conception and a more active admiration of those vital elements which bind men together' without recourse to 'the more transient forms on which an outworn teaching [i.e. Christianity] tends to make them dependent', she adds:

But, since you have read my books, you must perceive that the bent of my mind is conservative rather than destructive, and that denial has been wrung from me by hard experience—not adopted as a pleasant rebellion.[23]

---

[22] An example of the former tendency is Sandra M. Gilbert and Susan Gubar, *The Madwoman in the Attic: The Woman Writer and the Nineteenth-Century Literary Imagination* (New Haven, Conn., 1979), and of the latter Elaine Showalter, *A Literature of Their Own: British Women Novelists from Brontë to Lessing* (Princeton, NJ, 1977).

[23] George Eliot to Clifford Allbutt, Aug. 1868, *GEL*, iv. 472.

Her tolerant, 'conservative' attitude towards the religious beliefs she had rejected is evident also in her utterances on the role of women in society. Here, too, her thinking was bold, but not altogether iconoclastic. She was in favour of education and 'culture' for women—how could she not be? But in 'Woman in France', and in another article in which she directly addressed the 'woman question', 'Margaret Fuller and Mary Wollstonecraft' (1855), she stressed the different functions of the sexes. Comte's view of the softening role of women in society may well have coloured hers; in 'Woman in France' she writes:

Under every imaginable social condition, she will necessarily have a class of sensations and emotions—the maternal ones—which must remain unknown to man; and the fact of her comparative physical weakness, which, however it may have been exaggerated by a vicious civilization, can never be cancelled, introduces a distinctively feminine condition into the wondrous chemistry of the affections and sentiments, which inevitably gives rise to distinctive forms and combinations.

In 'Margaret Fuller and Mary Wollstonecraft' she argues wittily that it is in men's interests—the anonymous voice she adopts in these articles is consciously male—to encourage the education of women, so that they may become fit mates for thinking men:

There is a notion commonly entertained among men that an instructed woman, capable of having opinions, is likely to prove an impracticable yoke-fellow, always pulling one way when her husband wants to go the other, oracular in tone, and prone to give curtain lectures on metaphysics. But surely, so far as obstinacy is concerned, your unreasoning animal is the most unmanageable of creatures, where you are not allowed to settle the question by a cudgel, a whip and bridle, or even a string to the leg.

Rosamond Vincy in *Middlemarch* is the creature of George Eliot's imagination who most nearly embodies such an 'unreasoning animal'. With her narrow notions of a woman's role and her unimaginative expectation of a husband's duties towards her, she is shown to be the weaker vessel, but she nevertheless triumphs over her husband by her very refusal, or inability, to understand his point of view. Using the same metaphor as in the essay written nearly twenty years before, George Eliot writes: 'Lydgate was bowing his neck under the yoke', while Rosamond 'no more identified herself with him than if they had been creatures of different species and opposing interests'.[24]

Most of the novels address the woman problem through the plot as it relates to the heroine. Maggie in *The Mill on the Floss* is cleverer than her brother, who receives the classical education for which she has the aptitude he lacks. Maggie is full of complaints about her lot, and George Eliot obviously endorses her frustration. But the specific issue of education remains unresolved, as the plot moves away during the course of the novel to other concerns (though these still have to do with the unfairness of society's attitudes to women).[25] Dorothea's lack of opportunities is more fully aired in *Middlemarch*. The Prelude states baldly that 'no epic life' is possible for this modern St Theresa, 'foundress of nothing'. But the Finale balances precariously between expressions of regret that a woman of such potential has been reduced by her social position to being 'absorbed into the life of another', known only as a wife and mother, and more positive claims for Dorothea's influence, as Will Ladislaw's wife and helpmate, on the lives of others. The final sentence strikes a melancholy-optimistic note, offering only partial comfort to those looking for feminism in the novel:

But the effect of her being on those around her was incalculably diffusive: for the growing good of the world is partly dependent on unhistoric acts; and that things are not so ill with you and me as they might have been, is half owing to the number who lived faithfully a hidden life, and rest in unvisited tombs.

In letters to friends and to campaigners for women's education and women's suffrage George Eliot was equally cautious. She found it easier to give her unqualified support to Barbara Bodichon and Emily Davies, founders of Girton

---

[24] *Middlemarch*, ch. 58.
[25] See Rosemary Ashton, *The Mill on the Floss: A Natural History* (Boston, 1990), 94–103.

College, than she did to espouse openly the cause of political and social equality for women. Her remark to Charles Bray in 1857 is typical:

'Conscience goes to the hammering in of nails' is my Gospel. There can be no harm in preaching *that* to women, at any rate. But I should be sorry to undertake any more specific enunciation of doctrine on a question so entangled as the 'Woman Question'. The part of the Epicurean gods is always an easy one; but because I prefer it so strongly myself, I the more highly venerate those who are struggling in the thick of the contest.[26]

Though she was herself no 'mere' wife and mother (she and Lewes decided not to have children because of their anomalous marital situation), she often returned to the position that woman's special function was the maternal one. It is impossible to discount her sensitivity about her own peculiar position when considering her responses on this subject; on the other hand, it is also impossible to be sure that she would have been an unequivocal feminist had she not been, in this respect, a reluctant rebel and outcast. That she was herself acutely aware of this difficulty is clear from her reply in 1867 to John Morley, a supporter of J. S. Mill's proposed amendment to the Reform Bill which would have given women the vote. She disappointed Morley by declaring that 'there is a basis for a sublimer resignation in woman and a more regenerating tenderness in man', adding, 'the peculiarities of my own lot may have caused me to have idiosyncrasies rather than an average judgement'.[27]

Rather as she did in her early articles on the subject, George Eliot in her later years fell back on the argument that while women 'ought to have the same fund of truth placed within their reach as men have', the main reason for urging this was that they could then exercise an appropriate influence on, and be useful partners to, men. Besides, as she argued in 1869, a year before the Education Act stipulated compulsory education for all, 'we are very far from

---

[26] George Eliot to Charles Bray, 30 Oct. 1857, *GEL*, ii. 396.
[27] George Eliot to John Morley, 14 May 1867, ibid. viii. 402.

having found a perfect plan for educating men, let alone women'.[28]

This balancing of social and political concerns, particularly with reference to the relationship between the sexes, was characteristic. The article 'Woman in France' ends as follows:

Let the whole field of reality be laid open to woman as well as to man, and then that which is peculiar in her mental modification, instead of being, as it is now, a source of discord and repulsion between the sexes, will be found to be a necessary complement to the truth and beauty of life. Then we shall have that marriage of minds which alone can blend all the hues of thought and feeling in one lovely rainbow of promise for the harvest of human happiness.

Apt words from the woman living in harmony with Lewes, accepted socially in Germany as she was not, alas, to be on her return to England in March 1855, working on Spinoza, and helping Lewes with his translation of extracts for the *Life of Goethe*.

Not surprisingly, Marian's journalism immediately after their return from Germany often had a German subject. One of two articles she wrote for *Fraser's Magazine*, 'Liszt, Wagner, and Weimar' (July 1855), is reprinted here. Though much of it consists of a paraphrase of an article by Liszt, whom she met in Weimar, it has its interest as a statement of cautious welcome to the 'new music' of Wagner. As usual, the range of reference is impressively large, and Marian characteristically excuses her inability to appreciate Wagner's music fully by recourse to a biological analogy. Yearning for melody, she acknowledges that it may be

only a transitory phase of music, and that the musicians of the future may read the airs of Mozart and Beethoven and Rossini as scholars read the *Stabreim* [alliteration] and assonance of early poetry. We are but in 'the morning of the times', and must learn to think of ourselves as tadpoles unprescient of the future frog.

Two short articles on German subjects appeared in July 1855 in the *Leader*, the radical weekly newspaper which

[28] George Eliot to Mrs Nassau Senior, 4 Oct. 1869, ibid. v. 58.

Lewes had co-founded with Thornton Hunt in 1850. These articles illustrate how closely related in her mind were matters of literary and philosophical interest. In 'The Future of German Philosophy' she welcomes Otto Friedrich Gruppe's breaking away from the predominant school of German philosophy, the Hegelian 'system-mongers', 'spinners of elaborate cocoons', who disdain common sense and observation. Like Lewes, who had attacked Hegelianism and all *a priori* reasoning (i.e. reasoning independent of the experience of the senses) in favour of empiricism in his *Biographical History of Philosophy* (1845-6), she applauds the philosopher who 'renounces the attempt to climb to heaven by the rainbow bridge of "the high *priori* road", and is content humbly to use his muscles in treading the uphill *a posteriori* path which will lead, not indeed to heaven, but to an eminence whence we may see very bright and blessed things on earth'.

In the other essay for the *Leader* of July 1855, 'The Morality of *Wilhelm Meister*', the thinking is much the same. Written as a kind of trailer for Lewes's *Life of Goethe*, to be published the following November, it undertakes a robust defence of Goethe's notorious novel against the usual charge of immorality. What Goethe does, she writes, is to give us pictures of life without idealizing them; he 'quietly follows the stream of fact and of life; and waits patiently for the moral processes of nature as we all do for her material processes'. The vocabulary here recalls her insistence in 'The Progress of the Intellect' on the existence of 'undeviating law in the material and moral world'.

So well versed was Marian Evans in contemporary scientific thinking—for she knew the work of Lyell, Chambers, and Comte, and Lewes was, after all, a keen naturalist and physiologist[29]—that its language came easily to her. When Darwin's *Origin of Species* appeared late in 1859, she welcomed it as 'an elaborate exposition of the evidence in favour

---

[29] Lewes published several scientific works: *Sea-Side Studies* (1858), *The Physiology of Common Life*, 2 vols. (1859-60), *Studies in Animal Life* (1862), and *Problems of Life and Mind*, 5 vols. (1874-9).

of the Development Theory' which would help the world
get on 'step by step towards brave clearness and honesty'.[30]
The novel she was writing throughout 1859, *The Mill on
the Floss*, was, as we have seen, steeped in scientific metaphors for human progress (and also for tragic waste). It was
for his complex 'truth to nature' that she appreciated
Goethe, who had himself been an amateur scientist of talent
and enthusiasm.

Instead of punishing the wicked and rewarding the good
in his novel, Goethe allows some immorality to flourish,
while also subtly mixing good and bad qualities in his
characters. 'The line between the virtuous and the vicious',
writes Marian in her article, 'so far from being a necessary
safeguard to morality, is itself an immoral fiction.' It is a
bold plea for realism in art, on quite sophisticated grounds.
The tolerance which she shows towards Goethe's own 'large
tolerance' here is a foretaste of her authorial voice in the
novels. Though as George Eliot she was to intrude in a way
Goethe does not in order to persuade her readers to share
her view, she nevertheless shows a similar boldness,
grounded in accurate observation of life, to that which she
here identifies in Goethe. In *The Mill on the Floss* in
particular (which also 'borrows' its denouement, the boat
journey and forgetfulness of duty of a pair of illicit 'lovers',
from another Goethe novel, *Elective Affinities*), she displays
Maggie's dilemma in terms which are reminiscent of her
argument in the essay:

The great problem of the shifting relation between passion and
duty is clear to no man who is capable of apprehending it: the
question, whether the moment has come in which a man has fallen
below the possibility of a renunciation that will carry any efficacy,
and must accept the sway of a passion against which he had
struggled as a trespass, is one for which we have no master key
that will fit all cases.[31]

[30] George Eliot to Charles Bray, 25 Nov. 1859, and to Barbara Bodichon,
5 Dec. 1859, *GEL*, iii. 214, 227.
[31] *The Mill on the Floss*, bk. vii, ch. 2.

Brief though the *Wilhelm Meister* essay is, it is extremely important as a statement of Marian Evans's views on the duty of literature to reflect life, though not at all in terms of a simple, programmatic, 'coat-and-waistcoat' realism.[32] Rather literature ought to employ imaginative fictions in such a way as to extend the reader's experience and move him/her to a Spinozan sympathy with the species.

This was the theme also of one of her most important essays written during her critical *annus mirabilis*, 1855–6. 'The Natural History of German Life' (*Westminster Review*, July 1856), a review of Wilhelm Heinrich von Riehl's work on social and cultural history, brings together her philosophical, political, and artistic views. She wholly endorses Riehl's 'social-political-conservatism' in his history of Germany's peasant class, welcoming his analysis of 'the internal conditions and the external' in terms of 'the organism and its medium'. The subject draws from her several prophetic remarks about the need for literature, particularly fiction, to deal with the lower classes, and, moreover, to deal honestly and sympathetically with them. She who was soon to dare to demand our interest in the life of a country carpenter who speaks in dialect, Adam Bede, takes her cue from Riehl (and Ruskin, whom she also invokes) to denounce 'idyllic ploughmen' and 'opera peasants'. 'The greatest benefit we owe to the artist', she exclaims, 'whether painter, poet, or novelist, is the extension of our sympathies.'

This Wordsworthian ideal was to be the keynote of her early novels, as can be seen from the brief extracts included in this volume, following hard on 'The Natural History of German Life' and 'Silly Novels by Lady Novelists'. The ill-educated country clergyman Amos Barton is 'palpably and unmistakably commonplace', and *therefore*, in the spirit of Feuerbach and Spinoza, we should feel a sympathetic interest in him. The rustic life in *Adam Bede* is 'a monotonous

---

[32] This is Lewes's term in ch. 2 of his *Fortnightly Review* articles 'The Principles of Success in Literature' (reprinted by Gregg International Publishers with an introduction by Geoffrey Tillotson, 1969).

homely existence', and so we ought to pay attention to it, recognizing 'a fibre of sympathy' which connects us with 'that vulgar citizen who weighs out [our] sugar in a vilely assorted cravat and waistcoat'.

These are deliberately moralizing moments. If they are perhaps momentary failures of _art_, coming as they do within the fiction itself, we can see that the later novels, though still written by a knowing, guiding persona (in _Middlemarch_ the narrator expressly compares himself to Fielding, who also steps outside the story to comment on what he is doing[33]), are generally more skilful in making incarnate George Eliot's ideas. In _Daniel Deronda_, indeed, she experiments with a shifting point of view. The novel opens with a set of questions—'Was she beautiful or not beautiful?' 'Was the good or evil genius dominant in those beams?'—these being questions raised in the mind of one character, Daniel Deronda, by the sight of another, Gwendolen Harleth, at the gambling table. The answer given to such questions in the course of the novel is subtle and complex, even uncomfortable. As if recalling her claim in the _Wilhelm Meister_ essay that the line between the virtuous and the vicious is an artificial one, she allows it to remain unclear to Gwendolen, Daniel, and the reader how far Gwendolen has colluded in the death by drowning of her detested husband.

Many of the essays of 1855–6 deal with literary subjects, English and European. Included here are her excellent article on Heine, of whom she wrote elsewhere 'Nature one day resolved to make a witty German',[34] and her brief reviews of Tennyson's _Maud_, attacked for its ultra-conservatism and support for the disastrous Crimean War, and Browning's _Men and Women_, praised for its freshness and originality. She writes searchingly in the _Leader_ in March 1856 about Sophocles' _Antigone_, the tragedy of which she locates in the 'antagonism of valid claims' rather than the crude triumph of evil over good. Again, her critical thinking

---

[33] _Middlemarch_, ch. 15.
[34] 'Heine's Poems', _Leader_ (1 Sept. 1855), the first of four articles George Eliot wrote on Heine in 1855–6.

helped to form her own literary practice. The novels, beginning with *Adam Bede*, often invoke Greek tragedy in the portrayal of family life, linking the language of classical drama with that of modern science with characteristic daring: 'Family likeness has often a deep sadness in it. Nature, that great tragic dramatist, knits us together by bone and muscle, and divides us by the subtler web of our brains; blends yearning and repulsion; and ties us by our heartstrings to the beings that jar us at every movement.'[35]

In April 1856 she reviewed Ruskin's *Modern Painters*, volume III, praising, as she had done in passing in 'The Natural History of German Life', Ruskin's valuing of realistic portrayal over idealistic, while agreeing with his Wordsworthian view that imagination and invention are also necessary to render commonplace objects interesting.

Though again and again in these essays Marian Evans asserts the importance of the writer's duty to teach morality, she is aware of the dangers for the novelist of falling into mere preaching. Two brief reviews in 1855 of novels which fall into the trap, Charles Kingsley's *Westward Ho!* and Geraldine Jewsbury's *Constance Herbert*, make the point trenchantly. Kingsley 'drops' into homily when he should be 'giving us his higher sensibility as a medium, a delicate acoustic or optical instrument, bringing home to our coarser senses what would otherwise be unperceived by us'. And Geraldine Jewsbury is utterly confused, suggesting that 'duty looks stern, but all the while has her hand full of sugar-plums, with which she will reward us by-and-by'. The critic who writes so assuredly of what is not required in novel-writing met her own high standards of complexity when she herself turned to fiction.

The last essays included in this volume are representative of George Eliot's much reduced critical output in the years of her established fame as a novelist. 'A Word for the Germans' was written in 1865 for the new paper, the *Pall Mall Gazette*, of which Lewes was editorial adviser. In it George Eliot sums up what the nineteenth century generally,

[35] *Adam Bede* (1859), ch. 4.

as well as she personally, owes to German scholarship in the fields of philosophy and history. The erstwhile translator of Strauss and Feuerbach and appreciative reader of Goethe and Heine makes a strong claim for the need to know German, for 'the two other greatest literatures of the world are now impregnated with the results of German labour and German genius'.

Also included here is George Eliot's most obviously political piece. 'Address to Working Men, by Felix Holt' (1868) is a kind of appendix to the novel *Felix Holt, the Radical* (1866), which was written during the period leading up to the Reform Bill of 1867 and took for its subject the agitation surrounding the first Reform Bill of 1832. Blackwood, a genial Tory, asked her to write a piece for *Blackwood's Magazine* addressed by the fictional Felix (a very mild radical) to the real class of newly enfranchised working men. The result is this rather solemn address, unlikely perhaps to raise the enthusiasm of such men, if indeed, as Blackwood remarked, 'the poor fellows were capable of appreciating it'.[36] However, it illustrates clearly enough George Eliot's view, expressed early and late, that education is necessary to fit men for the 'heavy responsibility' of the franchise. She stresses the importance of community, of realizing 'the dependence of men on each other' and their 'common interest in preventing injury'. It is rather a statement of belief in the organic nature of society than a party-political utterance. In short, it is of a piece with her earlier opinions, formed in response to her reading of Feuerbach, Comte, Spinoza, and Riehl. The radicalism she endorsed was one which demanded reverence for tradition rather than mere uprooting.

Finally, I have included an essay which was not published in any periodical, but was written in a notebook of 1868, 'Notes on Form in Art'. While not analysing literary technique or the nature of the imagination in any detail—nowhere does George Eliot do so—these notes indicate her

[36] John Blackwood to George Eliot, 6 Dec. 1867, *GEL*, iv. 402.

adherence to the organic unity of a work of literature. It is the familiar Romantic view, given a typical modern twist by the insistence on detailed scientific observation and analogy:

Poetic Form was not begotten by thinking it out or framing it as a shell which should hold emotional expression, any more than the shell of an animal arises before the living creature; but emotion, by its tendency to repetition, i.e. rhythmic persistence in proportion as diversifying thought is absent, creates a form by the recurrence of its elements in adjustment with certain given conditions of sound, language, action, or environment. Just as the beautiful expanding curves of a bivalve shell are not first made for the reception of the unstable inhabitant, but grow and are limited by the simple rhythmic conditions of its growing life.

George Eliot's intelligent interest in science dates, as we have seen, from her early years with Lewes. 'Silly Novels' was written at Tenby, where he was zoologizing in preparation for his popular *Sea-Side Studies* (1858). Prefiguring the analogical habits of the narrators in the novels, she writes towards the end of this essay about the freedom allowed to fiction: 'Like crystalline masses, it may take any form, and yet be beautiful; we have only to pour in the right elements—genuine observation, humour, and passion.' These qualities are there in abundance in her novels. They are also to be found in unusual richness, along with strong argument, merciless criticism, and everywhere a humane intelligence at work, in her critical writings.

NOTE ON THE TEXT

GEORGE ELIOT'S periodical articles were not collected
during her lifetime. Shortly before her death she revised
five of her longer essays for republication. These appeared
in 1884 as *Essays and Leaves from a Notebook*, a volume
containing less than a tenth of her critical writing. In 1963
Thomas Pinney edited a much larger selection, *Essays of
George Eliot*, containing twenty-nine reviews and essays,
published with an excellent introduction and notes by Col-
umbia University Press. More recently A. S. Byatt and
Nicholas Warren have edited a miscellany of George Eliot's
non-fiction, *George Eliot: Selected Essays, Poems and Other
Writings*, for Penguin Classics (1990). I am indebted to both
these excellent editions.

Though many of the essays reproduced here also appear
in the other selections, there are differences of choice and
emphasis. My interest has been to trace George Eliot's
intellectual and artistic development from her earliest writings to her novels and beyond, with particular emphasis
falling on the essays of 1855–6 which immediately preceded
her first efforts at fiction. I include extracts from all three
of her translations—Strauss's *Life of Jesus* (1846), Feuerbach's *Essence of Christianity* (1854), and Spinoza's *Ethics*
(translated in 1854–5 but not published until 1981). These
translations are important indicators of her intellectual and
moral thinking. Spinoza and Feuerbach, in particular, influenced George Eliot's mature adherence to an ethical
system based on determinism, but a determinism rescued
from mere fatalism by the belief in human reason, sympathy,
and effort (Spinoza), and to a religion divorced from Christian dogma, known in George Eliot's day as the 'religion of
humanity' (Feuerbach).

Allowing, of course, for the difference of medium, these
are also the concerns of her fiction, from *Scenes of Clerical
Life* (1858) to *Daniel Deronda* (1876). This can be clearly

seen from the two extracts from her early fiction included in this volume, one from 'The Sad Fortunes of the Reverend Amos Barton', the first of the *Scenes of Clerical Life*, the other from *Adam Bede* (1859). The learned translator and wide-ranging critic Marian Evans can thus be seen emerging as the Victorian novelist George Eliot.

The essays are reproduced from the original periodicals—mainly the *Westminster Review* and the *Leader*—in which they were published. I have standardized the spelling and punctuation, which vary in the originals according to the house style of the periodical in which the essays first appeared. George Eliot often misquotes slightly—she probably quoted from memory often—and her errors are noted in the Explanatory Notes. In cases where George Eliot does not translate extracts in foreign languages, I do so in the Notes. George Eliot's own footnotes appear, numbered, at the bottom of the appropriate page of text. All other notes are to be found under 'Explanatory Notes' at the end of the volume. They are signalled in the text by an asterisk.

I am grateful to the Beinecke Rare Book and Manuscript Library of Yale University and to Jonathan Ouvry for permission to reproduce George Eliot's notebook essay, 'Notes on Form in Art', and an extract from her translation of Spinoza's *Ethics*. I have also to thank the editor of Salzburg Studies in English Literature for permission to reproduce the Spinoza from the text published in Salzburg in 1981 by Thomas Deegan.

SELECT BIBLIOGRAPHY

George Eliot's Fiction

MOST of George Eliot's novels are available in scholarly editions published in Oxford by the Clarendon Press. Paperback editions, with introduction and notes, are published by Oxford University Press (World's Classics series) and in the Penguin English Library series.

George Eliot's Non-Fiction

Essays and Leaves from a Notebook, ed. Charles Lee Lewes (London, 1884).

Essays of George Eliot, ed. Thomas Pinney (New York, 1963).

George Eliot: Selected Essays, Poems and Other Writings, ed. A. S. Byatt and Nicholas Warren (Harmondsworth, 1990).

Biography and Letters

Gordon S. Haight, *George Eliot and John Chapman* (New Haven, Conn., 1940).

Gordon S. Haight, *George Eliot: A Biography* (Oxford, 1969).

Ruby V. Redinger, *George Eliot: The Emergent Self* (London, 1975).

The George Eliot Letters, edited by Gordon S. Haight, 9 vols. (New Haven, Conn., 1954–5, 1978).

Criticism

George Levine, 'Determinism and Responsibility in the Works of George Eliot', *Publications of the Modern Language Association of America*, 77 (1962), 268–79.

Bernard J. Paris, *Experiments in Life: George Eliot's Quest for Values* (Detroit, 1965).

U. C. Knoepflmacher, *Religious Humanism and the Victorian Novel* (Princeton, NJ, 1965).

K. M. Newton, 'George Eliot, George Henry Lewes and Darwinism', *Durham University Journal*, 66 (1973–4), 278–93.

E. S. Shaffer, *'Kubla Khan' and The Fall of Jerusalem: The Mythological School in Biblical Criticism and Secular Literature 1770–1880* (Cambridge, 1975).

William Myers, 'George Eliot's Essays and Reviews 1849–57', *Prose Studies 1800–1900*, 1 (1978), 5–20.

George Levine, 'George Eliot's Hypothesis of Reality', *Nineteenth-Century Fiction*, 35 (1980), 1–28.

Rosemary Ashton, *The German Idea: Four English Writers and the Reception of German Thought 1800–1860* (Cambridge, 1980).

Rosemary Ashton, *George Eliot* (Oxford, 1983).

Gillian Beer, *Darwin's Plots: Evolutionary Narrative in Darwin, George Eliot, and Nineteenth-Century Fiction* (London, 1983).

William Myers, *The Teaching of George Eliot* (Leicester, 1984).

Sally Shuttleworth, *George Eliot and Nineteenth-Century Science: The Make-Believe of a Beginning* (Cambridge, 1984).

T. R. Wright, *The Religion of Humanity: The Impact of Comtean Positivism on Victorian Britain* (Cambridge, 1986).

Simon Dentith, *George Eliot* (Brighton, 1986).

Gillian Beer, *George Eliot* (Brighton, 1986).

Jennifer Uglow, *George Eliot* (London, 1987).

A CHRONOLOGY OF GEORGE ELIOT

1819	22 Nov.	Born Mary Ann Evans at Arbury, Warwickshire.
1825–7		At Miss Lathom's School, Attleborough.
1828–32		At Mrs Wallington's School, Nuneaton.
1832–5		At the Miss Franklins' School, Coventry.
1836	3 Feb.	Her mother Mrs Robert Evans dies.
1841	Mar.	Moves with her father to Foleshill, Coventry.
1842	Jan.–May	Refuses to go to Church.
1844–6		Translates Strauss's *The Life of Jesus*, 3 vols.
1849		Father dies; GE spends winter at Geneva.
1851	8 Jan.	Goes to live at 142 Strand, London.
1852–4		Edits the *Westminster Review*.
1854		Translates Feuerbach's *The Essence of Christianity*.
1854	20 July	Goes to Germany with G. H. Lewes.
1854–6		Writes articles for *Westminster Review*.
1856		Lewes encourages her to write fiction.
1857	Jan.	'Amos Barton' begins in *Blackwood's Magazine*.
1858	Jan.	*Scenes of Clerical Life*, 2 vols., published.
1859	12 Jan.	Studies floods for *The Mill on the Floss*.
1859	1 Feb.	*Adam Bede*, 3 vols., published.
1859	Sept.	Finds sites for Dorlcote Mill on the Trent.
1860	4 Apr.	*The Mill on the Floss*, 3 vols., published.
1861	1 Apr.	*Silas Marner* published.
1862	27 Feb.	Offered £10,000 for *Romola*.
1862	July	*Romola* begins in *Cornhill Magazine*.
1863	6 July	*Romola*, 3 vols., published.
1863	21 Aug.	Buys the Priory, 21 North Bank, Regent's Park.
1866	15 June	*Felix Holt*, 3 vols., published.
1868	29 Apr.	*The Spanish Gypsy* published.
1871	1 Dec.	*Middlemarch*, Book 1, published.
1872	1 Dec.	Concluded with Book VIII; published, 4 vols.
1874	May	*The Legend of Jubal and Other Poems* published.
1876	Feb.–Sept.	*Daniel Deronda* published in 8 Books.
1878	30 Nov.	Lewes dies.

1879	June	*Impressions of Theophrastus Such* published.
1880	6 May	Marries John Walter Cross.
1880	22 Dec.	Dies; buried in Highgate Cemetery.

Selected Critical Writings

From the Translation of Strauss's
The Life of Jesus (1846), Introduction

CRITERIA BY WHICH TO DISTINGUISH THE UNHISTORICAL IN THE GOSPEL NARRATIVE

HAVING shown the possible existence of the mythical and the legendary in the gospels, both on extrinsic and intrinsic grounds, and defined their distinctive characteristics, it remains in conclusion to inquire how their actual presence may be recognized in individual cases?

The mythus presents two phases; in the first place it is not history; in the second it is fiction, the product of the particular mental tendency of a certain community. These two phases afford the one a negative, the other a positive criterion, by which the mythus is to be recognized.

I. *Negative.* That an account is not historical—that the matter related could not have taken place in the manner described is evident,

First. When the narration is irreconcilable with the known and universal laws which govern the course of events. Now according to these laws, agreeing with all just philosophical conceptions and all credible experience, the absolute cause never disturbs the chain of secondary causes by single arbitrary acts of interposition, but rather manifests itself in the production of the aggregate of finite causalities, and of their reciprocal action. When therefore we meet with an account of certain phenomena or events of which it is either expressly stated or implied that they were produced immediately by God himself (divine apparitions—voices from heaven and the like), or by human beings possessed of supernatural powers (miracles, prophecies), such an account is *in so far* to be considered as not historical. And inasmuch as, in general, the intermingling of the spiritual world with the human is found only in unauthentic records, and is irreconcilable with all just conceptions; so narratives of angels and of devils, of their appearing in human shape and interfering with human concerns, cannot possibly be received as historical.

Another law which controls the course of events is the law of succession, in accordance with which all occurrences, not excepting the most violent convulsions and the most rapid changes, follow in a certain order of sequence of increase and decrease. If, therefore, we are told of a celebrated individual that he attracted already at his birth and during his childhood that attention which he excited in his manhood; that his followers at a single glance recognized him as being all that he actually was; if the transition from the deepest despondency to the most ardent enthusiasm after his death is represented as the work of a single hour; we must feel more than doubtful whether it is a real history which lies before us. Lastly, all those psychological laws, which render it improbable that a human being should feel, think, and act in a manner directly opposed to his own habitual mode and that of men in general, must be taken into consideration. As for example, when the Jewish Sanhedrim are represented as believing the declaration of the watch at the grave that Jesus was risen, and instead of accusing them of having suffered the body to be stolen away whilst they were asleep, bribing them to give currency to such a report. By the same rule it is contrary to all the laws belonging to the human faculty of memory, that long discourses, such as those of Jesus given in the fourth Gospel, could have been faithfully recollected and reproduced.

It is however true that effects are often far more rapidly produced, particularly in men of genius and by their agency, than might be expected; and that human beings frequently act inconsequently, and in opposition to their general modes and habits; the two last mentioned tests of the mythical character must therefore be cautiously applied, and in conjunction only with other tests.

Secondly. An account which shall be regarded as historically valid, must neither be inconsistent with itself, nor in contradiction with other accounts.

The most decided case falling under this rule, amounting to a positive contradiction, is when one account affirms what another denies. Thus, one gospel represents the first appearance of Jesus in Galilee as subsequent to the imprisonment of John the Baptist, whilst another Gospel remarks, long after Jesus had preached both in Galilee and in Judea, that 'John was not yet cast into prison.'*

When on the contrary, the second account, without absolutely contradicting the first, differs from it, the disagreement may be merely between the incidental particulars of the narrative; such as *time*, (the clearing of the Temple,) *place*, (the original residence of the parents of Jesus;) *number*, (the Gadarenes, the angels at the sepulchre;) *names*, (Matthew and Levi); or it may concern the essential substance of the history. In the latter case, sometimes the character and circumstances in one account differ altogether from those in another. Thus, according to one narrator, the Baptist recognizes Jesus as the Messiah destined to suffer; according to the other, John takes offence at his suffering condition. Sometimes an occurrence is represented in two or more ways, of which one only can be consistent with the reality; as when in one account Jesus calls his first disciples from their nets whilst fishing on the sea of Galilee, and in the other meets them in Judea on his way to Galilee. We may class under the same head instances where events or discourses are represented as having occurred on two distinct occasions, whilst they are so similar that it is impossible to resist the conclusion that both the narratives refer to the same event or discourse.

It may here be asked: is it to be regarded as a contradiction if one account is wholly silent respecting a circumstance mentioned by another? In itself, apart from all other considerations, the argumentum ex silentio* is of no weight; but it is certainly to be accounted of moment when, at the same time, it may be shown that had the author known the circumstance he could not have failed to mention it, and also that he must have known it had it actually occurred.

II. *Positive.* The positive characters of legend and fiction are to be recognized sometimes in the form, sometimes in the substance of a narrative.

If the form be poetical, if the actors converse in hymns, and in a more diffuse and elevated strain than might be expected from their training and situations, such discourses, at all events, are not to be regarded as historical. The absence of these marks of the unhistorical do not however prove the historical validity of the narration, since the mythus often wears the most simple and apparently historical form: in which case the proof lies in the substance.

If the contents of a narrative strikingly accords with certain ideas existing and prevailing within the circle from which the narrative proceeded, which ideas themselves seem to be the product of preconceived opinions rather than of practical experience, it is more or less probable, according to circumstances, that such a narrative is of mythical origin. The knowledge of the fact, that the Jews were fond of representing their great men as the children of parents who had long been childless, cannot but make us doubtful of the historical truth of the statement that this was the case with John the Baptist; knowing also that the Jews saw predictions every where in the writings of their prophets and poets, and discovered types of the Messiah in all the lives of holy men recorded in their Scriptures; when we find details in the life of Jesus evidently sketched after the pattern of these prophecies and prototypes, we cannot but suspect that they are rather mythical than historical.

The more simple characteristics of the legend, and of additions by the author, after the observations of the former section, need no further elucidation.

Yet each of these tests, on the one hand, and each narrative on the other, considered apart, will rarely prove more than the possible or probable unhistorical character of the record. The concurrence of several such indications, is necessary to bring about a more definite result. The accounts of the visit of the Magi, and of the murder of the innocents at Bethlehem, harmonize remarkably with the Jewish Messianic notion, built upon the prophecy of Balaam, respecting the star which should come out of Jacob; and with the history of the sanguinary command of Pharaoh.* Still this would not alone suffice to stamp the narratives as mythical. But we have also the corroborative facts that the described appearance of the star is contrary to the physical, the alleged conduct of Herod to the psychological laws; that Josephus,* who gives in other respects so circumstantial an account of Herod, agrees with all other historical authorities in being silent concerning the Bethlehem massacre; and that the visit of the Magi together with the flight into Egypt related in the one Gospel, and the presentation in the temple related in another Gospel, mutually exclude one another. Wherever, as in this instance, the several criteria of the mythical character concur, the result is certain, and certain in proportion to the accumulation of such grounds of evidence.

It may be that a narrative, standing alone, would discover but slight indications, or perhaps, might present no one distinct feature of the mythus; but it is connected with others, or proceeds from the author of other narratives which exhibit unquestionable marks of a mythical or legendary character; and consequently suspicion is reflected back from the latter, on the former. Every narrative, however miraculous, contains some details which might in themselves be historical, but which, in consequence of their connexion with the other supernatural incidents, necessarily become equally doubtful.

In these last remarks we are, to a certain extent, anticipating the question which is, in conclusion, to be considered: viz., whether the mythical character is restricted to those features of the narrative, upon which such character is actually stamped; and whether a contradiction between two accounts invalidate one account only, or both? That is to say, what is the precise boundary line between the historical and the unhistorical?—the most difficult question in the whole province of criticism.

In the first place, when two narratives mutually exclude one another, one only is thereby proved to be unhistorical. If one be true the other must be false, but though the one be false the other may be true. Thus, in reference to the original residence of the parents of Jesus, we are justified in adopting the account of Luke which places it at Nazareth, to the exclusion of that of Matthew, which plainly supposes it to have been at Bethlehem; and, generally speaking, when we have to choose between two irreconcilable accounts, in selecting as historical that which is the least opposed to the laws of nature, and has the least correspondence with certain national or party opinions. But upon a more particular consideration it will appear that, since one account is false, it is possible that the other may be so likewise: the existence of a mythus respecting some certain point, shows that the imagination has been active in reference to that particular subject; (we need only refer to the genealogies); and the historical accuracy of either of two such accounts cannot be relied upon, unless substantiated by its agreement with some other well authenticated testimony.

Concerning the different parts of one and the same narrative: it might be thought for example, that though the appearance of an angel, and his announcement to Mary that she should be the Mother of the Messiah, must certainly be regarded as unhistorical, still, that Mary should have indulged this hope before the birth of the child, is not in itself incredible. But what should have excited this hope in Mary's mind? It is at once apparent that that which is credible in itself is nevertheless unhistorical when it is so intimately connected with what is incredible that, if you discard the latter, you at the same time remove the basis on which the former rests. Again, any action of Jesus represented as a miracle, when divested of the marvellous, might be thought to exhibit a perfectly natural occurrence; with respect to some of the miraculous histories, the expulsion of devils for instance, this might with some limitation, be possible. But for this reason alone: in these instances, a cure, so instantaneous, and effected by a few words merely, as it is described in the Gospels, is not psychologically incredible; so that, the essential in these narratives remains untouched. It is different in the case of the healing of a man born blind. A natural cure could not have been effected otherwise than by a gradual process; the narrative states the cure to have been immediate; if therefore the history be understood to record a natural occurrence, the most essential particular is incorrectly represented, and consequently all security for the truth of the otherwise natural remainder is gone, and the real fact cannot be discovered without the aid of arbitrary conjecture.

The following examples will serve to illustrate the mode of deciding in such cases. According to the narrative, as Mary entered the house and saluted her cousin Elizabeth, who was then pregnant, the babe leaped in her womb, she was filled with the Holy Ghost, and she immediately addressed Mary as the mother of the Messiah. This account bears indubitable marks of an unhistorical character. Yet, it is not, in itself, impossible that Mary should have paid a visit to her cousin, during which every thing went on quite naturally. The fact is however that there are psychological difficulties connected with this journey of the betrothed; and that the visit, and even the relationship of the two women, seem to have originated entirely in the wish to exhibit a connexion between the mother of John the Baptist, and the mother of the Messiah. Or when in the history of the transfiguration it is stated, that the men who appeared with Jesus on the Mount were Moses and Elias; and that the brilliancy which illuminated Jesus was supernatural; it might seem here also that, after deducting the marvellous, the presence of two men and a bright morning beam might be retained as the historical facts. But the legend was predisposed, by virtue of the current idea concerning the relation of the Messiah to these two prophets, not merely to make any two men (whose persons, object, and conduct, if they were not what the narrative represents them, remain in the highest degree mysterious) into Moses and Elias, but to create the whole occurrence; and in like manner not merely to conceive of some certain illumination as a supernatural effulgence (which, if a natural one, is much exaggerated and misrepresented), but to create it at once after the pattern of the brightness which illumined the face of Moses on Mount Sinai.

Hence is derived the following rule. Where not merely the particular nature and manner of an occurrence is critically suspicious, its external circumstances represented as miraculous and the like; but where likewise the essential substance and groundwork is either inconceivable in itself, or is in striking harmony with some Messianic idea of the Jews of that age, then not the particular alleged course and mode of the transaction only, but the entire occurrence must be regarded as unhistorical. Where on the contrary, the form only, and not the general contents of the narration, exhibits the characteristics of the unhistorical, it is at least possible to suppose a kernel of historical fact; although we can never confidently decide whether this kernel of fact actually exists, or in what it consists; unless, indeed, it be discoverable from other sources. In legendary narratives, or narratives embellished by the writer, it is less difficult,—by divesting them of all that betrays itself as fictitious imagery, exaggeration, &c.—by endeavouring to abstract from them every extraneous adjunct and to fill up every hiatus—to succeed, proximately at least, in separating the historical groundwork.

The boundary line, however, between the historical and the unhistorical, in records, in which as in our Gospels this latter element is incorporated, will ever remain fluctuating and unsusceptible of precise attainment. Least of all can it be expected that the first comprehensive attempt to treat these records from a critical point of view should be successful in drawing a sharply defined line of demarcation. In the obscurity which criticism has produced, by the extinction of all lights hitherto held historical, the eye must accustom itself by degrees to discriminate objects with precision; and at all events the author of this work wishes especially to guard himself, in those places where he declares he knows not what happened, from the imputation of asserting that he knows that nothing happened.

Letter to Charles Bray, 21 October 1846

MY dear Friend

When I wrote to Cara* I complained that I had no news to tell her—but oh the mutations of this giddy planet! little did I think that ere another week passed away I should be an actress in scenes so novel as those which it has now become a duty of friendship to relate to you. But a truce to prefaces and palpitations. I will plunge at once in medias res.

The other day as I was sitting in my study, Mary* came with a rather risible cast of expression to deliver to me a card, saying that a gentleman was below requesting to see me. The name on the card ran thus—Professor Bücher-wurm, Moderig University.* Down I came, not a little elated at the idea that a live professor was in the house, and, as you know I have quite the average quantity of that valuable endowment which spiteful people call assurance, but which I dignify with the name of self possession, you will believe that I neither blushed nor made a nervous giggle in attempting to smile, as is the lot of some unfortunate young ladies who are immersed in youthful bashfulness.

And whom do you think I saw? A tall, gaunt personage with huge cheek bones, dull grey eyes, hair of a very light neutral tint, un grand nez retroussé, and very black teeth. As novel writers say, I give you at once what was the result of a survey carried on by degrees through a long interview. My professor's coat was threadbare enough for that of a first-rate genius, and his linen and skin dirty enough to have belonged to the Emperor Julian.* A profound reverence. I begged him to be seated, and this very begrimed professor began in sufficiently good English, 'Madam, you can form no preconception of my design in waiting on you.' I bowed. 'About a fortnight ago I came to London to seek—singular as it may seem to you—a *wife*.' (Surely, thought I, this poor man has escaped from a lunatic asylum, and I looked alternately at the door and the poker, measuring my distance from the two.) 'But,' my professor continued, 'there were certain qualifications which were indispensable to me in the person whom I could receive into that relation. I am a voluminous author—indeed my works already amount to some 20 vols.—my last publication in 5 vols. was a commentary on the book of Tobit.* I have also written a long dissertation on the Greek Digamma,* a treatise on Buddhism shewing that Christianity is entirely derived from this monstrous oriental superstition, and a very minute inquiry into the date, life and character of Cheops.* My chief work, however, and that by which I hope to confer a lasting benefit on mankind is yet on hand. It is a system of metaphysics which I doubt not will supersede the latest products of the German philosophic mind.

'But like most authors who, as our divine Schiller says, live citizens of the age to come,* my books are not appreciated in my own country. Now I wish that England should at least have the opportunity of profiting by them, and as I can find no indifferent person who will undertake a translation I am determined if possible to secure a translator in the person of a wife. I have made the most anxious and extensive inquiries in London after all female translators of German. I find them very abundant, but I require, besides ability to translate, a very decided ugliness of person and a sufficient fortune to supply a poor professor with coffee and tobacco, and an occasional draft of schwarzbier, as well as to contribute to the expenses of publication. After the most toilsome inquiries I have been referred to you, Madam, as presenting the required combination of attributes, and though I am rather disappointed to see that you have no beard, an attribute which I have ever regarded as the most unfailing indication of a strong-minded woman, I confess that in other respects your person at least comes up to my ideal.'

At this the professor bowed and coughed as waiting for my reply. I said that certainly I was taken by surprize, having long given up all hope of such an application as the present, but that I was decidedly pleased with the business-like tone of my suitor, and I thought no woman had been wooed in a more dignified manner since the days of the amazons, who were won with the sword. I thought it possible we might come to terms, always providing that he acceded to my irrevocable conditions. 'For you must know, learned Professor,' I said, 'that I require nothing more in a husband than to save me from the horrific disgrace of spinster-hood and to take me out of England. As negative conditions, my husband must neither expect me to love him nor to mend his clothes, and he must allow me about once in a quarter a sort of conjugal saturnalia in which I may turn the tables upon him, hector and scold and cuff him. At other times I will be a dutiful wife so far as the task of translation is concerned, and I promise to give to the English a lucid idea of your notions respecting Cheops and Tobit etc. As to my want of beard I trust that defect may be remedied, since I doubt not there must be creams and essences which gentlemen whose having in beard is but a younger brother's revenue* employ to cherish the too reluctant down, and it is an interesting physiological experiment yet to be tried, whether the feminine lip and chin may not be rendered fertile by this top-dressing.'

So we agreed to refer the matter to my Father. He, considering that it would probably be my last chance, at length consented though the professor peremptorily insisted on the wedding taking place next week, as he could not defer his literary projects for a longer period. My Father theorized a little on the undesirableness of long courtships, in order to reconcile his conscience, and accordingly the arrangements are made. On Wednesday next I become the Professorin and wend my way with my tocher* and my husband to Germany—never more to appear in this damp atmosphere and dull horizon. So if you wish to utter a last farewell, you must come home before next Wednesday.

I have ordered a magnificent wedding dress just to throw dust into the eyes of the Coventry people, but I have gone to no further expense in the matter of trousseau, as the Professor prefers as a female garb a man's coat, thrown over what are justly called the *petti*coats, so that the dress of a woman of genius may present the same sort of symbolical compromise between the masculine and feminine attire of which we have an example in the breastplate and petticoat of the immortal Joan.

I have requested Sara* to be my bridesmaid, but her notions are far too contracted for her to comprehend or sanction a scheme of matrimony so much beyond the views of the present age. But as I know that you, my dear Friend, hold the most enlightened and liberal views of these subjects, and regard all subjection to feeling in such affairs as a weakness, proper to small heads, under 20 inches in circumference, I doubt not you will honour my bridal with your presence.

J. A. Froude's *The Nemesis of Faith*
(1849)

ON certain red-letter days of our existence, it happens to us to discover among the *spawn* of the press, a book which, as we read, seems to undergo a sort of transfiguration before us. We no longer hold heavily in our hands an octavo of some hundred pages, over which the eye laboriously travels, hardly able to drag along with it the restive mind: but we seem to be in companionship with a spirit, who is transfusing himself into our souls, and is vitalizing them by his superior energy, that life, both outward and inward, presents itself to us for higher relief, in colours brightened and deepened—we seem to have been bathing in a pool of Siloam, and to have come forth reeling. The books which carry this magic in them are the true products of genius, and their influence, whether for good or evil, is to the influence of all the respectable results of mere talent and industry, as the mighty Nile to the dykes which receive and distribute its heaven-fed waters. Such a book is *The Nemesis of Faith*. We are sure that its author is a bright particular star,* though he sometimes leaves us in doubt whether he be not a fallen 'son of the morning'.* Much there is in the work of a questionable character: yet more which hardly falls within the scope of a newspaper editor's notice: but its trenchant remarks on some of our English conventions, its striking sketches of the dubious aspect which many chartered respectabilities are beginning to wear under the light of this nineteenth century, its suggestive hints as to the necessity of recasting the currency of our religion and virtue, that it may carry fresh and bright the stamp of the age's highest and best idea—these have a practical bearing, which may well excite the grave, perhaps the alarmed attention of some important classes among us. We will resign the work into the hands of judges of more ability, and more unquestioned credentials, only quoting one or two passages as a slight sample for our readers. Surely there is work for our augurs when a Clergyman writes thus of his co-ordinates:—

I cannot understand why, as a body, the Clergy are so fatally uninteresting: they who through all their waking hours ought to have for their one thought, the deepest and most absorbing interests of humanity. It is the curse of making it a profession—a road to get on upon, to succeed in life upon. The base stain is apparent in their very language, too, and an index of what they are. Their '*duty*'—what is it? To patter through the two Sunday's services. For a little money one of them will take the other's *duty* for him. And what do they all aim at? Getting livings!—not cures of souls, but *livings*: something which will keep their wretched bodies living in the comforts they have found indispensable. What business have they, any one of them, with a thought of what becomes of their poor wretched selves at all? To hear them preaching, to hear the words they use in these same duties of theirs, one would suppose they really believed that getting on, and getting rich, and getting comfortable, were quite the last things a Christian should propose to himself. They certainly say so. Alas! with the mass of them, the pulpit keeps its old meaning, and is but a stage. Off the stage there is the old prate of the old world stories, the patronage of this rich man and that, the vacant benefice or Cathedral stall. So and so, lucky fellow, has married a Bishop's daughter, and the Bishop himself has the best-dressed wife, and the best equipage in London: and oh, bitterest satire of all! the very pulpit eloquence with which they can paint the better life, the beauty of Christianity, is valued only as a means of advancing them into what they condemn . . . Oh, what a Clergyman might do! To have them all [the poor] for an hour at least each week, collected to be taught by him, really wishing to listen, if he will but take the trouble to understand them, and to learn what they require to be told. How sick one is of all sermons, such as they are! Why will men go on thrashing over and again the old withered straw that was thrashed out centuries ago, when every field is waving with fresh, and quit other crops craving for their hand . . .

But there are many other things besides what are in the Bible, which he (the Clergyman) ought to learn if he would assist the people to do what he tells them to do, if he would really give them rest from the painful vacancy of mind, which life spent in routine of never-ending work entails upon them; he should study their work, and the natural laws that are working in it: he should make another version of the Bible for them in what is for ever before their eyes, in the corn-field, in the meadow, in the work-shop, at the weaver's loom, in the market-places and in the warehouses . . . Let every flower have a second image to their eyes; let him bring in for witness to the love of the great Creator, every bird, every beast, every poorest insect; let the teeming earth tell of Him as in her unwearied labour-pangs she fashions up the material elements into the great rolling flood of life which ebbs and flows around them. They might do something, these Clergy, if they would go to work over this ground; labouring in good earnest would they be for the souls of mankind.

The following passage is at least as forcible:—

The men that write books, Carlyle says, are now the world's priests, the spiritual directors of mankind. No doubt they are; and it shows the folly and madness of trying still to enforce tests, that you do but silence a man in the pulpit, to send his voice along the press into every corner of the land. God abolished tests for all purposes, except of mischief and vexation, when he gave mankind the printing-press. What is the result of sustaining them, but that we are all at the mercy now of some clever self-assumer? and while our nominal teachers answer no end for us, except the hour's sleep on Sunday, the minds of all of us, from highest Lords to enlightened operatives, are formed in reading-rooms, in lecture-rooms, at the bar of public-houses, by all the shrewdest, and often the most worthless, novel writers or paper editors. Yet even this is better than nothing, better than that people should be left to their pulpit teachers, such as they are.*

R. W. Mackay's *The Progress of the Intellect* (1851)

THERE are many, and those not the least powerful thinkers and efficient workers amongst us, who are prone to underrate critical research into ancient modes of life and forms of thought, alleging that what it behoves us chiefly to ascertain is the truth which comes home to men's business and bosoms in these our days, and not by-gone speculations and beliefs which we can never fully comprehend, and with which we can only yet more imperfectly sympathize. Holding, with Auguste Comte,* that theological and metaphysical speculation have reached their limit, and that the only hope of extending man's sources of knowledge and happiness is to be found in positive science, and in the universal application of its principles; they urge that the thinkers who are in the van of human progress should devote their energies to the actual rather than to the retrospective.

There is, undeniably, truth in this view. It is better to discover and apply improved methods of draining our own towns, than to be able to quote Aristophanes in proof that the streets of Athens were in a state of unmacadamized muddiness—better to reason justly on some point of immediate concern, than to know the fallacies of the ancient sophists—better to look with 'awful eye'* at the starry heavens, and, under the teaching of Newton and Herschel, feel the immensity, the order, the sublimity of the universe, and of the forces by which it subsists, than to pore over the grotesque symbols, whereby the Assyrian or Egyptian shadowed forth his own more vague impression of the same great facts. But it would be a very serious mistake to suppose that the study of the past and the labours of criticism have no important practical bearing on the present. Our civilization, and, yet more, our religion, are an anomalous blending of lifeless barbarisms, which have descended to us like so many petrifactions from distant ages, with living ideas, the offspring of a true process of development. We are in bondage to terms and conceptions which, having had their root in conditions of thought no longer existing, have ceased to possess any vitality, and are for us as spells which have lost their virtue. The endeavour to spread enlightened ideas is perpetually counteracted by these *idola theatri*,* which have allied themselves, on the one hand with men's better sentiments, and on the other with institutions in whose defence are arrayed the passions and the interests of dominant classes. Now, though the teaching of positive truth is the grand means of expelling error, the process will be very much quickened if the negative argument serve as its pioneer; if, by a survey of the past, it can be shown how each age and each race has had a faith and a symbolism suited to its need and its stage of development, and that for succeeding ages to dream of retaining the spirit along with the forms of the past, is as futile as the embalming of the dead body in the hope that it may one day be resumed by the living soul.

But apart from this objective utility of critical research, it has certain highly advantageous influences on the mind which pursues it. There is so far justice in the common sarcasms against men of erudition *par excellence*, that they have rarely been distinguished for warmth of moral sympathy, or for fertility and grandeur of conception; but your eminently practical thinker is often beset by a narrowness of another kind. It may be doubted, whether a mind which has no susceptibility to the pleasure of changing its point of view, of mastering a remote form of thought, of perceiving identity of nature under variety of manifestation—a perception which resembles an expansion of one's own being, a pre-existence in the past—can possess the flexibility, the ready sympathy, or the tolerance, which characterizes a truly philosophic culture. Now and then, however, we meet with a nature which combines the faculty for amassing minute erudition with the largeness of view necessary to give it a practical bearing; a high appreciation of the genius of antiquity, with a profound belief in the progressive character of human development—in the eternal freshness of the founts of inspiration, a wonderful intuition of the mental conditions of past ages with an ardent participation in the most advanced ideas and most hopeful efforts of the present; a nature like some mighty river, which, in its long windings through unfrequented regions, gathers mineral and earthy treasures only more effectually to enrich and fertilize the cultivated valleys and busy cities which form the habitation of man.

Of such a nature, with valuable qualities thus 'antithetically mixt',* we have evidence in the work before us. It exhibits an industry in research which reminds us of Cudworth,* and for which, in recent literature, we must seek a parallel in Germany rather than in England, while its philosophy and its aims are at once lofty and practical. Scattered through its more abstruse disquisitions we find passages of pre-eminent beauty—gems into which are absorbed the finest rays of intelligence and feeling. We believe Mr Mackay's work is unique in its kind. England has been slow to use or to emulate the immense labours of Germany in the departments of mythology and biblical criticism,* but when once she does so, the greater solidity and directness of the English mind ensure a superiority of treatment.

The series of subjects which Mr Mackay has chosen as waymarks in tracing the 'Progress of the Intellect', are—after an introductory chapter on Intellectual Religion—Ancient Cosmogony; the Metaphysical Idea of God; the Moral Notion of God; the Theory of Mediation; the Hebrew Theory of Retribution and Immortality; the Messianic Theory; Christian Forms and Reforms; and Speculative Christianity. In the introductory dissertation on Intellectual Religion, he develops his view concerning the true basis and character of religion and morals, and the relation between ancient and modern ideas on these subjects, and it is perhaps here that he presents himself to the greatest advantage; this preliminary chapter is a sort of lofty, airy vestibule, in which we gather breath and courage to descend with the author into the crypts of citation and conjecture, into which he is about to introduce us. It is Mr Mackay's faith that divine revelation is not contained exclusively or pre-eminently in the facts and inspirations of any one age or nation, but is co-extensive with the history of human development, and is perpetually unfolding itself to our widened experience and investigation, as firmament upon firmament becomes visible to us in proportion to the power and range of our exploring instruments. The master key to this revelation, is the recognition of the presence of undeviating law in the material and moral world—of that invariability of sequence which is acknowledged to be the basis of physical science, but which is still perversely ignored in our social organization, our ethics and our religion. It is this invariability of sequence which can alone give value to experience and render education in the true sense possible. The divine yea and nay, the seal of prohibition and of sanction, are effectually impressed on human deeds and aspirations, not by means of Greek and Hebrew, but by that inexorable law of consequences, whose evidence is confirmed instead of weakened as the ages advance; and human duty is comprised in the earnest study of this law and patient obedience to its teaching. While this belief sheds a bright beam of promise on the future career of our race, it lights up what once seemed the dreariest region of history with new interest; every past phase of human development is part of that education of the race in which we are sharing; every mistake, every absurdity into which poor human nature has fallen, may be looked on as an experiment of which we may reap the benefit. A correct generalization gives significance to the smallest detail, just as the great inductions of geology demonstrate in every pebble the working of laws by which the earth has become adapted for the habitation of man. In this view, religion and philosophy are not merely conciliated, they are identical; or rather, religion is the crown and consummation of philosophy—the delicate corolla, which can only spread out its petals in all their symmetry and brilliance to the sun, when root and branch exhibit the conditions of a healthy and vigorous life. Mr Mackay's preliminary chapter has an independent value, and would be read with interest by many who might not care to follow him in his subsequent inquiry.

The dilemma of sensuousness and sentimentalism is thus excellently put:—

Religion often appears to be a mere sentiment, because the reason by which it should be disciplined requires long cultivation, and can only gradually assume its proper prominence and dignity. The faculties are seldom combined in its avowed service; and from its consequent misdirection has been inferred the impossibility of finding within the limits of the mind an effectual religious guide. It has even been said that religion has properly nothing to do with the head, but is exclusively an exercise of the heart and feelings; that all the teaching or education which can properly be called 'religious', consists 'in the formation of the temper and behaviour, the infusing of devotional feeling, and the implanting of Christian principles'. In other words, the highest faculty of the mind is not required in the service of him who bestowed it. Through this narrow view the sentiments are over-excited; the judgement becomes proportionately languid and incapable, the connexion between the theory of practice and duty* is unobserved, and dogmas are blindly learned without regard to their origin or meaning. Superficial religion has everywhere the same result; it fluctuates between the extremes of sensibility* and superstition, and exhibits in this respect a curious parallel to the analogous catastrophe of natural* philosophy. The uneducated feeling has only the alternative of unquestioning credulity, or of sacrificing and abrogating itself. This is the universal dilemma of artificial creeds; their votaries divide into formalists and sceptics, Pharisees and Sadducees; Calvinism, in our own days, has swung back to rationalism, and the symbolical forms of ancient religion are pronounced by a competent observer to have generally led to these extremes.[1] The passage is easy from one to the other. The devotional feeling of a Catholic of the middle age might have been destroyed, if the doctrines of Copernicus or Galileo had induced him to mistrust the infallibility of the Pope; and in the days of Sir Thomas Browne, it may have been correct to say that a disbelief in witchcraft implied 'a sort of atheism'. Horace was startled out of his irreligious philosophy by a clap of thunder; but if a heathen who saw an angry Hecate in the eclipsed moon could have understood a modern almanack, he might at once have fallen into the impiety from which Horace was a convert—Sec. 3, p. 9.

---

[1] Plutarch, *Isis and Osiris*, Ch. 67 [Mackay's note.]

Admirable again is the section on Faith, from which we cannot resist giving a long extract:—

Religion and science are inseparable. No object in nature, no subject of contemplation is destitute of a religious tendency and meaning. If religion be made to consist only in traditional and legendary forms, it is of course as distinguishable from science as the Mosaic cosmogony from geology; but if it be the *ascensio mentis in Deum per scalas creatarum rerum,** the evolving the grounds of hope, faith, and duty from the known laws of our being and the constitution of the universe; a religion may be said to include science as its minister, and antiquity, which beheld a divinity in all things, erred only in mistaking its intelligible character, and in making it a mere matter of mystic speculation. In a more limited sense, religion may be contrasted with science, as something beyond and above it; as beginning where science ends, and as a guide through the realms of the unknown. But the known and the unknown are intimately connected and correlative. A superstructure of faith can be securely built only on the foundations of the known. Philosophy and religion have one common aim; they are but different forms of answer to the same great question—that of man and his destination . . . Faith is, to a great extent, involuntary; it is a law or faculty of our nature, operating silently and intuitively to supply the imperfections of our knowledge. The boundary between faith and knowledge is, indeed, hard to distinguish. We are said to know our own impressions; to believe in their reality, or in the existence of an external* cause of them. It follows that the immediate as well as the more remote inferences from phenomena, are the blended fruit of faith and knowledge; and that though faith, properly speaking, is not knowledge, but the admission of certain inferences beyond knowledge, yet it is almost impossible, in tracing back the operations of the mind, to find any, even the most elementary inference, which is not in some degree a compound of both, and which may not ultimately be resolved into a consistent belief in the results of experience. Faith being thus the inseparable companion and offspring of knowledge, is, like it, liable to modification and correction; that which we call our knowledge of the ultimate purpose of existence being, in fact, only a belief or inference from experience, which would lose its rational value if it were supposed to be so complete and infallible as to exempt us from the necessity of further reflection. All human knowledge must partake of the imperfection of the faculties through which it is derived; and the limited and unsatisfactory character of what we know leaves a wide and most important void to be filled up by our belief. But the more imperfect our knowledge, the more necessary it becomes to examine with suspicion the foundations of the faith so closely connected with it. Faith, as opposed to credulity, and to that blind submission to inexplicable power which usurped its name in the ancient East, is an allegiance of the reason; and as the 'evidence of things unseen', stands on the verge of mysticism, its value must depend on the discretion with which it is formed and used. Like all the other faculties, the belief requires to be educated; as the feet are taught to walk, the lips and tongue to speak, so the capacity of belief must be taught how to build securely, yet not arrogantly, on the data of experience. Faith is not that belief of St Augustine, whose merit increased with the absurdity of the proposition, nor that which attributed to the instigation of God the real or projected murder of an only son. An irrational faith grew out of the opposite extreme of incredulity,* when men refused to believe the truth, unless authenticated by sensuous evidence that confounded their understandings. True faith is a belief in things probable; it is the assigning to certain inferences a hypothetical objectivity, and upon the conscious acknowledgement of this hypothetical character alone depends its advantage over fanaticism; its moral value and dignity. Between the opposite risks of credulity and scepticism, it must be guided by those broad principles of reason which all the faculties require for their regulation. Reason alone can in each case determine where credulity begins, and fix the limit beyond which the mind should cease to assign even a qualified objectivity to its own imaginations. In its advanced stages faith is a legitimate result of the calculation of probabilities; it may transcend experience, but can never absolutely contradict it. Faith and knowledge tend mutually to the confirmation and enlargement of each other; faith by verification being often transformed into knowledge, and every increase of knowledge supplying a wider and firmer basis of belief. Faith, as an inference from knowledge, should be consistently inferred from the whole of knowledge; since, when estranged and isolated, it loses its vitality, and the estrangement is as effectual when it is hastily and unfairly inferred as where it is wholly gratuitous. The same experience which is the source of knowledge being, therefore, the only legitimate foundation of faith, a sound faith cannot be derived from the anomalous and exceptional. It is the avidity for the marvellous, and the morbid eagerness for a cheap and easy solution of the mysteries of existence—a solution supposed to be implied in the conception of an arbitrary and unintelligible rule, which has ever retarded philosophy and stultified religion. Faith naturally arises out of the regular and undeviating. The same unerring uniformity, which alone made experience possible, was also the first teacher of the invisible things of God. It is this

> Elder Scripture, writ by God's own hand,
> Scripture authentic, uncorrupt by man,

which is set before every one, without note or comment, and which even Holy Writ points out as the most unquestionable authority by which, both in heaven and earth, the will of God is interpreted to mankind. If man is not permitted to solve the problem of existence, he is at least emboldened to hope, and to infer so much from its actual conditions as to feel confident as to its results. Faith takes up the problem exactly where knowledge leaves it, and, as from confounding the objects of the two have arisen the discords of sects and the puzzles of philosophy, so the discovery of their true relations and limits enables the mind to reconcile and account for the controversies of the past, and in some measure to penetrate the mysteries that occasioned them—vol. i, p. 35.

Having thus indicated the ground on which he takes his stand, Mr Mackay commences his survey and delineation of religious development, selecting that of the Hebrews and Greeks as the most typical and complete, and tracing it up to the period when the combination of the two modes of thought in the Alexandrian theosophy formed that web of metaphysical and religious dogma, which constitutes speculative Christianity. While the Hebrew and Greek religions are his main subject, he has not neglected the copious illustration to be drawn from the Persian, the Hindoo and the Northern mythologies, by indicating instances of analogy and of possible derivation, and thus the 'Progress of the Intellect', is, perhaps, the nearest approach in our language to a satisfactory natural history of religion. The third chapter on the 'Metaphysical Idea of God' is a rich mine of associated facts and ideas; but while admiring the range of learning which it exhibits, it is here that we begin to perceive the author's defects, or rather his redundancies. Some of his pages read like extracts from his common-place book, which must be, as Southey said of his own, an urn under the arm of a river-god, rather than like a digested result of study, intended to inform the general reader. Only a devotedness of research such as his own, can give interest and significance to the mass of allusions and particulars with which Mr Mackay overlays, rather than illustrates, his more general passages, which are usually at once profound and lucid. The popular lecturer on science comes before his audience with a selection of striking and apt experiments in readiness, and is silent as to the morning's preparation in the laboratory; and so the scholar, who would produce a work of general utility, must not drag his readers through the whole region of his own researches, but simply present them with an impressive *coup d'œil*. The occasional absence of this artistic working-up of materials diminishes the effectiveness of Mr Mackay's admirable work.

The introduction of a truly philosophic spirit into the study of mythology—an introduction for which we are chiefly indebted to the Germans—is a great step in advance of the superficial Lucian-like tone of ridicule adopted by many authors of the eighteenth century, or the orthodox prepossessions of writers such as Bryant,* who saw in the Greek legends simply misrepresentations of the authentic history given in the book of Genesis. The enlarged acquaintance with Hindoo literature, and with the monumental records of other ancient nations, which the last half century has brought us, has rendered more possible that wide comparison which is a requisite for all true, scientific generalization. O. Müller* says, obviously enough, that if we possessed no other access to Grecian antiquity than its mythology, a systematic and philosophic explanation of the latter would be impossible; and so while the mythology of one nation is studied apart from that of others, or while what is really mythology in the records of any one nation is not recognized as such, but, though it presents the ordinary mythical elements, is accounted for by a special theory; we shall never arrive at a just and full estimate of this phase of man's religious tendencies.

Mr Mackay holds, with Creuzer,* that the basis of all mythology was a nature-worship; that 'those interpreters are in the main right, who held that the heathen Pantheon, in its infinite diversity of names and personifications, was but a multitudinous, though in its origin, unconscious allegory, of which physical phenomena, and principally the heavenly bodies, were the fundamental types'. This primitive period of the myth, in which sacerdotal influence was in the ascendant, he thinks may be designated the Orphic or Cabiric, in distinction from the Epic period, which was characterized by a gradual merging of the mystic or religious feeling in the poetic. He says:—'Between the life-like Epic and the sombre Orphic style, between the picturesque and eventful romance, in which the gods are the mere machinery of a human drama, and the mystical symbols of theological metaphysics, there must have been many varieties in the treatment of religious legend, tending to reduce its fragmentary materials to the consistent and positive forms in which they are found in Homer.' In this theory, mythical conception, instead of being a step in advance of fetishism, is a decadence of the religious sentiment from that monotheistic or pantheistic impression to which it leaps by its first impulse; general ideas in the process of transmission, or simply as a necessary result of the laws of expression in the early stages of thought, resolve themselves into the crystalline forms of the legend. We will quote the author's own presentation of his opinion. Under the head of 'Relation of Monotheism to Symbolism', he says:—

It is impossible to assume any period of time at which the vague sense of Deity ceased to be a mere feeling and assumed a specific form, or became an 'idea'. The notion of external power must have been almost instantaneously associated with some external object; and the diversified reflections of the Divine easily came to be looked on as substantive and distinct divinities. But however infinite the variety of objects which helped to develop the notion of Deity, and eventually usurped its place, the notion itself was essentially a concentrated or monotheistic one. A vague monotheism resided in the earliest exertions of thought, being nearly identical with that impression of unity and connexion in sensible phenomena, which in its simplest form appears to rise independently of any effort of philosophical comparison. The power of generalization, or of seeing the one in the many, that first element both of science and of religion, is so nearly innate or instinctive as to have been termed by Plato a divine or Promethean gift; and the philosophical conception of the oneness of the universe and of its author, usually regarded as the last acquisition of civilization and reflection, appears to have been anticipated by a natural revelation, an indefinite dread of the aggregate of super-sensuous nature; which is said to be common even among savages. In this indefinite feeling must be sought, if anywhere, that conceptional monotheism of primitive ages, which like the virtues of the golden age, makes every successive epoch, unless it be the present, appear only as a stage in the progress of degeneracy and aberration. The genius of religion . . . does not wait for the co-operation of science in order to commence her task, the powers of combination are at work long before the maturity of the reason eventually found necessary to guide them; nay, the origin of religion, like that of civilization, may be said to be free from many of the corruptions attending its onward progress, which arise from the mind's inability to deal unembarrassed with the multitude of sensuous analogies. Generalization begins before a sufficient basis has been prepared to make it legitimate, and every successive step in the research into particulars seems to be in mysterious contradiction to the first hurried conclusion. Hence the universal blending of monotheism with polytheism, and the impossibility of discovering historically, which of the two is older or more original.

Mr Mackay's main proposition, that the substratum of religious symbolism was a worship or deification of the elements, is well sustained by the evidence; but he perhaps overstates the degree in which the monotheistic idea was originally co-existent with polytheistic personification. To the uncultured intellect, a plurality of divine agencies, analogous to the human, would seem, by their conflicting wills and influences, a natural explanation of physical and moral vicissitudes. As the impression of unity in nature gained force, these agencies would gradually become subordinate to a higher power, but the impression would at first be hardly more than a shadowy presentiment—one of those

> High instincts, before which our mortal nature
> Doth shudder like a guilty thing surprised.*

That allegorical elements exist to a considerable extent, in the divine, if not in the heroic myths of Greece, there is strong evidence, both presumptive and internal; and the allegorical interpretation, on the lowest estimate of its soundness, is far superior to the pragmatical or semi-historical, which, in endeavouring to show a nucleus of fact in the myths, exhibits an utter blindness to the mental state in which they originated, and simply substitutes an unpoetical fable for a poetical one. But owing to the manysidedness of all symbols, there is a peculiarly seductive influence in allegorical interpretation; and we observe that all writers who adopt it, though they set out with the largest admissions as to the spontaneous and unconscious character of mythical allegory, and the manifold modifications which have obscured it, acquire a sort of fanatical faith in their rule of interpretation, and fall into the mistake of supposing that the conscious allegorizing of a modern can be a correct reproduction of what they acknowledge to be unconscious allegorizing in the ancients. We do not see what unconscious allegory can mean, unless it be personification accompanied with belief, and with the spontaneous, vivid conception of a symbol, as opposed to the premeditated use of a poetical figure; and this belief would lead to an elaboration of the myth, in harmony rather with the attributed personality than with the true physical characteristics of the object personified. As a painter, in treating an allegorical subject, is led on by his artistic feeling to add one detail after another, until the specific idea with which he began becomes subordinate to the general effect; so the exuberant religious imagination of the Greek, which set out with a personification of the sun or the ocean, would generate myths having relation rather to the human symbol than to the real phenomena of its cosmical prototype. Hence it appears to us, that any attempt extensively to trace consistent allegory in the myths must fail. Nor need we regret it, since our interest in the subject is of a different nature from that of the ancient philosophical interpreters, who, living at a period when the myths still constituted the popular religion, were under the necessity of bringing them into accordance with their own moral and religious views. It is enough for us if we have sufficient insight into the myths to form an approximate conception of the state of mind which produced them, and to assign them their true rank in the scale of religious development. Mr Mackay has not escaped the influence of the allegorizing mania; he does not despair of finding the true cosmical meaning of the most natural human incidents in the Odyssey, or of the tragic conceptions of the dramatists; but if, like the alchymists, he is sometimes in quest of things not in *rerum naturâ*,* he, like them, elicits much that is suggestive in his search. To criticize details would carry us beyond our limits, and we shall do a greater service to the reader by referring him to the work itself, which, open it where he may, will offer both food and stimulus to his thought.

While the poets of Greece were giving to its religious thought a more and more sensuous expression, its philosophers were working out an opposite result; and Mr Mackay traces this subtilizing process until it reaches the Aristotelian theosophy, of which he gives a comprehensive and clear account.

It is in his theory concerning the religious development of the Hebrews, and in his treatment of their records, that Mr Mackay departs the most widely from prevalent opinion. The idea that many parts of the Old Testament have a mythical character, an idea which was necessary to conciliate them, as well with the philosophic Hebrewism of Philo, as with the Christian morality of Origen,* and which has long been familiar to German critics, is still startling to the English theological mind. No thinker of ordinary intelligence can fail to perceive, not merely difference in degree of completeness, but contrast, between the religious conceptions which represented the Deity as sanctioning or prescribing the cunning trickery of Jacob, or the savage cruelties of Joshua,* and those which preside over the sublime remonstrances of the prophets; but the explanation is still sought in the theory of accommodation, that is, the puerile

and unworthy religious conceptions invariably accompanying
an absence of intellectual culture, which in other nations are
referred to the general principles of human development,
are, in the case of the Hebrews, supposed to have been
benevolent falsities on the part of the true God, whereby
he allured a barbarous race to his recognition and worship.
On this theory, because Abraham had but limited notions
of honour and justice, God plagued Pharaoh and Abimelech* for being misled by the falsehoods of the father of the
faithful, and made those falsehoods redound to the temporal
advantage of his chosen servant; because the Israelites were
surrounded by examples of idolatrous and sacrificial observ-
ance, and had a strong propensity to imitate them, Jehovah,
in condescension to their weakness, prescribed for them a
ritual analogous in spirit and in symbolism to that of their
heathen neighbours: because they were a ferocious race,
eager to 'eat of the prey and drink the blood of the slain',*
a suitable vent for their destructive energies was found in
such requirements as the slaughter of three thousand in their
own camp, and the war of extermination against the Canaan-
ites, or in the especial injunction to Joshua to hough the
enemy's horses. The only argument by which the theory of
accommodation can be sustained is, that in conjunction with
that divine countenance of human vice and weakness which
it supposes, there were delivered and preserved certain
elements of superhuman truth which attest the specifically
divine origin of the religion—its distinctive character as a
revelation. Now, while the mythical theory does not exclude
that more enlarged idea of providential evolution, which sees
in the peculiar religious and political history of the Hebrews,
a preparation for ushering into the world a religion which
anticipates and fulfils the yearnings of man's spiritual nature, it delivers the understanding from a heavy burthen of
contradiction and absurdity, and the religious sentiment
from the admission of painful anomalies. The fact, that the
history of all other nations has a mythical period, urges a
strong presumption, that the Hebrew records will not present an exception in this respect, and an unprejudiced examination confirms this presumption. We find there not only

a generic similarity to the gentile myths, in a degrading conception of the divine attributes, with a corresponding crudeness and obliquity of moral views, in an ignorant interpretation of physical phenomena, a love of prodigy, and a lavish supposition of gratuitous miracle, but also a specific resemblance in symbolism. This is visible on a cursory glance, but a nearer investigation discloses overwhelming proof, that the Hebrew writings, far from meriting an exceptional confidence, require, from the evidence they exhibit that the Hebrew mind was peculiarly deficient in a true historical sense, special canons of caution in their interpretation. On applying the test of a critical analysis, the books of the Pentateuch resolve themselves into a compilation of distinct documents, differing in date and frequently in spirit and purpose, as may be seen from the variations and contradictions in their accounts of the same event; and the more ancient of these documents presents internal evidence, that it was not in existence earlier than the time of Samuel, about 400 years after Moses. The same artificial coherence, the same arbitrariness of classification and of titles, together with palpable inaccuracies and indications of partisanship, characterize large portions, not only of the remaining historical works, but also of the prophetic. Since these conclusions are denied by no competent critic uncommitted to the maintenance of certain tenets, it would be wise in our theological teachers, instead of struggling to retain a footing for themselves and their doctrine on the crumbling structure of dogmatic interpretation, to cherish those more liberal views of biblical criticism, which, admitting of a development of the Christian system corresponding to the wants and the culture of the age, would enable it to strike a firm root in man's moral nature, and to entwine itself with the growth of those new forms of social life to which we are tending. The spirit which doubts the ultimately beneficial tendency of inquiry, which thinks that morality and religion will not bear the broadest daylight our intellect can throw on them, though it may clothe itself in robes of sanctity and use pious phrases, is the worst form of atheism; while he who believes, whatever else he may deny, that the true and the

good are synonymous, bears in his soul the essential element
of religion. Viewed in this relation, the 'Progress of the
Intellect' is a valuable addition to recent examples of plain
speaking—of that παρρησία* which Paul held to be the
proper effect of confidence in the excellence of revelation,
whose manifestation was in the spirit, and not in the letter.

Before stating Mr Mackay's theory concerning the Hebrew history and religion, we must express our regret that
the force of his conclusions is weakened by his unduly
insisting on details difficult of proof, by a frequently infelicitous citation, and by his not giving due value to a free
poetical impulse in the figurative language of the Hebrews,
a deficiency which sometimes leads him into an almost
trivial literalness of interpretation. But notwithstanding
these occasional defects, the chapters which treat principally
of the Hebrews will repay a close study, both from their
suggestiveness, and the soundness of their general views.
Mr Mackay holds that the original God of the Israelites was
no other than the Nature-God, El or Ilus, worshipped in
Arabia, Palestine, and Phœnicia, with licentious and sanguinary rites, under the double aspect of Baal and Moloch; and
that the purer worship of Jehovah, inculcated by the
prophets, and established by Josiah, was a religious reformation among the Hebrews, generated by the growth in
civilization consequent on an enlarged commercial intercourse with foreign nations, and contemporaneous with a
movement of religious reform which took place throughout
Asia, about 700 BC, 'connected in India with the name of
Buddha, in Persia (or Media), with that of Zoroaster, and
a century later extending itself by Xenophanes and Heracli-
tus into Greece'. According to this theory, the calf-worship
in the wilderness and under the kings, the altars in the high
places, and the atrocities of the valley of Hinnom, were not
acts of apostasy, but of persistence in early barbarism. In
Mr Mackay's opinion, the account of the Passover, as it now
stands, is the veil which the purer conceptions of later
Hebrews cast over the ancient custom of sacrificing firstborn
children to the bloodthirsty El; the massacre of three thousand Israelites, represented in Exodus as retributive, was

probably sacrificial—a huge offering to the same demon, the rather that Aaron, the leader in the calf-worship, was not involved in the same destruction; the command by which God is said to have tempted Abraham, the vow of Jephthah, the slaughter of the seven descendants of Saul, whereby David sought to propitiate his God and avert a famine, are indications that human sacrifices were familiar to the Hebrews; above all, that 'passing of children through the fire', recorded of so many kings, and indignantly denounced by the prophets, as a practice habitual to the nation, is most probably to be interpreted as an actual immolation. The somewhat obscure passage, Amos 5: 25, 26—'Have ye offered unto me sacrifices and offerings in the wilderness forty years, O house of Israel? But ye have borne the tabernacle of your Moloch and Chiun, your images, the star of your God which ye made to yourselves'—Mr Mackay thinks important as conveying a denial of the early existence of a pure, Jehovistic religion. A disputed passage is, of course, dubious ground for an inference; but there is ample evidence of a less questionable kind, that the early Hebrew God, whether identical or not with any heathen deity, was of a character widely different from the one proclaimed by Micah, as requiring nothing of man but to do justly, to love mercy, and to walk humbly with God.

The original presiding Deity of Israel was, in Mr Mackay's words, 'emphatically the terrific God'. The Old Testament abounds in pictures of Divine operations that cannot be regarded as true delineations of the real character of Deity; but only distortions of it, analogous to those exhibited in the mythologies of other countries. The judicious reader of the Hebrew Scriptures, however orthodox his faith, cannot fail to perceive that they exhibit a progress from degrading to enlightened views of Divine nature and government. The writings of the prophets are full of protests against the conceptions of popular ignorance, and by continually expanding and purifying the Jewish ideas of Deity, prepared the way for the reception of the teachings of Christ. This view of the progressive character of 'revelation' does not depend for its evidence on minute points of criticism; it rests rather upon broad facts which are open to the apprehension of the most unlearned: and the 'Progress of the Intellect' abounds in statements which place them in the most forcible point of view. To a greater or less extent they are now recognized by Christians of all denominations, and it is impossible to take up the writings, or listen to the discourses of the leading men of any church or sect, without perceiving the influence which they have exerted upon their minds.

Mr Mackay's analysis and history of the theory of Mediation, from its earliest mythical embodiments, those 'flowers which fancy strewed before the youthful steps of Psyche, when she first set out in pursuit of the immortal object of her love', to its subtilization in philosophy—his delineation of the origin of Christianity as an expansion of the prophetic spiritualism, yet carrying within it certain elements of Jewish symbolism, which have arrested its true development and perverted its influence—his final sketch of the confluence of Greek Philosophy and Christianized Hebrewism—are admirable, both from their panoramic breadth and their richness in illustrative details. We can only recommend the reader to resort himself to this treasury of mingled thought and learning, and as a further inducement, we will quote the concluding passage from the section on the 'Mediation of Philosophy'.

The true religious philosophy of an imperfect being is not a system of creed, but, as Socrates thought, an infinite search or approximation. Finality is but another name for bewilderment or defeat, the common affectation of indolence and superstition, a temporary suspension of the mind's health arising from prejudice, and especially from the old error of clinging too closely to notions found instrumental in assisting it after they have ceased to be serviceable, and striving rather to defend and retain them, than to make them more correct. A remnant of the mythical lurks in the very sanctuary of science. Forms or theories ever fall short of nature, though they are ever tending to reach a position above nature, and may often be found really to include more than the maker of them at the time knew. To a certain extent they are reliable and complete; as a system of knowledge they are but intermediate and preparatory. As matter is the soul's necessary instrument, so ignorance, more or less mixed up with all its expressions and forms, may be said to be as it were the eyelid through which it gradually opens itself to the truth, admitting no more than it can for the time support, and, as through a veil, learning to support its lustre. The old religionists discovered a universal cause, personified it and prayed to it. The mere notion seemed not only to satisfy the religious feeling, but to solve all problems. Nations unanimously subscribed to the pious formula, which satisfied their imaginations, and pleased their vanity by cheating them into a belief that they were wise; but which, at the same time, supplanted nature by tradition, the sources of truth by artificial disguises, and at last paralysed the sentiment which gave birth to it. Science, unlike the rude expedient which stupefied without nourishing the mind, gratifies the religious feeling without arresting it, and opening out the barren mystery of the one into more explicit and manageable 'forms' expressing, not indeed his essence, but his will, feeds an endless enthusiasm by accumulating for ever new objects of pursuit. We have long experienced that knowledge is profitable; we are beginning to find out that it is moral, and shall at last discover it to be religious. Aristotle declared the highest and truest science to be that which is most disinterested; Bacon, treating science as separate from religion, asserted knowledge to be power, and held that truth must be tested by its fruits, that is, its instrumentality in promoting the right and the useful. Both assertions may be justified and reconciled by the fact that, while no real knowledge is powerless or fruitless, the fruits differ in refinement and value, the highest being unquestionably those disinterested gratifications which minister to the highest wants of the highest faculties, and which earned for philosophy the title of a divine love, realizing the mysterious longing of the soul, and promoting the accomplishment of its destiny,

> To rise in science as in bliss,
> Initiate in the secrets of the skies.

Woman in France: Madame de Sablé
(1854)

IN 1847, a certain Count Leopold Ferri died at Padua, leaving a library entirely composed of works written by women, in various languages, and this library amounted to nearly 32,000 volumes. We will not hazard any conjecture as to the proportion of these volumes which a severe judge, like the priest in Don Quixote, would deliver to the flames, but for our own part, most of those we should care to rescue would be the works of French women. With a few remarkable exceptions, our own feminine literature is made up of books which could have been better written by men; books which have the same relation to literature in general, as academic prize poems have to poetry: when not a feeble imitation, they are usually an absurd exaggeration of the masculine style, like the swaggering gait of a bad actress in male attire. Few English women have written so much like a woman as Richardson's Lady G.* Now, we think it an immense mistake to maintain that there is no sex in literature. Science has no sex: the mere knowing and reasoning faculties, if they act correctly, must go through the same process, and arrive at the same result. But in art and literature, which imply the action of the entire being, in which every fibre of the nature is engaged, in which every peculiar modification of the individual makes itself felt, woman has something specific to contribute. Under every imaginable social condition, she will necessarily have a class of sensations and emotions—the maternal ones—which must remain unknown to man; and the fact of her comparative physical weakness, which, however it may have been exaggerated by a vicious civilization, can never be cancelled, introduces a distinctively feminine condition into the wondrous chemistry of the affections and sentiments, which inevitably gives rise to distinctive forms and combinations.

A certain amount of psychological difference between man and woman necessarily arises out of the difference of sex, and instead of being destined to vanish before a complete development of woman's intellectual and moral nature, will be a permanent source of variety and beauty, as long as the tender light and dewy freshness of morning affect us differently from the strength and brilliancy of the mid-day sun. And those delightful women of France, who, from the beginning of the seventeenth to the close of the eighteenth century, formed some of the brightest threads in the web of political and literary history, wrote under circumstances which left the feminine character of their minds uncramped by timidity, and unstrained by mistaken effort. They were not trying to make a career for themselves; they thought little, in many cases not at all, of the public; they wrote letters to their lovers and friends, memoirs of their everyday lives, romances in which they gave portraits of their familiar acquaintances, and described the tragedy or comedy which was going on before their eyes. Always refined and graceful, often witty, sometimes judicious, they wrote what they saw, thought, and felt, in their habitual language, without proposing any model to themselves, without any intention to prove that women could write as well as men, without affecting manly views or suppressing womanly ones. One may say, at least with regard to the women of the seventeenth century, that their writings were but a charming accident of their more charming lives, like the petals which the wind shakes from the rose in its bloom. And it is but a twin fact with this, that in France alone woman has had a vital influence on the development of literature; in France alone the mind of woman has passed like an electric current through the language, making crisp and definite what is elsewhere heavy and blurred; in France alone, if the writings of women were swept away, a serious gap would be made in the national history.

Patriotic gallantry may perhaps contend that English women could, if they had liked, have written as well as their neighbours; but we will leave the consideration of that question to the reviewers of the literature that might have been. In the literature that actually is, we must turn to France for the highest examples of womanly achievement in almost every department. We confess ourselves unacquainted with the productions of those awful women of Italy, who held professional chairs, and were great in civil and canon law; we have made no researches into the catacombs of female literature, but we think we may safely conclude that they would yield no rivals to that which is still unburied; and here, we suppose, the question of pre-eminence can only lie between England and France. And to this day, Madame de Sévigné* remains the single instance of a woman who is supreme in a class of literature which has engaged the ambition of men; Madame Dacier* still reigns the queen of blue-stockings, though women have long studied Greek without shame;¹ Madame de Staël's* name still rises first to the lips when we are asked to mention a woman of great intellectual power; Madame Roland* is still the unrivalled type of the sagacious and sternly heroic, yet lovable woman; George Sand* is the unapproached artist who, to Jean Jacques'* eloquence and deep sense of external nature, unites the clear delineation of character and the tragic depth of passion. These great names, which mark different epochs, soar like tall pines amidst a forest of less conspicuous, but not less fascinating, female writers; and beneath these again are spread, like a thicket of hawthorns, eglantines, and honeysuckles, the women who are known rather by what they stimulated men to write, than by what they wrote themselves—the women whose tact, wit, and personal radiance, created the atmosphere of the *salon*, where literature, philosophy, and science, emancipated from the trammels of pedantry and technicality, entered on a brighter stage of existence.

What were the causes of this earlier development and more abundant manifestation of womanly intellect in

---

¹ Queen Christina, when Mme Dacier (then Mlle Le Fèvre) sent her a copy of her edition of 'Callimachus' wrote in reply;- 'Mais vous, de qui on m'assure que vous êtes une belle et agréable fille, n'avez vous pas honte de'être si savante?' ['But you, a handsome and pleasing maid, as I am told, are you not ashamed of being so learned?']

France? The primary one, perhaps, lies in the physiological characteristics of the Gallic race:—the small brain and vivacious temperament which permit the fragile system of woman to sustain the superlative activity requisite for intellectual creativeness; while, on the other hand, the larger brain and slower temperament of the English and Germans are, in the womanly organization, generally dreamy and passive. The type of humanity in the latter may be grander, but it requires a larger sum of conditions to produce a perfect specimen. Throughout the animal world, the higher the organization, the more frequent is the departure from the normal form; we do not often see imperfectly-developed or ill-made insects, but we rarely see a perfectly-developed, well-made man. And thus the *physique* of a woman may suffice as the substratum for a superior Gallic mind, but is too thin a soil for a superior Teutonic one. Our theory is borne out by the fact, that among our own countrywomen, those who distinguish themselves by literary production, more frequently approach the Gallic than the Teutonic type; they are intense and rapid rather than comprehensive. The woman of large capacity can seldom rise beyond the absorption of ideas; her physical conditions refuse to support the energy required for spontaneous activity; the voltaic-pile is not strong enough to produce crystallizations; phantasms of great ideas float through her mind, but she has not the spell which will arrest them, and give them fixity. This, more than unfavourable external circumstances, is, we think, the reason why woman has not yet contributed any new form to art, any discovery in science, any deep-searching inquiry in philosophy. The necessary physiological conditions are not present in her. That under more favourable circumstances in the future, these conditions may prove compatible with the feminine organization, it would be rash to deny. For the present, we are only concerned with our theory so far as it presents a physiological basis for the intellectual effectiveness of French women.

A secondary cause was probably the laxity of opinion and practice with regard to the marriage-tie. Heaven forbid that we should enter on a defence of French morals, most of all in relation to marriage! But it is undeniable, that unions formed in the maturity of thought and feeling, and grounded only on inherent fitness and mutual attraction, tended to bring women into more intelligent sympathy with men, and to heighten and complicate their share in the political drama. The quiescence and security of the conjugal relation, are doubtless favourable to the manifestation of the highest qualities by persons who have already attained a high standard of culture, but rarely foster a passion sufficient to rouse all the faculties to aid in winning or retaining its beloved object—to convert indolence into activity, indifference into ardent partisanship, dullness into perspicuity. Gallantry and intrigue are sorry enough things in themselves, but they certainly serve better to arouse the dormant faculties of woman than embroidery and domestic drudgery, especially when, as in the high society of France in the seventeenth century, they are refined by the influence of Spanish chivalry, and controlled by the spirit of Italian causticity. The dreamy and fantastic girl was awakened to reality by the experience of wifehood and maternity, and became capable of loving, not a mere phantom of her own imagination, but a living man, struggling with the hatreds and rivalries of the political arena; she espoused his quarrels, she made herself, her fortune, and her influence, the stepping-stones of his ambition; and the languid beauty, who had formerly seemed ready to 'die of a rose',* was seen to become the heroine of an insurrection. The vivid interest in affairs which was thus excited in woman, must obviously have tended to quicken her intellect, and give it a practical application; and the very sorrows—the heart-pangs and regrets which are inseparable from a life of passion—deepened her nature by the questioning of self and destiny which they occasioned, and by the energy demanded to surmount them and live on. No wise person, we imagine, wishes to restore the social condition of France in the seventeenth century, or considers the ideal programme of woman's life to be a *mariage de convenance* at fifteen, a career of gallantry from twenty to eight-and-thirty, and penitence and piety for the rest of her days. Nevertheless, that social condition had its good results, as much as the madly-superstitious Crusades had theirs.

But the most indisputable source of feminine culture and development in France was the influence of the *salons*; which, as all the world knows, were *réunions* of both sexes, where conversation ran along the whole gamut of subjects, from the frothiest *vers de société* to the philosophy of Descartes. Richelieu had set the fashion of uniting a taste for letters with the habits of polite society and the pursuits of ambition; and in the first quarter of the seventeenth century, there were already several hôtels in Paris, varying in social position from the closest proximity of the Court to the debatable ground of the aristocracy and the bourgeoisie, which served as a rendezvous for different circles of people, bent on entertaining themselves either by showing talent or admiring it. The most celebrated of these rendezvous was the Hôtel de Rambouillet, which was at the culmination of its glory in 1630, and did not become quite extinct until 1648, when, the troubles of the Fronde commencing, its *habitués* were dispersed or absorbed by political interests. The presiding genius of this *salon*, the Marquise de Rambouillet, was the very model of the woman who can act as an amalgam to the most incongruous elements; beautiful, but not preoccupied by coquetry or passion; an enthusiastic admirer of talent, but with no pretensions to talent on her own part; exquisitely refined in language and manners, but warm and generous withal; not given to entertain her guests with her own compositions, or to paralyse them by her universal knowledge. She had once *meant* to learn Latin, but had been prevented by an illness; perhaps she was all the better acquainted with Italian and Spanish productions, which, in default of a national literature, were then the intellectual pabulum of all cultivated persons in France who were unable to read the classics. In her mild, agreeable presence was accomplished that blending of the high-toned chivalry of Spain with the caustic wit and refined irony of Italy, which issued in the creation of a new standard of taste—the combination of the utmost exaltation in sentiment with the utmost simplicity of language. Women are peculiarly fitted to further such a combination,—first, from their greater tendency to mingle affection and imagination with passion, and thus subtilize it into sentiment; and next, from that dread of what over-taxes their intellectual energies, either by difficulty or monotony, which gives them an instinctive fondness for lightness of treatment and airiness of expression, thus making them cut short all prolixity and reject all heaviness. When these womanly characteristics were brought into conversational contact with the materials furnished by such minds as those of Richelieu, Corneille, the Great Condé, Balzac, and Bossuet, it is no wonder that the result was something piquant and charming. Those famous *habitués* of the Hôtel de Rambouillet did not, apparently, first lay themselves out to entertain the ladies with grimacing 'small-talk', and then take each other by the sword-knot to discuss matters of real interest in a corner; they rather sought to present their best ideas in the guise most acceptable to intelligent and accomplished women. And the conversation was not of literature only; war, politics, religion, the lightest details of daily news—everything was admissible, if only it were treated with refinement and intelligence. The Hôtel de Rambouillet was no mere literary *réunion*; it included *hommes d'affaires* and soldiers as well as authors, and in such a circle, women would not become *bas bleus* or dreamy moralizers, ignorant of the world and of human nature, but intelligent observers of character and events. It is easy to understand, however, that with the herd of imitators who, in Paris and the provinces, aped the style of this famous *salon*, simplicity degenerated into affectation, and nobility of sentiment was replaced by an inflated effort to outstrip nature, so that the *genre précieux* drew down the satire, which reached its climax in the *Précieuses Ridicules* and *Les Femmes Savantes*,* the former of which appeared in 1660, and the latter in 1673. But Madelon and Cathos are the lineal descendants of Mademoiselle Scudéry* and her satellites quite as much as of the Hôtel de Rambouillet. The society which assembled every Saturday in her *salon* was exclusively literary, and, although occasionally visited by a few persons of high birth, bourgeois in its tone, and enamoured of madrigals, sonnets, stanzas, and *bouts rimés*.* The affectation that decks trivial things in fine language, belongs essentially to a class which sees another above it, and is uneasy in the sense of its inferiority; and this affectation is precisely the opposite of the original *genre précieux*.

Another centre from which feminine influence radiated into the national literature was the Palais du Luxembourg, where Mademoiselle d'Orleans, in disgrace at court on account of her share in the Fronde, held a little court of her own, and for want of anything else to employ her active spirit, busied herself with literature. One fine morning, it occurred to this princess to ask all the persons who frequented her court, among whom were Madame de Sévigné, Madame de la Fayette, and La Rochefoucauld, to write their own portraits, and she at once set the example. It was understood that defects and virtues were to be spoken of with like candour. The idea was carried out; those who were not clever or not bold enough to write for themselves employing the pen of a friend.

'Such,' says M. Cousin, 'was the pastime of Mademoiselle and her friends during the years 1657 and 1658: from this pastime proceeded a complete literature. In 1659, Ségrais revised these portraits, added a considerable number in prose and even in verse, and published the whole in a handsome quarto volume, admirably printed, and now become very rare, under the title, *Divers Portraits*. Only thirty copies were printed, not for sale, but to be given as presents by Mademoiselle. The work had a prodigious success. That which had made the fortune of Mademoiselle de Scudéry's romances—the pleasure of seeing one's portrait a little flattered, curiosity to see that of others, the passion which the middle class always have had and will have for knowing what goes on in the aristocratic world (at that time not very easy of access), the names of the illustrious persons who were here for the first time described physically and morally with the utmost detail, great ladies transformed all at once into writers, and unconsciously inventing a new manner of writing, of which no book gave the slightest idea, and which was the ordinary manner of speaking of the aristocracy; this undefinable mixture of the natural, the easy, and at the same time of the agreeable, and supremely distinguished—all this charmed the court and the town, and very early in the year 1659 permission was asked of Mademoiselle to give a new edition of the privileged book for the use of the public in general.

The fashion thus set, portraits multiplied throughout France, until in 1688, La Bruyère adopted the form in his *Characters*, and ennobled it by divesting it of personality. We shall presently see that a still greater work than La Bruyère's also owed its suggestion to a woman, whose *salon* was hardly a less fascinating resort than the Hôtel de Rambouillet itself.

In proportion as the literature of a country is enriched and culture becomes more generally diffused, personal influence is less effective in the formation of taste and in the furtherance of social advancement. It is no longer the coterie which acts on literature, but literature which acts on the coterie; the circle represented by the word *public*, is ever widening, and ambition, poising itself in order to hit a more distant mark, neglects the successes of the *salon*. What was once lavished prodigally in conversation, is reserved for the volume, or the 'article'; and the effort is not to betray originality rather than to communicate it. As the old coach-roads have sunk into disuse through the creation of railways, so journalism tends more and more to divert information from the channel of conversation into the channel of the Press: no one is satisfied with a more circumscribed audience than that very indeterminate abstraction 'the public', and men find a vent for their opinions not in talk, but in 'copy'. We read the 'Athenaeum' askance at the tea-table, and take notes from the 'Philosophical Journal' at a soirée; we invite our friends that we may thrust a book into their hands, and presuppose an exclusive desire in the 'ladies' to discuss their own matters, 'that we may crackle the *Times*' at our ease. In fact, the evident tendency of things to contract personal communication within the narrowest limits makes us tremble lest some further development of the electric telegraph should reduce us to a society of mutes, or to a sort of insects, communicating by ingenious antennæ of our own invention. Things were far from having reached this pass in the last century; but even then, literature and society had outgrown the nursing of coteries, and although many *salons* of that period were worthy successors of the Hôtel de Rambouillet, they were simply a recreation, not an influence. Enviable evenings, no doubt, were passed in them; and if we could be carried back to any of them at will, we should hardly know whether to choose the Wednesday dinner at Madame Geoffrin's, with d'Alembert, Mademoiselle de l'Espinasse, Grimm, and the rest, or the graver society which, thirty years later, gathered round Condorcet and his lovely young wife. The *salon* retained its attractions, but its power was gone: the stream of life had become too broad and deep for such small rills to affect it.

A fair comparison between the Frenchwomen of the seventeenth century and those of the eighteenth would, perhaps, have a balanced result, though it is common to be a partisan on this subject. The former have more exaltation, perhaps more nobility of sentiment, and less consciousness in their intellectual activity—less of the *femme auteur*, which was Rousseau's horror in Madame d'Epinay; but the latter have a richer fund of ideas—not more ingenuity, but the materials of an additional century for their ingenuity to work upon. The women of the seventeenth century, when love was on the wane, took to devotion, at first mildly and by halves, as English women take to caps, and finally without compromise; with the women of the eighteenth century, Bossuet and Massillon had given way to Voltaire and Rousseau; and when youth and beauty failed, then they were thrown on their own moral strength.

M. Cousin is especially enamoured of the women of the seventeenth century, and relieves himself from his labours in philosophy by making researches into the original documents which throw light upon their lives. Last year he gave us some results of these researches, in a volume on the youth of the Duchesse de Longueville; and he has just followed it up with a second volume, in which he further illustrates her career by tracing it in connexion with that of her friend, Madame de Sablé. The materials to which he has had recourse for this purpose, are chiefly two celebrated collections of manuscripts: that of Conrart, the first secretary to the French Academy, one of those universally curious people who seem made for the annoyance of contemporaries and the benefit of posterity; and that of Valant, who was at once the physician, the secretary, and general steward of Madame de Sablé, and who, with or without her permission, possessed himself of the letters addressed to her by her numerous correspondents during the latter part of her life, and of various papers having some personal or literary interest attached to them. From these stores M. Cousin has selected many documents previously unedited; and though he often leaves us something to desire in the arrangement of his materials, this volume of his on Madame de Sablé is very acceptable to us, for she interests us quite enough to carry us through more than three hundred pages of rather scattered narrative, and through an appendix of correspondence in small type. M. Cousin justly appreciates her character as 'un heureux mélange de raison, d'esprit, d'agrément, et de bonté';* and perhaps there are few better specimens of the woman who is extreme in nothing, but sympathetic in all things; who affects us by no special quality, but by her entire being; whose nature has no *tons criards*,* but is like those textures which, from their harmonious blending of all colours, give repose to the eye, and do not weary us though we see them every day. Madame de Sablé is also a striking example of the one order of influence which woman has exercised over literature in France; and on this ground, as well as intrinsically, she is worth studying. If the reader agrees with us he will perhaps be inclined, as we are, to dwell a little on the chief points in her life and character.

Madeline de Souvré, daughter of the Marquis of Courtenvaux, a nobleman distinguished enough to be chosen as governor of Louis XIII, was born in 1599, on the threshold of that seventeenth century, the brilliant genius of which is mildly reflected in her mind and history. Thus, when in 1635 her more celebrated friend, Mademoiselle de Bourbon, afterwards the Duchesse de Longueville, made her appearance at the Hôtel de Rambouillet, Madame de Sablé had nearly crossed that table-land of maturity which precedes a woman's descent towards old age. She had been married, in

1614, to Philippe Emanuel de Laval-Montmorency, Seigneur de Bois-Dauphin, and Marquis de Sablé, of whom nothing further is known than that he died in 1640, leaving her the richer by four children, but with a fortune considerably embarrassed. With beauty and high rank added to the mental attractions of which we have abundant evidence, we may well believe that Madame de Sablé's youth was brilliant. For her beauty, we have the testimony of sober Madame de Motteville, who also speaks of her as having 'beaucoup de lumière et de sincérité'; and in the following passage very graphically indicates one phase of Madame de Sablé's character:—

The Marquise de Sablé was one of those whose beauty made the most noise when the Queen came into France. But if she was amiable, she was still more desirous of appearing so; this lady's self-love rendered her too sensitive to the regard which men exhibited towards her. There yet existed in France some remains of the politeness which Catherine de Médici had introduced from Italy, and the new dramas, with all the other works in prose and verse, which came from Madrid, were thought to have such great delicacy, that she (Madame de Sablé) had conceived a high idea of the gallantry which the Spaniards had learned from the Moors.

She was persuaded that men can, without crime, have tender sentiments for women—that the desire of pleasing them led men to the greatest and finest actions—roused their intelligence, and inspired them with liberality, and all sorts of virtues; but, on the other hand, women, who were the ornament of the world, and made to be served and adored, ought not to admit anything from them but their respectful attentions. As this lady supported her views with much talent and great beauty, she had given them authority in her time, and the number and consideration of those who continued to associate with her, have caused to subsist in our day what the Spaniards call *finezas*.

Here is the grand element of the original *femme précieuse*, and it appears further, in a detail also reported by Madame de Motteville, that Madame de Sablé had a passionate admirer in the accomplished Duc de Montmorency, and apparently reciprocated his regard; but discovering (at what period of their attachment is unknown) that he was raising a lover's eyes towards the Queen, she broke with him at once. 'I have heard her say,' tells Madame de Motteville, 'that her pride was such with regard to the Duc de Montmorency, that at the first demonstrations which he gave of his change, she refused to see him any more, being unable to receive with satisfaction attentions which she had to share with the greatest princess in the world.' There is no evidence, except the untrustworthy assertion of Tallemant de Réaux, that Madame de Sablé had any other liaison than this; and the probability of the negative is increased by the ardour of her friendships. The strongest of these was formed early in life with Mademoiselle Dona d'Attichy, afterwards Comtesse de Maure; it survived the effervescence of youth and the closest intimacy of middle age, and was only terminated by the death of the latter in 1663. A little incident in this friendship is so characteristic in the transcendentalism which was then carried into all the affections, that it is worth relating at length. Mademoiselle d'Attichy, in her grief and indignation at Richelieu's treatment of her relative, quitted Paris, and was about to join her friend at Sablé, when she suddenly discovered that Madame de Sablé, in a letter to Madame de Rambouillet, had said, that her greatest happiness would be to pass her life with Julie de Rambouillet, afterwards Madame de Montausier. To Anne d'Attichy this appears nothing less than the crime of *lèse-amitié*.* No explanations will appease her: she refuses to accept the assurance that the offensive expression was used simply out of unreflecting conformity to the style of the Hôtel de Rambouillet—that it was mere '*galimatias*'.* She gives up her journey, and writes a letter, which is the only one Madame de Sablé chose to preserve, when, in her period of devotion, she sacrificed the records of her youth. Here it is:—

I have seen this letter in which you tell me there is so much *galimatias*, and I assure you that I have not found any at all. On the contrary, I find everything very plainly expressed, and among others, one which is too explicit for my satisfaction—namely, what you have said to Madame de Rambouillet, that if you tried to imagine a perfectly happy life for yourself, it would be to pass it all alone with Mademoiselle de Rambouillet. You know whether any one can be more persuaded than I am of her merit; but I confess to you that that has not prevented me from being surprised that you could entertain a thought which did so great an injury to our friendship. As to believing that you said this to one, and wrote it to the other, simply for the sake of paying them an agreeable compliment, I have too high an esteem for your courage to be able to imagine that complaisance would cause you thus to betray the sentiments of your heart, especially on a subject in which, as they were unfavourable to me, I think you would have the more reason for concealing them, the affection which I have for you being so well-known to every one, and especially to Mademoiselle de Rambouillet, so that I doubt whether she will not have been more sensible of the wrong you have done me, than of the advantage you have given her. The circumstance of this letter falling into my hands, has forcibly reminded me of these lines of Bertaut:—

> Malheureuse est l'ignorance.
> Et plus malheureux le savoir.*

Having through this lost a confidence which alone rendered life supportable to me, it is impossible for me to take the journey so much thought of. For would there be any propriety in travelling sixty miles in this season, in order to burthen you with a person so little suited to you, that after years of a passion without parallel, you cannot help thinking that the greatest pleasure of your life would be to pass it without her? I return, then, into my solitude, to examine the defects which cause me so much unhappiness, and unless I can correct them, I should have less joy than confusion in seeing you.

It speaks strongly for the charm of Madame de Sablé's nature that she was able to retain so susceptible a friend as Mademoiselle d'Attichy in spite of numerous other friend-ships, some of which, especially that with Madame de Longueville, were far from lukewarm—in spite too of a tendency in herself to distrust the affection of others to-wards her, and to wait for advances rather than to make them. We find many traces of this tendency in the affec-tionate remonstrances addressed to her by Madame de Longueville, now for shutting herself up from her friends, now for doubting that her letters are acceptable. Here is a little passage from one of these remonstrances which indicates a trait of Madame de Sablé, and is in itself a bit of excellent sense, worthy the consideration of lovers and friends in general:—

I am very much afraid that if I leave to you the care of letting me know when I can see you, I shall be a long time without having that pleasure, and that nothing will incline you to procure it me, for I have always observed a certain lukewarmness in your friendship after our *explanations*, from which I have never seen you thoroughly recover; and that is why I dread explanations, for however good they may be in themselves, since they serve to reconcile people, it must always be admitted, to their shame, that they are at least the effect of a bad cause, and that if they remove it for a time they *sometimes leave a certain facility in getting angry again*, which, without diminishing friendship, renders its intercourse less agreeable. It seems to me that I find all this in your behaviour to me; so I am not wrong in sending to know if you wish to have me to-day.

It is clear that Madame de Sablé was far from having what Sainte-Beuve calls the one fault of Madame Necker—absolute perfection. A certain exquisiteness in her physical and moral nature was, as we shall see, the source of more than one weakness, but the perception of these weaknesses, which is indicated in Madame de Longueville's letters, heightens our idea of the attractive qualities which notwithstanding drew from her, at the sober age of forty, such expressions as these:—'I assure you that you are the person in all the world whom it would be most agreeable to me to see, and there is no one whose intercourse is a ground of truer satisfaction to me. It is admirable that at all times, and amidst all changes, the taste for your society remains in me; and, *if one ought to thank God for the joys which do not tend to salvation*, I should thank him with all my heart for having preserved that to me at a time in which he has taken away from me all others.'

Since we have entered on the chapter of Madame de Sablé's weaknesses, this is the place to mention what was the subject of endless raillery from her friends—her elaborate precaution about her health, and her dread of infection, even from diseases the least communicable. Perhaps this anxiety was founded as much on æsthetic as on physical grounds, on disgust at the details of illness as much as on dread of suffering: with a cold in the head or a bilious complaint, the exquisite *précieuse* must have been considerably less conscious of being 'the ornament of the world', and 'made to be adored'. Even her friendship, strong as it was, was not strong enough to overcome her horror of contagion; for when Mademoiselle de Bourbon, recently become Madame de Longueville, was attacked by small-pox, Madame de Sablé for some time had not courage to visit her, or even to see Mademoiselle de Rambouillet, who was assiduous in her attendance on the patient. A little correspondence *à propos* of these circumstances so well exhibits the graceful badinage in which the great ladies of that day were adepts, that we are tempted to quote one short letter.

Mlle de Rambouillet to the Marquise de Sablé

Mlle de Chalais (*dame de compagnie* to the Marquise) will please to read this letter to Madame la Marquise, *out of* a draught.

Madame,

I do not think it possible to begin my treaty with you too early, for I am convinced that between the first proposition made to me that I should see you, and the conclusion, you will have so many reflections to make, so many physicians to consult, and so many fears to surmount, that I shall have full leisure to air myself. The conditions which I offer to fulfil for this purpose are, not to visit you until I have been three days absent from the Hôtel de Condé (where Mme de Longueville was ill), to choose a frosty day, not to approach you within four paces, not to sit down on more than one seat. You may also have a great fire in your room, burn juniper in the four corners, surround yourself with imperial vinegar, with rue and wormwood. If you can feel yourself safe under these conditions, without my cutting off my hair, I swear to you to execute them religiously; and if you want examples to fortify you, I can tell you that the Queen consented to see M. Chaudebonne, when he had come directly from Mlle de Bourbon's room, and that Mme d'Aiguillon, who has good taste in such matters, and is free from reproach on these points, has just sent me word that if I did not go to see her, she would come to me.

Madame de Sablé betrays in her reply that she winces under this raillery, and thus provokes a rather severe though polite rejoinder, which, added to the fact that Madame de Longueville is convalescent, rouses her courage to the pitch of paying the formidable visit. Mademoiselle de Rambouillet, made aware, through their mutual friend Voiture, that her sarcasm has cut rather too deep, winds up the matter by writing that very difficult production, a perfectly conciliatory yet dignified apology. Peculiarities like this always deepen with age, and accordingly, fifteen years later, we find Madame D'Orleans, in her *Princesse de Paphlagonia*—a romance in which she describes her court, with the little quarrels and other affairs that agitated it—giving the following amusing picture, or rather caricature, of the extent to which Madame de Sablé carried her pathological mania, which seems to have been shared by her friend the Countess de Maure (Mademoiselle d'Attichy). In the romance, these two ladies appear under the names of the Princesse Parthénie and the Reine de Mionie.*

There was not an hour in the day in which they did not confer together on the means of avoiding death, and on the art of rendering themselves immortal. Their conferences did not take place like those of other people; the fear of breathing an air which was too cold or too warm, the dread lest the wind should be too dry or too moist—in short, the imagination that the weather might not be as temperate as they thought necessary for the preservation of their health, caused them to write letters from one room to the other. It would be extremely fortunate if these notes could be found, and formed into a collection. I am convinced that they would contain rules for the regimen of life, precautions even as to the proper time for applying remedies, and also remedies which Hippocrates and Galen, with all their science, never heard of. Such a collection would be very useful to the public, and would be highly profitable to the faculties of Paris and Montpelier. If these letters were discovered, great advantages of all kinds might be derived from them, for they were princesses who had nothing mortal about them but the *knowledge* that they were mortal. In their writings might be learned all politeness in style, and the most delicate manner of speaking on all subjects. There is nothing with which they were not acquainted; they knew the affairs of all the

States in the world, through the share they had in all the intrigues of its private members, either in matters of gallantry, as in other things on which their advice was necessary; either to adjust embroilments and quarrels, or to excite them, for the sake of the advantages which their friends could derive from them;—in a word, they were persons through whose hands the secrets of the whole world had to pass. The Princess Parthénie (Mme de Sablé) had a palate as delicate as her mind; nothing could equal the magnificence of the entertainments she gave; all the dishes were exquisite, and her cleanliness was beyond all that could be imagined. It was in their time that writing came into use; previously, nothing was written but marriage contracts, and letters were never heard of; thus it is to them that we owe a practice so convenient in intercourse.

Still later, in 1669, when the most uncompromising of the Port Royalists* seemed to tax Madame de Sablé with lukewarmness that she did not join them at Port-Royal des Champs, we find her writing to the stern M. de Sévigny: 'En vérité, je crois que je ne pourrois mieux faire que de tout quitter et de m'en aller là. Mais que deviendroient ces frayeurs de n'avoir pas de médecins à choisir, ni de chirurgien pour me saigner?'*

Mademoiselle, as we have seen, hints at the love of delicate eating, which many of Madame de Sablé's friends numbered among her foibles, especially after her religious career had commenced. She had a genius in *friandise*,* and knew how to gratify the palate without offending the highest sense of refinement. Her sympathetic nature showed itself in this as in other things: she was always sending *bonnes bouches** to her friends, and trying to communicate to them her science and taste in the affairs of the table. Madame de Longueville, who had not the luxurious tendencies of her friend, writes—'Je vous demande au nom de Dieu, que vous ne me prépariez aucun ragoût. Surtout ne me donnez point de festin. Au nom de Dieu, qu'il n'y ait rien que ce qu'on peut manger, car vous savez que c'est inutile pour moi; de plus j'en ai scrupule.'* But other friends had more appreciation of her niceties. Voiture thanks her for her melons, and assures her that they are better than those of yesterday;

Madame de Choisy hopes that her ridicule of Jansenism*
will not provoke Madame de Sablé to refuse her the receipt
for salad; and La Rochefoucauld writes: 'You cannot do me
a greater charity than to permit the bearer of this letter to
enter into the mysteries of your marmalade and your genuine preserves, and I humbly entreat you to do everything
you can in his favour. If I could hope for two dishes of
those preserves, which I did not deserve to eat before, I
should be indebted to you all my life.' For our own part,
being as far as possible from fraternizing with those spiritual
people who convert a deficiency into a principle, and pique
themselves on an obtuse palate as a point of superiority, we
are not inclined to number Madame de Sablé's *friandise*
amongst her defects. M. Cousin, too, is apologetic on this
point. He says:

It was only the excess of a delicacy which can be readily understood, and a sort of fidelity to the character of *précieuse*. As the
précieuse did nothing according to common usage, she could not
dine like another. We have cited a passage from Mme de Motteville, where Mme de Sablé is represented in her first youth at the
Hôtel de Rambouillet, maintaining that woman is born to be an
ornament to the world, and to receive the adoration of men. The
woman worthy of the name, ought always to appear above material
wants, and retain, even in the most vulgar details of life, something
distinguished and purified. Eating is a very necessary operation,
but one which is not agreeable to the eye. Mme de Sablé insisted
on its being conducted with a peculiar cleanliness. According to
her, it was not every woman who could with impunity be at table
in the presence of a lover; the first distortion of the face, she said,
would be enough to spoil all. Gross meals, made for the body
merely, ought to be abandoned to *bourgeoises*, and the refined
woman should appear to take a little nourishment merely to sustain
her, and even to divert her, as one takes refreshments and ices.
Wealth did not suffice for this; a particular talent was required.
Mme de Sablé was a mistress in this art. She had transported the
aristocratic spirit and the *genre précieux*, good breeding and good
taste, even into cookery. Her dinners, without any opulence, were
celebrated and sought after.

It is quite in accordance with all this, that Madame de
Sablé should delight in fine scents, and we find that she

did; for being threatened, in her Port Royal days, when she was at an advanced age, with the loss of smell, and writing for sympathy and information to Mère Agnès, who had lost that sense early in life, she receives this admonition from the stern saint: 'You would gain by this loss, my very dear sister, if you made use of it as a satisfaction to God, for having had too much pleasure in delicious scents.' Scarron describes her as

> La non pareille Bois-Dauphine,
> *Entre dames perle très fine,**

and the superlative delicacy implied by this epithet seems to have belonged equally to her personal habits, her affections, and her intellect.

Madame de Sablé's life, for anything we know, flowed on evenly enough until 1640, when the death of her husband threw upon her the care of an embarrassed fortune. She found a friend in Réné de Longueil, Seigneur de Maisons, of whom we are content to know no more than that he helped Madame de Sablé to arrange her affairs, though only by means of alienating from her family the estate of Sablé, that his house was her refuge during the blockade of Paris, in 1649, and that she was not unmindful of her obligations to him, when, subsequently, her credit could be serviceable to him at court. In the midst of these pecuniary troubles came a more terrible trial—the loss of her favourite son, the brave and handsome Guy de Laval, who, after a brilliant career in the campaigns of Condé, was killed at the siege of Dunkirk, in 1646, when scarcely four-and-twenty. The fine qualities of this young man had endeared him to the whole army, and especially to Condé, had won him the hand of the Chancellor Séguire's daughter, and had thus opened to him the prospect of the highest honours. His loss seems to have been the most real sorrow of Madame de Sablé's life. Soon after followed the commotions of the Fronde, which put a stop to social intercourse, and threw the closest friends into opposite ranks. According to Lenet, who relies on the authority of Gourville, Madame de Sablé was under strong obligations to the court, being in the receipt of a pension of 2,000 crowns; at all events, she adhered throughout to the Queen and Mazarin, but being as far as possible from a fierce partisan, and given both by disposition and judgement to hear both sides of a question, she acted as a conciliator, and retained her friends of both parties. The Countess de Maure, whose husband was the most obstinate of *frondeurs*,* remained throughout her most cherished friend, and she kept up a constant correspondence with the lovely and intrepid heroine of the Fronde, Madame de Longueville. Her activity was directed to the extinction of animosities, by bringing about marriages between the Montagues and Capulets of the Fronde—between the Prince de Condé, or his brother, and the niece of Mazarin, or between the three nieces of Mazarin and the sons of three noblemen who were distinguished leaders of the Fronde. Though her projects were not realized, her conciliatory position enabled her to preserve all her friendships intact, and when the political tempest was over, she could assemble around her in her residence, in the Place Royale, the same society as before. Madame de Sablé was now approaching her twelfth lustrum, and though the charms of her mind and character made her more sought after than most younger women, it is not surprising that, sharing as she did in the religious ideas of her time, the concerns of 'salvation' seemed to become pressing. A religious retirement, which did not exclude the reception of literary friends, or the care for personal comforts, made the most becoming frame for age and diminished fortune. Jansenism was then to ordinary Catholicism what Puseyism is to ordinary Church of Englandism in these days—it was a *recherché* form of piety unshared by the vulgar; and one sees at once that it must have special attractions for the *précieuse*. Madame de Sablé, then, probably about 1655 or 1656, determined to retire to Port Royal, not because she was already devout, but because she hoped to become so; as, however, she wished to retain the pleasure of intercourse with friends who were still worldly, she built for herself a set of apartments at once distinct from the monastery and attached to it. Here, with a comfortable establishment, consisting of her secretary, Dr

Valant, Mademoiselle de Chalais, formerly her *dame de compagnie*, and now become her friend; an excellent cook; a few other servants, and for a considerable time a carriage and coachman; with her best friends within a moderate distance, she could, as M. Cousin says, be out of the noise of the world without altogether forsaking it, preserve her dearest friendships, and have before her eyes edifying examples—'vaquer enfin à son aise aux soins de son salut et à ceux de sa santé'.*

We have hitherto looked only at one phase of Madame de Sablé's character and influence—that of the *précieuse*. But she was much more than this: she was the valuable, trusted friend of noble women and distinguished men; she was the animating spirit of a society whence issued a new form of French literature: she was the woman of large capacity and large heart, whom Pascal sought to please, to whom Arnauld submitted the Discourse prefixed to his Logic, and to whom La Rochefoucauld writes: 'Vous savez que je ne crois que vous êtes sûr de certains chapitres, et surtout sur les replis du cœur.'* The papers preserved by her secretary, Valant, show that she maintained an extensive correspondence with persons of various rank and character; that her pen was untiring in the interest of others; that men made her the depositary of their thoughts, women of their sorrows; that her friends were as impatient, when she secluded herself, as if they had been rival lovers and she a youthful beauty. It is into her ear that Madame de Longueville pours her troubles and difficulties, and that Madame de La Fayette communicates her little alarms, lest young Count de St Paul should have detected her intimacy with La Rochefoucauld.[2] The few of Madame de Sablé's letters which survive show

[2] The letter to which we allude has this charming little touch;—'Je hais comme la mort que les gens de son age puissent croire que j'ai des galanteries. Il semble qu'on leur parait cent ans des qu'on est plus vieille qu'eux, et ils sont tout propre à s'étonner qu'il y ait encore question des gens.' ['I hate like death the idea that people of his own age might believe me to have liaisons. To all appearances one is deemed to be a hundred years old the moment one is older than they—and they are all too prone to wonder at there still being men about one.']

that she excelled in that epistolary style which was the
speciality of the Hôtel de Rambouillet; one to Madame de
Montausier, in favour of M. Périer, the brother-in-law of
Pascal, is a happy mixture of good taste and good sense;
but amongst them all we prefer quoting one to the Duchesse
de la Trimouille. It is light and pretty, and made out of
almost nothing, like soap-bubbles.

Je crois qu'il n'y a que moi qui face si bien tout le contraire de
ce que je veux faire, car il est vrai qu'il n'y a personne que j'honore
plus que vous et j'ai si bien fait qu'il est quasi impossible que
vous le puissiez croire. Ce n'estoit pas assez pour vous persuader
que je suis indigne de vos bonnes grâces et de votre souvenir que
d'avoir manqué fort longtemps à vous écrire; il falloit encore
retarder quinze jours à me donner l'honneur de répondre à votre
lettre. En vérité, madame, cela me fait parôitre si coupable, que
vers tout autre que vous j'aimerois mieux l'etre en effct que
d'entreprendre une chose si difficile qu'est celle de me justifier.
Mais je me sens si innocente dans mon âme, et j'ai tant d'estime,
de respect et d'affection pour vous, qu'il me semble que vous
devez le connôitre à cent lieues de distance d'ici, encore que je
ne vous dise pas un mot. C'est ce que me donne le courage de
vous écrire à cette heure, mais non pas ce qui m'en a empêché si
longtemps. J'ai commencé à faillir par force, ayant eu beaucoup
de maux, et depuis je l'ai fait par honte, et je vous avoue que si
je n'avois à cette heure la confiance que vous m'avez donnée en
me rassurant, et celle que je tire de mes propres sentimens pour
vous, je n'oserois jamais entreprendre de vous faire souvenir de
moi; mais je m'assure que vous oublierez tout, sur la protestation
que je vous fais de ne me laisser plus endurceir en mes fautes et
de demeurer inviolablement, madame, votre, etc.*

Was not the woman, who could unite the ease and grace
indicated by this letter, with an intellect that men thought
worth consulting on matters of reasoning and philosophy,
with warm affections, untiring activity for others, no ambition as an authoress, and an insight into *confitures* and
ragoûts, a rare combination? No wonder that her *salon* at
Port-Royal was the favourite resort of such women as
Madame de La Fayette, Madame de Montausier, Madame
de Longueville, and Madame de Hautefort; and of such
men as Pascal, La Rochefoucauld, Nicole, and Domat. The

collections of Valant contain papers which show what were
the habitual subjects of conversation in this *salon*. Theology,
of course, was a chief topic; but physics and metaphysics
had their turn, and still more frequently morals, taken in
their widest sense. There were *Conferences on Calvinism*, of
which an abstract is preserved. When Rohault invented his
glass tubes to serve for the barometrical experiments, in
which Pascal had roused a strong interest, the Marquis de
Sourdis entertained the society with a paper, entitled *Why
Water Mounts in a Glass Tube*. Cartesianism was an exciting
topic here, as well as everywhere else in France; it had its
partisans and opponents; and papers were read, containing
Thoughts on the Opinions of M. Descartes. These lofty matters
were varied by discussions on love and friendship, on the
drama, and on most of the things in heaven and earth which
the philosophy of that day dreamt of. Morals—generalizations on human affections, sentiments, and conduct—seem
to have been the favourite theme; and the aim was to reduce
these generalizations to their briefest form of expression, to
give them the epigrammatic turn which made them portable
in the memory. This was the specialty of Madame de Sablé's
circle, and was, probably, due to her own tendency. As the
Hôtel de Rambouillet was the nursery of graceful letter-
writing, and the Luxembourg of 'portraits' and 'characters',
so Madame de Sablé's *salon* fostered that taste for the
sententious style, to which we owe, probably, some of the
best *Pensées* of Pascal, and, certainly, the *Maximes* of La
Rochefoucauld. Madame de Sablé herself wrote maxims,
which were circulated among her friends; and, after her
death, were published by the Abbé d'Ailly. They have the
excellent sense and nobility of feeling which we should
expect in everything of hers; but they have no stamp of
genius or individual character: they are, to the Maxims of
La Rochefoucauld, what the vase moulded in dull, heavy
clay, is to the vase which the action of fire has made light,
brittle, and transparent. She also wrote a treatise on Education, which is much praised by La Rochefoucauld and M.
d'Andilly; but which seems no longer to be found: probably
it was not much more elaborate than her so-called 'Treatise

on Friendship', which is but a short string of maxims. Madame de Sablé's forte was evidently not to write herself, but to stimulate others to write; to show that sympathy and appreciation which are as genial and encouraging as the morning sunbeams. She seconded a man's wit with under-standing—one of the best offices which womanly intellect has rendered to the advancement of culture; and the absence of originality made her all the more receptive towards the originality of others.

The manuscripts of Pascal show that many of the *Pensées*, which are commonly supposed to be raw materials for a great work on religion, were remodelled again and again, in order to bring them to the highest degree of terseness and finish, which would hardly have been the case if they had only been part of a quarry for a greater production. Thoughts which are merely collected as materials, as stones out of which a building is to be erected, are not cut into facets, and polished like amethysts or emeralds. Since Pascal was from the first in the habit of visiting Madame de Sablé at Port-Royal, with his sister, Madame Périer (who was one of Madame de Sablé's dearest friends), we may well suppose that he would throw some of his jewels among the large and small coin of maxims, which were a sort of subscrip-tion-money there. Many of them have an epigrammatic piquancy, which was just the thing to charm a circle of vivacious and intelligent women; they seem to come from a La Rochefoucauld, who has been dipped over again in philosophy and wit, and received a new layer. But whether or not Madame de Sablé's influence served to enrich the *Pensées* of Pascal, it is clear that but for her influence the *Maximes* of La Rochefoucauld would never have existed. Just as in some circles the effort is, who shall make the best puns (*horribile dictu!*), or the best charades, in the *salon* of Port-Royal the amusement was to fabricate maxims. La Rochefoucauld said, 'L'envie de faire des maximes se gagne comme le rhume.'* So far from claiming for himself the initiation of this form of writing, he accuses Jacques Esprit, another *habitué* of Madame de Sablé's *salon*, of having excited in him the taste for maxims, in order to trouble his repose. The said Esprit was an academician, and had been a frequenter of the Hôtel de Rambouillet. He had already published 'Maxims in Verse', and he subsequently produced a book called *La Fausseté des Vertus Humaines*, which seems to consist of Rochefoucauldism become flat with an infusion of sour Calvinism. Nevertheless, La Rochefoucauld seems to have prized him, to have appealed to his judgement, and to have concocted maxims with him, which he afterwards begs him to submit to Madame de Sablé. He sends a little batch of maxims to her himself, and asks for an equivalent in the shape of good eatables: 'Voilà tout ce que j'ai de maximes; mais comme je ne donne rien pour rien, je vous demande un potage aux carottes, un ragoût de mouton,' etc.* The taste and the talent enhanced each other; until, at last, La Rochefoucauld began to be conscious of his pre-eminence in the circle of maxim-mongers, and thought of a wider audience. Thus grew up the famous 'Maxims', about which little need be said. Every one is now convinced, or professes to be convinced, that, as to form, they are perfect, and that as to matter, they are at once undeniably true and miserably false; true as applied to that condition of human nature in which the selfish instincts are still dominant, false if taken as a representation of all the elements and possibilities of human nature. We think La Rochefoucauld himself wavered as to their universality, and that this wavering is indicated in the qualified form of some of the maxims; it occasionally struck him that the shadow of virtue must have a substance, but he had never grasped that substance—it had never been present to his consciousness.

It is curious to see La Rochefoucauld's nervous anxiety about presenting himself before the public as an author; far from rushing into print, he stole into it, and felt his way by asking private opinions. Through Madame de Sablé he sent manuscript copies to various persons of taste and talent, both men and women, and many of the written opinions which she received in reply are still in existence. The women generally find the maxims distasteful, but the men write approvingly. These men, however, are for the most part ecclesiastics who decry human nature that they may exalt divine grace. The coincidence between Augustinianism or Calvinism, with its doctrine of human corruption, and the hard cynicism of the maxims, presents itself in quite a piquant form in some of the laudatory opinions of La Rochefoucauld. One writer says:—'On ne pourroit faire une instruction plus propre à un catéchumène pour convertir à Dieu son esprit et sa volonté . . . Quand il n'y auroit que cet escrit au monde et l'Evangile je voudrois être chrétien. L'un m'apprendroit à connoistre mes misères, et l'autre à implorer mon libérateur.'* Madame de Maintenon sends word to La Rochefoucauld, after the publication of his work, that the Book of Job and the Maxims are her only reading!

That Madame de Sablé herself had a tolerably just idea of La Rochefoucauld's character, as well as of his maxims, may be gathered not only from the fact that her own maxims are as full of the confidence in human goodness which La Rochefoucauld wants, as they are empty of the style which he possesses, but also from a letter in which she replies to the criticisms of Madame de Schomberg. 'The author,' she says, 'derived the maxim on indolence from his own disposition, for never was there so great an indolence as his, and I think that his heart, inert as it is, owes this defect as much to his idleness as his will. It has never permitted him to do the last action for others; and I think that, amidst all his great desires and great hopes, he is sometimes indolent even on his own behalf.' Still she must have felt a hearty interest in the 'Maxims', as in some degree her foster-child, and she must also have had considerable affection for the author, who was lovable enough to those who observed the rule of Helvetius, and expected nothing from him. She not only assisted him, as we have seen, in getting criticisms, and carrying out the improvements suggested by them, but when the book was actually published, she prepared a notice of it for the only journal then existing—the *Journal des Savants*. This notice was originally a brief statement of the nature of the work, and the opinions which had been formed for and against it, with a moderate eulogy, in conclusion, on its good sense, wit, and insight into human nature. But when she submitted it to La Rochefoucauld he objected to the paragraph which stated the adverse opinion, and requested her to alter it. She, however, was either unable or unwilling to modify her notice, and returned it with the following note:—

Je vous envoie ce que j'ai pu tirer de ma teste pour mettre dans le *Journal des Savants*. J'y ai mis cet endroit qui vous est le plus sensible, afin que cela vous fasse surmonter la mauvaise honte qui vous fit mettre la préface sans y rien retrancher, et je n'ai pas craint de le mettre, parce que je suis assurée que vous ne le ferez pas imprimer, quand même le reste vous plairoit. Je vous assure aussi que je vous serai plus obligée, si vous en usez comme d'une chose qui servit à vous pour le corriger ou pour le jeter au feu. Nous autres grands auteurs, nous sommes trop riches pour craindre de rien perdre de nos productions. Mandez-moi ce qu'il vous semble de ce dictum.*

La Rochefoucauld availed himself of this permission, and 'edited' the notice, touching up the style, and leaving out the blame. In this revised form it appeared in the *Journal des Savants*. In some points, we see, the youth of journalism was not without promise of its future.

While Madame de Sablé was thus playing the literary confidante to La Rochefoucauld, and was the soul of a society whose chief interest was the *belles lettres*, she was equally active in graver matters. She was in constant intercourse or correspondence with the devout women of Port-Royal, and of the neighbouring convent of the Carmelites, many of whom had once been the ornaments of the court; and there is a proof that she was conscious of being highly valued by them in the fact that when the Princess Marie-Madeline, of the Carmelites, was dangerously ill, not being able or not daring to visit her, she sent her youthful portrait to be hung up in the sick-room, and received from the same Mère Agnès whose grave admonition we have quoted above, a charming note, describing the pleasure which the picture had given in the infirmary of 'Notre bonne Mère'. She was interesting herself deeply in the translation of the New Testament, which was the work of Sacy, Arnauld, Nicole, Le Maître, and the Duc de Luynes conjointly, Sacy having the principal share. We have mentioned that Arnauld asked her opinion on the Discourse prefixed to his *Logic*, and we may conclude from this that he had found her judgement valuable in many other cases. Moreover, the persecution of the Port-Royalists had commenced, and she was uniting with Madame de Longueville in aiding and protecting her pious friends. Moderate in her Jansenism, as in everything else, she held that the famous formulary denouncing the Augustinian doctrine, and declaring it to have been originated by Jansenius, should be signed without reserve, and, as usual, she had faith in conciliatory measures; but her moderation was no excuse for inaction. She was at one time herself threatened with the necessity of abandoning her residence at Port-Royal, and had thought of retiring to a religious house at Auteuil, a village near Paris. She did, in fact, pass some summers there, and she sometimes took refuge with her brother, the Commandeur de Souvré, with Madame de Montausier, or Madame de Longueville. The last was much bolder in her partisanship than her friend, and her superior wealth and position enabled her to give the Port-Royalists more efficient aid. Arnauld and Nicole resided five years in her house; it was under her protection that the translation of the New Testament was carried on and completed, and it was chiefly through her efforts that, in 1669, the persecution was brought to an end. Madame de Sablé co-operated with all her talent and interest in the same direction; but here, as elsewhere, her influence was chiefly valuable in what she stimulated others to do, rather than in what she did herself. It was by her that Madame de Longueville was first won to the cause of Port-Royal; and we find this ardent brave woman constantly seeking the advice and sympathy of her more timid and self-indulgent, but sincere and judicious friend.

In 1669, when Madame de Sablé had at length rest from these anxieties, she was at the good old age of seventy, but she lived nine years longer—years, we may suppose, chiefly dedicated to her spiritual concerns. This gradual, calm decay allayed the fear of death which had tormented her more vigorous days; and she died with tranquillity and trust. It is a beautiful trait of these last moments, that she desired not to be buried with her family, or even at Port-Royal, among her saintly and noble companions, but in the cemetery of her parish, like one of the people, without pomp or ceremony.

It is worth while to notice, that with Madame de Sablé, as with some other remarkable Frenchwomen, the part of her life which is richest in interest and results, is that which is looked forward to by most of her sex with melancholy as the period of decline. When between fifty and sixty, she had philosophers, wits, beauties, and saints clustering around her; and one naturally cares to know what was the elixir which gave her this enduring and general attraction. We think it was, in a great degree, that well-balanced development of mental powers which gave her a comprehension of varied intellectual processes, and a tolerance for varied forms of character, which is still rarer in women than in men. Here was one point of distinction between her and Madame de Longueville; and an amusing passage, which Sainte-Beuve has disinterred from the writings of the Abbé St Pierre, so well serves to indicate, by contrast, what we regard as the great charm of Madame de Sablé's mind, that we shall not be wandering from our subject in quoting it.

I one day asked M. Nicole what was the character of Mme de Longueville's intellect; he told me it was very subtle and delicate in the penetration of character, but very small, very feeble; and that her comprehension was extremely narrow in matters of science and reasoning, and on all speculations that did not concern matters of sentiment. For example, he added, I one day said to her that I could wager and demonstrate that there were in Paris, at least two inhabitants who had the same number of hairs, although I could not point out who these two men were. She told me, I could never be sure of it until I had counted the hairs of these two men. Here is my demonstration, I said:—I take it for granted that the head which is most amply supplied with hairs has not more than 200,000 and the head which is least so has but one hair. Now, if you suppose that 200,000 heads have each a different number of hairs, it necessarily follows that they have each one of the number of hairs which form the series from 1 to 200,000; for if it were supposed that there were two among these 200,000 who had the same number of hairs, I should have gained my wager. Supposing, then, that these 200,000 inhabitants have all a different number of hairs, if I add a single inhabitant who has hairs, and who has not more than 200,000, it necessarily follows that this number of hairs, whatever it may be, will be contained in the series from 1 to 200,000, and consequently will be equal to the number of hairs on one of the previous 200,000 inhabitants. Now as, instead of one inhabitant more than 200,000, there are nearly 800,000 inhabitants in Paris, you see clearly that there must be many heads which have an equal number of hairs, though I have not counted them. Still Mme de Longueville could never comprehend that this equality of hairs could be demonstrated, and always maintained that the only way of proving it was to count them.*

Surely, the most ardent admirer of feminine shallowness must have felt some irritation when he found himself arrested by this dead wall of stupidity, and have turned with relief to the larger intelligence of Madame de Sablé, who was not the less graceful, delicate, and feminine, because she could follow a train of reasoning, or interest herself in a question of science. In this combination consisted her pre-eminent charm: she was not a genius, not a heroine, but a woman whom men could more than love—whom they could make their friend, confidante, and counsellor; the sharer, not of their joys and sorrows only, but of their ideas and aims.

Such was Madame de Sablé, whose name is, perhaps, new to some of our readers, so far does it lie from the surface of literature and history. We have seen, too, that she was only one amongst a crowd—one in a firmament of feminine stars which, when once the biographical telescope is turned upon them, appear scarcely less remarkable and interesting. Now, if the reader recollects what was the position and average intellectual character of women in the high society of England during the reigns of James I and the two Charleses—the period through which Madame de Sablé's career extends—we think he will admit our position as to the early superiority of womanly development in France: and this fact, with its causes, has not merely an historical interest, it has an important bearing on the culture of women in the present day. Women become superior in France by being admitted to a common fund of ideas, to common objects of interest with men; and this must ever be the essential condition at once of true womanly culture and of true social well-being. We have no faith in feminine conversazioni, where ladies are eloquent on Apollo and Mars; though we sympathize with the yearning activity of faculties which, deprived of their proper material, waste themselves in weaving fabrics out of cobwebs. Let the whole field of reality be laid open to woman as well as to man, and then that which is peculiar in her mental modification, instead of being, as it is now, a source of discord and repulsion between the sexes, will be found to be a necessary complement to the truth and beauty of life. Then we shall have that marriage of minds which alone can blend all the hues of thought and feeling in one lovely rainbow of promise for the harvest of human happiness.

From the Translation of Feuerbach's
The Essence of Christianity (1854)

CONCLUDING APPLICATION

IN the contradiction between Faith and Love which has just
been exhibited,* we see the practical, palpable ground of
necessity that we should raise ourselves above Christianity,
above the peculiar stand-point of all religion. We have
shown that the substance and object of religion is altogether
human; we have shown that divine wisdom is human wisdom; that the secret of theology is anthropology; that the
absolute mind is the so-called finite subjective mind. But
religion is not conscious that its elements are human; on
the contrary, it places itself in opposition to the human, or
at least it does not admit that its elements are human. The
necessary turning-point of history is therefore the open
confession, that the consciousness of God is nothing else
than the consciousness of the species; that man can and
should raise himself only above the limits of his individuality, and not above the laws, the positive essential conditions of his species; that there is no other essence which
man can think, dream of, imagine, feel, believe in, wish for,
love and adore as the *absolute*, than the essence of human
nature itself.[1]

Our relation to religion is therefore not a merely negative,
but a critical one; we only separate the true from the
false;—though we grant that the truth thus separated from
falsehood is a new truth, essentially different from the old.
Religion is the first form of self-consciousness. Religions are

[1] Including external Nature; for as man belongs to the essence of Nature,—in opposition to common materialism; so Nature belongs to the
essence of man,—in opposition to subjective idealism; which is also the
secret of our 'absolute' philosophy, at least in relation to Nature. Only by
uniting man with Nature can we conquer the supranaturalistic egoism of
Christianity.

sacred because they are the traditions of the primitive self-consciousness. But that which in religion holds the first place,—namely, God,—is, as we have shown, in itself and according to truth, the second, for it is only the nature of man regarded objectively; and that which to religion is the second,—namely, man,—must therefore be constituted and declared the first. Love to man must be no derivative love; it must be original. If human nature is the highest nature to man, then practically also the highest and first law must be the love of man to man. *Homo homini Deus est*:—this is the great practical principle:—this is the axis on which revolves the history of the world. The relations of child and parent, of husband and wife, of brother and friend,—in general, of man to man,—in short, all the moral relations are *per se* religious. Life as a whole is, in its essential, substantial relations, throughout of a divine nature. Its religious consecration is not first conferred by the blessing of the priest. But the pretension of religion is that it can hallow an object by its essentially external co-operation; it thereby assumes to be itself the only holy power; besides itself it knows only earthly, ungodly relations; hence it comes forward in order to consecrate them and make them holy.

But marriage—we mean, of course, marriage as the free bond of love[2]—is sacred in itself, by the very nature of the union which is therein effected. That alone is a religious marriage, which is a true marriage, which corresponds to the essence of marriage—of love. And so it is with all moral relations. Then only are they moral,—then only are they enjoyed in a moral spirit, when they are regarded as sacred in themselves. True friendship exists only when the boundaries of friendship are preserved with religious conscientiousness, with the same conscientiousness with which the believer watches over the dignity of his God. Let friendship be sacred to thee, property sacred, marriage sacred,—sacred

[2] Yes, only as the free bond of love; for a marriage the bond of which is merely an external restriction, not the voluntary, contented self-restriction of love, in short, a marriage which is not spontaneously concluded, spontaneously willed, self-sufficing, is not a true marriage, and therefore not a truly moral marriage.

the well-being of every man; but let them be sacred *in and by themselves.*

In Christianity the moral laws are regarded as the commandments of God; morality is even made the criterion of piety; but ethics have nevertheless a subordinate rank, they have not in themselves a religious significance. This belongs only to faith. Above morality hovers God, as a being distinct from man, a being to whom the best is due, while the remnants only fall to the share of man. All those dispositions which ought to be devoted to life, to man,—all the best powers of humanity, are lavished on the being who wants nothing. The real cause is converted into an impersonal means, a merely conceptional, imaginary cause usurps the place of the true one. Man thanks God for those benefits which have been rendered to him even at the cost of sacrifice by his fellow-man. The gratitude which he expresses to his benefactor is only ostensible; it is paid, not to him, but to God. He is thankful, grateful to God, but unthankful to man.[3] Thus is the moral sentiment subverted in religion! Thus does man sacrifice man to God! The bloody human sacrifice is in fact only a rude, material expression of the inmost secret of religion. Where bloody human sacrifices are offered to God, such sacrifices are regarded as the highest thing, physical existence as the chief good. For this reason life is sacrificed to God, and it is so on extraordinary occasions; the supposition being that this is the way to show him the greatest honour. If Christianity no longer, at least in our day, offers bloody sacrifices to its God, this arises, to say nothing of other reasons, from the fact that physical existence is no longer regarded as the highest good. Hence the soul, the emotions are now offered to God, because these

[3] 'Because God does good through government, great men and creatures in general, people rush into error, lean on creatures and not on the Creator;—they do not look from the creature to the Creator. Hence it came that the heathens made gods of kings . . . For they cannot and will not perceive that the work or the benefit comes from God, and not merely from the creature, though the latter is a means, through which God works, helps us, and gives to us.'—Luther (T. iv. p. 237). [The reference is to Luther's 95 Theses, as included in Luther's *Sämmtliche Schriften und Werke* (Leipzig, 1729), the edition used by Feuerbach.]

are held to be something higher. But the common case is, that in religion man sacrifices some duty towards man—such as that of respecting the life of his fellow, of being grateful to him—to a religious obligation,—sacrifices his relation to man to his relation to God. The Christians, by the idea that God is without wants, and that he is only an object of pure adoration, have certainly done away with many pernicious conceptions. But this freedom from wants is only a metaphysical idea, which is by no means part of the peculiar nature of religion. When the need for worship is supposed to exist only on one side, the subjective side, this has the invariable effect of one-sidedness, and leaves the religious emotions cold; hence, if not in express words, yet in fact, there must be attributed to God a condition corresponding to the subjective need, the need of the worshipper, in order to establish reciprocity.[4] All the positive definitions of religion are based on reciprocity. The religious man thinks of God, because God thinks of him; he loves God, because God has first loved him. God is jealous of man; religion is jealous of morality;[5] it sucks away the best forces of

[4] 'They who honour me, I will honour, and they who despise me shall be lightly esteemed.'—1 Sam. ii. 30. 'Jam se, o bone pater, vermis vilissimus et odio dignissimus sempiterno, tamen confidit amari, quoniam se sentit amare, imo quia se amari præsentit, non redamare confunditur . . . Nemo itaque se amari diffidat, qui jam amat.'—Bernardus ad Thomam (Epist. 107). A very fine and pregnant sentence. If I exist not for God, God exists not for me; if I do not love, I am not loved. The *passive* is the *active* certain of itself, the object is the subject certain of itself. To love is to be man, to be loved is to be God. I am loved, says God; I love, says man. It is not until later that this is reversed, that the passive transforms itself into the active, and conversely.

[5] 'The Lord spake to Gideon: The people are too many, that are with thee, that I should give Midian into their hands; Israel might glorify itself against me and say: My hand has delivered me,'—*i.e.*, 'Ne Israel sibi tribuat, quæ mihi debentur.' Judges vii. 2. 'Thus saith the Lord: Cursed is the man that trusteth in man. But blessed is the man that trusteth in the Lord and whose hope is in the Lord.'—Jer. xvii. 5. 'God desires not our gold, body and possessions, but has given these to the emperor (that is, to the representative of the world, of the state), and to us through the emperor. But the heart, which is the greatest and best in man, he has reserved for himself;—this must be our offering to God—that we believe in him.'—Luther (xvi. p. 505).

morality; it renders to man only the things that are man's, but to God the things that are God's; and to Him is rendered true, living emotion,—the heart.

When in times in which peculiar sanctity was attached to religion, we find marriage, property, and civil law respected, this has not its foundation in religion, but in the original, natural sense of morality and right, to which the true social relations are sacred *as such*. He to whom the Right is not holy for its own sake, will never be made to feel it sacred by religion. Property did not become sacred because it was regarded as a divine institution; but it was regarded as a divine institution because it was felt to be in itself sacred. Love is not holy, because it is a predicate of God, but it is a predicate of God because it is in itself divine. The heathens do not worship the light or the fountain, because it is a gift of God, but because it has of itself a beneficial influence on man, because it refreshes the sufferer; on account of this excellent quality they pay it divine honours.

Wherever morality is based on theology, wherever the right is made dependent on divine authority, the most immoral, unjust, infamous things can be justified and established. I can found morality on theology only when I myself have already defined the divine being by means of morality. In the contrary case, I have no criterion of the moral and immoral, but merely an *un*moral, arbitrary basis, from which I may deduce anything I please. Thus, if I would found morality on God, I must first of all place it in God: for Morality, Right, in short, all substantial relations, have their only basis in themselves, can only have a real foundation— such as truth demands—when they are thus based. To place anything in God, or to derive anything from God, is nothing more than to withdraw it from the test of reason, to institute it as indubitable, unassailable, sacred, without rendering an account *why*. Hence self-delusion, if not wicked, insidious design, is at the root of all efforts to establish morality, right, on theology. Where we are in earnest about the right we need no incitement or support from above. We need no Christian rule of political right; we need only one which is rational, just, human. The right, the true, the good, has always its ground of sacredness in itself, in its quality. Where man is in earnest about ethics, they have in themselves the validity of a divine power. If morality has no foundation in itself, there is no inherent necessity for morality; morality is then surrendered to the groundless arbitrariness of religion.

Thus the work of the self-conscious reason in relation to religion is simply to destroy an illusion:—an illusion, however, which is by no means indifferent, but which, on the contrary, is profoundly injurious in its effect on mankind; which deprives man as well of the power of real life, as of the genuine sense of truth and virtue; for even love, in itself the deepest, truest emotion, becomes by means of religiousness merely ostensible, illusory, since religious love gives itself to man only for God's sake, so that it is given only in appearance to man, but in reality to God.

And we need only, as we have shown, invert the religious relations—regard that as an end which religion supposes to be a means—exalt that into the primary which in religion is subordinate, the accessory, the condition,—at once we have destroyed the illusion, and the unclouded light of truth streams in upon us.

From the Translation of Spinoza's *Ethics* (1854–5)

PART V: ON THE POWER OF THE INTELLECT, OR, ON HUMAN LIBERTY

PREFACE

I PASS at length to the other part of Ethics,* the object of which is to point out the way that leads to liberty. Herein, therefore, I shall treat of the power of reason, showing first, how far reason can control the passions, and next, in what consists the liberty or blessedness of the soul; whence we shall be able to appreciate the superiority of the wise man over the ignorant. In what way the intellect must be perfected and with what art the body must be tended, so that it can rightly perform its functions are points not included in our present inquiry; for the latter belongs to medicine, the former to logic. Hence, as I have said, I shall here consider solely the power of the mind or reason, and before all else I shall shew what amount and what kind of empire it has over the passions, as a means of restraining and governing them. For that we have not absolute power over our passions I have already demonstrated. The Stoics, indeed, supposed that they depend entirely on our Will, and that we can keep them under absolute control. Nevertheless, they were compelled by experience, though not by their principles, to admit, that considerable practice and effort are required in order to subdue and regulate the passions. Some one (if I rightly remember) has attempted to illustrate this by the example of two dogs, the one domestic, the other a hunting dog, which he succeeded in so training that the house-dog acquired and the hunting dog lost, the propensity to pursue hares. This opinion is not a little countenanced by Descartes. For he holds that the soul or mind is especially united to a certain part of the brain, called the pineal gland, by means of which the mind is conscious of all the motions that are excited in the body, and of external objects, and which the mind, by the mere fact that it wills, can move in various ways. This gland he supposes to be so placed in the centre of the brain that it can be moved by the smallest motion of the animal spirits. He further holds that this gland is suspended in the centre of the brain in as many different ways as the animal spirits have different ways of impinging upon it and that as many different impressions are made upon it as there are external objects which propel those animal spirits towards it; whence it results, that if the gland, owing to the impulses of the Will which moves it in various ways, be suspended in the same way in which it had once before been suspended when agitated by the animal spirits, then this gland in its turn propels and determines the animal spirits and places them in the same condition as when they were formerly reacted on by a similar suspension of the gland. Again, he holds that every volition of the mind is by nature united with a certain motion of some gland. For example, if any one has the will to look at a distant object, this volition causes his pupils to dilate; but if he thinks solely of dilating his pupil, it will be of no use for him to will this dilation, since Nature has not united the motion of the gland, which serves to impel the animal spirits towards the optic nerve so as to induce the dilatation or contraction of the pupil, with the will to dilate or contract the pupil, but only with the will to look at a remote or near object. Lastly, he holds that although each motion of this gland appears to be connected by nature with particular thoughts from the commencement of life, it can nevertheless be united with others by habit; and this he has attempted to prove in his treatise on the Passions, Part I. art. 50.* From these positions he concludes that no mind is so feeble that it cannot, when well directed, acquire absolute power over its passions. For these, as defined by him, are perceptions or sensations, or emotions of the soul, which belong especially to it, and which are produced, preserved and strengthened by some motion of the animal spirits. See Descartes, Pass. anim. part I. art. 27. As, however, we can unite any motion of [the] gland and consequently of the animal spirits to any volition, it follows that the determination of the will depends solely on our own power; if therefore we determine our will be certain and firm judgments, according to which we desire to regulate the actions of our lives, and if we connect the movement of the passions which we desire to have, with these judgments, we shall acquire an absolute empire over our passions. Such are options of this celebrated man (so far as I can gather them from his words); opinions which, if they were less ingenious, I should hardly believe to have been advanced by so great a mind. Indeed I cannot sufficiently express my surprise that a philosopher who firmly resolved not to deduce any thing save from self-evident principles, nor affirm any thing but what is clearly and distinctly perceived, and who so often reproached the Schoolmen because they sought to explain obscure things by occult qualities, should assume an hypothesis more occult than any occult quality. What, I ask, does he understand by the union of the mind and body? What clear and distinct conception, I say, has he of a thought immediately united with a certain minute portion of quantity? Truly, I wish he had explained this union by its proximate cause. But he had conceived the mind as so distinct from the body, that he could have assigned no particular cause either of this union or of the mind itself, and it would have been necessary for him to have recourse to the cause of the whole universe, i.e. to God. Again, I should like to know what degree of motion the mind can communicate to this pineal gland, and with how great an amount of force it can hold that gland suspended. For I do not know whether this gland be impelled more slowly or more quickly by the mind than by the animal spirits, and whether the movements of the passions, which we have closely united with firm judgments, may not be again disjoined from them by corporeal causes; in which case it would follow, that although the mind had firmly purposed to advance against dangers, and had joined a movement of audacity with this resolution, yet when the danger was seen, the gland might be so suspended that the mind could mediate nothing but flight. And in truth, since there is no ratio of will and motion, no possibility of comparison between the power or forces of the mind and those of body; the powers of the latter can never be determined by the powers of the former. Add to this, that the said gland is in fact not found so situated in the centre of the brain, that it can be this easily driven about in an endless variety of ways, and that all nerves do not extend to the cavities of the brain. To conclude: everything that Descartes asserts concerning the Will and its freedom I omit, having already more than sufficiently demonstrated its falsity. As then, according to what I have shown in the preceding Part, the power of the mind is determined by the intelligence alone; I shall derive the remedies of the passions (remedies which indeed I suppose all men to have in some degree experienced, but not to have accurately observed or distinctly perceived) solely from the knowledge of the mind; and from this also I shall deduce every thing that relates to blessedness.

Axioms

1. If two contrary actions be excited in the same subject, there must necessarily be a change either in one or both those actions before they can cease to be contrary.

2. The power of an effect is determined by the power of its cause in so far as its essence is explained or determined by that cause. (This axiom is evident from prop. 7, Part III.)

Propositions

Prop. I. According as thoughts and the ideas of things are ordered and concatenated in the mind, so precisely the affections of the body or the images of things are ordered and concatenated in the body.

Dem. The order and connexion of ideas is the same (by prop. 7, Part II) as the order and connexion of things, and *vice versa*, the order and connexion of things is the same (by coroll., prop. 6 and 7, Part II) as the order and connexion of ideas. Hence, as the order and connexion of ideas in the mind takes place according to the order and concatenation of the affections of the body (by prop. 18, Part II), so *vice versa* (by prop. 2, Part III) the order and connexion of the affections of the body takes place according to the order and concatenation of thoughts and of the ideas of things in the mind; q.e.d.

Prop. II. If we disjoin an emotion or affection of the soul from the idea of an external cause, and unite it with other ideas, then love or hatred towards the external cause, as also the fluctuations of the soul, which arise from these emotions, will be destroyed.

Dem. For that which constitutes the form of love or hatred, is pleasure or pain accompanying the idea of an external cause (by def. 6 and 7 of emot.). Hence this idea being removed, the form of love or hatred is removed likewise; and therefore these emotions, and all arising from them, are destroyed; q.e.d.

Prop. III. An emotion which is a passion, ceases to be a passion, as soon as we form a clear and distinct idea of it.

Dem. An emotion which is a passion is a confused idea (by the gen. def. of emot.). If therefore we form a clear and distinct idea of such an emotion, this idea is not distinguished from the emotion, so far as it belongs to the mind, except by reason (by prop. 21, Part II with schol.); and thus (by prop. 3, Part III) the emotion ceases to be a passion; q.e.d.

Coroll. The better we know or understand an emotion, therefore, the more it is in our power, and the less the mind suffers from it.

Prop. IV. There is no affection of the body, of which we cannot form some clear and distinct idea.

Dem. What is common to all cannot be conceived otherwise than adequately (by prop. 38, Part II). And thus (by prop. 12 and lemma 2 after schol., prop. 13, Part II) there is no affection of the body, of which we cannot form a clear and distinct conception; q.e.d.

Coroll. Hence it follows, that there is no emotion of which we cannot form a distinct and clear conception. For an emotion is the idea of an affection of the body (by gen. def. of affect.), and must therefore (by the preced. prop.) involve a clear and distinct conception.

Schol. Since there is nothing from which some effect does not follow (by prop. 36, Part I) and since whatever follows from an idea which is adequate in us [is] clearly and distinctly understood by us (by prop. 40, Part II); it is to be concluded that every one has the power, if not absolutely, at least in part, of clearly and distinctly understanding himself and his emotions and consequently of causing himself to suffer less from them. Hence, our efforts must chiefly be directed to attaining as far as possible a clear and distinct knowledge of every emotion, so that the mind may be determined by its emotion to think of that which it clearly and distinctly perceives and in which it altogether acquiesces; and that this emotion may thus be separated from the idea of an external cause and united with true ideas.* The result will be, that not only love, hatred etc. will be destroyed (by prop. 2, Part V) but that the appetites or desires which are wont to arise from such emotions, cannot be in excess (by prop. 61, Part IV). For it is important to observe, that it is one and the same appetite by which a man is said at one time to act, at another to suffer. For example, we have shown human nature to be so constituted, that every one desires that others should live according to his mind (see schol., prop. 31, Part III); which desire in a man who is not guided by reason, is a passion called ambition, and is not very different from pride; while, on the contrary, in another man, who lives according to the dictates of reason, it is an action or virtue, which is called piety. (See schol. 1, prop. 37, Part IV and dem. 2 of the same prop.) In the same way, all appetites or desires are passions so far alone as they arise from inadequate ideas; and are ranked as virtues when they are excited or generated by adequate ideas. For all desires by which we are determined to action, may arise as well from adequate as from inadequate ideas. See prop. 59, Part IV. And (to revert to the point whence I have digressed) there is not in our own power any conceivable antidote to the emotions superior to this, which consists in

the true knowledge or understanding of them, since the
mind has no other power than that of thinking and forming
adequate ideas, as we have shown above (by prop. 3, Part
III).

Liszt, Wagner, and Weimar (1855)

THE Weimar theatre opens about the middle of September. A very pretty theatre it is, and all its appointments show that the Grand Duke does not grudge expense for the sake of keeping up its traditional reputation. The opera here, as every one knows, has two special attractions: it is superintended by Liszt; and Wagner's operas, in many places consigned to the *Index Expurgatorius* of managers, are a standing part of the Weimar *répertoire*. Most London concert-goers, for whom Liszt has 'blazed the comet of a season',* think of him as certainly the archimagus of pianists, but as otherwise a man of no particular significance; as merely an erratic, flighty, artistic genius, who has swept through Europe, the Napoleon of the *salon*, carrying devastation into the hearts of countesses. A single morning's interview with him is enough to show the falsity of this conception.* In him Nature has not sacrificed the man to the artist; rather, as the blossom of the acacia is a glorious ornament to the tree, but we see it fall without regret because the tree itself is grand and beautiful, so if Liszt the pianist were unknown to you, or even did not exist, Liszt the man would win your admiration and love. See him for a few hours and you will be charmed by the originality of his conversation and the brilliancy of his wit; know him for weeks or months, and you will discern in him a man of various thought, of serious purpose, and of a moral nature which, in its mingled strength and gentleness, has the benignest influence on those about him.

The lovers of characteristic heads could hardly have a more interesting study than the head of Liszt. No wonder Ary Scheffer* is fond of painting him, and that the type of Liszt's face seems to haunt this artist in so many of his compositions. I never saw features having at once so strong and clear an outline and so rich a gamut of expression; at one moment you think what a capital face he has for a witch

in *Macbeth*, with knitted brow and preternatural grey light
in his eyes; at another, with head thrown back and nostril
dilated, he suggests a prophet in the moment of inspiration:
and then again, seated placidly silent amidst a group of gay
talkers, he is a perfect model of a St John. Scheffer has
seized something of the second expression in a picture in
which he expressly intended to introduce an idealization of
Liszt. The picture represents the three Magi, two of whom
are venerable bearded sages watching with bent head the
third—a young man in the likeness of Liszt—who is gazing
in ecstasy at the guiding light above them. In Liszt, of
course, there is baser metal mingled with the fine gold; and
besides this natural alloy, there is the tarnish contracted in
a life spent in the midst of adulation. Even an ordinary man
has to pass through so many 'mud baths' before he reaches
his fortieth year, and some of the mud will become ingrained
in the process. But, take him all in all, he is a glorious
creature—one of those men whom the ancients would have
imagined the son of a god or goddess, from their superiority
to the common clay of humanity.

It seems to be understood that we may write the more
freely of our personal admiration for musical and dramatic
artists, because their fame does not live after them, except
for a few short years in the eulogies of their superannuated
contemporaries, who are listened to with an incredulous
smile as *laudatores temporis acti*.* It is this fact which gives
a character of justice to the apparently excessive tribute of
adoration paid to a great actor, a great singer, or a great
instrumentalist; they have but their 'one crowded hour of
glorious life',* while the genius who can leave permanent
creations behind him knows that he shall live for the next
age more emphatically than for his own—an ideal life, if
you will, but happily one which is felt to be more real by
many a noble soul than the pudding and praise of the
present hour. Fame is but another word for the sympathy
of mankind with individual genius, and the great poet or
the great composer is sure that that sympathy will be given
some day, though his Paradise Lost will fetch only five
pounds, and his symphony is received with contemptuous

laughter, so he can transport himself from the present and live by anticipation in that future time when he will be thrilling men's minds and ravishing their ears. But the artist whose genius can only act through his physical presence has not this reversionary life; the memory of the *prima donna* scarcely outlives the flowers that are flung at her feet on her farewell night, and even the fame of a Garrick or a Siddons is simply a cold acquiescence in the verdict of the past. It is possible, however, that Liszt will turn out to be something more than one of those coruscating meteors, who come, are seen, and are extinguished in darkness; he is now devoting himself principally to composition, and may perhaps produce something perennial, though the opponents of the Wagner sect, of which Liszt is the great apostle, will not believe that any good can come out of Nazareth.

Liszt, indeed, has devoted himself with the enthusiasm of earnest conviction to the propaganda of Wagnerism: he has not only used his personal influence to get Wagner's operas put on the stage, but he has also founded a musical newspaper (*Neue Zeitschrift für Musik*), which is the organ of the Romantic School in music, and derives its chief value from the contributions of his pen. Much cheap ridicule has been spent on the 'music of the future';* a ridicule excused, perhaps, by the more than ordinary share Herr Wagner seems to have of a quality which is common to almost all innovators and heretics, and which their converts baptize as profound conviction, while the adherents of the old faith brand it as arrogance. It might be well, however, if the ridicule were arrested by the consideration that there never was an innovating movement which had not some negative value as a criticism of the prescriptive, if not any positive value as a lasting creation. The attempt at an innovation reveals a want that has not hitherto been met, and if the productions of the innovator are exaggerated symbols of the want, rather than symmetrical creations which have within them the conditions, of permanence—like an Owenite parallelogram,* an early poem of Wordsworth's, or an early picture of Overbeck's*—still they are protests which it is wiser to accept as strictures than to hiss down as absurdities. Without pretending to be a musical critic, one may be allowed to give an opinion as a person with an ear and a mind susceptible to the direct and indirect influences of music. In this character I may say that, though unable to recognize Herr Wagner's compositions as the ideal of the opera, and though, with a few slight exceptions, not deeply affected by his music on a first hearing, it is difficult to me to understand how any one who finds deficiencies in the opera as it has existed hitherto, can give fair attention to Wagner's theory, and his exemplification of it in his operas, without admitting that he has pointed out the direction in which the lyric drama must develop itself, if it is to be developed at all. Moreover, the musician who writes librettos for himself, which can be read with interest as dramatic poems, must be a man of no ordinary mind and accomplishments, and such a man, even when he errs, errs with ingenuity, so that his mistakes are worth studying.

Wagner would make the opera a perfect musical drama, in which feelings and situations spring out of *character*, as in the highest order of tragedy, and in which no dramatic probability or poetic beauty is sacrificed to musical effect. The drama must not be a mere pretext for the music; but music, drama, and spectacle must be blended, like the coloured rays in the sunbeam, so as to produce one undivided impression. The controversy between him and his critics is the old controversy between Gluck and Piccini, between the declamatory and melodic schools of music, with the same difference in comprehensiveness as between the disputes of La Motte and the Daciers about the value of the classics, and the disputes of the classical and romantic schools of literature in our own day. In its first period the opera aimed simply at the expression of feeling through melody; the second period, which has its culmination in the joint productions of Meyerbeer and Scribe, added the search for effective situations and a heightening of dramatic movement, which has led more and more to the predominance of the declamatory style and the subordination of melody. But in Meyerbeer's operas the grand object is to produce a climax of spectacle, situation, and orchestral effects; there is no attempt at the evolution of these from the true workings of human character and human passions; on the contrary, the characters seem to be a second thought, and with a few exceptions, such as Alice and Marcel,* are vague and uninteresting. Every opera-goer has remarked that *Robert* is a mere nose of wax; or has laughed at the pathos with which the fiend Bertram invites his son to go to the bottomless pit with him, instead of settling into respectability above ground; or has felt that *Jean, the Prophet*, is a feeble sketch, completely lost in the blaze of spectacle. Yet what a progress is there in the libretto of these operas compared with the libretto of *Der Freischütz*, which, nevertheless, was thought so good in its day that Goethe said Weber ought to divide the merit of success with Kind.* Even Weber's enchanting music cannot overcome the sense of absurdity when, in a drinking party of two, one of whom is sunk in melancholy, a man gets up and bursts into a rolling song which seems the very topmost wave in the high tide of bacchanalian lyrism; or when Caspar climbs a tree apparently for no other reason than because the *dénouement* requires him to be shot.

Now, says Wagner, this ascent from the warbling puppets of the early opera to the dramatic effects of Meyerbeer, only serves to bring more clearly into view the unattained summit of the true musical drama. An opera must be no mosaic of melodies stuck together with no other method than is supplied by accidental contrast, no mere succession of ill-prepared crises, but an organic whole, which grows up like a palm, its earliest portion containing the germ and prevision of all the rest. He will write no *part* to suit a *primo tenore*, and interpolate no *cantata* to show off the powers of a *prima donna assoluta*; those who sing his operas must be content with the degree of prominence which falls to them in strict consonance with true dramatic development and ordonnance. Such, so far as I understand it, is Wagner's theory of the opera*—surely a theory worth entertaining, and one which he has admirably exemplified so far as the libretto of his operas is concerned.

But it is difficult to see why this theory should entail the exclusion of melody to the degree at which he has arrived in *Lohengrin*,* unless we accept one of two suppositions: either that Wagner is deficient in melodic inspiration, or that his inspiration has been overridden by his system, which opposition has pushed to exaggeration. Certainly his *Fliegender Holländer*—a transition work, in which, as Liszt says, he only seeks to escape from the idols to which he has hitherto sacrificed, and has not yet reached the point of making war against them—is a charming opera; and *Tannhäuser* too is still the music of men and women, as well of Wagnerites; but *Lohengrin* to us ordinary mortals seemed something like the whistling of the wind through the keyholes of a cathedral, which has a dreamy charm for a little while, but by and bye you long for the sound even of a street organ to rush in and break the monotony. It may be safely said, that whatever the music of the future may be, it will not be a music which is in contradiction with a permanent element in human nature—the need for a frequent alternation of sensations or emotions; and this need is *not* satisfied in *Lohengrin*.

As to melody—who knows? It is just possible that melody, as we conceive it, is only a transitory phase of music, and that the musicians of the future may read the airs of Mozart and Beethoven and Rossini as scholars read the *Stabreim** and assonance of early poetry. We are but in 'the morning of the times',* and must learn to think of ourselves as tadpoles unprescient of the future frog. Still the tadpole is limited to tadpole pleasures; and so, in our state of development, we are swayed by melody. When, a little while after hearing *Lohengrin*, we happened to come on a party of musicians who were playing exquisitely a quartette of Beethoven's, it was like returning to the pregnant speech of men after a sojourn among glums and gowries.

This is a purely individual impression, produced even in spite of favourable prepossessions derived from hearing the *Fliegender Holländer* and *Tannhäuser*, and only accidentally in agreement with the judgment of anti-Wagner critics, who are certainly in the majority at present. Still, those who are familiar with the history of music during the last forty or fifty years, should be aware that the reception of new music by the majority of musical critics, is not at all a criterion of its ultimate success. A man of high standing, both as a composer and executant, told a friend of mine, that when a symphony of Beethoven's was first played at the Philharmonic, there was a general titter among the musicians in the orchestra, of whom he was one, at the idea of sitting seriously to execute such music! And as a proof that professed musicians are sometimes equally unfortunate in their predictions about music which begins by winning the ear of the public, he candidly avowed that when Rossini's music was first fascinating the world of opera-goers, he had joined in pronouncing it a mere passing fashion, that tickled only by its novelty. Not indeed that the contempt of musicians and the lash of critics is a pledge of future triumph: St Paul five times received forty stripes save one, but so did many a malefactor; and unsuccessful composers before they take consolation from the pooh-poohing or 'damnation' of good music, must remember how much bad music has had the same fate, from the time when Jean Jacques' oratorio set the teeth of all hearers on edge.*

If it were admissible for a person entirely without technical qualifications for judgment, to give an opinion on Wagner as a musician, I should say that his musical inspiration is not sufficiently predominant over his thinking and poetical power, for him to have the highest creative genius in music. So far as music is an art, one would think that the same rule applied to musicians as to other artists. Now, the greatest painters and sculptors have surely not been those who have been inspired through their intellect, who have first thought and then chosen a plastic symbol for their thought; rather, the symbol rushes in on their imagination before their slower reflection has seized any abstract idea embodied in it. Nay, perhaps the artist himself *never* seizes that idea, but his picture or his statue stands there an immortal symbol nevertheless. So the highest degree of musical inspiration must overmaster all other conceptions in the mind of the musical genius; and music will be great and ultimately triumphant over men's ears and souls in proportion as it is less a studied than an involuntary symbol. Of course in composing an oratorio or an opera, there is a prior conception of a theme; but while the composer in whom other mental elements outweigh his musical power will be preoccupied with the idea, the *meaning* he has to convey, the composer who is pre-eminently a musical genius, on the slightest hint of a passion or an action, will have all other modes of conception merged in the creation of music, which is for him the supreme language, the highest order of representation. All this may be wrong, and so may be my conjecture that Wagner is a composer of the reflective kind. We often enough mistake our own negations for a negation out of ourselves, as purblind people are apt to think the sun gives but a feeble light.

Certainly Wagner has admirably fulfilled his own requisition of organic unity in the opera. In his operas there is a gradual unfolding and elaboration of that fundamental contrast of emotions, that collision of forces, which is the germ of the tragedy; just as the leaf of the plant is successively elaborated into branching stem and compact bud and radiant corolla. The artifice, however, of making certain contrasted strains of melody run like coloured threads through the woof of an opera, and also the other dramatic device of using a particular melody or musical phrase as a sort of Ahnung or prognostication of the approach or action of a particular character, are not altogether peculiar to Wagner, though he lays especial stress on them as his own. No one can forget the recurring hymn of Marcel in the *Huguenots*, or the strain of the Anabaptists in the *Prophète*, which is continually contrasted with the joyous song or dance of the rustics. Wagner, however, has carried out these devices much more completely, and, in the *Fliegender Holländer* and *Tannhäuser*, with very impressive effect. With all my inability at present to enjoy his music as I have enjoyed that of Mozart, or Beethoven, or Mendelssohn, these two operas left in me a real desire to hear them again.

Wagner has wisely gone for the themes of his operas to the fresh and abundant source of early German poetry and legend, and the mode in which he expands and works up these themes shows a deep and refined poetic feeling. He was led to choose the story of the *Fliegender Holländer*—familiar to English ears as the 'Flying Dutchman'—by happening to read Heine's beautiful version of the legend on a sea voyage, when a storm occurred and gave vividness to his conception of the doomed mariner's fate. The legend tells how, long, long ago, a Dutch vessel, making for the Cape of Good Hope, was encountered by an obstinate storm; how, when the sailors entreated the captain to put back, he exclaimed, 'Not if I must live on the sea to all eternity!' and how, as a punishment for this blasphemy, he was condemned to wander about the ocean until the last day, and bring destruction to all ships which met him on their way. The angel of mercy, however, announced to him that he should be permitted to go on shore every seven years and marry: if the wife he chose proved untrue to him, she too would become the prey of the Evil One; but if he found a wife who would love him till death, her truth would expiate his guilt, and would open to him the gates of salvation. It is Heine's version of this legend which Wagner has expanded into a beautiful drama.

The first scene represents the rocky coast of Norway. It is night, and the sea is violent. A merchant ship is struggling with the storm, but at length manages to cast anchor. Daland, the captain, comes ashore to reconnoitre, and finds that the storm has thrown him seven miles from the accustomed haven, whither he was returning after a long absence. As the wind begins to be laid, he and his men go to rest, leaving a young pilot as a watch. The pilot tries to keep himself awake by singing a song to the south wind; but presently sleep conquers him so completely that he is undisturbed by the reawakening of the storm, through which glides in doomed safety, accompanied by mournful, mysterious music, the Hollander's black ship, with its red sails and ghastly crew. As the Hollander slowly descends to land, a strain that rises from the orchestra sounds like a sentence of doom, and recurs throughout the opera whenever his terrible fate is immediately operative. Leaning against a rock, the pale man soliloquizes on this new crisis in his destiny. Meanwhile morning breaks and rouses Daland, who, seeing the newly-arrived ship, hails it through the speaking-trumpet; but, to his amazement, receives no answer. Descrying the Hollander, he goes up to him, and asks him whence he comes. Then follows a scene in which the Hollander tells that he is a weary wanderer, and that he carries in his ship treasures from all climes, which he is ready to offer Daland if he will give him a home for a short time beneath his roof. Chests of precious things are brought from the ship; and the cupidity of Daland is so strongly excited, that when the Hollander asks to have his daughter as a wife, he persuades himself, with ready sophistry, that he is consulting his daughter's interest in consenting, and that the Hollander's open-handedness is a sign that he has a good heart. The storm is now allayed, and the ships weigh anchor. Daland's ship leads the way amid the joyous song of the sailors, and after it glides in dread silence the black ship with red sails.

The scene of the second act is a room in Daland's house, where his daughter Senta is sitting in dreamy sadness, gazing at a portrait of the unhappy Hollander which hangs on the wall; while round her a company of sprightly Norwegian maidens, presided over by Senta's nurse, are seated at their wheels, which mark the time of a charming song sung by them in chorus. The nurse becomes uneasy at Senta's rapt silence, and chides her for dwelling continually on this picture. The maidens join in her complaint, and jokingly tell Senta that her lover Eric will be jealous. Senta, disturbed in her reverie, asks the nurse to sing her the ballad about the Dutch captain; and when the nurse refuses, telling her to let the Dutch captain alone, she herself sings the wild and thrilling ballad; and by and bye, her companions, carried away by sympathy, join in the melancholy *refrain*. Exhausted by her emotion, she sinks fainting into her chair, while the maidens involuntarily sing *pianissimo* the conclusion of the ballad, asking where the 'pale man' will find the woman who will save him by her truth. Suddenly Senta rises, and singing in piercing tones, 'I am she!':

> Ich sei's die Dich durch ihre Treu erlöse!
> Mög' Gottes Engel mich Dir zeigen:
> Durch mich sollst Du das Heil erreichen!*

she rushes with outstretched arms to the picture. While all are trembling at this outburst, Eric enters, and announces the arrival of Senta's father, with his ship; the maidens rush out to greet their lovers and relatives, and Senta is left alone with Eric, who tenderly urges her to ask her father's sanction for their speedy marriage. Unsatisfied by her answers, he accuses her of dwelling on the image of the legendary captain, and when these reproaches only call out stronger evidence of Senta's absorption in this ideal being, he exclaims that Satan has ensnared her, and that he has been admonished of this in a dream. Senta sinks into her chair, eager to hear the dream, but exhausted by her emotions, and during Eric's narration, seems gradually to enter into a state of *clairvoyance*, in which the objects he describes as having appeared to him in a dream are actually present to her inward vision—the approach of the dark ship, the entrance of her father into their dwelling with the *pale man*, whom she runs to meet, and who passionately embraces her. 'And then', continues Eric, 'I saw you flee away on the sea'. At these words Senta, her cheek pale, and her eyes fixed, exclaims, 'I must be lost with him!'

> Er sucht mich auf, ich muss ihn sehn,
> Mit ihm muss ich zu grunde gehn!*

Eric, horror-struck at what he believes to be madness, rushes out. Senta turns again towards the portrait with affectionate gestures, as if it were a living being. While she is sunk in contemplation the door opens, and the *pale man* stands within its frame like a Vandyck picture. At this sight Senta gives a cry, but fixes her eye steadily on the apparition, as if gathering up her resolution to follow it till death. The Hollander returns her gaze with equal fixedness, and slowly advances into the room. Daland follows, puzzled at his daughter's astonishment, and asking her why she does not come to meet him. She embraces her father without turning away her eyes from the countenance of the stranger. In reply to her question, Daland tells her that the stranger possesses immense riches, that he is a banished wanderer, and hopes to find a new home with them. In a charming *aria* he exhorts her to receive the stranger well, and at length tells her that he has promised him her hand. Senta accepts this information with a melancholy gesture of acquiescence, and will not even turn her head to look at the casket of jewels which her father shows as a proof that he has consulted her welfare. At length Daland leaves them to make acquaintance with each other. They break silence by speaking apart of their amazement at the sudden realization of a long presentiment. At last the Hollander approaches Senta, and asks her if she will fulfil her father's promise. She replies, without revealing her knowledge of his secret, that whoever he may be, and whatever may be her lot in accepting him, she will obey her father. The unhappy man kneels at her feet, adoring her as a messenger from heaven, and they join in a duet of yearning desire that Senta may be the being who will bring him release. Then, with a movement of pride and generosity, unwilling to allow this self-sacrifice for his sake, the Hollander rises, and pointing out to Senta the sad lot to which she would unite herself in the bloom of youth, seeks to deter her from such an act of devotion. But Senta answers, that she knows woman's sacred duties, and will be true till death:

> Wohl kenn ich Weibes heil'ge Pflichten,
> Sei d'rum getrost, unsel'ger Mann!
> Lass' über Die das Schicksal richten
> Die seinem Spruche trotzen kann!
> Kenn' ich der Treue Hochgebot:—
> Wem ich sie weih', schenk ich die Eine,
> *Die Treue bis zum Tod!**

Exquisitely beautiful is Senta's declamation of these verses. The Hollander seems to drink hope and new life from her words, and both join in a glorious duet of triumphant love and confidence.

The third act opens with a sailors' festival. The scene is the haven where two ships lie at anchor. Daland's ship is decked with streamers, garlands, and lamps, and the crew are feasting and dancing; the mysterious ship meanwhile remaining in darkness and silence. Presently women come with fresh provisions, and the sailors playfully attempt to get possession of the baskets, but the women will not allow this, wishing to reserve some for the sailors of the rich bridegroom. Seeing none of these among the merry-makers, they go to the edge of the quay and call to the Dutch ship. The deck is empty, and no sign is made in answer. The women repeat their call again and again, the sailors joining in with jeers and laughter, but the same deathlike stillness continuing to reign in the mysterious ship, they begin to be alarmed, and hurry from the quay, trying to drown their terrors in new gaiety. When the women have left the scene, the fun becomes more riotous, and the sailors take up their original joyous song. In the moment when the bacchanalian shout of the refrain *Hussassahe! Johollohe!* is at its height, there floats on the Dutch ship a bluish flame, the crew suddenly rise out of the darkness, and, assembled round the masts, fill the air with a demoniacal chorus. At first Daland's crew are too much deafened by their own song to perceive this outburst of satanic harmony—this terrific response to their gay *refrain*; but by and bye they become aware of it, and ask each other whether it may not be a delusion of their wine-heated brains, or the work of evil spirits. To banish their fears, they continue their song, pitching it higher and higher, but are each time interrupted by the hellish *Huissa! Johohoe! Johohoe!* till at length they are reduced to complete silence by a tremendous *fortissimo*. The pale, white-bearded phantoms continue their unearthly chorus, until the swelling flood of diabolical song bursts into a torrent of still more diabolical laughter. The Norwegians cross themselves and rush from the spot in a panic. The whole scene is wonderfully effective, and the climax of the hellish chorus and hideous laughter is, I should think, not surpassed in its kind. In the stillness that succeeds, Senta appears, already attired in the pretty dress of the Norwegian bride. She is pursued by the importunities of Eric, who is visiting her with tender reproaches. The Hollander approaches and overhears him. In vain Senta tries to end the dialogue; Eric reminds her of all the tokens of kindness she has given him, tokens which he has interpreted as promises. Thus the Hollander learns that Senta has already loved, and thinks that she will perhaps one day regret the loss of this peaceful love, and repent her self-sacrifice, that she will at last forget her plighted troth, break her oath, and so fall to perdition. He loves her too well to expose her to this danger; he hastens to her, takes leave of her, and rushing towards his ship, calls to his sailors, 'To sea! To sea! for ever! all is over with thy truth and my salvation!' Senta rushes after him, holds him by the arm, and reproaches him for so lightly doubting her truth. Then the Hollander tells her the doom she would incur by being faithless to him, and that he is determined to renounce the hope of salvation, so that at all events *she* may be saved. In vain Senta assures him that she knows him, and the duties she has sworn to fulfil—that she will save *him*. He tells her she does not know him, and exclaiming that he is the Flying Hollander:

> Der Fliengender Holländer nennt man mich!

he breaks loose from her, springs on board and pushes off from land. Senta struggles out of the hands of her friends, whom Eric has summoned in his alarm, and, springing to the edge of a jutting rock, calls to the Hollander, to behold that she is true till death, and throws herself into the sea. In the same moment the Hollander's ship sinks into the waves, and presently the forms of Senta and her rescued lover are seen hovering above the waters in light and glory.[1]

In *Tannhäuser* the dramatic situations are more striking than in the *Fliegender Holländer*; indeed, I never saw an opera which had a more interesting succession of well-con-

[1] My recollection of Wagner's three greatest operas has been assisted by Liszt's charming analysis or rather paraphrase of them—that of the *Fliegender Holländer*, contained in five numbers of the *Neue Zeitschrift für Musik*, and that of *Tannhäuser* and *Lohengrin*, in his little work entitled, *Richard Wagner's Lohengrin und Tannhäuser*.

trasted effects. The libretto is founded on the old German *saga* of the Venusberg and the knightly minstrel Tannhäuser. On the introduction of Christianity into Germany, the clergy, finding it impossible to eradicate from the minds of the people the faith in their old gods, resorted to the plan of representing them as demons, and transforming the benign influences formerly attributed to them into malignant ones. Thus Holda, the genial goddess, whose yearly procession through the land made the meadows flourish, was thrust down into subterranean caverns, and her appearance above ground was represented as unpropitious. Later, by a not uncommon blending of names and ideas, Holda was merged into a Germanized conception of Venus, and she was made the symbol of seductive sensuality. Her chief dwelling was supposed to be in Thüringia, in the interior of the Hörselberg, near Eisenach, thence called the Venusberg. Here she held open court in a fairy palace, surrounded by her nymphs, naiads, and syrens, whose song was heard in the distance, and seduced mortals, who were the prey of impure desires, along unknown paths, to this grotto, where hell lay concealed under ensnaring ravishments, enticing them to everlasting destruction. Tannhäuser, the knight and minstrel, had, in one of the contests for the palm in song, won a brilliant victory, and with it the heart of the Princess Elizabeth of Thüringia. A short time after this he disappears, and no one can explain his absence. It is after the lapse of a year from this disappearance that the opera is supposed to commence. The curtain is drawn up on the interior of the Venusberg, with its nymphs and syrens dancing in rosy twilight, Venus lying on her couch, and Tannhäuser at her feet, with his harp in his hand. He has become weary of hectic sensualism, and tells her that he longs once more for the free air of the field and forest under the blue arch of heaven:

> —Sterblich, ach! bin ich geblieben,
> Un übergross ist mir dein Lieben;
> Wenn stets ein Gott geniessen kann,
> Bin ich dem Wechsel unterthan;
> Nicht Lust allein liegt mir am Herzen,
> *Aus Freuden sehn' ich mich nach schmerzen!**

Venus starts up enraged, and reminds him with bitter sarcasm that he is accursed through his residence with her, and that the world he desires to return to would reject him with horror. Then she attempts to lull his awakened conscience by blandishments; but he breaks loose at once from her threats and her fascinations, by an appeal to the Virgin, on whom his salvation depends. At the mention of this sacred name the whole scene of enchantment vanishes. Instead of the grotto we see the landscape round the Wartburg in the pure air of a spring morning. To the deafening sounds of the preceding scene follows a complete silence of the orchestra, and the soft, dreamy song of a shepherd seated on a neighbouring rock. Before Tannhäuser is awakened to complete consciousness of his deliverance, we hear in the distance the chorus of a band of pilgrims. In the pauses of their song the voice of the shepherd who recommends himself to their prayers forms a fresh contrast. The pilgrims approach, and pause before an image of the Virgin. Tannhäuser on hearing their song throws himself on his knees, and overwhelmed with gratitude for the mercy which has rescued him, repeats the penitent words of the pilgrims. The bells of the neighbouring church call believers to morning prayer, and at the same time the signals of a hunting horn heard, at various distances, heighten the impression of rural peace and sylvan loneliness. Soon after arrives the Landgrave with his hunt, and perceiving a knight who seems to be standing apart from the train of courtiers, approaches him, and recognizes Tannhäuser. Wolfram von Eschenbach, Tannhäuser's rival in the poetic art, and also in love for the Princess Elizabeth, at last by speaking of her prevails on Tannhäuser to take his old place among the minstrels, whom he had so often conquered, and who nevertheless mourned his absence. The name of Elizabeth is like a sunbeam to Tannhäuser, and he breaks into a song of joy, ending 'To her! To her!' As soon as his voice unites with the others, the septett commences a joyous allegro, the finale of which, interrupted by the sound of the hunting horn, forms the close of the first act.

The second act opens with the meeting between Elizabeth and Tannhäuser, generously brought about by Wolfram, and we have a duet of happy greeting. Elizabeth is dressed for the festival, which is about to commence—the contest of minstrels. During the entrance of the Landgrave and his guests, a fine march is played by the orchestra. A second march in another key accompanies the entrance of the minstrels. As soon as the guests have ranged themselves and the minstrels have entered, there is a deep silence. Wolfram rises first, his name having been drawn from the urn by Elizabeth. Like all the other minstrels he carries his harp in his hand, and the songs are all accompanied by this instrument in the orchestra. He sings in praise of spiritual love. Tannhäuser replies, intimating that true love demands something more than mere contemplation. Walther von der Vogelweide then rises, and admonishes Tannhäuser that his idea of love is too sensuous. Tannhäuser starts up, and sings again in ardent vindication of his former strain—that distant worship belongs to the stars, and other incomprehensible glories, but that which is near to us, and of like nature with us, is to be the object of tender love:

> Dem ziemt Genuss in freud'gem Triebe,
> Und im Genuss nur kenn' ich Liebe.*

He is interrupted by Biterolf, who impetuously and scornfully challenges Tannhäuser to a strife of weapons instead of song. Biterolf, like the other opponents of Tannhäuser, is encouraged with loud signs of applause, and Tannhäuser, provoked, answers him with scornful bitterness. Immediately there is a tumult and a clashing of swords. Wolfram tries to restore peace, and sings with new enthusiasm in honour of pure, exalted love. Tannhäuser, beside himself with indignation at the scorn and bitterness of which he is the object, scarcely hears Wolfram, and bursts into a song in praise of Venus, declaring that he alone knows what love is who has been in the Venusberg:

> Armsel'ge, die ihr Liebe nie genossen,
> Zieht hin, zieht in der Berg der Venus ein!*

A cry of horror arises at the mention of this unhallowed name. The noble ladies, shocked at this insult to their delicacy, flee from the hall; the men draw their swords and fall on the bold sinner, whose long absence is now explained. But Elizabeth, who on this fearful avowal is at first completely overwhelmed, suddenly throws herself as a shield before her lover. All are amazed that she can defend one who has so betrayed her, but she exclaims, 'What of me! But he—his salvation! Will you rob him of eternal salvation?' Overcome by her noble devotion, all retire, and Tannhäuser, melted into penitence and hope by this sublime love, rushes to unite himself with the pilgrims to Rome, whose chant is now heard without, there to seek forgiveness for his dreadful sin.

The third act opens with the return of pilgrims, whose procession winds through the same valley, near the Wartburg, where the Landgrave found Tannhäuser. Elizabeth, who has been awaiting his return through long days and nights of prayer and weeping, is wandering through this valley in the evening. A thrilling moment in the drama is that when Elizabeth scrutinizes the faces of all the pilgrims as they kneel before the image of the Virgin, in the hope of finding her lover among them. He is not there. As the pilgrims pass on, she sinks down before the image, and pours forth the anguish of her heart in a prayer for her lover. When she rises to return to the castle, Wolfram, who has approached in the interval, offers to accompany her, but in vain. Meanwhile the evening deepens, and in the gloom of twilight Tannhäuser, transformed from the brilliant knight and minstrel into a withered and ragged pilgrim, returns in solitude. Wolfram with difficulty recognizes him, and eagerly questions him concerning his fate, on which hangs the peace of Elizabeth. Tannhäuser only answers ironically, inquiring the way to the Venus Grotto. Struck with horror, Wolfram nevertheless will not give up the man who is beloved by Elizabeth; he continues his questions, and Tannhäuser at length gives him a description of his pilgrimage—how, full of penitence and thirsting for reconciliation, he had inflicted every possible penance on himself on his way to Rome; how, on the confession of his sin, the bishop had denied him absolution, declaring that the man who had been in the Venusberg could no more win pardon than the pastoral staff in his hand could bud with fresh green; and how, hopeless on earth and in heaven, he was now returning to the goddess who had predicted to him this rejection. (According to the legend, the bishop, after Tannhäuser had departed, found his pastoral staff had actually budded, as a reproof to his inexorable severity.) Tannhäuser now rises to take his way to the Venusberg, and the voices of the syrens are heard singing their old strain of enticement. Wolfram holds him back with all his force, but can only succeed in neutralizing the unholy charm by uttering the name of Elizabeth. Once more this name exercises its saving power. Immediately the seductive melodies are silenced, and Tannhäuser repeats the beloved name with the same rapture and hope as ever. At this moment a funeral procession approaches, bearing Elizabeth to the grave. He falls down beside the corpse, and exclaiming, 'Holy Elizabeth, pray for me!' dies. As soon as the long procession, led by the Landgrave, has filled the scene, the sun rises over the valley, and in the same moment all break into a chorus, 'Alleluja! he is saved!'—joined in by a band of pilgrims who have just come from Rome, bringing news of the salvation which has been announced to the inexorable bishop by the budding of his staff.

The theme of *Lohengrin*, which I must only allow myself to sketch very rapidly, is taken from the romantic poetry of the middle ages. To understand it we must know the legend of the *Holy Graal*. This was a dish made of a precious stone which fell from the crown of Lucifer on his expulsion from heaven. In this dish the Saviour blessed the bread and wine at the Last Supper, and Joseph of Arimathea received the blood that streamed from the wounded side of Jesus on the cross. Joseph of Arimathea brought the Holy Graal to the West, where it at length came under the charge of King Arthur and the Knights of the Round Table. A glorious temple was built for it on Mont Salvage, a mountain in Biscay, encircled with a forest of cedars and cypresses. Here it was served by loyal and brave knights, chosen by the Holy Graal itself, which, like the high priest's breastplate, had a mode of giving revelations. One of the bravest and most devout of these knights was Lohengrin, and the pathetic story of his championship and love for Elsa of Brabant forms the theme of the opera.

The scene of the first act is on the shores of the Scheldt. Henry the Fowler, the German King, has come into Brabant to summon its nobles to aid him, their feudal lord, in his war against the Hungarians. Frederic of Telramund, a rejected lover of Elsa or Alice, who by her brother's mysterious death has become Duchess of Brabant, seizes this occasion, under the instigation of his wife Ortruda, who is a sorceress, to accuse Elsa of her brother's murder. The truth is, that Ortruda herself has by her sorceries changed the brother into a swan, and that by this accusation of Elsa she means to clear the way for her own hereditary pretensions to the duchy. When Elsa denies the charge, Henry the Fowler decrees that an appeal shall be made to heaven by single combat, if Elsa can find a champion. She declares that she has seen a knight in a vision, who will come and defend her, and on the double summons of the trumpet, a boat is seen approaching along the Scheldt, drawn by a swan. From it lands a knight in silver armour, with a golden horn at his side, as seen by Elsa in her vision; while the swan sails slowly away again. Elsa recognises the knight with rapture, and in reply to his wish, promises to be his for ever, when he has cleared her name. Telramund is overthrown in the combat, and the act ends with the raising of Lohengrin and Elsa on shields, in sign that they are accepted rulers.

The second act opens in the town of Antwerp. It is night, and Frederic of Telramund, and his wife Ortruda, now sunk in disgrace and condemned to banishment, are seated on the steps of the cathedral, opposite the palace, which is lighted up. Ortruda, with stinging sarcasms, reproaches Frederic for his deep debasement, informs him that if the stranger knight is required to tell his name, and whence he comes, his power will be at an end, and suggests to him to betray Elsa into making this demand. At length, Elsa appears in the balcony, Frederic retires, and Ortruda, by her feigned penitence, induces Elsa to take her into the palace, so that in the morning she presents herself in the marriage-train. Her insinuations to Elsa, and the public accusation of Frederic that Lohengrin has won the combat by foul magic, which will be evident if he be required to disclose his name and origin, though repelled for the moment, prepare the way for the tragic *dénouement*. The act closes with the entrance of the marriage procession into the cathedral.

The third act is divided into two parts. In the first part we have an exquisitely pathetic scene between Lohengrin and Elsa in their bridal chamber. The doubts with which Frederic and Ortruda have poisoned her mind, are heightened when Lohengrin tells her that he has come from a glorious and happy lot, for which her love only is a full compensation. She dreads that he will yearn for that lot again—that he will one day forsake her, and in spite of his assurance that her doubt alone can separate them, she is led on to utter the fatal demand that he should tell her his name and whence he comes. The words Lohengrin has dreaded have scarcely passed her lips, when she sees Telramund and four other nobles, lurking with drawn swords near the door. Uttering a cry of terror, she calls to Lohengrin to seize his sword, and in a moment he is fallen on by Frederic, whom, however, he lays dead at his feet, to the dismay of the other nobles, who fall on their knees before him. Lohengrin tells them to carry the corpse before the king's judgment-seat, and with tender sadness summons Elsa to robe herself, that she too may appear in the king's presence, where he will reveal to her his name and origin. Then follows the second part of the act, which takes place on the banks of the Scheldt. Here Lohengrin declares, before the assembled court, that he is a knight of the Holy Graal, and that it is one of the laws of their society, that in whatever deed of virtuous valour a knight engages, he shall be triumphant so long as his office remains concealed, but the secret once betrayed, he must flee from the eyes of the uninitiated, and return to the temple on Mont Salvage. Complaining tones had been wafted to the Graal, revealing that a maiden was in distress, and while the knights were preparing to inquire of the sacred vessel whither one of them should be sent to relieve this distress, a swan came, leading a boat on the waters. Parcival, Lohengrin's father, knew this swan, that it was under an enchantment, and in obedience to a command of the sacred vessel, took it into the service of the Graal, that service being, after the lapse of a year, a means of dissolving every evil charm. Lohengrin was chosen as the champion of the distressed maiden, and committing himself to the guidance of the swan, was brought, as had been seen, to the shores of Brabant. But now, his bride having been seduced by guile to demand the betrayal of his name and office, he must part from her for ever. While Elsa and the rest are entreating him to stay, the swan is seen approaching once more along the Scheldt. Lohengrin turns to Elsa, and giving her his horn, his sword, and his ring, which she is to present to her brother when he shall return, released from enchantment by the power of the Holy Graal, he embraces her, and says a sad, lingering farewell:

> Leb wohl! leb wohl! leb wohl, mein süsses Weib!
> Leb wohl! mir zürnt der Graal wenn ich noch bleib!*

He has reached the shore, and is ready to step into the boat, when, hearing the scornful voice of Ortruda rejoicing that he is going without restoring Elsa's brother, he kneels down in silent prayer. Suddenly a white dove descends on his neck; he rises joyfully, and loosens the chain that holds the swan, which instantly sinks into the water, and in its place appears the youth Gottfried, Elsa's brother. Lohengrin springs into the boat, which is now guided by the dove instead of the swan, and glides away. Elsa casts one last look of joy on her brother, then turns to the water, exclaiming, 'My husband! my husband!'—sees that Lohengrin is already in the distance, and uttering a cry of anguish, sinks lifeless into the arms of her brother. At this moment the curtain falls.

Of these three operas, we heard the *Fliegender Holländer* to the greatest advantage, from the fact that the principal man's part, being a baritone, was filled by an excellent artist—Herr Milde. His wife sang admirably, as the heroine in each of the operas; but *Tannhäuser* and *Lohengrin* absolutely demand a tenor with a voice, and the first tenor at Weimar had only 'intentions.'

It is charming to see how real an amusement the theatre is to the Weimar people. The greater number of places are occupied by subscribers, and there is no fuss about toilette or escort. The ladies come alone, and slip quietly into their places without need of 'protection'—a proof of civilization perhaps more than equivalent to our preeminence in patent locks and carriage springs—and after the performance is over, you may see the same ladies following their servants, with lanterns, through streets innocent of gas, in which an oil lamp, suspended from a rope slung across from house to house, occasionally reveals to you the shafts of a cart or omnibus, conveniently placed for you to run upon them.

A yearly autumn festival at Weimar is the *Vogelschiessen*, or *Bird-shooting*; but the reader must not let his imagination wander at this word into fields and brakes. The bird here concerned is of wood, and the shooters, instead of wandering over breezy down and common, are shut up, day after day, in a room clouded with tobacco smoke, that they may take their turn at shooting with the rifle from the window of a closet about the size of a sentinel's box. However, this is a mighty enjoyment to the Thüringian yeomanry, and an occasion of profit to our friend Punch, and other itinerant performers; for while the *Vogelschiessen* lasts, a sort of fair is held in the field where the marksmen assemble.

Among the quieter every-day pleasures of the Weimarians, perhaps the most delightful is a stroll on a bright afternoon or evening to Belvedere, one of the Duke's summer residences, about two miles from Weimar. A glorious avenue of chesnut trees leads all the way from the town to the entrance of the grounds, which are open to all the world as much as to the Duke himself. Close to the palace and its subsidiary buildings there is an inn, for the accommodation of the good people who come to take dinner, or any other meal here, by way of holiday making. A sort of pavilion stands on a spot commanding a lovely view of Weimar and its valley, and here the Weimarians constantly come on summer and autumn evenings to smoke a cigar, or drink a cup of coffee. In one wing of the little palace, which is made smart by wooden cupolas, with gilt pinnacles, there is a saloon, which I recommend to the imitation of tasteful people in their country houses. It has no decoration but that of natural foliage: ivy is trained at regular intervals up the pure white walls, and all round the edge of the ceiling, so as to form pilasters and a cornice; ivy again, trained on trellis-work, forms a blind to the window, which looks towards the entrance-court; and beautiful ferns, arranged in tall baskets, are placed here and there against the walls. The furniture is of light cane-work. Another pretty thing here is the *Natur-Theater*—a theatre constructed with living trees, trimmed into walls and side scenes. We pleased ourselves for a little while with thinking that this was one of the places where Goethe acted in his own dramas, but we afterwards learned that it was not made until his acting days were over. The inexhaustible charm of Belvedere, however, is the grounds, which are laid out with a taste worthy of a first-rate landscape gardener. The tall and graceful limes, plane trees, and weeping birches, the little basins of water here and there, with fountains playing in the middle of them, and with a fringe of broad-leaved plants, or other tasteful bordering round them, the gradual descent towards the river, and the hill clothed with firs and pines on the opposite side, forming a fine dark background for the various and light foliage of the trees that ornament the gardens—all this we went again and again to enjoy, from the time when everything was of a vivid green until the Virginian creepers which festooned the silver stems of the birches were bright scarlet, and the touch of autumn had turned all the green to gold. One of the spots to linger in is at a semicircular seat against an artificial rock, on which are placed large glass globes of different colours. It is wonderful to see with what minute perfection the scenery around is painted in these globes. Each is like a pre-Rafaelite picture, with every little detail of gravelly walk, mossy bank, and delicately-leaved, interlacing boughs, presented in accurate miniature.

In the opposite direction to Belvedere lies Tiefurt, with its small park and tiny chateau, formerly the residence of the Duchess Amalia, the mother of Carl August, and the friend and patroness of Wieland, but now apparently serving as little else than a receptacle for the late Duke Carl Friederich's rather childish collections. In the second story there is a suite of rooms, so small that the largest of them does not take up as much space as a good dining table, and each of these doll-house rooms is crowded with prints, old china, and all sorts of knick-knacks and rococo wares. The park is a little paradise. The Ilm is seen here to the best advantage: it is clearer than at Weimar, and winds about gracefully between the banks, on one side steep, and cur-tained with turf and shrubs, or fine trees. It was here, at a point where the bank forms a promontory into the river, that Goethe and his court friends got up the performance of an operetta—*Die Fischerin*, by torchlight.* On the way to Tiefurt lies the Webicht, a beautiful wood, through which run excellent carriage roads and grassy footpaths. It was a rich enjoyment to skirt this wood along the Jena road, and see the sky arching grandly down over the open fields on the other side of us, the evening red flushing the west over the town, and the stars coming out as if to relieve the sun in its watch; or to take the winding road through the wood, under its tall overarching trees, now bending their mossy trunks forward, now standing with the stately erectness of lofty pillars; or to saunter along the grassy footpaths where the sunlight streamed through the fairy-like foliage of the silvery barked birches.

Stout pedestrians who go to Weimar will do well to make a walking excursion, as we did, to Ettersburg, a more distant summer residence of the Grand Duke, interesting to us beforehand as the scene of private theatricals and *sprees* in the Goethe days. We set out on one of the brightest and hottest mornings that August ever bestowed, and it required some resolution to trudge along the shadeless *chaussée*, which formed the first two or three miles of our way. One compensating pleasure was the sight of the beautiful mountain ash trees in full berry, which, alternately with cherry trees, border the road for a considerable distance. At last we rested from our broiling walk on the borders of a glorious pine wood, so extensive that the trees in the distance form a complete wall with their trunks, and so give one a twilight very welcome on a summer's noon. Under these pines you tread on a carpet of the softest moss, so that you hear no sound of a footstep, and all is as solemn and still as in the crypt of a cathedral. Presently we passed out of the pine wood into one of limes, beeches, and other trees of transparent and light foliage, and from this again we emerged into the open space of the Ettersburg Park in front of the *Schloss*, which is finely placed on an eminence commanding a magnificent view of the far-reaching woods. Prince Pückler Muskau* has been of service here by recommending openings to be made in the woods, in the taste of the English parks. The Schloss, which is a favourite residence of the Grand Duke, is a house of very moderate size, and no pretension of any kind. Its stuccoed walls, and doors long unacquainted with fresh paint, would look distressingly shabby to the owner of a villa at Richmond or Twickenham; but much beauty is procured here at slight expense, by the tasteful disposition of creepers on the balustrades, and pretty vases full of plants ranged along the steps, or suspended in the little piazza beneath them. A walk through a beech wood took us to the Mooshütte, in front of which stands the famous beech from whence Goethe denounced Jacobi's *Woldemar*.* The bark is covered with initials cut by him and his friends.

People who only allow themselves to be idle under the pretext of hydropathizing, may find all the apparatus necessary to satisfy their conscience at Bercka, a village seated in a lovely valley about six miles from Weimar. Now and then a Weimar family takes lodgings here for the summer, retiring from the quiet of the capital to the deeper quiet of Bercka; but generally the place seems not much frequented. It would be difficult to imagine a more peace-inspiring scene than this little valley. The hanging woods—the soft colouring and graceful outline of the uplands—the village, with its roofs and spire of a reddish violet hue, muffled in luxuriant trees—the white *Kurhaus* glittering on a grassy slope—the avenue of poplars contrasting its pretty primness with the wild bushy outline of the wood-covered hill, which rises abruptly from the smooth, green meadows—the clear winding stream, now sparkling in the sun, now hiding itself under soft grey willows—all this makes an enchanting picture. The walk to Bercka and back was a favourite expedition with us and a few Weimar friends, for the road thither is a pleasant one, leading at first through open cultivated fields, dotted here and there with villages, and then through wooded hills—the outskirts of the Thüringian Forest. We used not to despise the fine plums which hung in tempting abundance by the roadside; but we afterwards found that we had been deceived in supposing ourselves free to pluck them, as if it were the golden age, and that we were liable to a penalty of ten groschen for our depredations.

But I must not allow myself to be exhaustive on pleasures which seem monotonous when told, though in enjoying them one is as far from wishing them to be more various as from wishing for any change in the sweet sameness of successive summer days. I will only advise the reader who has yet to make excursions in Thüringia to visit Jena, less for its traditions than for its fine scenery, which makes it, as Goethe says, *ein allerliebster ort*—a delicious place, in spite of its dull, ugly streets; and exhort him, above all, to brave the discomforts of a postwagen for the sake of getting to Ilmenau. Here he will find the grandest pine-clad hills, with endless walks under their solemn shades; beech woods where every tree is a picture; an air that he will breathe with as conscious a pleasure as if he were taking iced water on a hot day; baths *ad libitum*, with a *douche* lofty and tremendous enough to invigorate the giant Cormoran;* and, more than all, one of the most interesting relics of Goethe, who had a great love for Ilmenau. This is the small wooden house, on the height called the Kickelhahn, where he often lived in his long retirements here, and where you may see written by his own hand, near the window-frame, those wonderful

lines—perhaps the finest expression yet given to the sense
of resignation inspired by the sublime calm of Nature:

> Ueber allen Gipfeln
> Ist Ruh,
> In allen Wipfeln
> Spürest du
> Kaum einen Hauch;
> Die Vögelein schweigen im Walde.
> Warte nur, balde
> Ruhest du auch.*

Charles Kingsley's *Westward Ho!* (1855)

EVERY ONE who was so happy as to go mushrooming in his early days, remembers his delight when, after picking up and throwing away heaps of dubious fungi, dear to naturalists but abhorred of cooks, he pounces on an unmistakable mushroom, with its delicate fragrance and pink lining tempting him to devour it there and then, to the prejudice of the promised dish for breakfast. We speak in parables, after the fashion of the wise, amongst whom Reviewers are always to be reckoned. The plentiful dubious fungi are the ordinary quarter's crop of novels, not all poisonous, but generally not appetizing, and certainly not nourishing; and the unmistakable mushroom is a new novel by Charles Kingsley. It seemed too long since we had any of that genuine description of external nature, not done after the poet's or the novelist's recipe, but flowing from spontaneous observation and enjoyment; any of that close, vigorous painting of outdoor life, which serves as myrrh and rich spices to embalm much perishable theorizing and offensive objurgation—too long since we had a taste of that exquisite lyrical inspiration to which we owe—

> O, Mary! go and call the cattle home
> Along the sands of Dee.*

After courses of 'psychological' novels (very excellent things in their way), where life seems made up of talking and journalizing, and men are judged almost entirely on 'carpet consideration',* we are ready to welcome a stirring historical romance, by a writer who, poet and scholar and social reformer as he is, evidently knows the points of a horse and has followed the hounds, who betrays a fancy for pigs, and becomes dithyrambic on the virtues of tobacco. After a surfeit of Hebes and Psyches, or Madonnas and Magdalens, it is a refreshment to turn to Kiss's Amazon.*

But this ruddy and, now and then, rather ferocious barbarism, which is singularly compounded in Mr Kingsley with the susceptibility of the poet and the warm sympathy of the philanthropist, while it gives his writings one of their principal charms, is also the source of their gravest fault. The battle and the chase seem necessary to his existence; and this Red Man's nature, planted in a pleasant rectory among corn fields and pastures, takes, in default of better game, to riding down capitalists and Jesuits, and fighting with that Protean personage—'the devil'. If, however, Mother Nature has made Mr Kingsley very much of a poet and philanthropist, and a little of a savage, her dry-nurse Habit has made him superlatively a preacher: he drops into the homily as readily as if he had been 'to the manner born';* and while by his artistic faculty he can transplant you into whatever scene he will, he can never trust to the impression that scene itself will make on you, but, true to his cloth, must always 'improve the occasion'. In these two points—his fierce antagonism and his perpetual hortative tendency—lie, to our thinking, the grand mistakes which enfeeble the effect of all Mr Kingsley's works, and are too likely to impede his production of what his high powers would otherwise promise—a fiction which might be numbered among our classics. Poet and artist in a rare degree, his passionate impetuosity and theological prepossessions inexorably forbid that he should ever be a philosopher; he sees, feels, and paints vividly, but he theorizes illogically and moralizes absurdly. If he would confine himself to his true sphere, he might be a teacher in the sense in which every great artist is a teacher—namely, by giving us his higher sensibility as a medium, a delicate acoustic or optical instrument, bringing home to our coarser senses what would otherwise be unperceived by us. But Mr Kingsley, unhappily, like so many other gifted men, has two steeds—his Pegasus and his hobby: the one he rides with a graceful *abandon*, to the admiration of all beholders; but no sooner does he get astride the other, than he becomes a feeble imitator of Carlyle's *manège*, and attempts to put his wooden toy to all the wonderful paces of the great Scotchman's fiery Tartar horse.

This imitation is probably not a conscious one, but arises
simply from the fact, that Mr Kingsley's impetuosity and
Boanerges' vein* give him an affinity for Carlyle's faults—
his one-sided judgement of character and his undiscriminating fulminations against the men of the present as tried by
some imaginary standard in the past. Carlyle's great merits
Mr Kingsley's powers are not fitted to achieve; his genius
lies in another direction. He has not that piercing insight
which every now and then flashes to the depth of things,
and alternating as it does with the most obstinate one-sidedness, makes Carlyle a wonderful paradox of wisdom and
wilfulness; he has not that awful sense of the mystery of
existence which continually checks and chastens the denunciations of the Teufelsdröckh;* still less has he the rich
humour, the keen satire, and the tremendous word-missiles,
which Carlyle hurls about as Milton's angels hurl the rocks.
But Mr Kingsley *can* scold; he *can* select one character for
unmixed eulogy and another for unmitigated vituperation;
he *can* undertake to depict a past age and try to make out
that it was the pattern of all heroisms now utterly extinct;
he *can* sneer at actual doings which are only a new form of
the sentiments he vaunts as the peculiar possession of his
pet period; he *can* call his own opinion God, and the
opposite opinion the Devil. Carlyle's love of the concrete
makes him prefer any proper name rather than an abstraction, and we are accustomed to smile at this in him, knowing
it to be mere Carlylian rhetoric; but with Mr Kingsley, who
has publicly made a vehement disclaimer of all heterodoxy,*
and wishes to be understood as believing 'all the doctrines
of the Catholic Church', we must interpret such phraseology
more literally. But enough of general remarks. Let us turn
to the particular work before us, where we shall find all the
writer's merits and faults in full blow. We abstain on
principle from telling the story of novels, which seems to
us something like stealing geraniums from your friend's
flower-pot to stick in your own button-hole: you spoil the
effect of his plant, and you secure only a questionable
ornament for yourself. We shall therefore be careful to give
the reader no hint of the domestic story around which Mr

Kingsley has grouped the historical scenes and characters of 'Westward Ho!'

Hardly any period could furnish a happier subject for an historical fiction than the one Mr Kingsley has here chosen. It is unhackneyed, and it is unsurpassed in the grandeur of its moral elements, and the picturesqueness and romance of its manners and events. Mr Kingsley has not brought only genius but much labour to its illustration. He has fed his strong imagination with all accessible material, and given care not only to the grand figures and incidents but to small details. One sees that he knows and loves his Devonshire at first hand, and he has evidently lingered over the description of the forests and savannahs and rivers of the New World, until they have become as vividly present to him as if they were part of his own experience. We dare not pronounce on the merit of his naval descriptions, but to us, landlubbers as we are, they seem wonderfully real, and not to smack at all of technicalities learned by rote over the desk. He has given a careful and loving study to the history and literature of the period, and whatever misrepresentation there is in the book, is clearly not due to ignorance but to prepossession: if he misrepresents, it is not because he has omitted to examine, but because he has examined through peculiar spectacles. In the construction of a story Mr Kingsley has never been felicitous; and the feebleness of his *dénouements* have been matter of amazement, even to his admirers. In this respect, 'Westward Ho!' though by no means criticism-proof, is rather an advance on his former works, especially in the winding-up. It is true, this winding-up reminds us a little of Jane Eyre but we prefer a partially borrowed beauty to an original bathos, which was what Mr Kingsley achieved in the later chapters of 'Alton Locke' and 'Yeast'. Neither is humour his forte. His Jack Brimblecombe is too much like a piece of fun *obligato*, after the manner of Walter Scott, who remains the unequalled model of historical romancists, however they may criticize him. Mr Kingsley's necessity for strong loves and strong hatreds, and his determination to hold up certain persons as models, is an obstacle to his successful delineation of character, in which he might otherwise excel. As it is, we can no more believe in and love his men and women than we could believe in and love the pattern-boy at school, always cited as a rebuke to our aberrations. Amyas Leigh would be a real, lovable fellow enough if he were a little less exemplary, and if Mr Kingsley would not make him a text to preach from, as we suppose he is accustomed to do with Joshua, Gideon, and David. Until he shakes off this parsonic habit he will not be able to create truly human characters, or to write a genuine historical romance. Where his prepossessions do not come into play, where he is not dealing with his model heroes, or where the drama turns on a single passion or motive, he can scarcely be rivalled in truthfulness and beauty of presentation; for in clothing passion with action and language, and in the conception of all that gives local colouring, he has his best gifts to aid him. Beautiful is that episode of Mr Oxenham's love, told by Salvation Yeo! Very admirable, too, is the felicity with which Mr Kingsley has seized the style and spirit of the Elizabethan writers, and reproduced them in the poetry and supposed quotations scattered through his story. But above all other charms in his writings, at least to us, is his scene-painting. Who does not remember the scene by the wood in 'Alton Locke', or that of the hunt at the beginning of 'Yeast'? And 'Westward Ho!' is wealthy in still greater beauties of the same kind. Here is a perfect gem. After a description of the old house at Stow, the residence of Sir Richard Grenvile, we read—

From the house on three sides, the hill sloped steeply down, and the garden where Sir Richard and Amyas were walking gave a truly English prospect. At one turn they could catch, over the western walls, a glimpse of the blue ocean flecked with passing sails; and at the next, spread far below them, range on range of fertile park, stately avenue, yellow autumn woodland, and purple heather moors, lapping over and over each other up the valley to the old British earthwork, which stood black and furze-grown on its conical peak; and standing out against the sky on the highest bank of hill which closed the valley to the east, the lofty tower of Kilkhampton church, rich with the monuments and offerings of five centuries of Grenviles. A yellow eastern haze hung soft over park, and wood, and moor; the red cattle lowed to each other as they stood brushing away the flies in the rivulet far below; the colts in the horse-park close on their right whinnied as they played together, and their sires from the Queen's park, on the opposite hill, answered them in fuller though fainter voices. A rutting stag made the still woodland rattle with his hoarse thunder, and rival far up the valley gave back a trumpet note of defiance, and was himself defied from heathery brows which quivered far away above, half seen through the veil of eastern mist. And close at home, upon the terrace before the house, amid romping spaniels and golden-haired children, sat Lady Grenvile herself, the beautiful Saint Leger of Annery, the central jewel of all that glorious place, and looked down at her noble children, and then up at her more noble husband, and round at that broad paradise of the west, till life seemed too full of happiness, and heaven of light.

It is pleasanter to linger over beauties such as these, than to point out faults; but unhappily, Mr Kingsley's faults are likely to do harm in other ways than in subtracting from the lustre of his fame, and a faithful reviewer must lift up his voice against them, whether men 'will hear, or whether they will forbear'.* Who that has any knowledge of our history and literature—that has felt his heart beat high at the idea of great crises and great deeds—that has any true recognition of the greatest poetry, and some of the greatest thoughts enshrined in our language, is not ready to pay the tribute of enthusiastic reverence to the Elizabethan age? In his glowing picture of that age, Mr Kingsley would have carried with him all minds in which there is a spark of nobleness, if he could have freed himself from the spirit of the partisan, and been content to admit that in the Elizabethan age, as in every other, human beings, human parties, and human deeds are made up of the most subtly intermixed good and evil. The battle of Armageddon in which all the saints are to fight on one side, has never yet come. It is perfectly true that, at certain epochs, the relations and tendencies of ideas and events are so clearly made out to minds of any superiority, that the best and ablest men are for the most part ranged under one banner: there was a point at which it must have become disgraceful to a cultivated mind not to accept the Copernican system, and in these days we are unable to draw any favourable inference concerning the intellect or morals of a man who advocates capital punishment for sheep-stealing or forgery. But things have never come to this pass with regard to Catholicism and Protestantism; and even supposing they had, Mr Kingsley's ethics seem to resemble too closely those of his bugbears the Dominicans, when he implies that it is a holy work for the 'Ayes' to hunt down the 'Noes' like so many beasts of prey. His view of history seems not essentially to differ from that we have all held in our childish days, when it seemed perfectly easy for us to divide mankind into the sheep and the goats, when we devoutly believed that our favourite heroes, Wallace and Bruce, and all who fought on their side, were 'good', while Edward and his soldiers were all 'wicked'; that all the champions of the Reformation were of un-exceptionable private character, and all the adherents of Popery consciously vicious and base. Doubtless the Elizabethan age bore its peculiar fruit of excellence, as every age has done which forms a nodus, a ganglion, in the historical development of humanity—as the age of Pericles produced the divinest sculptures, or the age of the Roman Republic the severe grandeur of Roman law and Roman patriotism, or as the core of the Middle Ages held the germ of chivalrous honour and reverential love. Doubtless the conquest of the Spanish Armada was virtually the triumph of light and freedom over darkness and bondage. What then? Is this a reason why Mr Kingsley should seem almost angry with us for not believing with the men of that day in the golden city of Manoa and the Gulf-stream, or scold by anticipation any one who shall dare to congratulate himself on being undeceived in these matters? Doubtless Drake, Hawkins, Frobisher, and the rest, were brave, energetic men—men of great will and in some sort of great faculty; but like all other human agents, they 'builded better than they knew',* and it would be as rational to suppose that the bee is an entomological Euclid, interested only in the solution of a problem, as to suppose that the motives of these mariners were as grand as the results of their work.

We had marked several passages as specimens of the small success which attends Mr Kingsley in his favourite exercise of deducing a moral, but our want of space obliges us to renounce the idea of quoting them, with the exception of one, which, we think, will in some degree justify our low estimate of Mr Kingsley's gifts as a philosophizer. Here is the passage—

Humboldt* has somewhere a curious passage; in which, looking on some wretched group of Indians, squatting stupidly round their fires, besmeared with grease and paint, and devouring ants and clay, he somewhat naïvely remarks, that were it not for science, which teaches us that such is the crude material of humanity, and this the state from which we have all risen, he should have been tempted rather to look upon those hapless beings as the last degraded remnants of some fallen and dying race. One wishes that the great traveller had been bold enough to yield to that temptation, which his own reason and common sense presented to him as the real explanation of the sad sight, instead of following the dogmas of a so-called science, which has not a fact whereon to base its wild notion, and must ignore a thousand facts in asserting it. His own good sense, it seems, coincided instinctively with the Bible doctrine, that man in a state of nature is a fallen being, doomed to death—a view which may be a sad one, but still one more honourable to poor humanity than the theory, that we all began as some sort of two-handed apes. It is surely more hopeful to believe that those poor Otomacs or Guahibas were not what they ought to be, than to believe that they were. It is certainly more complimentary to them, to think that they had been somewhat nobler and more prudent in centuries gone by, than that they were such blockheads as to have dragged on, the son after the father, for all the thousands of years which have elapsed since man was made, without having had wit enough to discover any better food than ants and clay.

Our voyagers, however, like those of their time, troubled their heads with no such questions. Taking the Bible story as they found it, they agreed with Humboldt's reason, and not with his science; or, to speak correctly, agreed with Humboldt's self, and not with the shallow anthropologic theories which happened to be in vogue fifty years ago; and their new hosts were in their eyes immortal souls like themselves, 'captived by the devil at his will', lost there in the pathless forests, likely to be lost hereafter.

Note the accuracy of Mr Kingsley's reasoning. Humboldt observes that, but for scientific data leading to an opposite conclusion, he could have imagined that a certain group of Indians were the remnants of a race which had sunk from a state of well-being to one of almost helpless barbarism. Hereupon, Mr Kingsley is sorry that Humboldt did not reject 'the dogmas of a so-called science', and rest in this conception which 'coincided with the Bible doctrine'; and he urges as one of his reasons for this regret, that it would be complimentary to the Otomacs and Guahibas to suppose that in centuries gone by, they had been nobler and more prudent. Now, so far as we are acquainted with the third chapter of Genesis, and with the copious exegeses of that chapter from Saint Paul downwards, the 'Bible doctrine' is *not* that man multiplied on the earth and formed communities and nations—amongst the rest, noble and prudent societies of Otomacs and Guahibas—in a state of innocence, and that *then* came the Fall. We have always understood that for the Fall 'we may thank Adam', and that consequently the very first Otomac or Guahiba was already 'captived by the devil', and 'likely to be lost hereafter'. Hence, what the question of the Otomacs and Guahibas having been nobler and more prudent in centuries gone by, can have to do with the doctrine of the Fall, we are at a loss to perceive. We will do no more than point to Mr Kingsley's cool arrogance in asserting that a man like Humboldt, the patriarch of scientific investigators, is 'misled by the dogmas of a so-called science, which has *not a fact* whereon to base its wild notions'. Indeed it is rather saddening to dwell on the occasional absurdities into which anomalous opinions can betray a man of real genius; and after all, the last word we have to say of 'Westward Ho!' is to thank Mr Kingsley for the great and beautiful things we have found in it, as our dominant feeling towards his works in general is that of high admiration.

Geraldine Jewsbury's *Constance Herbert*
(1855)

NEXT in interest to 'Westward Ho!' at least among the English novels of the quarter, is 'Constance Herbert'. Miss Jewsbury has created precedents for herself which make critics exacting towards her. We measure her work by her own standard, and find it deficient; when if measured by the standard of ordinary feminine novelists, it would perhaps seem excellent. We meet with some beauties in it which, coming from the author of the 'Half Sisters', we take as a matter of course, but we miss other beauties which she has taught us to expect; we feel that she is not equal to herself; and it is a tribute to her well-attested powers if we dwell on what has disappointed us, rather than on what has gratified us. An easy, agreeable style of narrative, some noble sentiments expressed in the quiet, unexaggerated way that indicates their source to be a deep spring of conviction and experience, not a mere rain-torrent of hearsay enthusiasm, with here and there a trait of character or conduct painted with the truthfulness of close observation, are merits enough to raise a book far above the common run of circulating library fiction; but they are not enough to make a good novel, or one worthy of Miss Jewsbury's reputation. 'Constance Herbert' is a *Tendenz-roman*; the characters and incidents are selected with a view to the enforcement of a principle. The general principle meant to be enforced is the unhesitating, uncompromising sacrifice of inclination to duty, and the special case to which this principle is applied in the novel, is the abstinence from marriage where there is an inheritance of insanity. So far, we have no difference of opinion with Miss Jewsbury. But the *mode* in which she enforces the principle, both theoretically in the *Envoi* and illustratively in the story of her novel, implies, we think, a false view of life, and virtually nullifies the very

magnanimity she inculcates. 'If,' she says in the *Envoi*, 'we
have succeeded in articulating any principle in this book, it
is to entreat our readers to have boldness to act up to the
sternest requirements that duty claims as right. Although it
may at the time seem to slay them, it will in the end prove
life. *Nothing they renounce for the sake of a higher principle,
will prove to have been worth the keeping.*' The italics are
ours, and we use them to indicate what we think false in
Miss Jewsbury's moral. This moral is illustrated in the novel
by the story of three ladies, who, after renouncing their
lovers, or being renounced by them, have the satisfaction of
feeling in the end that these lovers were extremely 'good-
for-nothing', and that they (the ladies) have had an excellent
riddance. In all this we can see neither the true doctrine of
renunciation, nor a true representation of the realities of
life; and we are sorry that a writer of Miss Jewsbury's
insight and sincerity should have produced three volumes
for the sake of teaching such copy-book morality. It is not
the fact that what duty calls on us to renounce, will
invariably prove 'not worth the keeping'; and if it *were* the
fact, renunciation would cease to be moral heroism, and
would be simply a calculation of prudence. Let us take the
special case which Miss Jewsbury has chosen as her illustration. It might equally happen that a woman in the
position of Constance Herbert, who renounces marriage
because she will not entail on others the family heritage of
insanity, had fixed her affections, not on an egotistic, shallow worldling like Philip Marchmont, but on a man who
was fitted to make the happiness of a woman's life, and
whose subsequent career would only impress on her more
and more deeply the extent of the sacrifice she had made
in refusing him. And it is this very perception that the thing
we renounce is precious, is something never to be compen-
sated to us, which constitutes the beauty and heroism of
renunciation. The only motive that renders such a resolution
as Constance Herbert's noble, is that keen sympathy with
human misery which makes a woman prefer to suffer for
the term of her own life, rather than run the risk of causing
misery to an indefinite number of other human beings; and

a mind influenced by such a motive will find no support in the very questionable satisfaction of discovering that objects once cherished were in fact worthless. The notion that duty looks stern, but all the while has her hand full of sugar-plums, with which she will reward us by and by, is the favourite cant of optimists, who try to make out that this tangled wilderness of life has a plan as easy to trace as that of a Dutch garden; but it really undermines all true moral development by perpetually substituting something extrinsic as a motive to action, instead of the immediate impulse of love or justice, which alone makes an action truly moral. This is a grave question to enter on *à propos* of a novel; but Miss Jewsbury is so emphatic in the enunciation of her moral, that she forces us to consider her book rather in the light of a homily than of a fiction—to criticize her doctrine rather than her story. On another point, too, we must remonstrate with her a little, chiefly because we value her influence, and should like to see it always in what seems to us the right scale. With the exception of Mr Harrop, who is simply a cipher awaiting a wife to give him any value, there is not a man in her book who is not either weak, perfidious, or rascally, while almost all the women are models of magnanimity and devotedness. The lions, i.e., the ladies, have got the brush in their hands with a vengeance now, and are retaliating for the calumnies of men from Adam downwards. Perhaps it is but fair to allow them a little exaggeration. Still we must meekly suggest that we cannot accept an *ex parte* statement, even from that paragon Aunt Margaret, as altogether decisive. Aunt Margaret tells us that in the bloom of youth and beauty, with virtues and accomplishments to correspond, she alienated her husband by pure devotion to him. 'No man,' she says, 'can bear entire devotion.' This reminds us of a certain toper, who after drinking a series of glasses of brandy-and-water one night, complained the next morning that the water did not agree with him. We are inclined to think that it is less frequently devotion which alienates men, than something infused in the devotion—a certain amount of silliness, or temper, or *exigeance*, for example, which, though given in small doses, will, if persevered in, have a strongly alterative effect. Men, in fact, are in rather a difficult position: in one ear a Miss Grace Lee,* or some such strong-minded woman, thunders that they demand to be worshipped, and abhor a woman who has any self-dependence; on the other, a melancholy Viola* complains that they never appreciate devotion, that they care only for a woman who treats them with indifference. A discouraging view of the case for both sexes! Seriously, we care too much for the attainment of a better understanding as to woman's true position, not to be sorry when a writer like Miss Jewsbury only adds her voice to swell the confusion on this subject.

Lord Brougham's Literature (1855)

IT is matter of very common observation that members of the 'privileged classes', who, either from want of work or want of ability to do their proper work, find their time hang rather heavily on their hands, try to get rid of it by employments which, if not self-imposed, they would think rather pitiable. Kings and emperors have turned their hands to making locks and sealing-wax; ambassadresses have collected old stockings for the sake of darning them; and we knew a wealthy old gentleman who devoted himself to making pokers, which he presented to all the ladies of his acquaintance. It is generally presumed of such people that if they had brains to enable them to do anything better, they would prosecute this voluntary artisanship with less zeal; still, the case of these incapables is one to be charitably smiled at or sighed over, not gravely rebuked: we graciously accept the present of their lock or their poker and say no more about it. But it would be a different affair if these voluntary artisans were to set up shop—if, for example, Lord A., or Sir B.C., or any other of the tribe of wealthy Englishmen to whom foreigners give the generic title of *milord*, were not only to amuse himself with making boots, but were to hire a shop frontage, with plate glass, and exhibit his clumsy wares to the public with as much pomp and circumstance as if he were a very Hoby,* thereby inducing snobbish people to set the fashion of wearing and crying up Lord A.'s boots, to the depreciation of really well-made articles, and to the great detriment both of human candour and the human foot. Political economists and bootmakers, lady-loves and orthopaedists, science and aesthetics, would vote the aristocratic Crispin* a nuisance.

A sufficiently close parallel to this hypothetic case is suggested by Lord Brougham's *Lives of Men of Letters*, the sight of which, republished in a cheap form, has, we confess, roused our critical gall. Relieved from the labours of his chancellorship, Lord Brougham, we suppose, found a good deal of leisure on his hands; and how did he employ it? By taking to what we may call literary lock and poker-making— by writing third-rate biographies in the style of a literary hack! Biographies, too, of men whose lives had already been depicted in all sorts of ways, and presented to us in all sorts of lights—like Prince Albert's face and legs. If we had found these 'Lives of Men of Letters' in a biographical dictionary, we should perhaps have thought them about up to the average of the piecework usually to be met with in such compilations; finding them, as we did more than ten years ago, in an *édition de luxe* adorned with portraits, and with Lord Brougham's name on the title-page, we felt some simmering indignation at such gratuitous mediocrities in a pretentious garb; and now that we see them in a cheaper reissue—as if there were any demand for these clumsy superfluities, these amateur locks and pokers—our indignation fairly boils over. We have not the slightest wish to be disrespectful to Lord Brougham. His name is connected with some of the greatest movements in the last half century, and in general, is on the side of the liberal and the just. But he has been a successful man; his reputation is fully equal to his merit; society is unanimous in pronouncing that he has done many things well and wisely; and there is, therefore, no reason why we should be reticent of our criticism where, in our opinion, he has done some things less wisely and *not* well.

The first thing that strikes us in these *Lives* is the slovenliness of their style, which is thrown almost ludicrously into relief by the fact that many of Lord Brougham's pages are occupied with criticism of other men's style. The hard-run literary man, who is every moment expecting the knock of the printer's boy, has reason enough to renounce fastidiousness; but his lordship, in the elegant ease of his library, with no call impending but that of the lunch or dinner-bell, might at least atone for the lack of originality by finish—might, if he has no jewels to offer us, at least polish his pebbles. How far he has done this we will let the reader judge by giving some specimens of the manner in which Lord Brougham contrives

To blunt a moral and to spoil a tale.*

One of his reproaches against Gibbon's style is, that it is 'prone to adopt false and mixed metaphors'; but we doubt whether the *Decline and Fall* could furnish us with a more typical specimen of that kind than one which he himself gives us in his life of Voltaire. 'Proofs also remain,' says Lord Brougham, 'which place beyond all doubt his (Voltaire's) kindness to several worthless men, who repaid it with the black ingratitude so commonly used as their *current coin* by the base and spiteful, who thus repay their benefactors and *salve their own wounded pride by pouring venom on the hand that saved or served them.*' Again, in the life of Johnson, we read: 'Assuredly, we may in vain search all the Mantuan *tracery of sweets* for any to excel them in the beauty of numbers.' It may be our ignorance of confectionery that prevents us from perceiving what 'tracery' can have to do with 'sweets'; as it is, however, we can only explain his lordship's metaphor by supposing *tracery* to be a misprint for *tea-tray*, since misprints abound in this volume. Lord Brougham is very frequently quite as infelicitous in his phrases, and in the structure of his sentences, as in his metaphors. For example: 'It is none of the least absurd *parts* of Condorcet's work, that he, being so well versed in physical and mathematical science, passes without any particular observation the writings of Voltaire on physical subjects, when he was so competent to pronounce an opinion upon their merits.' 'Condorcet was a man of science, no doubt, a good mathematician; but he was *in other respects* of a middling understanding and *violent feelings.*' 'The lady treated him with kindness, apparently as a child; his friend Saint Lambert did not much relish the matter, being unable to adopt his singular *habit* of *several lovers at one and the same time intimate* with one mistress.' The style of Rousseau's *Confessions*, we are told, is 'so exquisitely graphic without any effort, and so accommodated to its subject without any baseness, *that there hardly exists another example of the miracles which composition can perform.*' In the labour of turning his heavy sentences, his lordship is sometimes oblivious of logic. Speaking of Johnson's Latin verses to Mrs Thrale, he says: 'Such offences as "Littera Skaiae" (*sic*—a misprint, of course, for *litora*) for an Adonian in his Sapphics to "Thralia dulcis", would have called down his severe censure on any luckless wight of Paris or Edinburgh who should peradventure have perpetrated them; nor would his being the countryman of Polignac or of by far the finest of modern Latinists, Buchanan, have operated except as an aggravation of the fault.' Why should it?

Remembering Sydney Smith's verdict on Scotch 'wut',* we are not very much surprised to find that Lord Brougham has some anticipation of a Millennium when men will cease to perpetrate witticisms—when not only will the lion eat straw like the ox, but latter-day Voltaires will be as heavy as Scotch lawyers. At least, this is the only way in which we can interpret his peroration to the 'Life of Voltaire'. After an allusion in the previous sentence to 'the graces of his style' and 'the spirit of his *immortal* wit', we read: 'But if ever the time shall arrive when men, intent solely on graver matters, and bending their whole minds to things of solid importance, shall be careless of such light accomplishments, and the writings which now have so great a relish more or less openly tasted, shall pass into oblivion, then,' etc., etc. We confess that we shudder at such a Millennium as much as at one predicted by Dr Cumming, or planned by Robert Owen.*

Another striking characteristic of these *Lives of Men of Letters* is the way in which the writer ignores what is not only notorious to all the educated world, but notoriously well known to Lord Brougham. The long-faced gravity with which he discourses on Voltaire's ridicule of religious dogmas, and on Hume's abstinence from such ridicule, might lead a very ignorant reader to suppose that Lord Brougham had led a retired life, chiefly in clerical and senile society, and could only with difficulty imagine a man passing a joke on the Trinity. He says of Hume that 'occasionally his opinions were perceivable' in his conversation, and that one day the inscription on the staircase of the college library, *Christo et Musis has aedes sacrarunt cives Edinenses,** actually 'drew from the unbeliever an irreverent observation on the junction which the piety rather than the classical purity of the good town had made between the worship of the heathen and our own'. Astounding! Even this distant allusion to such irreverence might have had a pernicious effect by exciting in us an unhealthy desire to know what the irreverent observation was, had we not remembered that Hume had no wit, but only 'wut', so that his joke was probably a feeble one . . . A still more surprising example of Lord Brougham's ignoring system as a writer is his comment on Voltaire's relation to Madame du Châtelet. He thinks that on the whole there is no sufficient reason for questioning that it was Platonic, and the chief grounds he alleges for this conclusion are: that the laws of French society at *that* time, as well as now, were exceedingly rigorous, that the relation was recognized by all their friends, that Voltaire mentions Madame du Châtelet in his letters, and that Frederick II sent his regards to her! One would think it did not require Lord Brougham's extensive acquaintance with the history of French society in the days of Voltaire and Rousseau to know that, whatever may be the truth of his conclusion, the grounds by which he supports it must sound like irony rather than like a grave statement of fact; and, indeed, he himself,—on another page, having laid aside his ignoring spectacles, talks of Grimm being the 'professed lover of Madame d'Epinay', and of St Lambert being 'the avowed lover' of Madame d'Houdetot.

We had marked several other points for notice, especially that very remarkable criticism of Lord Brougham's on the *Nouvelle Héloïse*, in which he implies, that for a lover to remind his mistress that she had allowed him to kiss her, is to tell her what a 'forward, abandoned wanton she proved', and his supposition, that because Johnson was sometimes wandering all night in the streets with Savage, he must necessarily have indulged in certain vices 'in their more crapulous form' (an unfortunate suggestion to come from the Brougham of Jeffrey's letters, who is described as 'roaming the streets with the sons of Belial'). But we must remember that when indignation makes reviews instead of Juvenalian verses, the result is not equally enjoyable by the reader. So we restrain our noble rage, and say good bye now and for ever to Lord Brougham's *Lives of Men of Letters*, hoping that the next time we meet with any production of his we may be able to express admiration as strongly as we have just now expressed the reverse.

The Morality of *Wilhelm Meister* (1855)

PERHAPS Mr Lewes's *Life of Goethe*, which we now see advertised, may throw some new light on the structure and purpose of the much-debated novel—*Wilhelm Meister's Apprenticeship*. In the meantime, we are tempted by the appearance of a new translation to give the opinion which our present knowledge enables us to form on one or two aspects of this many-sided work.

Ask nineteen out of twenty moderately-educated persons what they think of *Wilhelm Meister*, and the answer will probably be—'I think it an immoral book; and besides, it is awfully dull: I was not able to read it.' Whatever truth there may be in the first half of this judgement, the second half is a sufficient guarantee that the book is not likely to do any extensive injury in English society. Parents may let it lie on the drawing-room table without scruple, in the confidence that for youthful minds of the ordinary cast it will have no attractions, and that the exceptional youthful mind which is strongly arrested by it is of too powerful and peculiar a character to be trained according to educational dogmas.

But is *Wilhelm Meister* an immoral book? We think not: on the contrary, we think that it appears immoral to some minds because its morality has a grander orbit than any which can be measured by the calculations of the pulpit and of ordinary literature. Goethe, it is sometimes said, seems in this book to be almost destitute of moral bias: he shows no hatred of bad actions, no warm sympathy with good ones; he writes like a passionless Mejnour,* to whom all human things are interesting only as objects of intellectual contemplation. But we question whether the direct exhibition of a moral bias in the writer will make a book really moral in its influence. Try this on the first child that asks you to tell it a story. As long as you keep to an apparently impartial narrative of facts you will have earnest eyes fixed on you

in rapt attention, but no sooner do you begin to betray
symptoms of an intention to moralize, or to turn the current
of facts towards a personal application, than the interest of
your hearer will slacken, his eyes will wander, and the moral
dose will be doubly distasteful from the very sweetmeat in
which you have attempted to insinuate it. One grand reason
of this is, that the child is aware you are talking *for it* instead
of *from yourself*, so that instead of carrying it along in a
stream of sympathy with your own interest in the story, you
give it the impression of contriving coldly and talking
artificially. Now, the moralizing novelist produces the same
effect on his mature readers; an effect often heightened by
the perception that the moralizing is rather intended to make
his book eligible for family reading than prompted by any
profound conviction or enthusiasm. Just as far from being
really moral is the so-called moral *dénouement*, in which
rewards and punishments are distributed according to those
notions of justice on which the novel-writer would have
recommended that the world should be governed if he had
been consulted at the creation. The emotion of satisfaction
which a reader feels when the villain of the book dies of
some hideous disease, or is crushed by a railway train,* is
no more essentially moral than the satisfaction which used
to be felt in whipping culprits at the cart-tail. So we dismiss
the charge of immorality against *Wilhelm Meister* on these
two counts—the absence of moral bias in the mode of
narration, and the comfortable issues allowed to questionable
actions and questionable characters.

But there is another ground for the same accusation which
involves deeper considerations. It is said that some of the
scenes and incidents are such as the refined moral taste of
these days will not admit to be proper subjects for art, that
to depict irregular relations in all the charms they really
have for human nature, and to associate lovely qualities with
vices which society makes a brand of outlawry, implies a
toleration which is at once a sign and a source of perverted
moral sentiment. Wilhelm's relation to Mariana, and the
charm which the reader is made to feel in the lawless
Philina, many incidents that occur during Wilhelm's life

with the players, and the stories of Lothario's loves in the present, preterite, and future, are shocking to the prevalent English. It is no answer to this objection to say—what is the fact—that Goethe's pictures are truthful, that the career of almost every young man brings him in contact with far more vitiating irregularities than any presented in the experience of Wilhelm Meister; for no one can maintain that *all* fact is a fit subject for art. The sphere of the artist has its limit somewhere, and the first question is, Has Goethe overstepped this limit, so that the mere fact of artistic representation is a mistake? The second: If his subjects are within the legitimate limits of art, is his mode of treatment such as to make his pictures pernicious? Surely the sphere of art extends wherever there is beauty either in form, or thought, or feeling. A ray of sunlight falling on the dreariest sandbank will often serve the painter for a fine picture; the tragedian may take for his subject the most hideous passions if they serve as the background for some divine deed of tenderness or heroism, and so the novelist may place before us every aspect of human life where there is some twist of love, or endurance, or helplessness to call forth our best sympathies. Balzac, perhaps the most wonderful writer of fiction the world has ever seen, has in many of his novels overstepped this limit. He drags us by his magic force through scene after scene of unmitigated vice, till the effect of walking among this human carrion is a moral nausea. But no one can say that Goethe has sinned in this way.

Everywhere he brings us into the presence of living, generous humanity—mixed and erring, and self-deluding, but saved from utter corruption by the salt of some noble impulse, some disinterested effort, some beam of good nature, even though grotesque or homely. And his mode of treatment seems to us precisely that which is really moral in its influence. It is without exaggeration; he is in no haste to alarm readers into virtue by melodramatic consequences; he quietly follows the stream of fact and of life; and waits patiently for the moral processes of nature as we all do for her material processes. The large tolerance of Goethe, which is markedly exhibited in *Wilhelm Meister*, is precisely that to which we point as the element of moral superiority. We all begin life by associating our passions with our moral prepossessions, by mistaking indignation for virtue, and many go through life without awaking from this illusion. These are the 'insupportables justes, qui du haut de leurs chaises d'or narguent les misères et les souffrances de l'humanité'.* But a few are taught by their own falls and their own struggles, by their experience of sympathy, and help and goodness in the 'publicans and sinners' of these modern days, that the line between the virtuous and vicious, so far from being a necessary safeguard to morality, is itself an immoral fiction. Those who have been already taught this lesson will at once recognize the true morality of Goethe's works. Like *Wilhelm Meister*, they will be able to love the good in a Philina, and to reverence the far-seeing efforts of a Lothario.*

The Future of German Philosophy (1855)

'THE age of systems is passed . . . System is the childhood of philosophy; the manhood of philosophy is investigation.' So says Professor Gruppe in the work of which we have given the title above, and we quote this dictum at the outset in order to propitiate those readers who might otherwise turn away with disgust from the mention of German philosophy, having registered a vow to trouble themselves no more with those spinners of elaborate cocoons—German system-mongers.*

Perhaps, however, there are some of our readers who would not require any such password from Professor Gruppe; for although he is better known in England as a writer on classical literature than as a philosopher, still it is likely that many German scholars amongst us are acquainted with his two philosophical works, *Antaeus*, published in 1831, and *Wendepunkt der Philosophie im neunzehnten Jahrhundert*, published in 1834. He is a man of very various accomplishments, and throws his active intellect with equal fervour and facility into many channels—into poetry and politics as well as into classical literature and philosophy. This versatility in authorship is rare among erudite Germans, and is held rather in suspicion by them, in spite of the fact that some of their greatest men—Lessing, Herder, Goethe, and Schiller—were productive in several departments. Those who decry versatility—and there are many who do so in other countries besides Germany—seem to forget the immense service rendered by the *suggestiveness* of versatile men, who come to a subject with fresh, unstrained minds. You have perhaps been spending much time and ingenuity in planning a house or in spinning a theory which seems to you to account satisfactorily for many things: an intelligent neighbour comes in, and you show him your plan, or explain to him your theory. He is not an accomplished architect, but he sees at once that you have put a door and a chimney in incompatible positions; he is not, perhaps, a profound thinker, but he makes an observation on your theory which directly shows you that it will not 'hold water'. Such is the service which the versatile man will often render to the patient, exclusive inquirer. To return to Professor Gruppe: he has vindicated his versatility by achieving more than an average success in more than one department; his *Ariadne* is one of the best books, if not the very best, we have on the Greek Drama; his *Cosmic System of the Greeks* is an ingenious application of scholarship; many of his lyrical poems have considerable merit; and his *Wendepunkt der Philosophie* is a striking philosophical work, showing much acumen and independent thought. In the work now before us, which was originally intended to be a mere pamphlet, but which has swelled to a volume of nearly three hundred pages, he rapidly (and somewhat too allusively for the general reader) restates the views contained in his earlier philosophical works, the *Antaeus* and the *Wendepunkt*—views which twenty years of additional study and considerable experience as a professor of Moral Philosophy in the University of Berlin have served to confirm and make clearer.

The object towards which Herr Gruppe chiefly directs his consideration is the Reformation of Logic, or the rectification of the *method* of philosophical inquiry, which, as he justly insists, is the essential preliminary to all true progress. It is, he says, simply to a reform in method that we owe all the splendid achievements of modern natural science, and it is only by the extension of that reform to every department of philosophical inquiry that here also any of what Bacon calls 'fruit' can be obtained. In fact, the gist of his philosophical labours is partly to map out the road which John Mill (to whose work he seems to have given imperfect attention)* has actually wrought out and made available. It is curious that while Locke is, on the one hand, accused of being the originator of the French Sensational Philosophy, he is, on the other hand, as in the present work, reproached for having formed a step towards the speculative systems of Germany, in admitting *ideas of reflection*, thus severing *ideas* from *things*. This, says Professor Gruppe, is the fundamental error of philosophy, and, from Parmenides downwards, has issued in nothing but the bewilderment of the human intellect. Kant's classification of Infinity and Universality as ideas *a priori*, and of Space and Time as purely subjective forms of the intelligence, is a further elaboration of this fundamental error. These abstract terms on which speculation has built its huge fabrics are simply the x and y by which we mark the boundary of our knowledge; they have no value except in connexion with the concrete. The abstract is derived from the concrete: what, then, can we expect from a philosophy the essence of which is the derivation of the concrete from the abstract? The chief argument in favour of *a priori* ideas, as insisted on by Leibnitz and Kant is, that they can never be arrived at by induction; that induction may lead to the *general* but never to the *universal*, and that, nevertheless, this idea of universality is found in speech and in thought with the mark of necessity. But this argument will not bear a rigid examination. The language of all peoples soon attains to the expressions *all*, *universal*, *necessary*, but these expressions have their origin purely in the observations of the senses; they are simply a practical expedient, and are valued only under certain well-known and presupposed conditions. To isolate such expressions, to operate with them apart from experience, to exalt their relative value into an absolute value, to deduce knowledge from them alone, and to make them a standing point higher than all experience—this, which is what Parmenides and all speculative philosophers since him have done, is an attempt to poise the universe on one's head, and no wonder if dizziness and delusion are the consequence.*

These views are familiar enough to us in England, but to find them urged by a German professor is not so familiar.

A system of logic, says Herr Gruppe, which assigns the first place to general ideas, and makes them prior to judgment, inverts the true order of things. The true object of investigation is the formation of ideas from judgments, and in order to ascertain the law of their formation, we must direct our observation to those cases in which a new judgment or perception occurs, and is embodied in language, to the mental process which takes [place when] a discovery in natural science is made and is expressed in words, to the development of language, and to the application of language by children. In these three ways the formation of general ideas is daily carried forward. According to these tests, every judgment exhibits itself as a comparison, or perception of likeness in the midst of difference: the metaphor is no mere ornament of speech, but belongs to its essence, though usage gradually dispenses with it. When we say the evening sky is red, the lily is white, it may seem as if red and white were independent, immediate ideas; not so, when we say the sky is rose-red or rosy, the lily snow-white or snowy. Again, when we hear a child call the neighbour's dog, not a dog, but *Caro*, because its own dog is named Caro, we see the origin of the idea of species, or of general ideas; this is the first step towards the remotest abstractions. A consideration of examples, taken from the doctrines of natural science, shows, what has hitherto been overlooked by logicians, that every true judgment inevitably alters the idea both of the subject and predicate. Thus, when we say granite is volcanic, we modify both the idea of granite and of the predicate volcanic: a new quality is attributed to granite, and the predicate volcanic receives a wider extension. Kant, then, was mistaken in regarding synthetical and analytical judgments as two distinct classes. The true statement is, that every analytical judgment has previously been synthetic, and every synthetic judgment is such only once, and immediately becomes analytic. By a synthetic judgment, the idea of the predicate passes into that of the subject, and is incorporated with it, so that when I repeat this judgment it is necessarily analytic. Thus, from the simple act of judgment we ascend to the formation of ideas, to their modification, and their generalisation. And by a series of ascending generalisations we are led to the most comprehensive, abstract ideas. But by the side of these abstract ideas, to which we attain by an ascent from positive particulars, there is another set of ideas which owe their origin to unprecise expressions and mere devices of language, by which we bridge over our ignorance or eke out our limitation, and singularly enough these are the very ideas which have been enthroned as the *absolute*.

Professor Gruppe, in common with many before him, makes war against the syllogism as a *petitio principii*, and even seems to reject it altogether as an instrument. He seems to us not to have rightly apprehended Mill's analysis of the syllogism and the function he assigns to it, since he makes it an objection to that writer's views that he gives an important place to deduction in his method. Deduction, as Mill shows, is not properly opposed to induction but to experiment, and is a means of registering and using the results of induction, indispensable to any great progress in science. But these are questions which this is not the place to discuss.

What then, asks Herr Gruppe in conclusion, is the future sphere of Philosophy? It must renounce metaphysics: it must renounce the ambitious attempt to form a theory of the universe, to know things in their causes and first principles. But in its function of determining logic or method, it is still the centre and heart of human knowledge, and it has to apply this method to the investigation of Psychology, with its subordinate department Aesthetics; to Ethics; and to the principles of Jurisprudence. A sufficient task!

These are rather abstruse subjects to enter on in a short space, but we have at least been able to present one point of interest to our readers, in the fact that a German professor of philosophy renounces the attempt to climb to heaven by the rainbow bridge of 'the high *priori* road', and is content humbly to use his muscles in treading the uphill *a posteriori* path which will lead, not indeed to heaven, but to an eminence whence we may see very bright and blessed things on earth.

Evangelical Teaching: Dr Cumming
(1855)

GIVEN, a man with moderate intellect, a moral standard not higher than the average, some rhetorical affluence and great glibness of speech, what is the career in which, without the aid of birth or money, he may most easily attain power and reputation in English society? Where is that Goshen* of mediocrity in which a smattering of science and learning will pass for profound instruction, where platitudes will be accepted as wisdom, bigoted narrowness as holy zeal, unctuous egoism as God-given piety? Let such a man become an evangelical preacher; he will then find it possible to reconcile small ability with great ambition, superficial knowledge with the prestige of erudition, a middling morale with a high reputation for sanctity. Let him shun practical extremes and be ultra only in what is purely theoretic: let him be stringent on predestination, but latitudinarian on fasting; unflinching in insisting on the Eternity of punishment, but diffident of curtailing the substantial comforts of Time; ardent and imaginative on the pre-millennial Advent of Christ, but cold and cautious towards every other infringement of the status quo. Let him fish for souls not with the bait of inconvenient singularity, but with the dragnet of comfortable conformity. Let him be hard and literal in his interpretation only when he wants to hurl texts at the heads of unbelievers and adversaries, but when the letter of the Scriptures presses too closely on the genteel Christianity of the nineteenth century, let him use his spiritualizing alembic and disperse it into impalpable ether. Let him preach less of Christ than of Anti-christ; let him be less definite in showing what sin is than in showing who is the Man of Sin, less expansive on the blessedness of faith than on the accursedness of infidelity. Above all, let him set up as an interpreter of prophecy, and rival Moore's

Almanack in the prediction of political events, tickling the interest of hearers who are but moderately spiritual by showing how the Holy Spirit has dictated problems and charades for their benefit, and how, if they are ingenious enough to solve these, they may have their Christian graces nourished by learning precisely to whom they may point as the 'horn that had eyes', 'the lying prophet', and the 'unclean spirits'.* In this way he will draw men to him by the strong cords of their passions, made reason-proof by being baptized with the name of piety. In this way he may gain a metropolitan pulpit; the avenues to his church will be as crowded as the passages to the opera; he has but to print his prophetic sermons and bind them in lilac and gold, and they will adorn the drawing-room table of all evangelical ladies, who will regard as a sort of pious 'light reading' the demonstration that the prophecy of the locusts whose sting is in their tail,* is fulfilled in the fact of the Turkish commander's having taken a horse's tail for his standard, and that the French are the very frogs predicted in the Revelations.

Pleasant to the clerical flesh under such circumstances is the arrival of Sunday! Somewhat at a disadvantage during the week, in the presence of working-day interests and lay splendours, on Sunday the preacher becomes the cynosure of a thousand eyes, and predominates at once over the Amphitryon* with whom he dines, and the most captious member of his church or vestry. He has an immense advantage over all other public speakers. The platform orator is subject to the criticism of hisses and groans. Counsel for the plaintiff expects the retort of counsel for the defendant. The honourable gentleman on one side of the House is liable to have his facts and figures shown up by his honourable friend on the opposite side. Even the scientific or literary lecturer, if he is dull or incompetent, may see the best part of his audience quietly slip out one by one. But the preacher is completely master of the situation: no one may hiss, no one may depart. Like the writer of imaginary conversations, he may put what imbecilities he pleases into the mouths of his antagonists, and swell with triumph when he has refuted

them. He may riot in gratuitous assertions, confident that
no man will contradict him; he may exercise perfect free-will
in logic, and invent illustrative experience; he may give an
evangelical edition of history with the inconvenient facts
omitted:—all this he may do with impunity, certain that
those of his hearers who are not sympathizing are not
listening. For the Press has no band of critics who go the
round of the churches and chapels, and are on the watch
for a slip or defect in the preacher, to make a 'feature' in
their article: the clergy are, practically, the most irrespon-
sible of all talkers. For this reason, at least, it is well that
they do not always allow their discourses to be merely
fugitive, but are often induced to fix them in that black and
white in which they are open to the criticism of any man
who has the courage and patience to treat them with thorough freedom of speech and pen.

It is because we think this criticism of clerical teaching
desirable for the public good, that we devote some pages to
Dr Cumming. He is, as every one knows, a preacher of
immense popularity, and of the numerous publications in
which he perpetuates his pulpit labours, all circulate widely,
and some, according to their title-page, have reached the
sixteenth thousand. Now our opinion of these publications
is the very opposite of that given by a newspaper eulogist:
we do *not* 'believe that the repeated issues of Dr Cumming's
thoughts are having a beneficial effect on society', but the
reverse; and hence, little inclined as we are to dwell on his
pages, we think it worth while to do so, for the sake of
pointing out in them what we believe to be profoundly
mistaken and pernicious. Of Dr Cumming personally we
know absolutely nothing: our acquaintance with him is
confined to a perusal of his works, our judgement of him
is founded solely on the manner in which he has written
himself down on his pages. We know neither how he looks
nor how he lives. We are ignorant whether, like St Paul, he
has a bodily presence that is weak and contemptible, or
whether his person is as florid and as prone to amplification
as his style. For aught we know, he may not only have the
gift of prophecy, but may bestow the profits of all his works

to feed the poor, and be ready to give his own body to be burned with as much alacrity as he infers the everlasting burning of Roman-catholics and Puseyites.* Out of the pulpit he may be a model of justice, truthfulness, and the love that thinketh no evil; but we are obliged to judge of his charity by the spirit we find in his sermons, and shall only be glad to learn that his practice is, in many respects, an amiable *non sequitur* from his teaching.

Dr Cumming's mind is evidently not of the pietistic order. There is not the slightest leaning towards mysticism in his Christianity—no indication of religious raptures, of delight in God, of spiritual communion with the Father. He is most at home in the forensic view of Justification, and dwells on salvation as a scheme rather than as an experience. He insists on good works as the sign of justifying faith, as labours to be achieved to the glory of God, but he rarely represents them as the spontaneous, necessary outflow of a soul filled with Divine love. He is at home in the external, the polemical, the historical, the circumstantial, and is only episodically devout and practical. The great majority of his published sermons are occupied with argument or philippic against Romanists and unbelievers, with 'vindications' of the Bible, with the political interpretation of prophecy, or the criticism of public events; and the devout aspiration, or the spiritual and practical exhortation, is tacked to them as a sort of fringe in a hurried sentence or two at the end. He revels in the demonstration that the Pope is the Man of Sin; he is copious on the downfall of the Ottoman empire; he appears to glow with satisfaction in turning a story which tends to show how he abashed an 'infidel'; it is a favourite exercise with him to form conjectures of the process by which the earth is to be burned up, and to picture Dr Chalmers and Mr Wilberforce* being caught up to meet Christ in the air, while Romanists, Puseyites, and infidels are given over to gnashing of teeth. But of really spiritual joys and sorrows, of the life and death of Christ as a manifestation of love that constrains the soul, of sympathy with that yearning over the lost and erring which made Jesus weep over Jerusalem, and prompted the sublime prayer,

'Father, forgive them', of the gentler fruits of the Spirit, and the peace of God which passeth understanding—of all this, we find little trace in Dr Cumming's discourses.

His style is in perfect correspondence with this habit of mind. Though diffuse, as that of all preachers must be, it has rapidity of movement, perfect clearness, and some aptness of illustration. He has much of that literary talent which makes a good journalist—the power of beating out an idea over a large space, and of introducing far-fetched *à propos*. His writings have, indeed, no high merit: they have no originality or force of thought, no striking felicity of presentation, no depth of emotion. Throughout nine volumes we have alighted on no passage which impressed us as worth extracting, and placing among the 'beauties' of evangelical writers, such as Robert Hall, Foster the Essayist, or Isaac Taylor.* Everywhere there is commonplace cleverness, nowhere a spark of rare thought, of lofty sentiment, or pathetic tenderness. We feel ourselves in company with a voluble retail talker, whose language is exuberant but not exact, and to whom we should never think of referring for precise information, or for well-digested thought and experience. His argument continually slides into wholesale assertion and vague declamation, and in his love of ornament he frequently becomes tawdry. For example, he tells us ('Apocalyptic Sketches', p.265), that 'Botany weaves around the cross her amaranthine garlands; and Newton comes from his starry home—Linnaeus from his flowery resting-place—and Werner and Hutton from their subterranean graves at the voice of Chalmers, to acknowledge that all they learned and elicited in their respective provinces, has only served to show more clearly that Jesus of Nazareth is enthroned on the riches of the universe':—and so prosaic an injunction to his hearers as that they should choose a residence within an easy distance of church, is magnificently draped by him as an exhortation to prefer a house 'that basks in the sunshine of the countenance of God'. Like all preachers of his class, he is more fertile in imaginative paraphrase than in close exposition, and in this way he gives us some remarkable fragments of what we may call the romance of Scripture, filling up the outline of the record with an elaborate colouring quite undreamed of by more literal minds. The serpent, he informs us, said to Eve, 'Can it be so? Surely you are mistaken, that God hath said you shall die, a creature so fair, so lovely, so beautiful. It is impossible. *The laws of nature and physical science tell you that my interpretation is correct*; you shall not die. I can tell you by my own experience as an angel that you shall be as gods, knowing good and evil' (Apoc. Sketches, p.294). Again, according to Dr Cumming, Abel had so clear an idea of the Incarnation and Atonement, that when he offered his sacrifice 'he must have said, "I feel myself a guilty sinner, and that in myself I cannot meet thee alive; I lay on thine altar this victim, and I shed its blood as my testimony that mine should be shed; and I look for forgiveness and undeserved mercy through Him who is to bruise the serpent's head, and whose atonement this typifies" ' ('Occasional Discourses', vol i, p.23). Indeed, his productions are essentially ephemeral; he is essentially a journalist, who writes sermons instead of leading articles, who, instead of venting diatribes against her Majesty's Ministers, directs his power of invective against Cardinal Wiseman and the Puseyites,—instead of declaiming on public spirit, perorates on the 'glory of God'. We fancy he is called, in the more refined evangelical circles, an 'intellectual preacher'; by the plainer sort of Christians, a 'flowery preacher'; and we are inclined to think that the more spiritually-minded class of believers, who look with greater anxiety for the kingdom of God within them than for the visible advent of Christ in 1864, will be likely to find Dr Cumming's declamatory flights and historico-prophetical exercitations as little better than 'clouts o' cauld parritch'.*

Such is our general impression from his writings after an attentive perusal. There are some particular characteristics which we shall consider more closely, but in doing so we must be understood as altogether declining any doctrinal discussion. We have no intention to consider the grounds of Dr Cumming's dogmatic system, to examine the principles of his prophetic exegesis, or to question his opinion concerning the little horn, the river Euphrates, or the seven vials.* We identify ourselves with no one of the bodies whom he regards it as his special mission to attack: we give our adhesion neither to Romanism, Puseyism, nor to that anomalous combination of opinions which he introduces to us under the name of Infidelity. It is simply as spectators that we criticize Dr Cumming's mode of warfare, and we concern ourselves less with what he holds to be Christian truth than with his manner of enforcing that truth, less with the doctrines he teaches than with the moral spirit and tendencies of his teaching.

One of the most striking characteristics of Dr Cumming's writings is *unscrupulosity of statement.* His motto apparently is, *Christianitatem, quocunque modo, Christianitatem;** and the only system he includes under the term Christianity is Calvinistic Protestantism. Experience has so long shown that the human brain is a congenial nidus for inconsistent beliefs, that we do not pause to inquire how Dr Cumming, who attributes the conversion of the unbelieving to the Divine Spirit, can think it necessary to co-operate with that Spirit by argumentative white lies. Nor do we for a moment impugn the genuineness of his zeal for Christianity, or the sincerity of his conviction that the doctrines he preaches are necessary to salvation; on the contrary, we regard the flagrant unveracity that we find on his pages as an indirect result of that conviction—as a result, namely, of the intellectual and moral distortion of view which is inevitably produced by assigning to dogmas, based on a very complex structure of evidence, the place and authority of first truths. A distinct appreciation of the value of evidence—in other words, the intellectual perception of truth—is more closely allied to truthfulness of statement, or the moral quality of veracity, than is generally admitted. There is not a more pernicious fallacy afloat in common parlance, than the wide distinction made between intellect and morality. Amiable impulses without intellect, man may have in common with dogs and horses; but morality, which is specifically human, is dependent on the regulation of feeling by intellect. All human beings who can be said to be in any degree moral have their impulses guided, not indeed always by their own intellect, but by the intellect of human beings who have gone before them, and created traditions and associations which have taken the rank of laws. Now that highest moral habit, the constant preference of truth both theoretically and practically, pre-eminently demands the co-operation of the intellect with the impulses; as is indicated by the fact that it is only found in anything like completeness in the highest class of minds. In accordance with this we think it is found that, in proportion as religious sects exalt feeling above intellect, and believe themselves to be guided by direct inspiration rather than by a spontaneous exertion of their faculties—that is, in proportion as they are removed from rationalism—their sense of truthfulness is misty and confused. No one can have talked to the more enthusiastic Methodists and listened to their stories of miracles without perceiving that they require no other passport to a statement than that it accords with their wishes and their general conception of God's dealings; nay, they regard as a symptom of sinful scepticism an inquiry into the evidence for a story which they think unquestionably tends to the glory of God, and in retailing such stories, new particulars, further tending to his glory, are 'borne in' upon their minds. Now, Dr Cumming, as we have said, is no enthusiastic pietist: within a certain circle—within the mill of evangelical orthodoxy, his intellect is perpetually at work; but that principle of sophistication which our friends the Methodists derive from the predominance of their pietistic feelings, is involved for him in the doctrine of verbal inspiration; what is for them a state of emotion submerging the intellect, is with him a formula imprisoning the intellect, depriving it of its proper function—the free search for truth—and making it the mere servant-of-all-work to a foregone conclusion. Minds fettered by this doctrine no longer inquire concerning a proposition whether it is attested by sufficient evidence, but whether it accords with Scripture; they do not search for facts, as such, but for facts that will bear out their doctrine. They become accustomed to reject the more direct evidence in favour of the less direct, and where adverse evidence

reaches demonstration they must resort to devices and ex-
pedients in order to explain away contradiction. It is easy
to see that this mental habit blunts not only the perception
of truth, but the sense of truthfulness, and that the man
whose faith drives him into fallacies, treads close upon the
precipice of falsehood.

We have entered into this digression for the sake of
mitigating the inference that is likely to be drawn from that
characteristic of Dr Cumming's works to which we have
pointed. He is much in the same intellectual condition as
that professor of Padua,* who, in order to disprove Galileo's
discovery of Jupiter's satellites, urged that as there were
only seven metals there could not be more than seven
planets—a mental condition scarcely compatible with candour. And we may well suppose that if the Professor had
held the belief in seven planets, and no more, to be a
necessary condition of salvation, his mental vision would
have been so dazed that even if he had consented to look
through Galileo's telescope, his eyes would have reported
in accordance with his inward alarms rather than with the
external fact. So long as a belief in propositions is regarded
as indispensable to salvation, the pursuit of truth *as such* is
not possible, any more than it is possible for a man who is
swimming for his life to make meteorological observations
on the storm which threatens to overwhelm him. The sense
of alarm and haste, the anxiety for personal safety, which
Dr Cumming insists upon as the proper religious attitude,
unmans the nature, and allows no thorough, calm-thinking,
no truly noble, disinterested feeling. Hence, we by no means
suspect that the unscrupulosity of statement with which we
charge Dr Cumming, extends beyond the sphere of his
theological prejudices; we do not doubt that, religion apart,
he appreciates and practises veracity.

A grave general accusation must be supported by details,
and in adducing these, we purposely select the most obvious
cases of misrepresentation—such as require no argument to
expose them, but can be perceived at a glance. Among Dr
Cumming's numerous books, one of the most notable for
unscrupulosity of statement is the 'Manual of Christian

Evidences', written, as he tells us in his Preface, not to give the deepest solutions of the difficulties in question, but to furnish Scripture-readers, City Missionaries, and Sunday-school Teachers, with a 'ready reply' to sceptical arguments. This announcement that *readiness* was the chief quality sought for in the solutions here given, modifies our inference from the other qualities which those solutions present; and it is but fair to presume, that when the Christian disputant is not in a hurry, Dr Cumming would recommend replies less ready and more veracious. Here is an example of what in another place[1] he tells his readers is 'change in their pocket . . . a little ready argument which they can employ, and therewith answer a fool according to his folly'. From the nature of this argumentative small coin, we are inclined to think Dr Cumming understands answering a fool according to his folly to mean, giving him a foolish answer. We quote from the 'Manual of Christian Evidences', p.62.

Some of the gods which the heathen worshipped were among the greatest monsters that ever walked the earth. Mercury was a thief; and because he was an expert thief, he was enrolled among the gods. Bacchus was a mere sensualist and drunkard; and therefore he was enrolled among the gods. Venus was a dissipated and abandoned courtesan; and therefore she was enrolled among the goddesses. Mars was a savage, that gloried in battle and in blood; and therefore he was deified and enrolled among the gods.

Does Dr Cumming believe the purport of these sentences? If so, this passage is worth handing down as his theory of the Greek myth—as a specimen of the astounding ignorance which was possible in a metropolitan preacher, AD 1854. And if he does not believe them . . . The inference must then be, that he thinks delicate veracity about the ancient Greeks is not a Christian virtue, but only a 'splendid sin' of the unregenerate. This inference is rendered the more probable by our finding, a little further on, that he is not more scrupulous about the moderns, if they come under his definition of 'Infidels'. But the passage we are about to

[1] *Lectures on the Book of Daniel*, p. 6.

quote in proof of this has a worse quality than its discrepancy with fact. Who that has a spark of generous feeling, that rejoices in the presence of good in a fellow-being, has not dwelt with pleasure on the thought that Lord Byron's unhappy career was ennobled and purified towards its close by a high and sympathetic purpose, by honest and energetic efforts for his fellow-men? Who has not read with deep emotion those last pathetic lines, beautiful as the afterglow of sunset, in which love and resignation are mingled with something of a melancholy heroism? Who has not lingered with compassion over the dying scene at Missolonghi—the sufferer's inability to make his farewell messages of love intelligible, and the last long hours of silent pain? Yet for the sake of furnishing his disciples with a 'ready reply', Dr Cumming can prevail on himself to inoculate them with a bad-spirited falsity like the following:

We have one striking exhibition of *an infidel's brightest thoughts*, in some lines *written in his dying moments* by a man, gifted with great genius, capable of prodigious intellectual prowess, but of worthless principle and yet more worthless practices—I mean the celebrated Lord Byron. He says—

> Though gay companions o'er the bowl
> Dispel awhile the sense of ill,
> Though pleasure fills the maddening soul,
> The heart—*the heart* is lonely still.
>
> Ay, but to die, and go, alas!
> Where all have gone and all must go;
> To be the *Nothing* that I was,
> Ere born to life and living woe!
>
> Count o'er the joys thine hours have seen,
> Count o'er thy days from anguish free,
> And know, whatever thou hast been,
> 'Tis *something better* not to be.
>
> Nay, for myself, so dark my fate
> Through every turn of life hath been,
> *Man* and the *world* so much *I hate*,
> I care not when I quit the scene.*

It is difficult to suppose that Dr Cumming can have been so grossly imposed upon—that he can be so ill-informed as really to believe that these lines were 'written' by Lord Byron in his dying moments; but, allowing him the full benefit of that possibility, how shall we explain his introduction of this feebly rabid doggerel as 'an infidel's brightest thoughts'?

In marshalling the evidences of Christianity, Dr Cumming directs most of his arguments against opinions that are either totally imaginary, or that belong to the past rather than to the present, while he entirely fails to meet the difficulties actually felt and urged by those who are unable to accept Revelation. There can hardly be a stronger proof of misconception as to the character of free-thinking in the present day, than the recommendation of Leland's* 'Short and Easy Method with the Deists'—a method which is unquestionably short and easy for preachers disinclined to reconsider their stereotyped modes of thinking and arguing, but which has quite ceased to realize those epithets in the conversion of Deists. Yet Dr Cumming not only recommends this book, but takes the trouble himself to write a feebler version of its arguments. For example, on the question of the genuineness and authenticity of the New Testament writings, he says:—'If, therefore, at a period long subsequent to the death of Christ, a number of men had appeared in the world, drawn up a book which they christened by the name of Holy Scripture, and recorded these things which appear in it as facts when they were only the fancies of their own imagination, surely the *Jews* would have instantly reclaimed that no such events transpired, that no such person as Jesus Christ appeared in their capital, and that *their* crucifixion of Him, and their alleged evil treatment of his apostles, were mere fictions.'[2] It is scarcely necessary to say that, in such argument as this, Dr Cumming is beating the air. He is meeting a hypothesis which no one holds, and totally missing the real question. The only type of 'infidel' whose existence Dr Cumming recognizes is that fossil personage

---

[2] *Manual of Christian Evidence*, p. 81.

who 'calls the Bible a lie and a forgery'. He seems to be ignorant—or he chooses to ignore the fact—that there is a large body of eminently instructed and earnest men who regard the Hebrew and Christian Scriptures as a series of historical documents, to be dealt with according to the rules of historical criticism, and that an equally large number of men, who are not historical critics, find the dogmatic scheme built on the letter of the Scriptures opposed to their profoundest moral convictions. Dr Cumming's infidel is a man who, because his life is vicious, tries to convince himself that there is no God, and that Christianity is an imposture, but who is all the while secretly conscious that he is opposing the truth, and cannot help 'letting out' admissions 'that the Bible is the Book of God'. We are favoured with the following 'Creed of the Infidel':—

I believe that there is no God, but that matter is God, and God is matter; and that it is no matter whether there is any God or not. I believe also that the world was not made, but that the world made itself, or that it had no beginning, and that it will last for ever. I believe that man is a beast; that the soul is the body, and that the body is the soul; and that after death there is neither body nor soul. I believe that there is no religion, that *natural religion is the only religion, and all religion unnatural.* I believe not in Moses; I believe in the first philosophers. I believe not in the evangelists; I believe in Chubb, Collins, Toland, Tindal, and Hobbes. I believe in Lord Bolingbroke, and I believe not in Saint Paul. I believe not in revelation; *I believe in tradition: I believe in the Talmud: I believe in the Koran*; I believe not in the Bible. I believe in Socrates; I believe in Confucius; I believe in Mahomet; I believe not in Christ. And lastly, *I believe* in all unbelief.

The intellectual and moral monster whose creed is this complex web of contradictions, is, moreover, according to Dr Cumming, a being who unites much simplicity and imbecility with his Satanic hardihood—much tenderness of conscience with his obdurate vice. Hear the 'proof':—

I once met with an acute and enlightened infidel, with whom I reasoned day after day, and for hours together; I submitted to him the internal, the external, and the experimental evidences, but made no impression on his scorn and unbelief. At length I entertained a suspicion that there was something morally, rather than intellectually wrong, and that the bias was not in the intellect, but in the heart; one day therefore I said to him—'I must now state my conviction, and you may call me uncharitable, but duty compels me; you are living in some known and gross sin.' *The man's countenance became pale; he bowed and left me (Manual of Christian Evidences, p.254).*

Here we have the remarkable psychological phenomenon of an 'acute and enlightened' man who, deliberately purposing to indulge in a favourite sin, and regarding the Gospel with scorn and unbelief, is, nevertheless, so much more scrupulous than the majority of Christians, that he cannot 'embrace sin and the Gospel simultaneously'; who is so alarmed at the Gospel in which he does not believe, that he cannot be easy without trying to crush it; whose acuteness and enlightenment suggest to him, as a means of crushing the Gospel, to argue from day to day with Dr Cumming; and who is withal so naïve that he is taken by surprise when Dr Cumming, failing in argument, resorts to accusation, and so tender in conscience that, at the mention of his sin, he turns pale and leaves the spot. If there be any human mind in existence capable of holding Dr Cumming's 'Creed of the Infidel', of at the same time believing in tradition and 'believing in all unbelief', it must be the mind of the infidel just described, for whose existence we have Dr Cumming's *ex officio* word as a theologian; and to theologians we may apply what Sancho Panza says of the bachelors of Salamanca,* that they never tell lies—except when it suits their purpose.

The total absence from Dr Cumming's theological mind of any demarcation between fact and rhetoric is exhibited in another passage, where he adopts the dramatic form:—

Ask the peasant on the hills—*and I have asked amid the mountains of Braemar and Dee-side*,—'How do you know that this book is Divine, and that the religion you profess is true? You never read Paley?' 'No, I never heard of him.'—'You have never read Butler?' 'No, I have never heard of him.'—'Nor Chalmers?' 'No, I do not know him.'—'You have never read any books on evidence?' 'No, I have read no such books.'—'Then, how do you know this book is true?' 'Know it! Tell me that the Dee, the Clunie, and the Garrawalt, the streams at my feet, do not run; that the winds do not sigh amid the gorges of these blue hills; that the sun does not kindle the peaks of Loch-na-Gar; tell me my heart does not beat, and I will believe you; but do not tell me the Bible is not Divine. I have found its truth illuminating my footsteps; its consolations sustaining my heart. May my tongue cleave to my mouth's roof, and my right hand forget its cunning, if I ever deny what is my deepest inner experience, that this blessed book is the book of God' (*Church before the Flood*, p.35).

Dr Cumming is so slippery and lax in his mode of presentation, that we find it impossible to gather whether he means to assert, that this is what a peasant on the mountains of Braemar *did* say, or that it is what such a peasant *would* say: in the one case, the passage may be taken as a measure of his truthfulness; in the other, of his judgement.

His own faith, apparently, has not been altogether intuitive, like that of his rhetorical peasant, for he tells us (Apoc. Sketches, p.405), that he has himself experienced what it is to have religious doubts. 'I was tainted while at the University by this spirit of scepticism. I thought Christianity might not be true. The very possibility of its being true was the thought I felt I must meet and settle. Conscience could give me no peace till I had settled it. I read, and I have read from that day, for fourteen or fifteen years, till this, and now I am as convinced, upon the clearest evidence, that this book is the book of God as that I now address you.' This experience, however, instead of impressing on him the fact that doubt may be the stamp of a truth-loving mind—that *sunt quibus non credidisse honor est, et fidei futurae pignus**— seems to have produced precisely the contrary effect. It has not enabled him even to conceive the condition of a mind 'perplext in faith but pure in deeds',* craving light, yearning for a faith that will harmonize and cherish its highest powers and aspirations, but unable to find that faith in dogmatic Christianity. His own doubts apparently were of a different kind. Nowhere in his pages have we found a humble, candid, sympathetic attempt to meet the difficulties that may be felt by an ingenuous mind. Everywhere he supposes that the doubter is hardened, conceited, consciously shutting his eyes to the light—a fool who is to be answered according to his folly—that is, with ready replies made up of reckless assertions, of apocryphal anecdotes, and, where other resources fail, of vituperative imputations. As to the reading which he has prosecuted for fifteen years—*either* it has left him totally ignorant of the relation which his own religious creed bears to the criticism and philosophy of the nineteenth century, *or* he systematically blinks that criticism and that philosophy; and instead of honestly and seriously endeavouring to meet and solve what he knows to be the real difficulties, contents himself with setting up popinjays to shoot at, for the sake of confirming the ignorance and winning the cheap admiration of his evangelical hearers and readers. Like the Catholic preacher who, after throwing down his cap and apostrophizing it as Luther, turned to his audience and said, 'You see this heretical fellow has not a word to say for himself', Dr Cumming, having drawn his ugly portrait of the infidel, and put arguments of a convenient quality into his mouth, finds a 'short and easy method' of confounding this 'croaking frog'.

In his treatment of infidels, we imagine he is guided by a mental process which may be expressed in the following syllogism: Whatever tends to the glory of God is true; it is for the glory of God that infidels should be as bad as possible; therefore, whatever tends to show that infidels are as bad as possible is true. All infidels, he tells us, have been men of 'gross and licentious lives'. Is there not some well-known unbeliever, David Hume, for example, of whom even Dr Cumming's readers may have heard as an exception? No matter. Some one suspected that he was *not* an exception, and as that suspicion tends to the glory of God, it is one for a Christian to entertain (see 'Man. of Ev.', p.73).—If we were unable to imagine this kind of self-sophistication, we should be obliged to suppose that, relying on the ignorance of his evangelical disciples, he fed them with direct and conscious falsehoods. 'Voltaire,' he informs them, 'declares there is no God'; he was 'an anti-theist, that is, one who deliberately and avowedly opposed and hated God;

who swore in his blasphemy that he would dethrone him';
and 'advocated the very depths of the lowest sensuality'.
With regard to many statements of a similar kind, equally
at variance with truth, in Dr Cumming's volumes, we
presume that he has been misled by hearsay or by the
secondhand character of his acquaintance with free-thinking
literature. An evangelical preacher is not obliged to be
well-read. Here, however, is a case which the extremest
supposition of educated ignorance will not reach. Even
books of 'evidences' quote from Voltaire the line—

> Si Dieu n'existait pas, il faudrait l'inventer;*

even persons fed on the mere whey and buttermilk of
literature, must know that in philosophy Voltaire was nothing if not a theist—must know that he wrote not against
God, but against Jehovah, the God of the Jews, whom he
believed to be a false God—must know that to say Voltaire
was an atheist on this ground is as absurd as to say that
a Jacobite opposed hereditary monarchy, because he declared the Brunswick family had no title to the throne.
That Dr Cumming should repeat the vulgar fables
about Voltaire's death,* is merely what we might expect from the specimens we have seen of his illustrative
stories. A man whose accounts of his own experience are
apocryphal, is not likely to put borrowed narratives to any
severe test.

The alliance between intellectual and moral perversion is
strikingly typified by the way in which he alternates from
the unveracious to the absurd, from misrepresentation to
contradiction. Side by side with the adduction of 'facts' such
as those we have quoted, we find him arguing on one page
that the Trinity was too grand a doctrine to have been
conceived by man, and was *therefore* Divine; and on another
page, that the Incarnation *had* been preconceived by man,
and is *therefore* to be accepted as Divine. But we are less
concerned with the fallacy of his 'ready replies', than with
their falsity; and even of this we can only afford space for
a very few specimens. Here is one: 'There is a *thousand times*
more proof that the Gospel of John was written by him than

there is that the 'Ανάβασις was written by Xenophon, or the Ars Poetica by Horace.' If Dr Cumming had chosen Plato's Epistles or Anacreon's Poems, instead of the Anabasis or the Ars poetica, he would have reduced the extent of the falsehood, and would have furnished a ready reply which would have been equally effective with his Sunday-school teachers and their disputants. Hence we conclude this prodigality of mis-statement, this exuberance of mendacity, is an effervescence of zeal *in majorem gloriam Dei*. Elsewhere he tells us that 'the idea of the author of the *Vestiges** is, that man is the development of a monkey, that the monkey is the embryo man, so that *if you keep a baboon long enough, it will develop itself into a man*'. How well Dr Cumming has qualified himself to judge of the ideas in 'that very unphilosophical book', as he pronounces it, may be inferred from the fact that he implies the author of the 'Vestiges' to have *originated* the nebular hypothesis.

In the volume from which the last extract is taken, even the hardihood of assertion is surpassed by the suicidal character of the argument. It is called 'The Church before the Flood', and is devoted chiefly to the adjustment of the question between the Bible and Geology. Keeping within the limits we have prescribed to ourselves, we do not enter into the matter of this discussion; we merely pause a little over the volume in order to point out Dr Cumming's mode of treating the question. He first tells us that 'the Bible has not a single scientific error in it'; that '*its slightest intimations of scientific principles or natural phenomena have in every instance been demonstrated to be exactly and strictly true*', and he asks:—

How is it that Moses, with no greater education than the Hindoo or the ancient philosopher, has written his book, touching science at a thousand points, so accurately, that scientific research has discovered no flaws in it; and yet in those investigations which have taken place in more recent centuries, it has not been shown that he has committed one single error, or made one solitary assertion which can be proved by the maturest science, or by the most eagle-eyed philosopher, to be incorrect, scientifically or historically?

According to this, the relation of the Bible to Science should be one of the strong points of apologists for Revelation: the scientific accuracy of Moses should stand at the head of their evidences; and they might urge with some cogency, that since Aristotle, who devoted himself to science, and lived many ages after Moses, does little else than err ingeniously, this fact, that the Jewish Lawgiver, though touching science at a thousand points, has written nothing that has not been 'demonstrated to be exactly and strictly true', is an irrefragable proof of his having derived his knowledge from a supernatural source. How does it happen, then, that Dr Cumming forsakes this strong position? How is it that we find him, some pages further on, engaged in reconciling Genesis with the discoveries of science, by means of imaginative hypotheses and feats of 'interpretation'? Surely, that which has been demonstrated to be exactly and strictly true does not require hypothesis and critical argument, in order to show that it may *possibly* agree with those very discoveries by means of which its exact and strict truth has been demonstrated. And why should Dr Cumming suppose, as we shall presently find him supposing, that men of science hesitate to accept the Bible, because it appears to contradict their discoveries? By his own statement, that appearance of contradiction does not exist; on the contrary, it has been demonstrated that the Bible precisely agrees with their discoveries. Perhaps, however, in saying of the Bible that its 'slightest intimations of scientific principles or natural phenomena have in every instance been demonstrated to be exactly and strictly true', Dr Cumming merely means to imply that theologians have found out a way of explaining the biblical text so that it no longer, in their opinion, appears to be in contradiction with the discoveries of science. One of two things, therefore: either, he uses language without the slightest appreciation of its real meaning; or, the assertions he makes on one page are directly contradicted by the arguments he urges on another.

Dr Cumming's principles—or, we should rather say, confused notions—of biblical interpretation, as exhibited in this volume, are particularly significant of his mental calibre. He says ('Church before the Flood', p.93):

Men of science, who are full of scientific investigation and ena-moured of scientific discovery, will hesitate before they accept a book which, they think, contradicts the plainest and the most unequivocal disclosures they have made in the bowels of the earth, or among the stars of the sky. To all these we answer, as we have already indicated, there is not the least dissonance between God's written book and the most mature discoveries of geological science. One thing, however, there may be; *there may be a contradiction between the discoveries of geology and our preconceived interpretations of the Bible.* But this is not because the Bible is wrong, but because our interpretation is wrong. (The italics in all cases are our own.)

Elsewhere he says:

It seems to me plainly evident that the record of Genesis, when read fairly, and not in the light of our prejudices,—*and mind you, the essence of Popery is to read the Bible in the light of our opinions, instead of viewing our opinions in the light of the Bible, in its plain and obvious sense,*—falls in perfectly with the assertion of geologists.

On comparing these two passages, we gather that when Dr Cumming, under stress of geological discovery, assigns to the biblical text a meaning entirely different from that which, on his own showing, was universally ascribed to it for more than three thousand years, he regards himself as 'viewing his opinions in the light of the Bible in its plain and obvious sense'! Now he is reduced to one of two alternatives: either, he must hold that the 'plain and obvious meaning' of the whole Bible differs from age to age, so that the criterion of its meaning lies in the sum of knowledge possessed by each successive age—the Bible being an elastic garment for the growing thought of mankind; or, he must hold that some portions are amenable to this criterion, and others not so. In the former case, he accepts the principle of interpretation adopted by the early German rationalists; in the latter case, he has to show a further criterion by which we can judge what parts of the Bible are elastic and what rigid. If he says that the interpretation of the text is rigid wherever it treats of doctrines necessary to salvation, we answer, that for doctrines to be necessary to salvation they must first be true; and in order to be true, according to his own principle, they must be founded on a correct interpretation of the biblical text. Thus he makes the necessity of doctrines to salvation the criterion of infallible interpretation, and infallible interpretation the criterion of doctrines being necessary to salvation. He is whirled round in a circle, having, by admitting the principle of novelty in interpretation, completely deprived himself of a basis. That he should seize the very moment in which he is most palpably betraying that he has no test of biblical truth beyond his own opinion, as an appropriate occasion for flinging the rather novel reproach against Popery that its essence is to 'read the Bible in the light of our opinions', would be an almost pathetic self-exposure, if it were not disgusting. Imbecility that is not even meek, ceases to be pitiable and becomes simply odious.

Parenthetic lashes of this kind against Popery are very frequent with Dr Cumming, and occur even in his more devout passages, where their introduction must surely disturb the spiritual exercises of his hearers. Indeed, Roman-catholics fare worse with him even than infidels. Infidels are the small vermin—the mice to be bagged *en passant*. The main object of his chase—the rats which are to be nailed up as trophies—are the Roman-catholics. Romanism is the masterpiece of Satan; but reassure yourselves! Dr Cumming has been created. Antichrist is enthroned in the Vatican; but he is stoutly withstood by the Boanerges of Crown Court. The personality of Satan as might be expected, is a very prominent tenet in Dr Cumming's discourses; those who doubt it are, he thinks, 'generally specimens of the victims of Satan as a triumphant seducer'; and it is through the medium of this doctrine that he habitually contemplates Roman-catholics. They are the puppets of which the devil holds the strings. It is only exceptionally that he speaks of them as fellow-men, acted on by the same desires, fears, and hopes as himself; his *rule* is to hold them up to his hearers as foredoomed instruments of Satan, and vessels of wrath. If he is obliged to admit that they are 'no shams', that they are 'thoroughly in earnest'—that is because they are inspired by hell, because they are under an 'infra-natural' influence. If their missionaries are found wherever Protestant missionaries go, this zeal in propagating their faith is not in them a consistent virtue, as it is in Protestants, but a 'melancholy fact', affording additional evidence that they are instigated and assisted by the devil. And Dr Cumming is inclined to think that they work miracles, because that is no more than might be expected from the known ability of Satan who inspires them.[3] He admits indeed, that 'there is a fragment of the Church of Christ in the very bosom of that awful apostasy',[4] and that there are members of the Church of Rome in glory; but this admission is rare and episodical—is a declaration, *pro forma*, about as influential on the general disposition and habits as an aristocrat's profession of democracy.

This leads us to mention another conspicuous characteristic of Dr Cumming's teaching—the *absence of genuine charity*. It is true that he makes large profession of tolerance and liberality within a certain circle; he exhorts Christians to unity; he would have Churchmen fraternize with Dissenters, and exhorts these two branches of God's family to defer the settlement of their differences till the millennium. But the love thus taught is the love of the *clan*, which is the correlative of antagonism to the rest of mankind. It is not sympathy and helpfulness towards men as men, but towards men as Christians, and as Christians in the sense of a small minority. Dr Cumming's religion may demand a tribute of love, but it gives a charter to hatred; it may enjoin charity, but it fosters all uncharitableness. If I believe that God tells me to love my enemies, but at the same time hates His own enemies and requires me to have one will with Him, which has the larger scope, love or hatred? And we refer to those pages of Dr Cumming's in which he opposes Roman-catholics, Puseyites, and infidels—pages which form

---

[3] *Signs of the Times*, p. 38.
[4] *Apocalyptic Sketches*, p. 234.

the larger proportion of what he has published—for proof
that the idea of God which both the logic and spirit of his
discourses keep present to his hearers, is that of a God who
hates his enemies, a God who teaches love by fierce denunciations of wrath—a God who encourages obedience to his
precepts by elaborately revealing to us that his own government is in precise opposition to those precepts. We know
the usual evasions on this subject. We know Dr Cumming
would say that even Roman-catholics are to be loved and
succoured as men; that he would help even that 'unclean
spirit', Cardinal Wiseman,* out of a ditch. But who that is
in the slightest degree acquainted with the action of the
human mind, will believe that any genuine and large charity
can grow out of an exercise of love which is always to have
an *arrière-pensée* of hatred? Of what quality would be the
conjugal love of a husband who loved his spouse as a wife,
but hated her as a woman? It is reserved for the regenerate
mind, according to Dr Cumming's conception of it, to be
'wise, amazed, temperate and furious, loyal and neutral, in
a moment'. Precepts of charity uttered with faint breath at
the end of a sermon are perfectly futile, when all the force
of the lungs has been spent in keeping the hearer's mind
fixed on the conception of his fellow-men, not as fellow-
sinners and fellow-sufferers, but as agents of hell, as automata through whom Satan plays his game upon earth,—not
on objects which call forth their reverence, their love, their
hope of good even in the most strayed and perverted, but
on a minute identification of human things with such symbols as the scarlet whore, the beast out of the abyss,
scorpions whose sting is in their tails, men who have the
mark of the beast, and unclean spirits like frogs. You might
as well attempt to educate a child's sense of beauty by
hanging its nursery with the horrible and grotesque pictures
in which the early painters represented the Last Judgement,
as expect Christian graces to flourish on that prophetic
interpretation which Dr Cumming offers as the principal
nutriment of his flock. Quite apart from the critical basis
of that interpretation, quite apart from the degree of truth
there may be in Dr Cumming's prognostications—questions

into which we do not choose to enter—his use of prophecy must be *a priori* condemned in the judgement of right-minded persons, by its results as testified in the net moral effect of his sermons. The best minds that accept Christianity as a divinely inspired system, believe that the great end of the Gospel is not merely the saving but the educating of men's souls, the creating within them of holy dispositions, the subduing of egotistical pretensions, and the perpetual enhancing of the desire that the will of God—a will synonymous with goodness and truth—may be done on earth. But what relation to all this has a system of interpretation which keeps the mind of the Christian in the position of a spectator at a gladiatorial show, of which Satan is the wild beast in the shape of the great red dragon, and two thirds of mankind the victims—the whole provided and got up by God for the edification of the saints? The demonstration that the Second Advent is at hand, if true, can have no really holy, spiritual effect; the highest state of mind inculcated by the Gospel is resignation to the disposal of God's providence—'Whether we live we live unto the Lord; whether we die, we die unto the Lord'* not an eagerness to see a temporal manifestation which shall confound the enemies of God and give exaltation to the saints; it is to dwell in Christ by spiritual communion with his nature, not to fix the date when He shall appear in the sky. Dr Cumming's delight in shadowing forth the downfall of the Man of Sin, in prognosticating the battle of Gog and Magog, and in advertising the pre-millennial Advent, is simply the transportation of political passions on to a so-called religious platform; it is the anticipation of the triumph of 'our party', accomplished by our principal men being 'sent for' into the clouds. Let us be understood to speak in all seriousness. If we were in search of amusement, we should not seek for it by examining Dr Cumming's works in order to ridicule them. We are simply discharging a disagreeable duty in delivering our opinion that, judged by the highest standard even of ortho-dox Christianity, they are little calculated to produce—

A closer walk with God,
A calm and heavenly frame;*

but are more likely to nourish egoistic complacency and pretension, a hard and condemnatory spirit towards one's fellow-men, and a busy occupation with the minutiæ of events, instead of a reverent contemplation of great facts and a wise application of great principles. It would be idle to consider Dr Cumming's theory of prophecy in any other light,—as a philosophy of history or a specimen of biblical interpretation; it bears about the same relation to the extension of genuine knowledge as the astrological 'house' in the heavens bears to the true structure and relations of the universe.

The slight degree in which Dr Cumming's faith is imbued with truly human sympathies, is exhibited in the way he treats the doctrine of Eternal Punishment. *Here* a little of that readiness to strain the letter of the Scriptures which he so often manifests when his object is to prove a point against Romanism, would have been an amiable frailty if it had been applied on the side of mercy. When he is bent on proving that the prophecy concerning the Man of Sin, in the Second Epistle to the Thessalonians, refers to the Pope, he can extort from the innocent word καθίσαι the meaning *cathedrize*, though why we are to translate 'He as God cathedrizes in the temple of God', any more than we are to translate 'cathedrize here, while I go and pray yonder',* it is for Dr Cumming to show more clearly than he has yet done. But when rigorous literality will favour the conclusion that the greater proportion of the human race will be eternally miserable—*then* he is rigorously literal.

He says:

The Greek words, εἰς τους αἰῶνας των αἰώνων here translated 'everlasting', signify literally 'unto the ages of ages'; 161-αἰεί ὤν, 'always being', that is, everlasting, ceaseless existence. Plato uses the word in this sense when he says, 'The gods that live for ever.' *But I must also admit*, that this word is used several times in a limited extent,—as for instance, 'The everlasting hills'. Of course, this does not mean that there never will be a time when the hills will cease to stand; the expression here is evidently figurative, but it implies eternity. The hills shall remain as long as the earth lasts, and no hand has power to remove them but that Eternal One which first called them into being; *so the state of the soul* remains the same after death as long as the soul exists, and no one has power to alter it. The same word is often applied to denote the existence of God—'the Eternal God'. Can we limit the word when applied to Him? Because occasionally used in a limited sense, we must not infer it is always so. 'Everlasting' plainly means in Scripture 'without end'; it is only to be explained figuratively when it is evident it cannot be interpreted in any other way.

We do not discuss whether Dr Cumming's interpretation accords with the meaning of the New Testament writers: we simply point to the fact that the text becomes elastic for him when he wants freer play for his prejudices, while he makes it an adamantine barrier against the admission that mercy will ultimately triumph,—that God, i.e., Love, will be all in all. He assures us that he does not 'delight to dwell on the misery of the lost': and we believe him. That misery does not seem to be a question of feeling with him, either one way or the other. He does not merely resign himself to the awful mystery of eternal punishment; he contends for it. Do we object, he asks,[5] to everlasting happiness? then why object to everlasting misery?—reasoning which is perhaps felt to be cogent by theologians who anticipate the everlasting happiness for themselves, and the everlasting misery for their neighbours.

The compassion of some Christians has been glad to take refuge in the opinion, that the Bible allows the supposition of annihilation for the impenitent: but the rigid sequence of Dr Cumming's reasoning will not admit of this idea. He sees that flax is made into linen, and linen into paper; that paper, when burnt, partly ascends as smoke and then again descends in rain, or in dust and carbon. 'Not one particle of the original flax is lost, although there may be not one particle that has not undergone an entire change: annihilation is not, but change of form is. *It will be thus with our bodies at the resurrection*. The death of the body means not annihilation. *Not one feature of the face* will be annihilated.' Having established the perpetuity of the body by this close

[5] *Manual of Christian Evidence*, p. 184.

and clear analogy, namely, that *as* there is a total change in the particles of flax in consequence of which they no longer appear as flax, *so* there will *not* be a total change in the particles of the human body, but they will reappear as the human body, he does not seem to consider that the perpetuity of the body involves the perpetuity of the soul, but requires separate evidence for this, and finds such evidence by begging the very question at issue; namely, by asserting that the text of the Scriptures implies 'the perpetuity of the punishment of the lost, and the consciousness of the punishment which they endure'. Yet it is drivelling like this which is listened to and lauded as eloquence by hundreds, and which a Doctor of Divinity can believe that he has his 'reward as a saint' for preaching and publishing!

One more characteristic of Dr Cumming's writings, and we have done. This is the *perverted moral judgement* that everywhere reigns in them. Not that this perversion is peculiar to Dr Cumming: it belongs to the dogmatic system which he shares with all evangelical believers. But the abstract tendencies of systems are represented in very different degrees, according to the different characters of those who embrace them; just as the same food tells differently on different constitutions: and there are certain qualities in Dr Cumming that cause the perversion of which we speak to exhibit itself with peculiar prominence in his teaching. A single extract will enable us to explain what we mean.

The 'thoughts' are evil. If it were possible for human eye to discern and to detect the thoughts that flutter round the heart of an unregenerate man—to mark their hue and their multitude, it would be found that they are indeed 'evil'. We speak not of the thief, and the murderer, and the adulterer, and such like, whose crimes draw down the cognizance of earthly tribunals, and whose unenviable character it is to take the lead in the paths of sin; but we refer to the men who are marked out by their practice of many of the seemliest moralities of life—by the exercise of the kindliest affections, and the interchange of the sweetest reciprocities—and of these men, if unrenewed and unchanged, we pronounce that their thoughts are evil. To ascertain this, we must refer to the object around which our thoughts ought continually to circulate.

The Scriptures assert that this object is *the glory of God*; that for this we ought to think, to act, and to speak; and that in thus thinking, acting, and speaking, there is involved the purest and most endearing bliss. Now it will be found true of the most amiable men, that with all their good society and kindliness of heart, and all their strict and unbending integrity, they never or rarely think of the glory of God. The question never occurs to them—Will this redound to the glory of God? Will this make his name more known, his being more loved, his praise more sung? And just inasmuch as their every thought comes short of this lofty aim, in so much does it come short of good, and entitle itself to the character of evil. If the glory of God is not the absorbing and the influential aim of their thoughts, then they are evil; but God's glory never enters into their minds. They are amiable, because it chances to be one of the constitutional tendencies of their individual character, left uneffaced by the Fall; and *they are just and upright, because they have perhaps no occasion to be otherwise, or find it subservient to their interests to maintain such a character* (Occasional Discourses, vol i, p. 8).

Again we read (p. 236):

There are traits in the Christian character which the mere worldly man cannot understand. He can understand the outward morality, but he cannot understand the inner spring of it; he can understand Dorcas's liberality to the poor, but he cannot penetrate the ground of Dorcas's liberality. *Some men give to the poor because they are ostentatious, or because they think the poor will ultimately avenge their neglect; but the Christian gives to the poor, not only because he has sensibilities like other men*, but because inasmuch as ye did it to the least of these my brethren ye did it unto me.

Before entering on the more general question involved in these quotations, we must point to the clauses we have marked with italics, where Dr Cumming appears to express sentiments which, we are happy to think, are not shared by the majority of his brethren in the faith. Dr Cumming, it seems, is unable to conceive that the natural man can have any other motive for being just and upright than that it is useless to be otherwise, or that a character for honesty is profitable; according to his experience, between the feelings of ostentation and selfish alarm and the feeling of love to Christ, there lie no sensibilities which can lead a man to relieve want. Granting, as we should prefer to think, that it is Dr Cumming's exposition of his sentiments which is deficient rather than his sentiments themselves, still, the fact that the deficiency lies precisely here, and that he can overlook it not only in the haste of oral delivery but in the examination of proof-sheets, is strongly significant of his mental bias—of the faint degree in which he sympathizes with the disinterested elements of human feeling, and of the fact, which we are about to dwell upon, that those feelings are totally absent from his religious theory. Now, Dr Cumming invariably assumes that, in fulminating against those who differ from him, he is standing on a moral elevation to which they are compelled reluctantly to look up; that his theory of motives and conduct is in its loftiness and purity a perpetual rebuke to their low and vicious desires and practice. It is time he should be told that the reverse is the fact; that there are men who do not merely cast a superficial glance at his doctrine, and fail to see its beauty or justice, but who, after a close consideration of that doctrine, pronounce it to be subversive of true moral development, and therefore positively noxious. Dr Cumming is fond of showing up the teaching of Romanism, and accusing it of undermining true morality: it is time he should be told that there is a large body, both of thinkers and practical men, who hold precisely the same opinion of his own teaching—with this difference, that they do not regard it as the inspiration of Satan, but as the natural crop of a human mind where the soil is chiefly made up of egoistic passions and dogmatic beliefs.

Dr Cumming's theory, as we have seen, is that actions are good or evil according as they are prompted or not prompted by an exclusive reference to the 'glory of God'. God, then, in Dr Cumming's conception, is a being who has no pleasure in the exercise of love and truthfulness and justice, considered as effecting the well-being of his creatures; He has satisfaction in us only in so far as we exhaust our motives and dispositions of all relation to our fellow-beings, and replace sympathy with men by anxiety for the 'glory of God'. The deed of Grace Darling, when she took a boat in the storm to rescue drowning men and women, was not good if it was only compassion that nerved her arm and impelled her to brave death for the chance of saving others; it was only good if she asked herself—Will this redound to the glory of God? The man who endures tortures rather than betray a trust, the man who spends years in toil in order to discharge an obligation from which the law declares him free, must be animated not by the spirit of fidelity to his fellow-man, but by a desire to make 'the name of God more known'. The sweet charities of domestic life—the ready hand and the soothing word in sickness, the forbearance towards frailties, the prompt helpfulness in all efforts and sympathy in all joys, are simply evil if they result from a 'constitutional tendency', or from dispositions disciplined by the experience of suffering and the perception of moral loveliness. A wife is not to devote herself to her husband out of love to him and a sense of the duties implied by a close relation—she is to be a faithful wife for the glory of God; if she feels her natural affections welling up too strongly, she is to repress them; it will not do to act from natural affection—she must think of the glory of God. A man is to guide his affairs with energy and discretion, not from an honest desire to fulfil his responsibilities as a member of society and a father, but—that 'God's praise may be sung'. Dr Cumming's Christian pays his debts for the glory of God; were it not for the coercion of that supreme motive, it would be evil to pay them. A man is not to be just from a feeling of justice; he is not to help his fellow-men out of good-will to his fellow-men: he is not to be a tender husband and father out of affection: all these natural muscles and fibres are to be torn away and replaced by a patent steel-spring—anxiety for the 'glory of God'.

Happily, the constitution of human nature forbids the complete prevalence of such a theory. Fatally powerful as religious systems have been, human nature is stronger and wider than religious systems, and though dogmas may hamper, they cannot absolutely repress its growth: build walls round the living tree as you will, the bricks and mortar have by and by to give way before the slow and sure operation of the sap. But next to that hatred of the enemies of God which is the principle of persecution, there perhaps has been no perversion more obstructive of true moral development than this substitution of a reference to the glory of God for the direct promptings of the sympathetic feelings. Benevolence and justice are strong only in proportion as they are directly and inevitably called into activity by their proper objects: pity is strong only because we are strongly impressed by suffering; and only in proportion as it is compassion that speaks through the eyes when we soothe, and moves the arm when we succour, is a deed strictly benevolent. If the soothing or the succour be given because another being wishes or approves it, the deed ceases to be one of benevolence, and becomes one of defence, of obedience, of self-interest, or vanity. Accessory motives may aid in producing an *action*, but they presuppose the weakness of the direct motive; and conversely, when the direct motive is strong, the action of accessory motives will be excluded. If then, as Dr Cumming inculcates, the glory of God is to be 'the absorbing and the influential aim' in our thoughts and actions, this must tend to neutralize the human sympathies; the stream of feeling will be diverted from its natural current in order to feed an artificial canal. The idea of God is really moral in its influence—it really cherishes all that is best and loveliest in man—only when God is contemplated as sympathizing with the pure elements of human feeling, as possessing infinitely all those attributes which we recognize to be moral in humanity. In this light, the idea of God and the sense of His presence intensify all noble feeling, and encourage all noble effort, on the same principle that human sympathy is found a source of strength: the brave man feels braver when he knows that another stout heart is beating time with his; the devoted woman who is wearing out her years in patient effort to alleviate suffering or save vice from the last stages of degradation, finds aid in the pressure of a friendly hand which tells her that there is one who understands her deeds, and in her place would do the like. The idea of a God who not only sympathizes with all we feel and endure for our fellow-men, but who will pour new life into our too languid love, and give firmness to our vacillating purpose, is an extension and multiplication of the effects produced by human sympathy; and it has been intensified for the better spirits who have been under the influence of orthodox Christianity, by the contemplation of Jesus as 'God manifest in the flesh'. But Dr Cumming's God is the very opposite of all this: he is a God who instead of sharing and aiding our human sympathies, is directly in collision with them; who instead of strengthening the bond between man and man, by encouraging the sense that they are both alike the objects of His love and care, thrusts himself between them and forbids them to feel for each other except as they have relation to Him. He is a God, who, instead of adding his solar force to swell the tide of those impulses that tend to give humanity a common life in which the good of one is the good of all, commands us to check those impulses, lest they should prevent us from thinking of His glory. It is in vain for Dr Cumming to say that we are to love man for God's sake: with the conception of God which his teaching presents, the love of man for God's sake involves, as his writings abundantly show, a strong principle of hatred. We can only love one being for the sake of another when there is an habitual delight in associating the idea of those two beings— that is, when the object of our indirect love is a source of joy and honour to the object of our direct love: but, according to Dr Cumming's theory, the majority of mankind—the majority of his neighbours—are in precisely the opposite relation to God. His soul has no pleasure in them, they belong more to Satan than to Him, and if they contribute to His glory, it is against their will. Dr Cumming then can only love *some* men for God's sake; the rest he must in consistency *hate* for God's sake.

There must be many, even in the circle of Dr Cumming's admirers, who would be revolted by the doctrine we have just exposed, if their natural good sense and healthy feeling were not early stifled by dogmatic beliefs, and their reverence misled by pious phrases. But as it is, many a rational question, many a generous instinct, is repelled as the suggestion of a supernatural enemy, or as the ebullition of human pride and corruption. This state of inward contradiction can be put an end to only by the conviction that the free and diligent exertion of the intellect, instead of being a sin, is a part of their responsibility—that Right and Reason are synonymous. The fundamental faith for man is faith in the result of a brave, honest, and steady use of all his faculties:—

> Let knowledge grow from more to more
> But more of reverence in us dwell;
> That mind and soul according well
> May make one music as before,
> But vaster.*

Before taking leave of Dr Cumming, let us express a hope that we have in no case exaggerated the unfavourable character of the inferences to be drawn from his pages. His creed often obliges him to hope the worst of men, and to exert himself in proving that the worst is true; but thus far we are happier than he. We have no theory which requires us to attribute unworthy motives to Dr Cumming, no opinions, religious or irreligious, which can make it a gratification to us to detect him in delinquencies. On the contrary, the better we are able to think of him as a man, while we are obliged to disapprove him as a theologian, the stronger will be the evidence for our conviction, that the tendency towards good in human nature has a force which no creed can utterly counteract, and which ensures the ultimate triumph of that tendency over all dogmatic perversions.

Tennyson's *Maud* (1855)

IF we were asked who among contemporary authors is likely to live in the next century, the name that would first and most unhesitatingly rise to our lips is that of Alfred Tennyson. He, at least, while belonging emphatically to his own age, while giving a voice to the struggles and the far-reaching thoughts of this nineteenth century, has those supreme artistic qualities which must make him a poet for all ages. As long as the English language is spoken, the word-music of Tennyson must charm the ear; and when English has become a dead language, his wonderful concentration of thought into luminous speech, the exquisite pictures in which he has blended all the hues of reflection, feeling, and fancy, will cause him to be read as we read Homer, Pindar, and Horace. Thought and feeling, like carbon, will always be finding new forms for themselves, but once condense them into the diamonds of poetry, and the form, as well as the element, will be lasting. This is the sublime privilege of the artist—to be present with future generations, not merely through the indirect results of his work, but through his immediate creations; and of all artists the one whose works are least in peril from the changing conditions of humanity, is the highest order of poet, who has received—

> Aus Morgenduft gewebt und Sonnenklarheit
> Der Dichtung Schleier aus der Hand der Wahrheit.*

Such a poet, by the suffrage of all competent judges among his countrymen, is Tennyson. His 'Ulysses' is a pure little ingot of the same gold that runs through the ore of the Odyssey. It has the 'large utterance' of the early epic, with that rich fruit of moral experience which it has required thousands of years to ripen. The 'Morte d'Arthur' breathes the intensest spirit of chivalry in the pure and serene air of unselfish piety; and it falls on the ear with the rich, soothing melody of a *Dona nobis* swelling through the aisles of a

cathedral. 'Locksley Hall' has become, like Milton's minor
poems, so familiar that we dare not quote it; it is the object
of a sort of family affection which we all cherish, but think
it is not good taste to mention. Then there are his idylls,
such as the 'Gardener's Daughter',—works which in their
kind have no rival, either in the past or present. But the
time would fail us to tell of all we owe to Tennyson, for,
with two or three exceptions, every poem in his two volumes
is a favourite. The 'Princess', too, with all that criticism has
to say against it, has passages of inspiration and lyrical gems
inbedded in it, which make it a fresh claim on our gratitude.
But, last and greatest, came 'In Memoriam', which to us
enshrines the highest tendency of this age, as the Apollo
Belvedere* expressed the presence of a free and vigorous
human spirit amidst a decaying civilization. Whatever was the
immediate prompting of 'In Memoriam', whatever the form
under which the author represented his aim to himself, the
deepest significance of the poem is the sanctification of human
love as a religion. If, then, the voice that sang all these undying
strains had remained for ever after mute, we should have had
no reason to reproach Tennyson with gifts inadequately used;
we should rather have rejoiced in the thought that one who
has sown for his fellow-men so much—

> generous seed,
> Fruitful of further thought and deed*

should at length be finding rest for his wings in a soft nest
of home affections, and be living idylls, instead of writing
them.

We could not prevail on ourselves to say what we think
of 'Maud', without thus expressing our love and admiration
of Tennyson. For that optical law by which an insignificant
object, if near, excludes very great and glorious things that
lie in the distance, has its moral parallel in the judgements
of the public: men's speech is too apt to be exclusively
determined by the unsuccessful deed or book of to-day,
the successful doings and writings of past years being for
the moment lost sight of. And even seen in the light of the
most reverential criticism, the effect of 'Maud' cannot be

favourable to Tennyson's fame. Here and there only it contains a few lines in which he does not fall below himself. With these slight exceptions, he is everywhere saying, if not something that would be better left unsaid, something that he had already said better; and the finest sentiments that animate his other poems are entirely absent. We have in 'Maud' scarcely more than a residuum of Alfred Tennyson; the wide-sweeping intellect, the mild philosophy, the healthy pathos, the wondrous melody, have almost all vanished, and left little more than a narrow scorn which piques itself on its scorn of narrowness, and a passion which clothes itself in exaggerated conceits. While to his other poems we turn incessantly with new distress that we cannot carry them all in our memory, of 'Maud' we must say, if we say the truth, that excepting only a few passages, we wish to forget it as we should wish to forget a bad opera. And this not only because it wants the charms of mind and music which belong to his other poetry, but because its tone is throughout morbid; it opens to us the self revelations of a morbid mind, and what it presents as the cure for this mental disease is itself only a morbid conception of human relations.

But we will abstain from general remarks, and make the reader acquainted with the plan and texture of the poem. It opens, like the gates of Pandemonium, 'with horrible discord and jarring sound',*—with harsh and rugged hexameters, in which the hero, who is throughout the speaker, tells us something of his history and his views of society. It is impossible to suppose that, with so great a master of rhythm as Tennyson, this harshness and ruggedness are otherwise than intentional; so we must conclude that it is a device of his art thus to set our teeth on edge with his verses when he means to rouse our disgust by his descriptions; and that, writing of disagreeable things, he has made it a rule to write disagreeably. These hexameters, weak in logic and grating in sound, are undeniably strong in expression, and eat themselves with phosphoric eagerness into our memory, in spite of our will. The hero opens his story by telling us how 'long since' his father was found dead in 'the

dreadful hollow behind the little wood', supposed to have
committed suicide in despair at the ruin entailed on him by
the failure of a great speculation; and he paints with terrible
force that crisis in his boyhood:

> I remember the time, for the roots of my hair were stirr'd
> By a shuffled step, by a dead weight trail'd, by a whisper'd fright,
> And my pulses closed their gates with a shock on my heart as
>   I heard
> The shrill-edged shriek of a mother divide the shuddering night.

An old neighbour 'dropt off gorged' from that same
speculation, and is now lord of the broad estate and the
hall. These family sorrows and mortifications the hero regards as a direct result of the anti-social tendencies of Peace,
which he proceeds to expose to us in all its hideousness;
looking to war as the immediate curative for unwholesome
lodging of the poor, adulteration of provisions, child-mur-
der, and wife-beating—an effect which is as yet by no
means visible in our police reports. It seems indeed that,
in the opinion of our hero, nothing short of an invasion
of our own coasts is the consummation devoutly to be
wished:

> For I trust if an enemy's fleet came yonder round by the hill,
> And the rushing battle-bolt sang from the three-decker out of
>   the foam,
> That the smoothfaced snubnosed rogue would leap from his
>   counter and till,
> And strike, if he could, were it but with his cheating yardwand,
>   home.

From his deadly hatred of retail traders and susceptibility
as to the adulteration of provisions, we were inclined to
imagine that this modern Conrad,* with a 'devil in his
sneer', but not a 'laughing devil', had in his reduced circumstances taken a London lodging and endured much
peculation in the shape of weekly bills, and much indigestion
arising from unwholesome bread and beer. But no: we
presently learn that he resides in a lone house not far from
the Hall, and can still afford to keep 'a man and a maid.'
And now, he says, the family is coming home to the Hall;

the old bloodsucker, with his son and a daughter, Maud, whom he remembers as a little girl, 'with her sweet purse-mouth, when my father dangled the grapes.' He is determined not to fall in love with her, and the glance he gets of her as she passes in her carriage, assures him that he is in no danger from her 'cold and clear-cut face',—

> Faultily faultless, icily regular, splendidly null,
> Dead perfection, no more.

However, he does not escape from this first glance without the 'least little touch of the spleen', which the reader foresees is the germinal spot that is to develop itself into love. The first lines of any beauty in the poem are those in which he describes the 'cold and clear-cut face,' breaking his sleep, and haunting him 'star-sweet on a gloom profound,' till he gets up and walks away the wintry night in his own dark garden. Then Maud seems to look haughtily on him as she returns his bow, and he makes fierce resolves to flee from the cruel madness of love, and more especially from the love of Maud, who is 'all unmeet for a wife;' but presently he hears her voice, which has a more irresistible magic even than her face. By-and-bye she looks more benignantly on him, but his suspicious heart dares not sun itself in her smile, lest her brother—

> That jewell'd mass of millinery,
> That oil'd and curl'd Assyrian Bull,

may have prompted her to this benignity as a mode of canvassing for a vote at the coming election. A fresh circumstance is now added in the form of a new-made lord, apparently a suitor of Maud's—

> a captain, a padded shape,
> A bought commission, a waxen face,
> A rabbit mouth that is ever agape.

Very indignant is our hero with this lord's grand-father, for having made his fortune by a coal-mine, though the consideration that the said grandfather is now in 'a blacker pit', is somewhat soothing to his chafed feelings. In the denunciations we have here of new-made fortunes, new titles, new houses, and new suits of clothes, it is evidently Mr. Tennyson's aversion, and not merely his hero's morbid mood, that speaks; and we must say, that this immense expenditure of gall on trivial social phases, seems to us intrinsically petty and snobbish. The gall presently overflows, as gall is apt to do, without any visible sequence of association, on Mr Bright,* who is denounced as—

> This broad-brimm'd hawker of holy things,
> Whose ear is stuft with his cotton, and rings
> Even in dreams to the chink of his pence.

In a second edition of 'Maud', we hope these lines will no longer appear on Tennyson's page: we hope he will by that time have recovered the spirit in which he once wrote how the 'wise of heart'

> Would love the gleams of good that broke
> From either side, nor veil his eyes.*

On the next page, he gives us an agreeable change of key in a little lyric, which will remind the German reader of Thekla's song.* Here is the second stanza:

> Let the sweet heavens endure
>   Not close and darken above me,
> Before I am quite, quite sure
>   That there is one to love me;
> Then let come what come may
>   To a life that has been so sad,
>   I shall have had my day.

At length, after many alternations of feeling and metre, our hero becomes assured that he is Maud's accepted lover, and atones for rather a silly outburst, in which he requests the sky to

> Blush from West to East
> Blush from East to West,
> Till the West is East,
> Blush it thro' the West,

by some very fine lines, of which we can only afford to
quote the concluding ones:

> Is that enchanted moan only the swell
> Of the long waves that roll in yonder bay?
> And hark the clock within, the silver knell
> Of twelve sweet hours that past in bridal white,
> And died to live, long as my pulses play;
> But now by this my love has closed her sight
> And given false death her hand, and stol'n away
> To dreamful wastes where footless fancies dwell
> Among the fragments of the golden day.
> May nothing there her maiden grace affright!
> Dear heart, I feel with thee the drowsy spell.
> My bride to be, my evermore delight,
> My own heart's heart and ownest own, farewell.
> It is but for a little space I go:
> And ye meanwhile far over moor and fell
> Beat to the noiseless music of the night!
> Has our whole earth gone nearer to the glow
> Of your soft splendours that you look so bright?
> I have climb'd nearer out of lonely Hell.
> Beat, happy stars, timing with things below,
> Beat with my heart more blest than heart can tell,
> Blest, but for some dark undercurrent woe
> That seems to draw—but it shall not be so:
> Let all be well, be well.

We are now approaching the crisis of the story. A grand
dinner and a dance are to be held at the Hall, and the hero,
not being invited, waits in the garden till the festivities are
over, that Maud may then come out and show herself to him
in all the glory of her ball-dress. Here occurs the invocation, which has been deservedly admired and quoted by every
critic:

> Come into the garden, Maud,
>   For the black bat, night, has flown,—
> Come into the garden, Maud,
>   I am here at the gate alone;
> And the woodbine spices are wafted abroad,
>   And the musk of the roses blown.

* * *

> For a breeze of morning moves,
>   And the planet of Love is on high,
> Beginning to faint in the light that she loves
>   On a bed of daffodil sky,—
> To faint in the light of the sun she loves,
>   To faint in his light, and to die.

Very exquisite is that descriptive bit, in the second stanza, where the music of the verse seems to faint and die like the star. Still the whole poem, which is too long for us to quote, is very inferior, as a poem of the Fancy, to the 'Talking Oak'. We do not, for a moment, believe in the sensibility of the roses and lilies in Maud's garden, as we believe in the thrills felt to his 'inmost ring' by the 'Old Oak of Summer Chace.'* This invocation is the topmost note of the lover's joy. The interview in the garden is disturbed by the 'Assyrian Bull', and the 'padded shape'. A duel follows, in which the brother is killed. And now we find the hero an exile on the Breton coast, where, from delivering some stanzas of Natural Theology *à propos* of a shell, he proceeds to retrace the sad memories of his love, until he becomes mad. We have then a Bedlam soliloquy, in which he fancies himself dead, and mingles with the images of Maud, her father, and her brother, his early-fixed idea—the police reports. From this madness he is recovered by the news that the Allies have declared war against Russia; whereupon he bursts into a paean, that

> the long, long canker of Peace is over and done.

It is possible, no doubt, to allegorize all this into a variety of edifying meanings; but it remains true, that the ground-notes of the poem are nothing more than hatred of peace and the Peace Society, hatred of commerce and coal-mines, hatred of young gentlemen with flourishing whiskers and padded coats, adoration of a clear-cut face, and faith in War as the unique social regenerator. Such are the sentiments, and such is the philosophy embodied in 'Maud'; at least, for plain people not given to allegorizing; and it, perhaps, speaks well for Tennyson's genius, that it has refused to aid him much on themes so little worthy of his greatest self.

Of the smaller poems, which, with the well-known 'Ode', make up the volume, 'The Brook' is rather a pretty idyll, and 'The Daisy' a graceful, unaffected recollection of Italy; but no one of them is remarkable enough to be ranked with the author's best poems of the same class.

Margaret Fuller and Mary
Wollstonecraft (1855)

THE dearth of new books just now gives us time to recur to less recent ones which we have hitherto noticed but slightly; and among these we choose the late edition of Margaret Fuller's *Woman in the Nineteenth Century*, because we think it has been unduly thrust into the background by less comprehensive and candid productions on the same subject. Notwithstanding certain defects of taste and a sort of vague spiritualism and grandiloquence which belong to all but the very best American writers, the book is a valuable one: it has the enthusiasm of a noble and sympathetic nature, with the moderation and breadth and large allowance of a vigorous and cultivated understanding. There is no exaggeration of woman's moral excellence or intellectual capabilities; no injudicious insistence on her fitness for this or that function hitherto engrossed by men; but a calm plea for the removal of unjust laws and artificial restrictions, so that the possibilities of her nature may have room for full development, a wisely stated demand to disencumber her of the

> Parasitic forms
> That seem to keep her up, but drag her down—
> And leave her field to burgeon and to bloom
> From all within her, make herself her own
> To give or keep, to live and learn and be
> All that not harms distinctive womanhood.*

It is interesting to compare this essay of Margaret Fuller's, published in its earliest form in 1843, with a work on the position of woman, written between sixty and seventy years ago—we mean Mary Wollstonecraft's *Rights of Woman*.* The latter work was not continued beyond the first volume; but so far as this carries the subject, the comparison, at least in relation to strong sense and loftiness of moral tone, is not at all disadvantageous to the woman of the last century. There is in some quarters a vague prejudice against the *Rights of Woman* as in some way or other a reprehensible book, but readers who go to it with this impression will be surprised to find it eminently serious, severely moral, and withal rather heavy—the true reason, perhaps, that no edition has been published since 1796, and that it is now rather scarce. There are several points of resemblance, as well as of striking difference, between the two books. A strong understanding is present in both; but Margaret Fuller's mind was like some regions of her own American continent, where you are constantly stepping from the sunny 'clearings' into the mysterious twilight of the tangled forest—she often passes in one breath from forcible reasoning to dreamy vagueness; moreover, her unusually varied culture gives her great command of illustration. Mary Wollstonecraft, on the other hand, is nothing if not rational; she has no erudition, and her grave pages are lit up by no ray of fancy. In both writers we discern, under the brave bearing of a strong and truthful nature, the beating of a loving woman's heart, which teaches them not to undervalue the smallest offices of domestic care or kindliness. But Margaret Fuller, with all her passionate sensibility, is more of the literary woman, who would not have been satisfied without intellectual production; Mary Wollstonecraft, we imagine, wrote not at all for writing's sake, but from the pressure of other motives. So far as the difference of date allows, there is a striking coincidence in their trains of thought; indeed, every important idea in the *Rights of Woman*, except the combination of home education with a common day-school for boys and girls, reappears in Margaret Fuller's essay.

One point on which they both write forcibly is the fact that, while men have a horror of such faculty or culture in the other sex as tends to place it on a level with their own, they are really in a state of subjection to ignorant and feeble-minded women. Margaret Fuller says:—

Wherever man is sufficiently raised above extreme poverty or brutal stupidity, to care for the comforts of the fireside, or the bloom and ornament of life, woman has always power enough, if she choose to exert it, and is usually disposed to do so, in proportion to her ignorance and childish vanity. Unacquainted with the importance of life and its purposes, trained to a selfish coquetry and love of petty power, she does not look beyond the pleasure of making herself felt at the moment, and governments are shaken and commerce broken up to gratify the pique of a female favourite. The English shopkeeper's wife does not vote, but it is for her interest that the politician canvasses by the coarsest flattery.

Again:—

All wives, bad or good, loved or unloved, inevitably influence their husbands from the power their position not merely gives, but necessitates of colouring evidence and infusing feelings in hours when the—patient, shall I call him?—is off his guard.

Hear now what Mary Wollstonecraft says on the same subject:—

Women have been allowed to remain in ignorance and slavish dependence many, very many years, and still we hear of nothing but their fondness of pleasure and sway, their preference of rakes and soldiers, their childish attachment to toys, and the vanity that makes them value accomplishments more than virtues. History brings forward a fearful catalogue of the crimes which their cunning has produced, when the weak slaves have had sufficient address to overreach their masters ... When, therefore, I call women slaves, I mean in a political and civil sense; for indirectly they obtain too much power, and are debased by their exertions to obtain illicit sway ... The libertinism, and even the virtues of superior men, will always give women of some description great power over them; and these weak women, under the influence of childish passions and selfish vanity, *will throw a false light over the objects which the very men view with their eyes who ought to enlighten their judgement.* Men of fancy, and those sanguine characters who mostly hold the helm of human affairs in general, relax in the society of women; and surely I need not cite to the most superficial reader of history the numerous examples of vice and oppression which the private intrigues of female favourites have produced; not to dwell on the mischief that naturally arises from the blundering interposition of well-meaning folly. *For in the transactions of business it is much better to have to deal with a knave than a fool, because a knave adheres to some plan, and any plan of reason may be seen through sooner than a sudden flight of folly.* The power which vile and foolish women have had over wise men who possessed sensibility is notorious.

There is a notion commonly entertained among men that an instructed woman, capable of having opinions, is likely to prove an impracticable yoke-fellow, always pulling one way when her husband wants to go the other, oracular in tone, and prone to give curtain lectures on metaphysics. But surely, so far as obstinacy is concerned, your unreasoning animal is the most unmanageable of creatures, where you are not allowed to settle the question by a cudgel, a whip and bridle, or even a string to the leg. For our own parts, we see no consistent or commodious medium between the old plan of corporal discipline and that thorough education of women which will make them rational beings in the highest sense of the word. Wherever weakness is not harshly controlled it must *govern*, as you may see when a strong man holds a little child by the hand, how he is pulled hither and thither, and wearied in his walk by his submission to the whims and feeble movements of his companion. A really cultured woman, like a really cultured man, will be ready to yield in trifles. So far as we see, there is no indissoluble connexion between infirmity of logic and infirmity of will, and a woman quite innocent of an opinion in philosophy, is as likely as not to have an indomitable opinion about the kitchen. As to airs of superiority, no woman ever had them in consequence of true culture, but only because her culture was shallow or unreal, only as a result of what Mrs Malaprop* well calls 'the ineffectual qualities in a woman'—mere acquisitions carried about, and not knowledge thoroughly assimilated so as to enter into the growth of the character.

To return to Margaret Fuller, some of the best things she says are on the folly of absolute definitions of woman's nature and absolute demarcations of woman's mission. 'Nature,' she says, 'seems to delight in varying the arrangements, as if to show that she will be fettered by no rule; and we must admit the same varieties that she admits.' Again: 'If nature is never bound down, nor the voice of inspiration stifled, that is enough. We are pleased that women should write and speak, if they feel need of it, from having something to tell; but silence for ages would be no misfortune, if that silence be from divine command, and not from man's tradition.' And here is a passage, the beginning of which has been often quoted:—

If you ask me what offices they (women) may fill, I reply—any. I do not care what case you put; let them be sea-captains if you will. I do not doubt there are women well fitted for such an office, and, if so, I should be as glad as to welcome the Maid of Saragossa, or the Maid of Missolonghi, or the Suliote heroine, or Emily Plater. I think women need, especially at this juncture, a much greater range of occupation than they have, to rouse their latent powers . . . In families that I know, some little girls like to saw wood, others to use carpenter's tools. Where these tastes are indulged, cheerfulness and good-humour are promoted. Where they are forbidden, because 'such things are not proper for girls', they grow sullen and mischievous. Fourier* had observed these wants of women, as no one can fail to do who watches the desires of little girls, or knows the *ennui* that haunts grown women, except where they make to themselves a serene little world by art of some kind. He, therefore, in proposing a great variety of employments, in manufactures or the care of plants and animals, allows for one third of women as likely to have a taste for masculine pursuits, one third of men for feminine . . . I have no doubt, however, that a large proportion of women would give themselves to the same employments as now, because there are circumstances that must lead them. Mothers will delight to make the nest soft and warm. Nature would take care of that; no need to clip the wings of any bird that wants to soar and sing, or finds in itself the strength of pinion for a migratory flight unusual to its kind. The difference would be that *all* need not be constrained to employments for which *some* are unfit.

A propos of the same subject, we find Mary Wollstonecraft offering a suggestion which the women of the United States have already begun to carry out. She says:—

Women, in particular, all want to be ladies. Which is simply to have nothing to do, but listlessly to go they scarcely care where, for they cannot tell what. But what have women to do in society? I may be asked, but to loiter with easy grace; surely you would not condemn them all to suckle fools and chronicle small beer. No. *Women might certainly study the art of healing, and be physicians as well as nurses* . . . Business of various kinds they might likewise pursue, if they were educated in a more orderly manner . . . Women would not then marry for a support, as men accept of places under government, and neglect the implied duties.

Men pay a heavy price for their reluctance to encourage self-help and independent resources in women. The precious meridian years of many a man of genius have to be spent in the toil of routine, that an 'establishment' may be kept up for a woman who can understand none of his secret yearnings, who is fit for nothing but to sit in her drawing-room like a doll-Madonna in her shrine. No matter. Anything is more endurable than to change our established formulæ about women, or to run the risk of looking up to our wives instead of looking down on them. *Sit divus, dummodo non sit vivus* (let him be a god, provided he be not living), said the Roman magnates of Romulus; and so men say of women, let them be idols, useless absorbents of precious things, provided we are not obliged to admit them to be strictly fellow-beings, to be treated, one and all, with justice and sober reverence.

On one side we hear that woman's position can never be improved until women themselves are better; and, on the other, that women can never become better until their position is improved—until the laws are made more just, and a wider field opened to feminine activity. But we constantly hear the same difficulty stated about the human race in general. There is a perpetual action and reaction between individuals and institutions; we must try and mend both by little and little—the only way in which human things can be mended. Unfortunately, many over-zealous champions of women assert their actual equality with men— nay, even their moral superiority to men—as a ground for their release from oppressive laws and restrictions. They lose strength immensely by this false position. If it were true, then there would be a case in which slavery and ignorance nourished virtue, and so far we should have an argument for the continuance of bondage. But we want freedom and culture for woman, because subjection and ignorance have debased her, and with her, Man; for—

> If she be small, slight-natured, miserable,
> How shall men grow?*

Both Margaret Fuller and Mary Wollstonecraft have too much sagacity to fall into this sentimental exaggeration. Their ardent hopes of what women may become do not prevent them from seeing and painting women as they are. On the relative moral excellence of men and women Mary Wollstonecraft speaks with the most decision:—

Women are supposed to possess more sensibility, and even humanity, than men, and their strong attachments and instantaneous emotions of compassion are given as proofs; but the clinging affection of ignorance has seldom anything noble in it, and may mostly be resolved into selfishness, as well as the affection of children and brutes. I have known many weak women whose sensibility was entirely engrossed by their husbands; and as for their humanity, it was very faint indeed, or rather it was only a transient emotion of compassion. Humanity does not consist 'in a squeamish ear', says an eminent orator. 'It belongs to the mind as well as to the nerves.' But this kind of exclusive affection, though it degrades the individual, should not be brought forward as a proof of the inferiority of the sex, because it is the natural consequence of confined views; for even women of superior sense, having their attention turned to little employments and private plans, rarely rise to heroism, unless when spurred on by love! and love, as an heroic passion, like genius, appears but once in an age. I therefore agree with the moralist who asserts 'that women have seldom so much generosity as men'; and that their narrow affections, to which justice and humanity are often sacrificed, render the sex apparently inferior, especially as they are commonly inspired by men; but I contend that the heart would expand as the understanding gained strength, if women were not depressed from their cradles.

We had marked several other passages of Margaret Fuller's for extract, but as we do not aim at an exhaustive treatment of our subject, and are only touching a few of its points, we have, perhaps, already claimed as much of the reader's attention as he will be willing to give to such desultory material.

Thomas Carlyle (1855)

IT has been well said that the highest aim in education is analogous to the highest aim in mathematics, namely, to obtain not *results* but *powers*, not particular solutions, but the means by which endless solutions may be wrought. He is the most effective educator who aims less at perfecting specific acquirements than at producing that mental condition which renders acquirements easy, and leads to their useful application; who does not seek to make his pupils moral by enjoining particular courses of action, but by bringing into activity the feelings and sympathies that must issue in noble action. On the same ground it may be said that the most effective writer is not he who announces a particular discovery, who convinces men of a particular conclusion, who demonstrates that this measure is right and that measure is wrong; but he who rouses in others the activities that must issue in discovery, who awakes men from their indifference to the right and the wrong, who nerves their energies to seek for the truth and live up to it at whatever cost. The influence of such a writer is dynamic. He does not teach men how to use sword and musket, but he inspires their souls with courage and sends a strong will into their muscles. He does not, perhaps, enrich your stock of data, but he clears away the film from your eyes that you may search for data to some purpose. He does not, perhaps, convince you, but he strikes you, undeceives you, animates you. You are not directly fed by his books, but you are braced as by a walk up to an alpine summit, and yet subdued to calm and reverence as by the sublime things to be seen from that summit.

Such a writer is Thomas Carlyle. It is an idle question to ask whether his books will be read a century hence: if they were all burnt as the grandest of Suttees on his funeral pile, it would be only like cutting down an oak after its acorns have sown a forest. For there is hardly a superior or active mind of this generation that has not been modified by Carlyle's writings; there has hardly been an English book written for the last ten or twelve years that would not have been different if Carlyle had not lived. The character of his influence is best seen in the fact that many of the men who have the least agreement with his opinions are those to whom the reading of *Sartor Resartus* was an epoch in the history of their minds.* The extent of his influence may be best seen in the fact that ideas which were startling novelties when he first wrote them are now become common-places. And we think few men will be found to say that this influence on the whole has not been for good. There are plenty who question the justice of Carlyle's estimates of past men and past times, plenty who quarrel with the exaggerations of the *Latter-Day Pamphlets*, and who are as far as possible from looking for an amendment of things from a Carlylian theocracy with the 'greatest man', as a Joshua who is to smite the wicked (and the stupid) till the going down of the sun. But for any large nature, those points of difference are quite incidental. It is not as a theorist, but as a great and beautiful human nature, that Carlyle influences us. You may meet a man whose wisdom seems unimpeachable, since you find him entirely in agreement with yourself; but this oracular man of unexceptionable opinions has a green eye, a wiry hand, and altogether a *Wesen*, or demeanour, that makes the world look blank to you, and whose unexceptionable opinions become a bore; while another man who deals in what you cannot but think 'dangerous paradoxes', warms your heart by the pressure of his hand, and looks out on the world with so clear and loving an eye, that nature seems to reflect the light of his glance upon your own feeling. So it is with Carlyle. When he is saying the very opposite of what we think, he says it so finely, with such hearty conviction—he makes the object about which we differ stand out in such grand relief under the clear light of his strong and honest intellect—he appeals so constantly to our sense of the manly and the truthful—that we are obliged to say 'Hear! hear!' to the writer before we can give the decorous 'Oh! oh!' to his opinions.

Much twaddling criticism has been spent on Carlyle's style. Unquestionably there are some genuine minds, not at all given to twaddle, to whom his style is antipathetic, who find it as unendurable as an English lady finds peppermint. Against antipathies there is no arguing; they are misfortunes. But instinctive repulsion apart, surely there is no one who can read and relish Carlyle without feeling that they could no more wish him to have written in another style than they could wish gothic architecture not to be gothic, or Raffaelle not to be Raffaellesque. It is the fashion to speak of Carlyle almost exclusively as a philosopher; but, to our thinking, he is yet more of an artist than a philosopher. He glances deep down into human nature, and shows the causes of human actions; he seizes grand generalizations, and traces them in the particular with wonderful acumen; and in all this he is a philosopher. But, perhaps, his greatest power lies in concrete presentation. No novelist has made his creations live for us more thoroughly than Carlyle has made Mirabeau and the men of the French Revolution, Cromwell and the Puritans. What humour in his pictures! Yet what depth of appreciation, what reverence for the great and god-like under every sort of earthly mummery!

It is several years now since we read a work of Carlyle's *seriatim*, but this our long-standing impression of him as a writer we find confirmed by looking over Mr Ballantyne's selection. Such a volume as this is surely a benefit to the public, for alas! Carlyle's works are still dear, and many who would like to have them are obliged to forgo the possession of more than a volume or two. Through this good service of Mr Ballantyne's, however, they may now obtain for a moderate sum a large collection of extracts—if not the best that could have been made, still very precious ones.

To make extracts from a book of extracts may at first seem easy, and to make extracts from a writer so well known may seem superfluous. The *embarras de richesses* and the length of the passages make the first not easy; and as to the second, why, we have reread these passages so often in the volumes, and now again in Mr Ballantyne's selection, that we cannot suppose any amount of repetition otherwise than agreeable. We will, however, be sparing. Here is

David, the Hebrew King

On the whole, we make too much of faults: the details of the business hide the real centre of it. Faults? The greatest of faults, I should say, is to be conscious of none. Readers of the Bible above all, one would think, might know better. Who is called there 'the man according to God's own heart'? David, the Hebrew King, had fallen into sins enough; blackest crimes; there was no want of sins. And thereupon the unbelievers sneer and ask, Is this your man according to God's heart? The sneer, I must say, seems to me but a shallow one. What are faults, what are the outward details of a life, if the inner secret of it, the remorse, temptations, true, often-baffled, never-ended struggle of it, be forgotten? 'It is not in man that walketh to direct his steps.' Of all acts is not, for a man, *repentance* the most divine? The deadliest sin, I say, were that same supercilious consciousness of no sin;—that is death; the heart so conscious is divorced from sincerity, humility, and fact; is dead: it is 'pure' as dead dry sand is pure. David's life and history, as written for us in those Psalms of his, I consider to be the truest emblem ever given of a man's moral progress and warfare here below. All earnest souls will ever discern in it the faithful struggle of an earnest human soul towards what is good and best. Struggle often baffled, sore baffled, down as into entire wreck; yet a struggle never ended; ever, with tears, repentance, true unconquerable purpose, begun anew. Poor human nature! Is not a man's walking, in truth, always that: 'a succession of falls'? Man can do no other. In this wild element of a Life, he has to struggle onwards; now fallen, deep-abased; and ever, with tears, repentance, with bleeding heart, he has to rise again, struggle again still onwards. That his struggle *be* a faithful unconquerable one: that is the question of questions.*

In another way how excellent is this on

The Worth of Formulas

What we call 'Formulas' are not in their origin bad; they are indispensably good. Formula is *method*, habitude, found wherever man is found. Formulas fashion themselves as Paths do, as beaten Highways, leading towards some sacred or high object, whither many men are bent. Consider it. One man, full of heartfelt earnest impulse, finds out a way of doing somewhat—were it of uttering his soul's reverence for the Highest, were it but of fitly saluting his fellow-man. An inventor was needed to do that, a *poet*; he has articulated the dim-struggling thought that dwelt in his own and many hearts. This is his way of doing that; these are his footsteps, the beginning of a 'Path'. And now see: the second man travels naturally in the footsteps of his foregoer: it is the *easiest* method. In the footsteps of his foregoer; yet with improvements, changes where such seem good; at all events with enlargements, the Path ever *widening* itself as more travel it;—till at last there is a broad Highway whereon the whole world may travel and drive. While there remains a City or Shrine, or any Reality to drive to, at the farther end, the Highway shall be right welcome! When the City is gone, we will forsake the Highway. In this manner all Institutions, Practices, Regulated Things in the world have come into existence, and gone out of existence. Formulas all begin by being *full* of substance; you may call them the *skin*, the articulation into shape, into limbs and skin, of a substance that is already there: *they* had not been there otherwise. Idols, as we said, are not idolatrous till they become doubtful, empty for the worshipper's heart. Much as we talk against Formulas, I hope no one of us is ignorant withal of the high significance of *true* Formulas; that they were, and will ever be, the indispensablest furniture of our habitation in this world.*

Finally, this characteristic passage tempts us:—

The Apes of the Dead Sea

Perhaps few narratives in History or Mythology are more significant than that Moslem one, of Moses and the Dwellers by the Dead Sea. A tribe of men dwelt on the shores of that same Asphaltic Lake; and having forgotten, as we are all prone to do, the inner facts of Nature, and taken up with the falsities and outer semblances of it, were fallen into sad conditions—verging indeed towards a certain far deeper Lake. Whereupon it pleased kind Heaven to send them the Prophet Moses, with an instructive word of warning, out of which might have sprung 'remedial measures' not a few. But no: the men of the Dead Sea discovered, as the valet-species always does in heroes or prophets, no comeliness in Moses; listened with real tedium to Moses, with light grinning, or with splenetic sniffs and sneers, affecting even to yawn; and signified, in short, that they found him a humbug, and even a bore. Such was the candid theory these men of the Asphalt Lake formed to themselves of Moses, that probably he was a humbug, that certainly he was a bore. Moses withdrew; but Nature and her rigorous veracities did not withdraw. The Men of the Dead Sea, when we next went to visit them, were all 'changed into Apes'; sitting on the trees there, grinning now in the most *un*affected manner; gibbering and chattering *complete* nonsense; finding the whole Universe now a most undisputable Humbug! The Universe has *become* a Humbug to the Apes who thought it one! There they sit and chatter, to this hour; only I think, every Sabbath there returns to them a bewildered half-consciousness, half-reminiscence; and they sit, with their wizened smoke-dried visages, and such an air of supreme tragicality as Apes may; looking out, through those blinking smoke-bleared eyes of theirs, into the wonderfulest universal smoky Twilight and undecipherable disordered Dusk of Things; wholly an Uncertainty, Unintelligibility, they and it; and for commentary thereon, here and there an unmusical chatter or mew:—truest, tragicalest Humbug conceivable by the mind of man or ape! They made no use of their souls; and *so* have lost them. Their worship on the Sabbath now is to roost there, with unmusical screeches, and half remember that they had souls. Didst thou never, O Traveller, fall in with parties of this tribe? Meseems they are grown somewhat numerous in our day.*

German Wit: Heinrich Heine (1856)

'NOTHING,' says Goethe, 'is more significant of men's character than what they find laughable.'* The truth of this observation would perhaps have been more apparent if he had said *culture* instead of character. The last thing in which the cultivated man can have community with the vulgar is their jocularity; and we can hardly exhibit more strikingly the wide gulf which separates him from them, than by comparing the object which shakes the diaphragm of a coal-heaver with the highly complex pleasure derived from a real witticism. That any high order of wit is exceedingly complex, and demands a ripe and strong mental development, has one evidence in the fact that we do not find it in boys at all in proportion to their manifestation of other powers. Clever boys generally aspire to the heroic and poetic rather than the comic, and the crudest of all their efforts are their jokes. Many a witty man will remember how in his school days a practical joke, more or less Rabelaisian, was for him the *ne plus ultra* of the ludicrous. It seems to have been the same with the boyhood of the human race. The history and literature of the ancient Hebrews gives the idea of a people who went about their business and their pleasure as gravely as a society of beavers; the smile and the laugh are often mentioned metaphorically, but the smile is one of complacency, the laugh is one of scorn. Nor can we imagine that the facetious element was very strong in the Egyptians; no laughter lurks in the wondering eyes and the broad calm lips of their statues. Still less can the Assyrians have had any genius for the comic: the round eyes and simpering satisfaction of their ideal faces belong to a type which is not witty, but the cause of wit in others. The fun of these early races was, we fancy, of the after-dinner kind—loud-throated laughter over the wine-cup, taken too little account of in sober moments to enter as an element into their Art, and differing as much from the laughter of a Chamfort* or a Sheridan as the gastronomic enjoyment of an ancient Briton, whose dinner had no other 'removes' than from acorns to beechmast and back again to acorns, differed from the subtle pleasures of the palate experienced by his turtle-eating descendant. In fact they had to live seriously through the stages which to subsequent races were to become comedy, as those amiable-looking pre-Adamite amphibia which Professor Owen has restored for us in effigy at Sydenham, took perfectly *au sérieux* the grotesque physiognomies of their kindred.* Heavy experience in their case as in every other, was the base from which the salt of future wit was to be made.

Humour is of earlier growth than Wit, and it is in accordance with this earlier growth that it has more affinity with the poetic tendencies, while Wit is more nearly allied to the ratiocinative intellect. Humour draws its materials from situations and characteristics; Wit seizes on unexpected and complex relations. Humour is chiefly representative and descriptive; it is diffuse, and flows along without any other law than its own fantastic will; or it flits about like a will-o'-the-wisp, amazing us by its whimsical transitions. Wit is brief and sudden, and sharply defined as a crystal; it does not make pictures, it is not fantastic; but it detects an unsuspected analogy or suggests a startling or confounding inference. Every one who has had the opportunity of making the comparison will remember that the effect produced on him by some witticisms is closely akin to the effect produced on him by subtle reasoning which lays open a fallacy or absurdity, and there are persons whose delight in such reasoning always manifests itself in laughter. This affinity of Wit with ratiocination is the more obvious in proportion as the species of wit is higher and deals less with words and with superficialities than with the essential qualities of things. Some of Johnson's most admirable witticisms consist in the suggestion of an analogy which immediately exposes the absurdity of an action or proposition; and it is only their ingenuity, condensation, and instantaneousness which lift them from reasoning into Wit—they are *reasoning raised to a higher power*. On the other hand,

Humour, in its higher forms, and in proportion as it associates itself with the sympathetic emotions, continually passes into poetry: nearly all great modern humorists may be called prose poets.

Some confusion as to the nature of humour has been created by the fact, that those who have written most eloquently on it have dwelt almost exclusively on its higher forms, and have defined humour in general as the *sympathetic* presentation of incongruous elements in human nature and life; a definition which only applies to its later development. A great deal of humour may co-exist with a great deal of barbarism, as we see in the Middle Ages; but the strongest flavour of the humour in such cases will come, not from sympathy, but more probably from triumphant egoism or intolerance; at best it will be the love of the ludicrous exhibiting itself in illustrations of successful cunning and of the *lex talionis*, as in *Reineke Fuchs*,* or shaking off in a holiday mood the yoke of a too exacting faith, as in the old Mysteries. Again, it is impossible to deny a high degree of humour to many practical jokes, but no sympathetic nature can enjoy them. Strange as the genealogy may seem, the original parentage of that wonderful and delicious mixture of fun, fancy, philosophy, and feeling which constitutes modern humour, was probably the cruel mockery of a savage at the writhings of a suffering enemy—such is the tendency of things towards the good and beautiful on this earth. Probably the reason why high culture demands more complete harmony with its moral sympathies in humour than in wit, is that humour is in its nature more prolix—that it has not the direct and irresistible force of wit. Wit is an electric shock, which takes us by violence, quite independently of our predominant mental disposition; but humour approaches us more deliberately and leaves us masters of ourselves. Hence it is, that while coarse and cruel humour has almost disappeared from contemporary literature, coarse and cruel wit abounds: even refined men cannot help laughing at a coarse *bon mot* or a lacerating personality, if the 'shock' of the witticism is a powerful one; while mere fun will have no power over them if it jar on their moral taste.

Hence, too, it is, that while wit is perennial, humour is liable to become superannuated.

As is usual with definitions and classifications, however, this distinction between wit and humour does not exactly represent the actual fact. Like all other species, Wit and Humour overlap and blend with each other. There are *bons mots*, like many of Charles Lamb's which are a sort of facetious hybrids, we hardly know whether to call them witty or humorous; there are rather lengthy descriptions or narratives, which, like Voltaire's *Micromégas*,* would be humorous if they were not so sparkling and antithetic, so pregnant with suggestion and satire, that we are obliged to call them witty. We rarely find wit untempered by humour, or humour without a spice of wit; and sometimes we find them both united in the highest degree in the same mind, as in Shakespeare and Molière. A happy conjunction this, for wit is apt to be cold, and thin-lipped, and Mephisto-phelean in men who have no relish for humour, whose lungs do never crow like Chanticleer at fun and drollery; and broad-faced, rollicking humour needs the refining influence of wit. Indeed, it may be said that there is no really fine writing in which wit has not an implicit, if not an explicit action. The wit may never rise to the surface, it may never flame out into a witticism; but it helps to give brightness and transparency, it warns off from flights and exaggerations which verge on the ridiculous—in every *genre* of writing it preserves a man from sinking into the *genre ennuyeux*. And it is eminently needed for this office in humorous writing; for as humour has no limits imposed on it by its material, no law but its own exuberance, it is apt to become prepos-terous and wearisome unless checked by wit, which is the enemy of all monotony, of all lengthiness, of all exaggera-tion.

Perhaps the nearest approach Nature has given us to a complete analysis, in which wit is as thoroughly exhausted of humour as possible, and humour as bare as possible of wit, is in the typical Frenchman and the typical German. Voltaire, the intensest example of pure wit, fails in most of his fictions from his lack of humour. *Micromégas* is a perfect tale, because, as it deals chiefly with philosophic ideas and does not touch the marrow of human feeling and life, the writer's wit and wisdom were all-sufficient for his purpose. Not so with *Candide*. Here Voltaire had to give pictures of life as well as to convey philosophic truth and satirè, and here we feel the want of humour. The sense of the ludicrous is continually defeated by disgust, and the scenes, instead of presenting us with an amusing or agreeable picture, are only the frame for a witticism. On the other hand, German humour generally shows no sense of measure, no instinctive tact; it is either floundering and clumsy as the antics of a leviathan, or laborious and interminable as a Lapland day, in which one loses all hope that the stars and quiet will ever come. For this reason, Jean Paul,* the greatest of German humorists, is unendurable to many readers, and frequently tiresomc to all. Here, as elsewhere, the German shows the absence of that delicate perception, that sensibility to gradation, which is the essence of tact and taste, and the necessary concomitant of wit. All his subtlety is reserved for the region of metaphysics. For *Identität* in the abstract, no one can havc an acuter vision, but in the concrete he is satisfied with a very loose approximation. He has the finest nose for *Empirismus* in philosophical doctrine, but the presence of more or less tobacco-smoke in the air he breathes is imperceptible to him. To the typical German— *Vetter Michel*—it is indifferent whether his door-lock will catch, whether his tea-cup be more or less than an inch thick; whether or not his book have every other leaf unstitched; whether his neighbour's conversation be more or less of a shout; whether he pronounce *b* or *p*, *t* or *d*; whether or not his adored one's teeth be few and far between. He has the same sort of insensibility to gradations in time. A German comedy is like a German sentence: you see no reason in its structure why it should ever come to an end, and you accept the conclusion as an arrangement of Providence rather than of the author. We have heard Germans use the word *Langeweile*, the equivalent for ennui, and we have secretly wondered *what* it can be that produces ennui in a German. Not the longest of long tragedies, for we have known him to pronounce that *höchst fesselnd* (*so* enchaining!); not the heaviest of heavy books, for he delights in that as *gründlich* (deep, sir, deep!); not the slowest of journeys in a *Post-wagen*, for the slower the horses, the more cigars he can smoke before he reaches his journey's end. German ennui must be something as superlative as Barclay's treble X,* which, we suppose, implies an extremely unknown quantity of stupefaction.

It is easy to see that this national deficiency in nicety of perception must have its effect on the national appreciation and exhibition of humour. You find in Germany ardent admirers of Shakespeare, who tell you that what they think most admirable in him is his *Wortspiel*, his verbal quibbles; and one of these, a man of no slight culture and refinement, once cited to a friend of ours Proteus's joke in *The Two Gentlemen of Verona*—'Nod, I? why that's Noddy,' as a transcendent specimen of Shakespearian wit.* German facetiousness is seldom comic to foreigners, and an Englishman with a swelled cheek might take up *Kladderadatsch*, the German *Punch*, without any danger of agitating his facial muscles. Indeed, it is a remarkable fact that, among the five great races concerned in modern civilization, the German race is the only one which, up to the present century, had contributed nothing classic to the common stock of European wit and humour; for *Reineke Fuchs* cannot be regarded as a peculiarly Teutonic product. Italy was the birth-place of Pantomime and the immortal Pulcinello; Spain had produced Cervantes; France had produced Rabelais and Molière, and classic wits innumerable; England had yielded Shakespeare and a host of humorists. But Germany had borne no great comic dramatist, no great satirist, and she has not yet repaired the omission; she had not even produced any humorist of a high order. Among her great writers, Lessing is the one who is the most specifically witty. We feel the implicit influence of wit—the 'flavour of mind'—throughout his writings; and it is often concentrated into pungent satire, as every reader of the *Hamburgische Dramaturgie** remembers. Still, Lessing's name has not become European through his wit, and his charming comedy, *Minna von Barnhelm*, has won no place on a foreign stage. Of course, we do not pretend to an exhaustive acquaintance with German literature; we not only admit— we are sure, that it includes much comic writing of which we know nothing. We simply state the fact, that no German production of that kind, before the present century, ranked as European; a fact which does not, indeed, determine the *amount* of the national facetiousness, but which is quite decisive as to its *quality*. Whatever may be the stock of fun which Germany yields for home consumption, she has provided little for the palate of other lands.—All honour to her for the still greater things she has done for us! She has fought the hardest fight for freedom of thought, has produced the grandest inventions, has made magnificent contributions to science, has given us some of the divinest poetry, and quite the divinest music, in the world. No one reveres and treasures the products of the German mind more than we do. To say that that mind is not fertile in wit, is only like saying that excellent wheat land is not rich pasture; to say that we do not enjoy German facetiousness, is no more than to say, that though the horse is the finest of quadrupeds, we do not like him to lay his hoof playfully on our shoulder. Still, as we have noticed that the pointless puns and stupid jocularity of the boy may ultimately be developed into the epigrammatic brilliancy and polished playfulness of the man; as we believe that racy wit and chastened delicate humour are inevitably the results of invigorated and refined mental activity; we can also believe that Germany will, one day, yield a crop of wits and humorists.

Perhaps there is already an earnest of that future crop in the existence of Heinrich Heine, a German born with the present century, who, to Teutonic imagination, sensibility, and humour, adds an amount of *esprit* that would make him brilliant among the most brilliant of Frenchmen. True, this unique German wit is half a Hebrew; but he and his ancestors spent their youth in German air, and were reared on *Wurst* and *Sauerkraut*, so that he is as much a German as a pheasant is an English bird, or a potato an Irish vegetable. But whatever else he may be, Heine is one of the most remarkable men of this age: no echo, but a real voice, and therefore, like all genuine things in this world, worth studying; a surpassing lyric poet, who has uttered our feelings for us in delicious song; a humorist, who touches leaden folly with the magic wand of his fancy, and transmutes it into the fine gold of art—who sheds his sunny smile on human tears, and makes them a beauteous rainbow on the cloudy background of life; a wit, who holds in his mighty hand the most scorching lightnings of satire; an artist in prose literature, who has shown even more completely than Goethe the possibilities of German prose; and—in spite of all charges against him, true as well as false—a lover of freedom, who has spoken wise and brave words on behalf of his fellow-men. He is, moreover, a suffering man, who, with all the highly-wrought sensibility of genius, has to endure terrible physical ills; and as such he calls forth more than an intellectual interest. It is true, alas! that there is a heavy weight in the other scale—that Heine's magnificent powers have often served only to give electric force to the expression of debased feeling, so that his works are no Phidian statue* of gold, and ivory, and gems, but have not a little brass, and iron, and miry clay mingled with the precious metal. The audacity of his occasional coarseness and personality is unparalleled in contemporary literature, and has hardly been exceeded by the licence of former days. Hence, before his volumes are put within the reach of immature minds, there is need of a friendly penknife to exercise a strict censorship. Yet, when all coarseness, all scurrility, all Mephistophelean contempt for the reverent feelings of other men, is removed, there will be a plenteous remainder of exquisite poetry, of wit, humour, and just thought. It is apparently too often a congenial task to write severe words about the transgressions committed by men of genius, especially when the censor has the advantage of being himself a man of *no* genius, so that those transgressions seem to him quite gratuitous; *he*, forsooth, never lacerated any one by his wit, or gave irresistible piquancy to a coarse allusion, and his indignation is not mitigated by any knowledge of the temptation that lies in transcendent power. We are also apt to measure what a gifted man has done by our arbitrary conception of what he might have done, rather than by a comparison of his actual doings with our own or those of other ordinary men. We make ourselves over-zealous agents of heaven, and demand that our brother should bring usurious interest for his five Talents, forgetting that it is less easy to manage five Talents than two.* Whatever benefit there may be in denouncing the evil, it is after all more edifying, and certainly more cheering, to appreciate the good. Hence, in endeavouring to give our readers some account of Heine and his works, we shall not dwell lengthily on his failings; we shall not hold the candle up to dusty, vermin-haunted corners, but let the light fall as much as possible on the nobler and more attractive details. Our sketch of Heine's life, which has been drawn from various sources, will be free from everything like intrusive gossip, and will derive its colouring chiefly from the autobiographical hints and descriptions scattered through his own writings. Those of our readers who happen to know nothing of Heine, will in this way be making their acquaintance with the writer while they are learning the outline of his career.

We have said that Heine was born with the present century; but this statement is not precise, for we learn that, according to his certificate of baptism, he was born 12 December 1799.* However, as he himself says, the important point is, that he was born, and born on the banks of the Rhine, at Düsseldorf, where his father was a merchant. In his 'Reisebilder' he gives us some recollections, in his wild poetic way, of the dear old town where he spent his childhood, and of his schoolboy troubles there. We shall quote from these in butterfly fashion, sipping a little nectar here and there, without regard to any strict order:—

I first saw the light on the banks of that lovely stream, where Folly grows on the green hills, and in autumn is plucked, pressed, poured into casks, and sent into foreign lands. Believe me, I yesterday heard some one utter folly which, in anno 1811, lay in a bunch of grapes I then saw growing on the Johannisberg . . . Mon Dieu! If I had only such faith in me that I could remove mountains, the Johannisberg would be the very mountain I should send for wherever I might be; but as my faith is not so strong, imagination must help me, and it transports me at once to the lovely Rhine . . . I am again a child, and playing with other children on the Schlossplatz, at Düsseldorf on the Rhine. Yes, madam, there was I born; and I note this expressly, in case, after my death, seven cities—Schilda, Krähwinkel, Polkwitz, Bockum, Dülken, Göttingen, and Schöppenstädt—should contend for the honour of being my birth-place. Düsseldorf is a town on the Rhine; sixteen thousand men live there, and many hundred thousand men besides lie buried there . . . Among them, many of whom my mother says, that it would be better if they were still living; for example, my grandfather and my uncle, the old Herr von Geldern and the young Herr von Geldern, both such celebrated doctors, who saved so many men from death, and yet must die themselves. And the pious Ursula, who carried me in her arms when I was a child, also lies buried there, and a rosebush grows on her grave; she loved the scent of roses so well in life, and her heart was pure rose-incense and goodness. The knowing old Canon, too, lies buried there. Heavens, what an object he looked when I last saw him! *He was made up of nothing but mind and plasters*, and nevertheless studied day and night, as if he were alarmed lest the worms should find an idea too little in his head. And the little William lies there, and for this I am to blame. We were school-fellows in the Franciscan monastery, and were playing on that side of it where the Düssel flows between stone walls, and I said—'William, fetch out the kitten that has just fallen in'—and merrily he went down on to the plank which lay across the brook, snatched the kitten out of the water, but fell in himself, and was dragged out dripping and dead. *The kitten lived to a good old age* . . . Princes in that day were not the tormented race as they are now; the crown grew firmly on their heads, and at night they drew a nightcap over it, and slept peacefully, and peacefully slept the people at their feet; and when the people waked in the morning, they said—'Good morning, father!'—and the princes answered—'Good morning, dear children!' But it was suddenly quite otherwise; for when we awoke one morning at Düsseldorf, and were ready to say—'Good morning, father!'—lo! the father was gone away; and in the whole town there was nothing but dumb sorrow, everywhere a sort of funeral disposition; and people glided along silently to the market, and read the long placard placed on the door of the Town Hall. It was dismal weather; yet the lean tailor, Kilian, stood in his nankeen jacket which he usually wore only in the house, and his blue worsted stockings hung down so that his naked legs peeped out mournfully, and his thin lips trembled while he muttered the announcement to himself. And an old soldier read rather louder, and at many a word a crystal tear trickled down to his brave old moustache. I stood near him and wept in company, and asked him—'*Why we wept?*' He answered—'The Elector has abdicated.' And then he read again, and at the words, 'for the long-manifested fidelity of my subjects' and 'hereby set you free from your allegiance', he wept more than ever. It is strangely touching to see an old man like that, with faded uniform and scarred face, weep so bitterly all of a sudden. While we were reading, the electoral arms were taken down from the Town Hall; everything had such a desolate air, that it was as if an eclipse of the sun were expected ... I went home and wept, and wailed out—'The Elector has abdicated!' In vain my mother took a world of trouble to explain the thing to me. I knew what I knew; I was not to be persuaded, but went crying to bed, and in the night dreamed that the world was at an end.

The next morning, however, the sun rises as usual, and Joachim Murat is proclaimed Grand Duke, whereupon there is a holiday at the public school, and Heinrich (or Harry, for that was his baptismal name, which he afterwards had the good taste to change), perched on the bronze horse of the Electoral statue, sees quite a different scene from yesterday's:—

The next day the world was again all in order, and we had school as before, and things were got by heart as before—the Roman emperors, chronology, the nouns in *im*, the *verba irregularia*, Greek, Hebrew, geography, mental arithmetic!—heaven! my head is still dizzy with it—all must be learned by heart! And a great deal of this came in very conveniently for me in after life. For if I had not known the Roman kings by heart, it would subsequently have been quite indifferent to me whether Niebuhr had proved or had not proved that they never really existed ... But oh! the trouble I had at school with the endless dates. And with arithmetic it was still worse. What I understood best was subtraction, for that has a very practical rule: 'Four can't be taken from three, therefore I must borrow one.' But I advise every one in such a case to borrow a few extra pence, for no one can tell what may happen ... As for Latin, you have no idea, madam, what a complicated affair it is. The Romans would never have found time to conquer the world if they had first had to learn Latin. Luckily for them, they already knew in their cradles what nouns have their accusative in *im*. I, on the contrary, had to learn them by heart in the sweat of my brow; nevertheless, it is fortunate for me that I know them . . . and the fact that I have them at my finger-ends if I should ever happen to want them suddenly, affords me much inward repose and consolation in many troubled hours of life . . . Of Greek I will not say a word, I should get too much irritated. The monks in the middle ages were not so far wrong when they maintained that Greek was an invention of the devil. God knows the suffering I endured over it . . . . With Hebrew it went somewhat better, for I had always a great liking for the Jews, though to this very hour they crucify my good name; but I could never get on so far in Hebrew as my watch, which had much familiar intercourse with pawnbrokers, and in this way contracted many Jewish habits—for example, it wouldn't go on Saturdays.

Heine's parents were apparently not wealthy, but his education was cared for by his uncle, Solomon Heine, a great banker in Hamburg, so that he had no early pecuniary disadvantages to struggle with. He seems to have been very happy in his mother, who was not of Hebrew, but of Teutonic blood; he often mentions her with reverence and affection, and in the 'Buch der Lieder' there are two exquisite sonnets addressed to her, which tell how his proud spirit was subdued by the charm of her presence, and how her love was the home of his heart after restless weary wanderings:—

> Wie mächtig auch mein stolzer Muth sich blähe,
> In deiner selig süssen, trauten Nähe
> Ergreift mich oft ein demuthvolle Zagen.
>
> Und immer irrte ich nach Liebe, immer
> Nach Liebe, doch die Liebe fand ich nimmer,
> Und kehrte um nach Hause, krank und trübe.
> Doch da bist du entgegen mir gekommen,
> Und ach! was da in deinem Aug' geschwommen,
> Das war die süsse, langgesuchte Liebe.*

He was at first destined for a mercantile life, but Nature declared too strongly against this plan. 'God knows,' he has lately said in conversation with his brother, 'I would willingly have become a banker, but I could never bring myself to that pass. I very early discerned that bankers would one day be the rulers of the world.' So commerce was at length given up for law, the study of which he began in 1819 at the University of Bonn. He had already published some poems in the corner of a newspaper, and among them was one on Napoleon, the object of his youthful enthusiasm. This poem, he says in a letter to St René Taillandier, was written when he was only sixteen. It is still to be found in the 'Buch der Lieder' under the title 'Die Grenadiere', and it proves that even in its earliest efforts his genius showed a strongly specific character.

It will be easily imagined that the germs of poetry sprouted too vigorously in Heine's brain for jurisprudence to find much room there. Lectures on history and literature, we are told, were more diligently attended than lectures on law. He had taken care, too, to furnish his trunk with abundant editions of the poets, and the poet he especially studied at that time was Byron. At a later period we find his taste taking another direction, for he writes, 'Of all authors, Byron is precisely the one who excites in me the most intolerable emotion; whereas Scott, in every one of his works, gladdens my heart, soothes, and invigorates me.' Another indication of his bent in these Bonn days, was a newspaper essay, in which he attacked the Romantic school; and here also he went through that chicken-pox of authorship—the production of a tragedy. Heine's tragedy—'Almansor'—is, as might be expected, better than the majority of these youthful mistakes. The tragic collision lies in the conflict between natural affection and the deadly hatred of religion and of race—in the sacrifice of youthful lovers to the strife between Moor and Spaniard, Moslem and Christian. Some of the situations are striking, and there are passages of considerable poetic merit; but the characters are little more than shadowy vehicles for the poetry, and there is a want of clearness and probability in the structure. It was published two years later, in company with another tragedy, in one act, called 'William Ratcliffe', in which there is rather a feeble use of the Scotch second-sight after the manner of the Fate in the Greek tragedy. We smile to find Heine saying of his tragedies, in a letter to a friend soon after their publication: 'I know they will be terribly cut up, but I will confess to you in confidence that they are very good, better than my collection of poems, which are not worth a shot.' Elsewhere he tells us, that when, after one of Paganini's concerts, he was passionately complimenting the great master on his violin-playing, Paganini interrupted him thus: 'But how were you pleased with my *bows*?'

In 1820 Heine left Bonn for Göttingen. He there pursued his omission of law studies; and at the end of three months he was rusticated for a breach of the laws against duelling. While there, he had attempted a negotiation with Brockhaus for the printing of a volume of poems, and had endured that first ordeal of lovers and poets—a refusal. It was not until a year after, that he found a Berlin publisher for his first volume of poems, subsequently transformed, with additions, into the 'Buch der Lieder'. He remained between two and three years at Berlin, and the society he found there seems to have made these years an important epoch in his culture. He was one of the youngest members of a circle which assembled at the house of the poetess Elise von Hohenhausen, the translator of Byron—a circle which included Chamisso, Varnhagen*, and Rahel (Varnhagen's wife). For Rahel, Heine had a profound admiration and regard; he afterwards dedicated to her the poems included under the title 'Heimkehr', and he frequently refers to her or quotes her in a way that indicates how he valued her influence. According to his friend, F. von Hohenhausen, the opinions concerning Heine's talent were very various among his Berlin friends, and it was only a small minority that had any presentiment of his future fame. In this minority was Elise von Hohenhausen, who proclaimed Heine as the Byron of Germany; but her opinion was met with much head-shaking and opposition. We can imagine how precious was such a recognition as hers to the young poet, then only two or three and twenty, and with by no means an impressive personality for superficial eyes. Perhaps even the deep-sighted were far from detecting in that small, blond, pale young man, with quiet, gentle manners, the latent powers of ridicule and sarcasm—the terrible talons that were one day to be thrust out from the velvet paw of the young leopard.

It was apparently during this residence in Berlin that Heine united himself with the Lutheran Church. He would willingly, like many of his friends, he tells us, have remained free from all ecclesiastical ties if the authorities there had not forbidden residence in Prussia, and especially in Berlin, to every one who did not belong to one of the positive religions recognized by the State.

As Henri IV once laughingly said, '*Paris vaut bien une messe*,' so I might with reason say, '*Berlin vaut bien une prêche*';* and I could afterwards, as before, accommodate myself to the very enlightened Christianity, filtrated from all superstition, which could then be had in the churches of Berlin, and which was even free from the divinity of Christ, like turtle-soup without turtle.

At the same period, too, Heine became acquainted with Hegel. In his lately published 'Geständnisse' (Confessions), he throws on Hegel's influence over him the blue light of demoniacal wit, and confounds us by the most bewildering double-edged sarcasms; but that influence seems to have been at least more wholesome than the one which produced the mocking retractations of the 'Geständnisse'. Through all his self-satire, we discern that in those days he had something like real earnestness and enthusiasm, which are certainly not apparent in his present theistic confession of faith.

On the whole, I never felt a strong enthusiasm for this philosophy, and conviction on the subject was out of the question. I never was an abstract thinker, and I accepted the synthesis of the Hegelian doctrine without demanding any proof, since its consequences flattered my vanity. I was young and proud, and it pleased my vainglory when I learned from Hegel that the true God was not, as my grandmother believed, the God who lives in heaven, but myself here upon earth. This foolish pride had not in the least a pernicious influence on my feelings, on the contrary, it heightened these to the pitch of heroism. I was at that time so lavish in generosity and self-sacrifice, that I must assuredly have eclipsed the most brilliant deeds of those good *bourgeois* of virtue who acted merely from a sense of duty, and simply obeyed the laws of morality.

His sketch of Hegel is irresistibly amusing; but we must warn the reader that Heine's anecdotes are often mere devices of style by which he conveys his satire or opinions. The reader will see that he does not neglect an opportunity of giving a sarcastic lash or two, in passing, to Meyerbeer, for whose music he has a great contempt. The sarcasm conveyed in the substitution of *reputation* for *music* and *journalists* for *musicians*, might perhaps escape any one unfamiliar with the sly and unexpected turns of Heine's ridicule.

To speak frankly, I seldom understood him, and only arrived at the meaning of his words by subsequent reflection. I believe he wished not to be understood; and hence his practice of sprinkling his discourse with modifying parentheses; hence, perhaps, his preference for persons of whom he knew that they did not understand him, and to whom he all the more willingly granted the honour of his familiar acquaintance. Thus every one in Berlin wondered at the intimate companionship of the profound Hegel with the late Heinrich Beer, a brother of Giacomo Meyerbeer, who is universally known by his reputation, and who has been celebrated by the cleverest journalists. This Beer, namely Heinrich, was a thoroughly stupid fellow, and indeed was afterwards actually declared imbecile by his family, and placed under guardianship, because instead of making a name for himself in art or in science by means of his great fortune, he squandered his money on childish trifles; and, for example, one day bought 6,000 thalers' worth of walking-sticks. This poor man, who had no wish to pass either for a great tragic dramatist, or for a great star-gazer, or for a laurel-crowned musical genius, a rival of Mozart and Rossini, and preferred giving his money for walking-sticks—this degenerate Beer enjoyed Hegel's most confidential society; he was the philosopher's bosom friend, his Pylades, and accompanied him everywhere like his shadow. The equally witty and gifted Felix Mendelssohn once sought to explain this phenomenon, by maintaining that Hegel did not understand Heinrich Beer. I now believe, however, that the real ground of that intimacy consisted in this—Hegel was convinced that no word of what he said was understood by Heinrich Beer; and he could therefore, in his presence, give himself up to all the intellectual outpourings of the moment. In general, Hegel's conversation was a sort of monologue, sighed forth by starts in a noiseless voice; the odd roughness of his expressions often struck me, and many of them have remained in my memory. One beautiful starlight evening we stood together at the window, and I, a young man of one-and-twenty, having just had a good dinner and finished my coffee, spoke with enthusiasm of the stars, and called them the habitations of the departed. But the master muttered to himself, 'The stars! hum! hum! The stars are only a brilliant leprosy on the face of the heavens.' 'For God's sake,' I cried, 'is there, then, no happy place above, where virtue is rewarded after death?' But he, staring at me with his pale eyes, said, cuttingly, 'So you want a bonus for having taken care of your sick mother, and refrained from poisoning your worthy brother?' At these words he looked anxiously round, but appeared immediately set at rest when he observed that it was only Heinrich Beer, who had approached to invite him to a game at whist.

In 1823, Heine returned to Göttingen to complete his career as a law student, and this time he gave evidence of advanced mental maturity, not only by producing many of the charming poems subsequently included in the 'Reise-bilder', but also by prosecuting his professional studies diligently enough to leave Göttingen, in 1825, as *Doctor juris*. Hereupon he settled at Hamburg as an advocate, but his profession seems to have been the least pressing of his occupations. In those days, a small blond young man, with the brim of his hat drawn over his nose, his coat flying open, and his hands stuck in his trouser-pockets, might be seen stumbling along the streets of Hamburg, staring from side to side, and appearing to have small regard to the figure he made in the eyes of the good citizens. Occasionally an inhabitant, more literary than usual, would point out this young man to his companion as *Heinrich Heine*; but in general, the young poet had not to endure the inconvenien-ces of being a lion. His poems were devoured, but he was not asked to devour flattery in return. Whether because the fair Hamburgers acted in the spirit of Johnson's advice to Hannah More*—to 'consider what her flattery was worth before she choked him with it'—or for some other reason,

Heine, according to the testimony of August Lewald, to whom we owe these particulars of his Hamburg life, was left free from the persecution of tea-parties. Not, however, from another persecution of genius—nervous headaches, which some persons, we are told, regarded as an improbable fiction, intended as a pretext for raising a delicate white hand to his forehead. It is probable that the sceptical persons alluded to were themselves untroubled with nervous head-ache, and that their hands were *not* delicate. Slight details these, but worth telling about a man of genius, because they help us to keep in mind that he is, after all, our brother, having to endure the petty every-day ills of life as we have; with this difference, that his heightened sensibility converts what are mere insect stings for us into scorpion stings for him.

It was, perhaps, in these Hamburg days that Heine paid the visit to Goethe, of which he gives us this charming little picture:—

When I visited him in Weimar, and stood before him, I involuntarily glanced at his side to see whether the eagle was not there with the lightning in his beak. I was nearly speaking Greek to him; but, as I observed that he understood German, I stated to him in German, that the plums on the road between Jena and Weimar were very good. I had for so many long winter nights thought over what lofty and profound things I would say to Goethe, if ever I saw him. And when I saw him at last, I said to him, that the Saxon plums were very good! And Goethe smiled.

During the next few years, Heine produced the most popular of all his works—those which have won him his place as the greatest of living German poets and humorists. Between 1826 and 1829, appeared the four volumes of the 'Reisebilder' (Pictures of Travel), and the 'Buch der Lieder' (Book of Songs)—a volume of lyrics, of which it is hard to say whether their greatest charm is the lightness and finish of their style, their vivid and original imaginativeness, or their simple, pure sensibility. In his 'Reisebilder,' Heine carries us with him to the Harz, to the isle of Norderney, to his native town Düsseldorf, to Italy, and to England, sketching scenery and character, now with the wildest, most fantastic humour, now with the finest idyllic sensibility,— letting his thoughts wander from poetry to politics, from criticism to dreamy reverie, and blending fun, imagination, reflection, and satire in a sort of exquisite, ever-varying shimmer, like the hues of the opal.

Heine's journey to England did not at all heighten his regard for the English. He calls our language the 'hiss of egoism' (*Zischlaute des Egoismus*); and his ridicule of English awkwardness is as merciless as—English ridicule of German awkwardness. His antipathy towards us seems to have grown in intensity, like many of his other antipathies; and in his *Vermischte Schriften* he is more bitter than ever. Let us quote one of his philippics; since bitters are understood to be wholesome.

It is certainly a frightful injustice to pronounce sentence of con- demnation on an entire people. But with regard to the English, momentary disgust might betray me into this injustice; and on looking at the mass, I easily forget the many brave and noble men who distinguished themselves by intellect and love of freedom. But these, especially the British poets, were always all the more glaringly in contrast with the rest of the nation; they were isolated martyrs to their national relations; and, besides, great geniuses do not belong to the particular land of their birth: they scarcely belong to this earth, the Golgotha of their sufferings. The mass—the English blockheads, God forgive me!—are hateful to me in my inmost soul; and I often regard them not at all as my fellow-men, but as miserable automata—machines, whose motive power is egoism. In these moods, it seems to me as if I heard the whizzing wheel-work by which they think, feel, reckon, digest, and pray: their praying, their mechanical Anglican church-going, with the gilt Prayer-book under their arms, their stupid, tiresome Sunday, their awkward piety, is most of all odious to me. I am firmly convinced that a blaspheming Frenchman is a more pleasing sight for the Divinity than a praying Englishman.

On his return from England, Heine was employed at Munich in editing the *Allgemeinen Politischen Annalen*, but in 1830 he was again in the north, and the news of the July Revolution surprised him on the island of Heligoland. He has given us a graphic picture of his democratic enthusiasm in those days in some letters, apparently written from Heligoland, which he has inserted in his book on Börne.* We quote some passages, not only for their biographic interest as showing a phase of Heine's mental history, but because they are a specimen of his power in that kind of dithyrambic writing which, in less masterly hands, easily becomes ridiculous:—

The thick packet of newspapers arrived from the Continent with these warm, glowing-hot tidings. They were sunbeams wrapped up in packing-paper, and they inflamed my soul till it burst into the wildest conflagration . . . It is all like a dream to me; especially the name, Lafayette, sounds to me like a legend out of my earliest childhood. Does he really sit again on horseback, commanding the National Guard? I almost fear it may not be true, for it is in print. I will myself go to Paris, to be convinced of it with my bodily eyes . . . It must be splendid, when he rides through the streets, the citizen of two worlds, the god-like old man, with his silver locks streaming down his sacred shoulder . . . He greets, with his dear old eyes, the grandchildren of those who once fought with him for freedom and equality . . . It is now sixty years since he returned from America with the Declaration of Human Rights, the decalogue of the world's new creed, which was revealed to him amid the thunders and lightnings of cannon . . . And the tri-coloured flag waves again on the towers of Paris, and its streets resound with the Marseillaise! . . . It is all over with my yearning for repose. I now know again what I will do, what I ought to do, what I must do . . . I am the son of the Revolution, and seize again the hallowed weapons on which my mother pronounced her magic benediction . . . Flowers! flowers! I will crown my head for the death-fight. And the lyre too, reach me the lyre, that I may sing a battle-song . . . Words like flaming stars, that shoot down from the heavens, and burn up the palaces, and illuminate the huts . . . Words like bright javelins, that whirr up to the seventh heaven and strike the pious hypocrites who have skulked into the Holy of Holies . . . I am all joy and song, all sword and flame! Perhaps, too, all delirium . . . One of those sunbeams wrapped in brown paper has flown to my brain, and set my thoughts aglow. In vain I dip my head into the sea. No water extinguishes this Greek fire . . . Even the poor Heligolanders shout for joy, although they have only a sort of dim instinct of what has occurred. The fisherman who yesterday took me over to the little sand island, which is the bathing-place here, said to me smilingly, 'The poor people have won!' Yes; instinctively the people comprehend such events, perhaps better than we, with all our means of knowledge. Thus Frau von Varnhagen once told me that when the issue of the Battle of Leipzig was not yet known, the maid-servant suddenly rushed into the room with the sorrowful cry, 'The nobles have won!' . . . This morning another packet of newspapers is come. I devour them like manna. Child that I am, affecting details touch me yet more than the momentous whole. Oh, if I could but see the dog Medor . . . The dog Medor brought his master his gun and cartridge-box, and when his master fell, and was buried with his fellow-heroes in the Court of the Louvre, there stayed the poor dog like a monument of faithfulness, sitting motionless on the grave, day and night, eating but little of the food that was offered him—burying the greater part of it in the earth, perhaps as nourishment for his buried master!

The enthusiasm which was kept thus at boiling heat by imagination, cooled down rapidly when brought into contact with reality. In the same book he indicates, in his caustic way, the commencement of that change in his political *temperature*—for it cannot be called a change in opinion— which has drawn down on him immense vituperation from some of the patriotic party, but which seems to have resulted simply from the essential antagonism between keen wit and fanaticism.

On the very first days of my arrival in Paris, I observed that things wore, in reality, quite different colours from those which had been shed on them, when in perspective, by the light of my enthusiasm. The silver locks which I saw fluttering so majestically on the shoulders of Lafayette, the hero of two worlds, were metamorphosed into a brown perruque, which made a pitiable covering for a narrow skull. And even the dog Medor, which I visited in the Court of the Louvre, and which, encamped under tri-coloured flags and trophies, very quietly allowed himself to be fed—he was not at all the right dog, but quite an ordinary brute, who assumed to himself merits not his own, as often happens with the French; and, like many others, he made a profit out of the glory of the Revolution . . . He was pampered and patronized, perhaps promoted to the highest posts, while the true Medor, some days after the battle, modestly slunk out of sight, like the true people who created the Revolution.

That it was not merely interest in French politics which sent Heine to Paris in 1831, but also a perception that German air was not friendly to sympathizers in July revolutions, is humorously intimated in the 'Geständnisse'.

I had done much and suffered much, and when the sun of the July Revolution arose in France, I had become very weary, and needed some recreation. Also, my native air was every day more unhealthy for me, and it was time I should seriously think of a change of climate. I had visions: the clouds terrified me, and made all sorts of ugly faces at me. It often seemed to me as if the sun were a Prussian cockade; at night I dreamed of a hideous black eagle, which gnawed my liver; and I was very melancholy. Add to this, I had become acquainted with an old Berlin Justizrath, who had spent many years in the fortress of Spandau, and he related to me how unpleasant it is when one is obliged to wear irons in winter. For myself I thought it very unchristian that the irons were not warmed a trifle. If the irons were warmed a little for us they would not make so unpleasant an impression, and even chilly natures might then bear them very well; it would be only proper consideration, too, if the fetters were perfumed with essence of roses and laurels, as is the case in this country (France). I asked my Justizrath whether he often got oysters to eat at Spandau? He said, No; Spandau was too far from the sea. Moreover, he said meat was very scarce there, and there was no kind of *volaille* except flies, which fell into one's soup . . . Now, as I really needed some recreation, and, as Spandau is too far from the sea for oysters to be got there, and the Spandau fly-soup did not seem very appetizing to me, as, besides all this, the Prussian chains are very cold in winter, and could not be conducive to my health, I resolved to visit Paris.

Since this time Paris has been Heine's home, and his best prose works have been written either to inform the Germans on French affairs or to inform the French on German philosophy and literature. He became a correspondent of the *Allgemeine Zeitung*, and his correspondence, which extends, with an interruption of several years, from 1831 to 1844, forms the volume entitled 'Französische Zustände' (French Affairs), and the second and third volume of his 'Vermischte

Schriften'. It is a witty and often wise commentary on public men and public events: Louis Philippe, Casimir Périer, Thiers, Guizot, Rothschild, the Catholic party, the Socialist party, have their turn of satire and appreciation, for Heine deals out both with an impartiality which made his less favourable critics—Börne, for example—charge him with the rather incompatible sins of reckless caprice and venality. Literature and art alternate with politics: we have now a sketch of George Sand, or a description of one of Horace Vernet's pictures,—now a criticism of Victor Hugo, or of Liszt,—now an irresistible caricature of Spontini, or Kalkbrenner,*—and occasionally the predominant satire is relieved by a fine saying or a genial word of admiration. And all is done with that airy lightness, yet precision of touch, which distinguishes Heine beyond any living writer. The charge of venality was loudly made against Heine in Germany: first, it was said that he was paid to write; then, that he was paid to abstain from writing; and the accusations were supposed to have an irrefragable basis in the fact that he accepted a stipend from the French government. He has never attempted to conceal the reception of that stipend, and we think his statement (in the 'Vermischte Schriften') of the circumstances under which it was offered and received, is a sufficient vindication of himself and M. Guizot from any dishonour in the matter.

It may be readily imagined that Heine, with so large a share of the Gallic element as he has in his composition, was soon at his ease in Parisian society, and the years here were bright with intellectual activity and social enjoyment. 'His wit,' wrote August Lewald, 'is a perpetual gushing fountain; he throws off the most delicious descriptions with amazing facility, and sketches the most comic characters in conversation.' Such a man could not be neglected in Paris, and Heine was sought on all sides—as a guest in distinguished salons, as a possible proselyte in the circle of the Saint Simonians. His literary productiveness seems to have been furthered by this congenial life, which, however, was soon to some extent embittered by the sense of exile; for since 1835 both his works and his person have been the object of denunciation by the German governments. Between 1833 and 1845 appeared the four volumes of the 'Salon', 'Die Romantische Schule' (both written, in the first instance, in French), the book on Börne, 'Atta Troll', a romantic poem, 'Deutschland', an exquisitely humorous poem, describing his last visit to Germany, and containing some grand passages of serious writing; and the 'Neue Gedichte', a collection of lyrical poems. Among the most interesting of his prose works are the second volume of the 'Salon', which contains a survey of religion and philosophy in Germany, and the 'Romantische Schule', a delightful introduction to that phase of German literature known as the Romantic school. The book on Börne, which appeared in 1840, two or three years after the death of that writer, excited great indignation in Germany, as a wreaking of vengeance on the dead, an insult to the memory of a man who had worked and suffered in the cause of freedom—a cause which was Heine's own. Börne, we may observe parenthetically for the information of those who are not familiar with recent German literature, was a remarkable political writer of the ultra-liberal party in Germany, who resided in Paris at the same time with Heine: a man of stern, uncompromising partisanship and bitter humour. Without justifying Heine's production of this book, we see excuses for him which should temper the condemnation passed on it. There was a radical opposition of nature between him and Börne; to use his own distinction, Heine is a Hellene—sensuous, realistic, exquisitely alive to the beautiful; while Börne was a Nazarene—ascetic, spiritualistic, despising the pure artist as destitute of earnestness. Heine has too keen a perception of practical absurdities and damaging exaggerations ever to become a thorough-going partisan; and with a love of freedom, a faith in the ultimate triumph of democratic principles, of which we see no just reason to doubt the genuineness and consistency, he has been unable to satisfy more zealous and one-sided liberals by giving his adhesion to their views and measures, or by adopting a denunciatory tone against those in the opposite ranks. Börne could not forgive what he regarded as Heine's epicurean indifference and artistic dalliance, and he at length gave vent to his antipathy in savage attacks on him through the press, accusing him of utterly lacking character and principle, and even of writing under the influence of venal motives. To these attacks Heine remained absolutely mute—from contempt according to his own account; but the retort, which he resolutely refrained from making during Börne's life, comes in this volume published after his death with the concentrated force of long-gathering thunder. The utterly inexcusable part of the book is the caricature of Börne's friend, Madame Wohl, and the scurrilous insinuations concerning Börne's domestic life. It is said, we know not with how much truth, that Heine had to answer for these in a duel with Madame Wohl's husband, and that, after receiving a serious wound, he promised to withdraw the offensive matter from a future edition. That edition, however, has not been called for. Whatever else we may think of the book, it is impossible to deny its transcendent talent—the dramatic vigour with which Börne is made present to us, the critical acumen with which he is characterized, and the wonderful play of wit, pathos, and thought which runs through the whole. But we will let Heine speak for himself, and first we will give part of his graphic description of the way in which Börne's mind and manners grated on his taste:—

To the disgust which, in intercourse with Börne, I was in danger of feeling towards those who surrounded him, was added the annoyance I felt from his perpetual talk about politics. Nothing but political argument, and again political argument, even at table, where he managed to hunt me out. At dinner, when I so gladly forget all the vexations of the world, he spoiled the best dishes for me by his patriotic gall, which he poured as a bitter sauce over everything. Calf's feet, *à la maître d'hôtel*, then my innocent *bonne bouche*, he completely spoiled for me by Job's tidings from Germany, which he scraped together out of the most unreliable newspapers. And then his accursed remarks, which spoiled one's appetite! . . . This was a sort of table-talk which did not greatly exhilarate me, and I avenged myself by affecting an excessive, almost impassioned indifference for the objects of Börne's enthusiasm. For example, Börne was indignant that immediately on my arrival in Paris, I had nothing better to do than to write for

German papers a long account of the Exhibition of Pictures. I omit all discussion as to whether that interest in Art which induced me to undertake this work was so utterly irreconcilable with the revolutionary interests of the day: but Börne saw in it a proof of my indifference towards the sacred cause of humanity, and I could in my turn spoil the taste of his patriotic *sauerkraut* for him by talking all dinner-time of nothing but pictures, of Robert's 'Reapers', Horace Vernet's 'Judith', and Scheffer's 'Faust' . . . That I never thought it worth while to discuss my political principles with him it is needless to say; and once when he declared that he had found a contradiction in my writings, I satisfied myself with the ironical answer, 'You are mistaken, *mon cher*; such contradictions never occur in my works, for always before I begin to write, I read over the statement of my political principles in my previous writings, that I may not contradict myself, and that no one may be able to reproach me with apostasy from my liberal principles.'

And here is his own account of the spirit in which the book was written:—

I was never Börne's friend, nor was I ever his enemy. The displeasure which he could often excite in me was never very important, and he atoned for it sufficiently by the cold silence which I opposed to all his accusations and raillery. While he lived I wrote not a line against him, I never thought about him, I ignored him completely; and that enraged him beyond measure. If I now speak of him, I do so neither out of enthusiasm nor out of uneasiness; I am conscious of the coolest impartiality. I write here neither an apology nor a critique, and as in painting the man I go on my own observation, the image I present of him ought perhaps to be regarded as a real portrait. And such a monument is due to him—to the greater wrestler who, in the arena of our political games, wrestled so courageously, and earned, if not the laurel, certainly the crown of oak leaves. I give an image with his true features, without idealization—the more like him the more honourable for his memory. He was neither a genius nor a hero; he was no Olympian god. He was a man, a denizen of this earth; he was a good writer and a great patriot . . . Beautiful delicious peace, which I feel at this moment in the depths of my soul! Thou rewardest me sufficiently for everything I have done and for everything I have despised . . . I shall defend myself neither from the reproach of indifference nor from the suspicion of venality. I have for years, during the life of the insinuator, held such self-justification unworthy of me; now even decency demands silence. That would be a frightful spectacle!—polemics between Death and Exile! Dost thou stretch out to me a beseeching hand from the grave? Without rancour I reach mine towards thee . . . See how noble it is and pure! It was never soiled by pressing the hands of the mob, any more than by the impure gold of the people's enemy. In reality thou hast never injured me . . . In all thy insinuations there is not a *louis-d'or*'s worth of truth.

In one of these years Heine was married, and, in deference to the sentiments of his wife, married according to the rites of the Catholic Church. On this fact busy rumour afterwards founded the story of his conversion to Catholicism, and could of course name the day and the spot on which he abjured Protestantism. In his 'Geständnisse' Heine publishes a denial of this rumour; less, he says, for the sake of depriving the Catholics of the solace they may derive from their belief in a new convert, than in order to cut off from another party the more spiteful satisfaction of bewailing his instability:—

That statement of time and place was entirely correct. I was actually on the specified day in the specified church, which was, moreover, a Jesuit church, namely Saint Sulpice; and I then went through a religious act. But this act was no odious abjuration, but a very innocent conjugation; that is to say, my marriage, already performed according to the civil law, there received the ecclesiastical consecration, because my wife, whose family are staunch Catholics, would not have thought her marriage sacred enough without such a ceremony. And I would on no account cause this beloved being any uneasiness or disturbance in her religious views.

For sixteen years—from 1831 to 1847—Heine lived that rapid concentrated life which is known only in Paris; but then, alas! stole on the 'days of darkness', and they were to be many. In 1847 he felt the approach of the terrible spinal disease which has for seven years chained him to his bed in acute suffering. The last time he went out of doors, he tells us, was in May 1848:—

With difficulty I dragged myself to the Louvre, and I almost sank down as I entered the magnificent hall where the ever-blessed goddess of beauty, our beloved Lady of Milo, stands on her pedestal. At her feet I lay long, and wept so bitterly that a stone must have pitied me. The goddess looked compassionately on me, but at the same time disconsolately, as if she would say: Dost thou not see, then, that I have no arms, and thus cannot help thee?

Since 1848, then, this poet, whom the lovely objects of Nature have always 'haunted like a passion', has not descended from the second storey of a Parisian house; this man of hungry intellect has been shut out from all direct observation of life, all contact with society, except such as is derived from visitors to his sick-room. The terrible nervous disease has affected his eyes; the sight of one is utterly gone, and he can only raise the lid of the other by lifting it with his finger. Opium alone is the beneficent genius that stills his pain. We hardly know whether to call it an alleviation or an intensification of the torture that Heine retains his mental vigour, his poetic imagination, and his incisive wit; for if this intellectual activity fills up a blank, it widens the sphere of suffering. His brother described him in 1851 as still, in moments when the hand of pain was not too heavy on him, the same Heinrich Heine, poet and satirist by turns. In such moments, he would narrate the strangest things in the gravest manner. But when he came to an end, he would roguishly lift up the lid of his right eye with his finger to see the impression he had produced; and if his audience had been listening with a serious face, he would break into Homeric laughter. We have other proof than personal testimony that Heine's disease allows his genius to retain much of its energy, in the 'Romanzero', a volume of poems published in 1851, and written chiefly during the first three years of his illness; and in the first volume of the 'Vermischte Schriften', also the product of recent years. Very plaintive is the poet's own description of his condition, in the epilogue to the 'Romanzero':—

Do I really exist? My body is so shrunken that I am hardly anything but a voice; and my bed reminds me of the singing grave of the magician Merlin, which lies in the forest of Brozeliand, in

Brittany, under tall oaks whose tops soar like green flames towards heaven. Aha! I envy thee those trees and the fresh breeze that moves their branches, brother Merlin, for no green leaf rustles about my mattress-grave in Paris, where early and late I hear nothing but the rolling of vehicles, hammering, quarrelling, and piano-strumming. A grave without repose, death without the privileges of the dead, who have no debts to pay, and need write neither letters nor books—that is a piteous condition. Long ago the measure has been taken for my coffin and for my necrology, but I die so slowly, that the process is tedious for me as well as my friends. But patience; everything has an end. You will one day find the booth closed where the puppet-show of my humour has so often delighted you.

As early as 1850, it was rumoured that since Heine's illness a change had taken place in his religious views; and as rumour seldom stops short of extremes, it was soon said that he had become a thorough pietist, Catholics and Protestants by turns claiming him as a convert. Such a change in so uncompromising an iconoclast, in a man who had been so zealous in his negations as Heine, naturally excited considerable sensation in the camp he was supposed to have quitted, as well as in that he was supposed to have joined. In the second volume of the 'Salon', and in the 'Romantische Schule', written in 1834 and 1835, the doctrine of Pantheism is dwelt on with a fervour and unmixed seriousness which show that Pantheism was then an animating faith to Heine, and he attacks what he considers the false spiritualism and asceticism of Christianity as the enemy of true beauty in Art, and of social well-being. Now, however, it was said that Heine had recanted all his heresies; but from the fact that visitors to his sick-room brought away very various impressions as to his actual religious views, it seemed probable that his love of mystification had found a tempting opportunity for exercise on this subject, and that, as one of his friends said, he was not inclined to pour out unmixed wine to those who asked for a sample out of mere curiosity. At length, in the epilogue to the 'Romanzero', dated 1851, there appeared, amidst much mystifying banter, a declaration that he had embraced Theism and the belief in a future life, and what chiefly lent an air of seriousness and reliability to this affirmation, was the fact that he took care to accompany it with certain negations:—

As concerns myself, I can boast of no particular progress in politics; I adhered (after 1848) to the same democratic principles which had the homage of my youth, and for which I have ever since glowed with increasing fervour. In theology, on the contrary, I must accuse myself of retrogression, since, as I have already confessed, I returned to the old superstition—to a personal God. This fact is, once for all, not to be stifled, as many enlightened and well-meaning friends would fain have had it. But I must expressly contradict the report that my retrograde movement has carried me as far as to the threshold of a Church, and that I have even been received into her lap. No: my religious convictions and views have remained free from any tincture of ecclesiasticism; no chiming of bells has allured me, no altar-candles have dazzled me. I have dallied with no dogmas, and have not utterly renounced my reason.

This sounds like a serious statement. But what shall we say to a convert who plays with his newly-acquired belief in a future life, as Heine does in the very next page? He says to his reader:—

Console thyself; we shall meet again in a better world, where I also mean to write thee better books. I take for granted that my health will there be improved, and that Swedenborg has not deceived me. He relates, namely, with great confidence, that we shall peacefully carry on our old occupations in the other world, just as we have done in this; that we shall there preserve our individuality unaltered, and that death will produce no particular change in our organic development. Swedenborg is a thoroughly honourable fellow, and quite worthy of credit in what he tells us about the other world, where he saw with his own eyes the persons who had played a great part on our earth. Most of them, he says, remained unchanged, and busied themselves with the same things as formerly; they remained stationary, were old-fashioned, *roco-co*—which now and then produced a ludicrous effect. For example, our dear Dr Martin Luther kept fast by his doctrine of Grace, about which he had for 300 years daily written down the same mouldy arguments—just in the same way as the late Baron Ekstein, who during twenty years printed in the *Allgemeine Zeitung* one and the same article, perpetually chewing over again the old cud of jesuitical doctrine. But, as we have said, all persons who once figured here below were not found by Swedenborg in such a state of fossil immutability: many had considerably developed their character, both for good and evil, in the other world; and this gave rise to some singular results. Some who had been heroes and saints on earth had *there* sunk into scamps and good-for-nothings; and there were examples, too, of a contrary transformation. For instance, the fumes of self-conceit mounted to Saint Anthony's head when he learned what immense veneration and adoration had been paid to him by all Christendom; and he who here below withstood the most terrible temptations, was now quite an impertinent rascal and dissolute gallows-bird, who vied with his pig in rolling himself in the mud. The chaste Susanna, from having been excessively vain of her virtue, which she thought indomitable, came to a shameful fall, and she who once so gloriously resisted the two old men, was a victim to the seductions of the young Absalom, the son of David. On the contrary, Lot's daughters had in the lapse of time become very virtuous, and passed in the other world for models of propriety: the old man, alas! had stuck to the wine-flask.

In his 'Geständnisse', the retractation of former opinions and profession of Theism are renewed, but in a strain of irony that repels our sympathy and baffles our psychology. Yet what strange, deep pathos is mingled with the audacity of the following passage!—

What avails it me, that enthusiastic youths and maidens crown my marble bust with laurel, when the withered hands of an aged nurse are pressing Spanish flies behind my ears? What avails it me, that all the roses of Shiraz glow and waft incense for me? Alas! Shiraz is 2,000 miles from the Rue d'Amsterdam, where, in the wearisome loneliness of my sickroom, I get no scent except it be, perhaps, the perfume of warmed towels. Alas! God's satire weighs heavily on me. The great Author of the universe, the Aristophanes of Heaven, was bent on demonstrating, with crushing force, to me, the little, earthly, German Aristophanes, how my wittiest sarcasms are only pitiful attempts at jesting in comparison with His, and how miserably I am beneath Him in humour, in colossal mockery.

For our own part, we regard the paradoxical irreverence with which Heine professes his theoretical reverence as pathological, as the diseased exhibition of a predominant tendency urged into anomalous action by the pressure of pain and mental privation—as the delirium of wit starved of its proper nourishment. It is not for us to condemn, who have never had the same burthen laid on us; it is not for pygmies at their ease to criticize the writhings of the Titan chained to the rock.

On one other point we must touch before quitting Heine's personal history. There is a standing accusation against him in some quarters of wanting political principle, of wishing to denationalize himself, and of indulging in insults against his native country. Whatever ground may exist for these accusations, that ground is not, so far as we see, to be found in his writings. He may not have much faith in German revolutions and revolutionists; experience, in his case as in that of others, may have thrown his millennial anticipations into more distant perspective; but we see no evidence that he has ever swerved from his attachment to the principles of freedom, or written anything which to a philosophic mind is incompatible with true patriotism. He has expressly denied the report that he wished to become naturalized in France; and his yearning towards his native land and the accents of his native language is expressed with a pathos the more reliable from the fact that he is sparing in such effusions. We do not see why Heine's satire of the blunders and foibles of his fellow-countrymen should be denounced as the crime of *lèse-patrie*, any more than the political caricatures of any other satirist. The real offences of Heine are his occasional coarseness and his unscrupulous personalities, which are reprehensible, not because they are directed against his fellow-countrymen, but because they are *personalities*. That these offences have their precedents in men whose memory the world delights to honour does not remove their turpitude, but it is a fact which should modify our condemnation in a particular case; unless, indeed, we are to deliver our judgements on a principle of compensation—making up for our indulgence in one direction by our severity in another. On this ground of coarseness and personality, a true bill may be found against Heine; *not*, we think, on the ground that he has laughed at what is laughable in his compatriots. Here is a specimen of the satire under which we suppose German patriots wince:—

Rhenish Bavaria was to be the starting-point of the German revolution. Zweibrücken was the Bethlehem in which the infant Saviour—Freedom—lay in the cradle, and gave whimpering promise of redeeming the world. Near his cradle bellowed many an ox, who afterwards, when his horns were reckoned on, showed himself a very harmless brute. It was confidently believed that the German revolution would begin in Zweibrücken, and everything was there ripe for an outbreak. But, as has been hinted, the tender-heartedness of some persons frustrated that illegal undertaking. For example, among the Bipontine conspirators there was a tremendous braggart, who was always loudest in his rage, who boiled over with the hatred of tyranny, and this man was fixed on to strike the first blow, by cutting down a sentinel who kept an important post . . . 'What!' cried the man, when this order was given him—'What!—me! Can you expect so horrible, so bloodthirsty an act of me? I—*I*, kill an innocent sentinel? I, who am father of a family! And this sentinel is perhaps also father of a family. One father of a family kill another father of a family? Yes! Kill—murder!'

In political matters, Heine, like all men whose intellect and taste predominate too far over their impulses to allow of their becoming partisans, is offensive alike to the aristocrat and the democrat. By the one he is denounced as a man who holds incendiary principles, by the other as a half-hearted 'trimmer'. He has no sympathy, as he says, with 'that vague, barren pathos, that useless effervescence of enthusiasm, which plunges, with the spirit of a martyr, into an ocean of generalities, and which always reminds me of the American sailor, who had so fervent an enthusiasm for General Jackson, that he at last sprang from the top of a mast into the sea, crying, *I die for General Jackson!*'

But thou liest, Brutus, thou liest, Cassius, and thou, too, liest, Asinius, in maintaining that my ridicule attacks those ideas which are the precious acquisition of Humanity, and for which I myself have so striven and suffered. No! for the very reason that those ideas constantly hover before the poet in glorious splendour and majesty, he is the more irresistibly overcome by laughter when he sees how rudely, awkwardly, and clumsily those ideas are seized and mirrored in the contracted minds of contemporaries ... There are mirrors which have so rough a surface that even an Apollo reflected in them becomes a caricature, and excites our laughter. *But we laugh then only at the caricature, not at the god.*

For the rest, why should we demand of Heine that he should be a hero, a patriot, a solemn prophet, any more than we should demand of a gazelle that it should draw well in harness? Nature has not made him of her sterner stuff—not of iron and adamant, but of pollen of flowers, the juice of the grape, and Puck's mischievous brain, plenteously mixing also the dews of kindly affection and the gold-dust of noble thoughts. It is, after all, a *tribute* which his enemies pay him when they utter their bitterest dictum, namely, that he is '*nur Dichter*'—only a poet. Let us accept this point of view for the present, and, leaving all consideration of him as a man, look at him simply as a poet and literary artist.

Heine is essentially a lyric poet. The finest products of his genius are

> Short swallow flights of song that dip
> Their wings in tears, and skim away,*

and they are so emphatically songs that, in reading them, we feel as if each must have a twin melody born in the same moment and by the same inspiration. Heine is too impressible and mercurial for any sustained production; even in his short lyrics his tears sometimes pass into laughter and his laughter into tears; and his longer poems, 'Atta Troll' and 'Deutschland', are full of Ariosto-like transitions. His song has a wide compass of notes: he can take us to the shores of the Northern Sea and thrill us by the sombre sublimity of his pictures and dreamy fancies; he can draw forth our tears by the voice he gives to our own sorrows, or to the sorrows of 'Poor Peter'; he can throw a cold shudder over us by a mysterious legend, a ghost story, or a still more ghastly rendering of hard reality; he can charm us by a quiet idyll, shake us with laughter at his overflowing fun, or give us a piquant sensation of surprise by the ingenuity of his transitions from the lofty to the ludicrous. This last power is not, indeed, essentially poetical; but only a poet can use it with the same success as Heine, for only a poet can poise our emotion and expectation at such a height as to give effect to the sudden fall. Heine's greatest power as a poet lies in his simple pathos, in the ever varied but always natural expression he has given to the tender emotions. We may perhaps indicate this phase of his genius by referring to Wordsworth's beautiful little poem, 'She dwelt among the Untrodden Ways'; the conclusion—

> She dwelt alone, and few could know
> When Lucy ceased to be;
> But she is in her grave, and, oh!
> The difference to me—*

is entirely in Heine's manner; and so is Tennyson's poem of a dozen lines, called 'Circumstance'. Both these poems have Heine's pregnant simplicity. But, lest this comparison should mislead, we must say that there is no general resemblance between either Wordsworth, or Tennyson, and Heine. Their greatest qualities lie quite away from the light, delicate lucidity, the easy, rippling music, of Heine's style. The distinctive charm of his lyrics may best be seen by comparing them with Goethe's. Both have the same masterly, finished simplicity and rhythmic grace; but there is more thought mingled with Goethe's feeling—his lyrical genius is a vessel that draws more water than Heine's, and, though it seems to glide along with equal ease, we have a sense of greater weight and force accompanying the grace of its movement. But, for this very reason, Heine touches our hearts more strongly; his songs are all music and feeling—they are like birds that not only enchant us with their delicious notes, but nestle against us with their soft breasts, and make us feel the agitated beating of their hearts. He indicates a whole sad history in a single quatrain: there is not an image in it, not a thought; but it is beautiful, simple, and perfect as a 'big round tear'—it is pure feeling breathed in pure music:—

> Anfangs wollt' ich fast verzagen
> Und ich glaubt' ich trug es nie,
> Und ich hab' es doch getragen,—
> Aber fragt mich nur nicht, wie.[1]

He excels equally in the more imaginative expression of feeling: he represents it by a brief image, like a finely-cut cameo; he expands it into a mysterious dream, or dramatizes it in a little story, half ballad, half idyll; and in all these forms his art is so perfect, that we never have a sense of artificiality or of unsuccessful effort; but all seems to have developed itself by the same beautiful necessity that brings forth vine-leaves and grapes and the natural curls of child-hood. Of Heine's humorous poetry, 'Deutschland' is the most charming specimen—charming, especially, because its wit and humour grow out of a rich loam of thought. 'Atta Troll' is more original, more various, more fantastic; but it is too great a strain on the imagination to be a general favourite. We have said, that feeling is the element in which Heine's poetic genius habitually floats; but he can occasion-ally soar to a higher region, and impart deep significance to picturesque symbolism; he can flash a sublime thought over the past and into the future; he can pour forth a lofty strain of hope or indignation. Few could forget, after once hearing them, the stanzas at the close of 'Deutschland', in which he warns the King of Prussia not to incur the irredeemable hell which the injured poet can create for him—the *singing flames* of a Dante's *terza rima*!

> Kennst du die Hölle des Dante nicht,
> Die schrecklichen Terzetten?
> Wen da der Dichter hineingesperrt
> Den kann kein Gott mehr retten.
>
> Kein Gott, kein Heiland, erlöst ihn je
> Aus diesen singenden flammen!
> Nimm dich in Acht, das wir dich nicht
> Zu solcher Hölle verdammen.*

[1] At first I was almost in despair, and I thought I could never bear it, and yet I have borne it—only do not ask me *how*?

As a prosaist, Heine is, in one point of view, even more distinguished than as a poet. The German language easily lends itself to all the purposes of poetry; like the ladies of the Middle Ages, it is gracious and compliant to the Troubadours. But as these same ladies were often crusty and repulsive to their unmusical mates, so the German language generally appears awkward and unmanageable in the hands of prose writers. Indeed, the number of really fine German prosaists before Heine, would hardly have exceeded the numerating powers of a New Hollander, who can count three and no more. Persons the most familiar with German prose testify that there is an extra fatigue in reading it, just as we feel an extra fatigue from our walk when it takes us over ploughed clay. But in Heine's hands German prose, usually so heavy, so clumsy, so dull, becomes, like clay in the hands of the chemist, compact, metallic, brilliant; it is German in an *allotropic* condition. No dreary, labyrinthine sentences in which you find 'no end in wandering mazes lost';* no chains of adjectives in linked harshness long drawn out; no digressions thrown in as parentheses; but crystalline definiteness and clearness, fine and varied rhythm, and all that delicate precision, all those felicities of word and cadence, which belong to the highest order of prose. And Heine has proved—what Madame de Stäel seems to have doubted—that it is possible to be witty in German; indeed, in reading him, you might imagine that German was pre-eminently the language of wit, so flexible, so subtle, so piquant does it become under his management. He is far more an artist in prose than Goethe. He has not the breadth and repose, and the calm development which belong to Goethe's style, for they are foreign to his mental character; but he excels Goethe in susceptibility to the manifold qualities of prose, and in mastery over its effects. Heine is full of variety, of light and shadow: he alternates between epigrammatic pith, imaginative grace, sly allusion, and daring piquancy; and athwart all these there runs a vein of sadness, tenderness, and grandeur which reveals the poet. He continually throws out those finely-chiselled sayings which stamp themselves on the memory, and become familiar by quotation. For example: 'The People have time enough, they are immortal; kings only are mortal.'—'Wherever a great soul utters its thoughts, there is Golgotha.'—'Nature wanted to see how she looked, and she created Goethe.'—'Only the man who has known bodily suffering is truly a *man*; his limbs have their Passion-history, they are spiritualized.' He calls Rubens 'this Flemish Titan, the wings of whose genius were so strong that he soared as high as the sun, in spite of the hundred weight of Dutch cheeses that hung on his legs.' Speaking of Börne's dislike to the calm creations of the true artist, he says, 'He was like a child which, insensible to the glowing significance of a Greek statue, only touches the marble and complains of cold.'

The most poetic and specifically humorous of Heine's prose writings are the 'Reisebilder'. The comparison with Sterne is inevitable here; but Heine does not suffer from it, for if he falls below Sterne in raciness of humour, he is far above him in poetic sensibility and in reach and variety of thought. Heine's humour is never persistent, it never flows on long in easy gaiety and drollery; where it is not swelled by the tide of poetic feeling, it is continually dashing down the precipice of a witticism. It is not broad and unctuous; it is aerial and sprite-like, a momentary meeting-place between his poetry and his wit. In the 'Reisebilder' he runs through the whole gamut of his powers, and gives us every hue of thought, from the wildly droll and fantastic to the sombre and the terrible. Here is a passage almost Dantesque in conception:—

Alas! one ought in truth to write against no one in this world. Each of us is sick enough in this great lazaretto, and many a polemical writing reminds me involuntarily of a revolting quarrel, in a little hospital at Cracow, of which I chanced to be a witness, and where it was horrible to hear how the patients mockingly reproached each other with their infirmities: how one who was wasted by consumption jeered at another who was bloated by dropsy; how one laughed at another's cancer in the nose, and this one again at his neighbour's locked-jaw or squint, until at last the delirious fever-patient sprang out of bed and tore away the cover-

ings from the wounded bodies of his companions, and nothing was
to be seen but hideous misery and mutilation.

And how fine is the transition in the very next chapter,
where, after quoting the Homeric description of the feasting
gods, he says:—

Then suddenly approached, panting, a pale Jew, with drops of
blood on his brow, with a crown of thorns on his head, and a
great cross laid on his shoulders; and he threw the cross on the
high table of the gods, so that the golden cups tottered, and the
gods became dumb and pale, and grew ever paler, till they at last
melted away into vapour.

The richest specimens of Heine's wit are perhaps to be
found in the works which have appeared since the 'Reisebilder'. The years, if they have intensified his satirical
bitterness, have also given his wit a finer edge and polish.
His sarcasms are so subtly prepared and so slily allusive,
that they may often escape readers whose sense of wit is
not very acute; but for those who delight in the subtle and
delicate flavours of style, there can hardly be any wit more
irresistible than Heine's. We may measure its force by the
degree in which it has subdued the German language to its
purposes, and made that language brilliant in spite of a long
hereditary transmission of dullness. As one of the most
harmless examples of his satire, take this on a man who has
certainly had his share of adulation:—

Assuredly it is far from my purpose to depreciate M. Victor
Cousin. The titles of this celebrated philosopher even lay me under
an obligation to praise him. He belongs to that living pantheon of
France, which we call the peerage, and his intelligent legs rest on
the velvet benches of the Luxembourg. I must indeed sternly
repress all private feelings which might seduce me into an excessive
enthusiasm. Otherwise I might be suspected of servility; for M.
Cousin is very influential in the State by means of his position
and his tongue. This consideration might even move me to speak
of his faults as frankly as of his virtues. Will he himself disapprove
of this? Assuredly not. I know that we cannot do higher honour
to great minds than when we throw as strong a light on their
demerits as on their merits. When we sing the praises of a
Hercules, we must also mention that he once laid aside the lion's

skin and sat down to the distaff: what then? he remains notwith-standing a Hercules! So when we relate similar circumstances concerning M. Cousin, we must nevertheless add, with discriminating eulogy: *M. Cousin, if he has sometimes sat twaddling at the distaff, has never laid aside the lion's skin* ... It is true that, having been suspected of demagogy, he spent some time in a German prison, just as Lafayette and Richard Cœur de Lion. But that M. Cousin there in his leisure hours studied Kant's *Critique of Pure Reason* is to be doubted on three grounds. First, this book is written in German. Secondly, in order to read this book, a man must understand German. Thirdly, M. Cousin does not understand German ... I fear I am passing unawares from the sweet waters of praise into the bitter ocean of blame. Yes, on one account I cannot refrain from bitterly blaming M. Cousin; namely, that he who loves truth far more than he loves Plato and Tenneman, is unjust to himself when he wants to persuade us that he has borrowed something from the philosophy of Schelling and Hegel. Against this self-accusation, I must take M. Cousin under my protection. On my word and conscience! this honourable man has not stolen a jot from Schelling and Hegel, and if he brought home anything of theirs, it was merely their friendship. That does honour to his heart. But there are many instances of such false self-accusation in psychology. I knew a man who declared that he had stolen silver spoons at the king's table; and yet we all knew that the poor devil had never been presented at court, and accused himself of stealing these spoons to make us believe that he had been a guest at the palace. No! In German philosophy M. Cousin has always kept the sixth commandment; here he has never pocketed a single idea, not so much as a salt-spoon of an idea. All witnesses agree in attesting that in this respect M. Cousin is honour itself ... I prophesy to you that the renown of M. Cousin, like the French Revolution, will go round the world! I hear some one wickedly add: Undeniably the renown of M. Cousin is going round the world, and *it has already taken its departure from France*.

The following 'symbolical myth' about Louis Philippe is very characteristic of Heine's manner:—

I remember very well that immediately on my arrival (in Paris) I hastened to the Palais-Royal to see Louis Philippe. The friend who conducted me told me that the king now appeared on the terrace only at stated hours, but that formerly he was to be seen at any time for five francs. 'For five-francs!' I cried, with amazement; 'does he then show himself for money?' 'No; but he is shown for money, and it happens in this way:—There is a society of *claqueurs, marchands de contremarques*, and such riff-raff, who offered every foreigner to show him the king for five francs: if he would give ten francs, he might see the king raise his eyes to heaven, and lay his hand protestingly on his heart; if he would give twenty francs, the king would sing the Marseillaise. If the foreigner gave five francs, they raised a loud cheering under the king's windows, and his Majesty appeared on the terrace, bowed and retired. If ten francs, they shouted still louder, and gesticulated as if they had been possessed, when the king appeared, who then, as a sign of silent emotion, raised his eyes to heaven, and laid his hand on his heart. English visitors, however, would sometimes spend as much as twenty francs, and then the enthusiasms mounted to the highest pitch: no sooner did the king appear on the terrace, then the Marseillaise was struck up and roared out frightfully, until Louis Philippe, perhaps only for the sake of putting an end to the singing, bowed, laid his hand on his heart, and joined in the Marseillaise. Whether, as is asserted, he beat time with his foot, I cannot say.'

One more quotation, and it must be our last:—

O the women! We must forgive them much, for they love much—and many. Their hate is properly only love turned inside out. Sometimes they attribute some delinquency to us, because they think they can in this way gratify another man. When they write, they have always one eye on the paper and the other on a man; and this is true of all authoresses, except the Countess Hahn-Hahn, who has only one eye.*

Robert Browning's *Men and Women* (1856)

WE never read Heinsius*—a great admission for a reviewer—but we learn from M. Arago that that formidably erudite writer pronounces Aristotle's works to be characterized by a *majestic obscurity which repels the ignorant*. We borrow these words to indicate what is likely to be the first impression of a reader who, without any previous familiarity with Browning, glances through his two new volumes of poems. The less acute he is, the more easily will he arrive at the undeniable criticism, that these poems have a 'majestic obscurity', which repels not only the ignorant but the idle. To read poems is often a substitute for thought: fine-sounding conventional phrases and the sing-song of verse demand no co-operation in the reader; they glide over his mind with the agreeable unmeaningness of 'the compliments of the season', or a speaker's exordium on 'feelings too deep for expression'. But let him expect no such drowsy passivity in reading Browning. Here he will find no conventionality, no melodious commonplace, but freshness, originality, sometimes eccentricity of expression; no didactic laying-out of a subject, but dramatic indication, which requires the reader to trace by his own mental activity the underground stream of thought that jets out in elliptical and pithy verse. To read Browning he must exert himself, but he will. exert himself to some purpose. If he finds the meaning difficult of access, it is always worth his effort—if he has to dive deep, 'he rises with his pearl'. Indeed, in Browning's best poems he makes us feel that what we took for obscurity in him was superficiality in ourselves. We are far from meaning that all his obscurity is like the obscurity of the stars, dependent simply on the feebleness of men's vision. On the contrary, our admiration for his genius only makes us feel the more acutely that its inspirations are too often straitened by the garb of whimsical mannerism with which he clothes them. This mannerism is even irritating sometimes, and should at least be kept under restraint in *printed* poems, where the writer is not merely indulging his own vein, but is avowedly appealing to the mind of his reader.

Turning from the ordinary literature of the day to such a writer as Browning, is like turning from Flotow's music, made up of well-pieced shreds and patches, to the distinct individuality of Chopin's Studies or Schubert's Songs. Here, at least, is a man who has something of his own to tell us, and who can tell it impressively, if not with faultless art. There is nothing sickly or dreamy in him: he has a clear eye, a vigorous grasp, and courage to utter what he sees and handles. His robust energy is informed by a subtle, penetrating spirit, and this blending of opposite qualities gives his mind a rough piquancy that reminds one of a russet apple. His keen glance pierces into all the secrets of human character, but, being as thoroughly alive to the outward as to the inward, he reveals those secrets, not by a process of dissection, but by dramatic painting. We fancy his own description of a poet applies to himself:—

> He stood and watched the cobbler at his trade,
> The man who slices lemons into drink,
> The coffee-roaster's brazier, and the boys
> That volunteer to help him at the winch.
> He glanced o'er books on stalls with half an eye,
> And fly-leaf ballads on the vendor's string,
> And broad-edge bold-print posters by the wall.
> *He took such cognizance of men and things,*
> *If any beat a horse, you felt he saw;*
> *If any cursed a woman, he took note;*
> *Yet stared at nobody,—they stared at him,*
> *And found, less to their pleasure than surprise,*
> *He seemed to know them and expect as much.* *

Browning has no soothing strains, no chants, no lullabys; he rarely gives voice to our melancholy, still less to our gaiety; he sets our thoughts at work rather than our emotions. But though eminently a thinker, he is as far as possible from prosaic; his mode of presentation is always concrete,

artistic, and, where it is most felicitous, dramatic. Take, for
example, 'Fra Lippo Lippi', a poem at once original and
perfect in its kind. The artist-monk, Fra Lippo, is supposed
to be detected by the night-watch roaming the streets of
Florence, and while sharing the wine with which he makes
amends to the Dogberrys * for the roughness of his tongue,
he pours forth the story of his life and his art with the racy
conversational vigour of a brawny genius under the influence
of the Care-dispeller.

> I was a baby when my mother died
> And father died and left me in the street.
> I starved there, God knows how, a year or two
> On fig-skins, melon-parings, rinds and shucks,
> Refuse and rubbish. One fine frosty day
> My stomach being empty as your hat,
> The wind doubled me up and down I went.
> Old aunt Lapaccia trussed me with one hand,
> (Its fellow was a stinger as I knew)
> And so along the wall, over the bridge,
> By the straight cut to the convent. Six words, there,
> While I stood munching my first bread that month:
> 'So, boy, you're minded,' quoth the good fat father
> Wiping his own mouth, 'twas refection time,—
> 'To quit this very miserable world?
> Will you renounce' . . . The mouthful of bread? thought I;
> By no means! Brief, they made a monk of me.

> 'Let's see what the urchin's fit for'—that came next.
> Not overmuch their way, I must confess.
> Such a to-do! they tried me with their books.
> Lord, they'd have taught me Latin in pure waste!
> *Flower o' the clove,*
> *All the Latin I construe is, 'amo' I love!*
> But, mind you, when a boy starves in the streets
> Eight years together as my fortune was,
> Watching folk's faces to know who will fling
> The bit of half-stripped grape-bunch he desires,
> And who will curse or kick him for his pains—
> Which gentleman processional and fine,
> Holding a candle to the Sacrament,

Will wink and let him lift a plate and catch
The droppings of the wax to sell again,
Or holla for the Eight and have him whipped,—
How say I?—nay, which dog bites, which lets drop
His bone from the heap of offal in the street!
—The soul and sense of him grow sharp alike,
He learns the look of things, and none the less
For admonitions from the hunger-pinch.
I had a store of such remarks, be sure,
Which, after I found leisure, turned to use:
I drew men's faces on my copy-books,
Scrawled them within the antiphonary's marge,
Joined legs and arms to the long music-notes,
Found nose and eyes and chin for A's and B's,
And made a string of pictures of the world
Betwixt the ins and outs of verb and noun,
On the wall, the bench, the door. The monks looked black.
'Nay,' quoth the Prior, 'turn him out, d'ye say?
In no wise. Lose a crow and catch a lark.
What if at last we get our man of parts,
We Carmelites, like those Camaldolese
And Preaching Friars, to do our church up fine
And put the front on it that ought to be!'
And hereupon they bade me daub away.
Thank you! my head being crammed, their walls a blank,
Never was such prompt disemburdening.
First, every sort of monk, the black and white,
I drew them fat and lean: then, folks at church,
From good old gossips waiting to confess
Their cribs of barrel-droppings, candle-ends,—
To the breathless fellow at the altar-foot,
Fresh from his murder, safe and sitting there
With the little children round him in a row
Of admiration, half for his beard and half
For that white anger of his victim's son
Shaking a fist at him with one fierce arm,
Signing himself with the other because of Christ,
(*Whose sad face on the cross sees only this*
After the passion of a thousand years)
Till some poor girl, her apron o'er her head
Which the intense eyes looked through, came at eve

   .   .   .

On tip-toe, said a word, dropped in a loaf,
Her pair of ear-rings and a bunch of flowers
The brute took growling, prayed, and then was gone.
I painted all, then cried ''tis ask and have—
Choose, for more's ready!'—laid the ladder flat,
And showed my covered bit of cloister-wall.
The monks closed in a circle and praised loud
Till checked (taught what to see and not to see,
Being simple bodies), 'that's the very man!
Look at the boy who stoops to pat the dog!
That woman's like the Prior's niece who comes
To care about his asthma: it's the life!'
But there my triumph's straw-fire flared and funked—
Their betters took their turn to see and say:
The Prior and the learned pulled a face
And stopped all that in no time. 'How? what's here?
Quite from the mark of painting, bless us all!
Faces, arms, legs and bodies like the true
As much as pea and pea! it's devil's-game!
Your business is not to catch men with show,
With homage to the perishable clay,
But lift them over it, ignore it all,
Make them forget there's such a thing as flesh.
Your business is to paint the souls of men—
Man's soul, and it's a fire, smoke . . . no it's not . . .
It's vapour done up like a new-born babe—
(In that shape when you die it leaves your mouth)
It's . . . well, what matters talking, it's the soul!
Give us no more of body than shows soul.

   .   .   .

Have it all out!' Now, is this sense, I ask?
A fine way to paint soul, by painting body
So ill, the eye can't stop there, must go further
And can't fare worse! Thus, yellow does for white
When what you put for yellow's simply black,
And *any sort of meaning looks intense*
When all beside itself means and looks nought.
Why can't a painter lift each foot in turn,
Left foot and right foot, go a double step,
Make his flesh liker and his soul more like,
Both in their order? Take the prettiest face,

   .   .   .

The Prior's niece . . . patron-saint—is it so pretty
You can't discover if it means hope, fear,
Sorrow or joy? won't beauty go with these?
Suppose I've made her eyes all right and blue,
Can't I take breath and try to add life's flash,
And then add soul and heighten them threefold?
Or say there's beauty with no soul at all—
(I never saw it—put the case the same—)
If you get simple beauty and nought else,
You get about the best thing God invents,—
That's somewhat. And you'll find the soul you have missed,
Within yourself when you return Him thanks!

    You be judge!
You speak no Latin more than I, belike—
However, you're my man, you've seen the world
—The beauty and the wonder and the power,
The shapes of things, their colours, lights and shades,
Changes, surprises,—and God made it all!
—For what? do you feel thankful, ay or no,
For this fair town's face, yonder river's line,
The mountain round it and the sky above,
Much more the figures of man, woman, child,
These are the frame to? What's it all about?
To be passed o'er, despised? or dwelt upon,
Wondered at? oh, this last of course, you say.
But why not do as well as say,—paint these
Just as they are, careless what comes of it?
God's works—paint anyone, and count it crime
To let a truth slip. Don't object, 'His works
Are here already—nature is complete:
Suppose you reproduce her—(which you can't)
There's no advantage! you must beat her, then.'
For, don't you mark, we're made so that we love
First when we see them painted, things we have passed
Perhaps a hundred times nor cared to see;
And so they are better, painted—better to us,
Which is the same thing. *Art was given for that—*
God uses us to help each other so,
Lending our minds out.

Extracts cannot do justice to the fine dramatic touches by
which Fra Lippo is made present to us, while he throws

out this instinctive Art-criticism. And extracts from 'Bishop Blougram's Apology', an equally remarkable poem of what we may call the dramatic-psychological kind, would be still more ineffective. 'Sylvester Blougram, styled *in partibus Episcopus*', is talking

> Over the glass's edge when dinner's done,
> And body gets its sop and holds its noise
> And leaves soul free a little,

with 'Gigadibs the literary man', to whom he is bent on proving by the most exasperatingly ingenious sophistry, that the theory of life on which he grounds his choice of being a bishop, though a doubting one, is wiser in the moderation of its ideal, with the certainty of attainment, than the Giga-dibs theory, which aspires after the highest and attains nothing. The way in which Blougram's motives are dug up from below the roots, and laid bare to the very last fibre, not by a process of hostile exposure, not by invective or sarcasm, but by making himself exhibit them with a self-complacent sense of supreme acuteness, and even with a crushing force of worldly common sense, has the effect of masterly satire. But the poem is too strictly consecutive for any fragments of it to be a fair specimen. Belonging to the same order of subtle yet vigorous writing are the 'Epistle of Karshish, the Arab Physician', 'Cleon', and 'How it Strikes a Contemporary'. 'In a Balcony' is so fine, that we regret it is not a complete drama instead of being merely the sugges-tion of a drama. One passage especially tempts us to extract.

> All women love great men
> If young or old—it is in all the tales—
> Young beauties love old poets who can love—
> Why should not he the poems in my soul,
> The love, the passionate faith, the sacrifice,
> The constancy? I throw them at his feet.
> Who cares to see the fountain's very shape
> And whether it be a Triton's or a Nymph's
> That pours the foam, makes rainbows all around?
> You could not praise indeed the empty conch;
> *But I'll pour floods of love and hide myself.*

These lines are less rugged than is usual with Browning's blank verse; but generally, the greatest deficiency we feel in his poetry is its want of music. The worst poems in his new volumes are, in our opinion, his lyrical efforts; for in these, where he engrosses us less by his thought, we are more sensible of his obscurity and his want of melody. His lyrics, instead of tripping along with easy grace, or rolling with a torrent-like grandeur, seem to be struggling painfully under a burthen too heavy for them; and many of them have the disagreeable puzzling effect of a charade, rather than the touching or animating influence of song. We have said that he is never prosaic; and it is remarkable that in his blank verse, though it is often colloquial, we are never shocked by the sense of a sudden lapse into prose. Wordsworth is, on the whole, a far more musical poet than Browning, yet we remember no line in Browning so prosaic as many of Wordsworth's, which in some of his finest poems have the effect of bricks built into a rock. But we must also say that though Browning never flounders helplessly on the plain, he rarely soars above a certain table-land—a footing between the level of prose and the topmost heights of poetry. He does not take possession of our souls and set them aglow, as the greatest poets—the greatest artists do. We admire his power, we are not subdued by it. Language with him does not seem spontaneously to link itself into song, as sounds link themselves into melody in the mind of the creative musician; he rather seems by his commanding powers to compel language into verse. He has *chosen* verse as his medium; but of our greatest poets we feel that they had no choice: Verse chose them. Still we are grateful that Browning chose this medium: we would rather have 'Fra Lippo Lippi' than an essay on Realism in Art; we would rather have 'The Statue and the Bust' than a three-volumed novel with the same moral; we would rather have 'Holy Cross-Day' than 'Strictures on the Society for the Emancipation of the Jews'.

By way of counterbalancing our judgement, we will give a parting quotation from one of the most musical of the rhymed poems.

My perfect wife, my Leonor,
    Oh, heart my own, oh, eyes, mine too,
Whom else could I dare look backward for,
    With whom beside should I dare pursue
    The path grey heads abhor?

For it leads to a crag's sheer edge with them;
    Youth, flowery all the way, there stops—
Not they; age threatens and they contemn,
    Till they reach the gulf wherein youth drops,
    One inch from our life's safe hem!

My own, confirm me! If I tread
    This path back, is it not in pride
To think how little I dreamed it led
    To an age so blest that by its side
    Youth seems the waste instead!

My own, see where the years conduct!
    At first, 'twas something our two souls
Should mix as mists do: each is sucked
    Into each now; on, the new stream rolls,
    Whatever rocks obstruct. *

The *Antigone* and Its Moral (1856)

'LO! here a little volume but great Book'—a volume small enough to slip into your breast pocket, but containing in fine print one of the finest tragedies of the single dramatic poet who can be said to stand on a level with Shakespeare. Sophocles is the crown and flower of the classic tragedy as Shakespeare is of the romantic: to borrow Schlegel's comparison, which cannot be improved upon, they are related to each other as the Parthenon to Strasburg Cathedral. *

The opinion which decries all enthusiasm for Greek literature as 'humbug', was put to an excellent test some years ago by the production of the *Antigone* at Drury Lane. The translation then adopted was among the feeblest by which a great poet has ever been misrepresented; yet so completely did the poet triumph over the disadvantages of his medium and of a dramatic motive foreign to modern sympathies, that the Pit was electrified, and Sophocles, over a chasm of two thousand years, once more swayed the emotions of a popular audience. And no wonder. The *Antigone* has every quality of a fine tragedy, and fine tragedies can never become mere mummies for Hermanns and Böckhs* to dispute about: they must appeal to perennial human nature, and even the ingenious dullness of translators cannot exhaust them of their passion and their poetry.

E'en in their ashes live their wonted fires.*

We said that the dramatic motive of the *Antigone* was foreign to modern sympathies, but it is only superficially so. It is true we no longer believe that a brother, if left unburied, is condemned to wander a hundred years without repose on the banks of the Styx; we no longer believe that to neglect funeral rites is to violate the claims of the infernal deities. But these beliefs are the accidents and not the substance of the poet's conception. The turning point of the tragedy is not, as it is stated to be in the argument prefixed to this edition, 'reverence for the dead and the importance of the sacred rites of burial', but the *conflict* between these and obedience to the State. Here lies the dramatic collision: the impulse of sisterly piety which allies itself with reverence for the Gods, clashes with the duties of citizenship; two principles, both having their validity, are at war with each. Let us glance for a moment at the plot.

Eteocles and Polynices, the brothers of Antigone, have slain each other in battle before the gates of Thebes, the one defending his country, the other invading it in conjunction with foreign allies. Hence Creon becomes, by the death of these two sons of Oedipus, the legitimate ruler of Thebes, grants funeral honours to Eteocles, but denies them to Polynices, whose body is cast out to be the prey of beasts and birds, a decree being issued that death will be the penalty of an attempt to bury him. In the second scene of the play Creon expounds the motive of his decree to the Theban elders, insisting in weighty words on the duty of making all personal affection subordinate to the well-being of the State. The impulses of affection and religion which urge Antigone to disobey this proclamation are strengthened by the fact that in her last interview with her brother he had besought her not to leave his corpse unburied. She determines to brave the penalty, buries Polynices, is taken in the act and brought before Creon, to whom she does not attempt to deny that she knew of the proclamation, but declares that she deliberately disobeyed it, and is ready to accept death as its consequence. It was not Zeus, she tells him—it was not eternal Justice that issued that decree. The proclamation of Creon is not so authoritative as the unwritten law of the Gods, which is neither of today nor of yesterday, but lives eternally, and none knows its beginning.

> Οὐ γάρ τι νῦν γε κἀχθές, ἀλλ' ἀεί ποτε
> Ζῇ ταῦτα, κοὐδεὶς οἶδεν ἐξ ὅτου 'φάνη.*

Creon, on his side, insists on the necessity to the welfare of the State that he should be obeyed as legitimate ruler, and becomes exasperated by the calm defiance of Antigone. She is condemned to death. Haemon, the son of Creon, to whom Antigone is betrothed, remonstrates against this judgement in vain. Teiresias also, the blind old soothsayer, alarmed by unfavourable omens, comes to warn Creon against persistence in a course displeasing to the Gods. It is not until he has departed, leaving behind him the denunciation of coming woes, that Creon's confidence begins to falter, and at length, persuaded by the Theban elders, he reverses his decree, and proceeds with his followers to the rocky tomb in which Antigone has been buried alive, that he may deliver her. It is too late. Antigone is already dead; Haemon commits suicide in the madness of despair, and the death of his mother Eurydice on hearing the fatal tidings, completes the ruin of Creon's house.

It is a very superficial criticism which interprets the character of Creon as that of a hypocritical tyrant, and regards Antigone as a blameless victim. Coarse contrasts like this are not the materials handled by great dramatists. The exquisite art of Sophocles is shown in the touches by which he makes us feel that Creon, as well as Antigone, is contending for what he believes to be the right, while both are also conscious that, in following out one principle, they are laying themselves open to just blame for transgressing another; and it is this consciousness which secretly heightens the exasperation of Creon and the defiant hardness of Antigone. The best critics have agreed with Böckh in recognizing this balance of principles, this antagonism between valid claims; they generally regard it, however, as dependent entirely on the Greek point of view, as springing simply from the polytheistic conception, according to which the requirements of the Gods often clashed with the duties of man to man.

But, is it the fact that this antagonism of valid principles is peculiar to polytheism? Is it not rather that the struggle between Antigone and Creon represents that struggle between elemental tendencies and established laws by which the outer life of man is gradually and painfully being brought into harmony with his inward needs? Until this harmony is perfected, we shall never be able to attain a great right without also doing a wrong. Reformers, martyrs, revolutionists, are never fighting against evil only; they are also placing themselves in opposition to a good—to a valid principle which cannot be infringed without harm. Resist the payment of ship-money, you bring on civil war; preach against false doctrines, you disturb feeble minds and send them adrift on a sea of doubt; make a new road, and you annihilate vested interests; cultivate a new region of the earth, and you exterminate a race of men. Wherever the strength of a man's intellect, or moral sense, or affection brings him into opposition with the rules which society has sanctioned, *there* is renewed the conflict between Antigone and Creon; such a man must not only dare to be right, he must also dare to be wrong—to shake faith, to wound friendship, perhaps, to hem in his own powers. Like Antigone, he may fall a victim to the struggle, and yet he can never earn the name of a blameless martyr any more than the society—the Creon he has defied, can be branded as a hypocritical tyrant.

Perhaps the best moral we can draw is that to which the Chorus points—that our protest for the right should be seasoned with moderation and reverence, and that lofty words—μεγάλοι λόγοι—are not becoming to mortals.

John Ruskin's *Modern Painters*, Vol. III
(1856)

OUR table this time does not, according to the favourite
metaphor, 'groan' under the light literature of the quarter,
for the quarter has not been very productive; but, in compensation, we ourselves groan under it rather more than
usual, for the harvest is principally of straw, and few grains
of precious corn remain after the winnowing. We except one
book, however, which is a rich sheaf in itself, and will serve
as bread, and seed-corn too, for many days. We mean the
new volume of Mr Ruskin's 'Modern Painters', to which he
appropriately gives the subordinate title, 'Of Many Things'.
It may be taken up with equal pleasure whether the reader
be acquainted or not with the previous volumes, and no
special artistic culture is necessary in order to enjoy its
excellences or profit by its suggestions. Every one who cares
about nature, or poetry, or the story of human development—every one who has a tinge of literature, or philosophy, will find something that is for him and that will
'gravitate to him' in this volume. Since its predecessors
appeared, Mr Ruskin has devoted ten years to the loving
study of his great subject—the principles of art; which, like
all other great subjects, carries the student into many fields.
The critic of art, as he tells us, 'has to take *some* note of
optics, geometry, geology, botany, and anatomy; he must
acquaint himself with the works of all great artists, and with
the temper and history of the times in which they lived; he
must be a fair metaphysician, and a careful observer of the
phenomena of natural scenery'. And when a writer like Mr
Ruskin brings these varied studies to bear on one great
purpose, when he has to trace their common relation to a
grand phase of human activity, it is obvious that he will
have a great deal to say which is of interest and importance
to others besides painters. The fundamental principles of all

just thought and beautiful action or creation are the same, and in making clear to ourselves what is best and noblest in art, we are making clear to ourselves what is best and noblest in morals; in learning how to estimate the artistic products of a particular age according to the mental attitude and external life of that age, we are widening our sympathy and deepening the basis of our tolerance and charity.

Of course, this treatise 'Of Many Things' presents certain old characteristics and new paradoxes which will furnish a fresh text to antagonistic critics; but, happily for us, and happily for our readers, who probably care more to know what Mr Ruskin says than what other people think he *ought* to say, we are not among those who are more irritated by his faults than charmed and subdued by his merits. When he announces to the world in his Preface, that he is incapable of falling into an illogical deduction—that, whatever other mistakes he may commit, he cannot possibly draw an inconsequent conclusion, we are not indignant, but amused, and do not in the least feel ourselves under the necessity of picking holes in his arguments in order to prove that he is not a logical Pope. We value a writer not in proportion to his freedom from faults, but in proportion to his positive excellences—to the variety of thought he contributes and suggests, to the amount of gladdening and energizing emotions he excites. Of what comparative importance is it that Mr Ruskin undervalues this painter, or overvalues the other, that he sometimes glides from a just argument into a fallacious one, that he is a little absurd here, and not a little arrogant there, if, with all these collateral mistakes, he teaches truth of infinite value, and *so* teaches it that men will listen? The truth of infinite value that he teaches is *realism*—the doctrine that all truth and beauty are to be attained by a humble and faithful study of nature, and not by substituting vague forms, bred by imagination on the mists of feeling, in place of definite, substantial reality. The thorough acceptance of this doctrine would remould our life; and he who teaches its application to any one department of human activity with such power as Mr Ruskin's, is a prophet for his generation. It is not enough simply to teach truth; that may be done, as we all know, to empty walls, and within the covers of unsaleable books; we want it to be so taught as to compel men's attention and sympathy. Very correct singing of very fine music will avail little without a *voice* that can thrill the audience and take possession of their souls. Now, Mr Ruskin has a voice, and one of such power, that whatever error he may mix with his truth, he will make more converts to that truth than less erring advocates who are hoarse and feeble. Considered merely as a writer, he is in the very highest rank of English stylists. The vigour and splendour of his eloquence are not more remarkable than its precision, and the delicate truthfulness of his epithets. The fine *largo* of his sentences reminds us more of De Quincey than of any other writer, and his tendency to digressiveness is another and less admirable point of resemblance to the English Opium-eater. Yet we are not surprised to find that he does not mention De Quincey among the favourite writers who have influenced him, for Mr Ruskin's style is evidently due far more to innate faculty than to modifying influences; and though he himself thinks that his constant study of Carlyle must have impressed itself on his language as well as his thought, we rarely detect this. In the point of view from which he looks at a subject, in the correctness of his descriptions, and in a certain rough flavour of humour, he constantly reminds us of Carlyle, but in the mere tissue of his style, scarcely ever. But while we are dilating on Mr Ruskin's general characteristics, we are robbing ourselves of the room we want for what is just now more important—namely, telling the reader something about the contents of the particular volume before us.

It opens with a discussion of the 'Grand Style', which, after an analysis and dismissal of Sir Joshua Reynolds's opinion, that it consists in attending to what is invariable, 'the great and general ideas only inherent in universal nature', Mr Ruskin concludes to be 'the suggestion by the imagination of noble grounds for noble emotions'. The conditions on which this result depends are, first, *the choice of noble subjects*, i.e., subjects which involve wide interests and profound passions, as opposed to those which involve narrow interests and slight passions. And the choice which characterizes the school of high art, is seen as much in the treatment of the subject as the selection. 'For the artist who sincerely chooses the noblest subject, will also choose chiefly to represent what makes that subject noble, namely, the various heroism or other noble emotions of the persons represented.' But here two dangers present themselves: that of superseding expression by technical excellence, as when Paul Veronese makes the Supper at Emmaus a background to the portraits of two children playing with a dog; and that of superseding technical excellence by expression.

This is usually done under the influence of another kind of vanity. The artist desires that men should think he has an elevated soul, affects to despise the ordinary excellence of art, contemplates with separated egotism the course of his own imaginations or sensations, and refuses to look at the real facts around about him, in order that he may adore at leisure the shadow of himself. He lives in an element of what he calls tender emotions and lofty aspirations; which are, in fact, nothing more than very ordinary weaknesses or instincts, contemplated through a mist of pride.

The second condition of greatness of style is *love of beauty*—the tendency to introduce into the conception of the subject as much beauty as is possible, consistently with truth.

The corruption of the schools of high art, so far as this particular quality is concerned, consists in the sacrifice of truth to beauty. Great art dwells on all that is beautiful; but false art omits or changes all that is ugly. Great art accepts Nature as she is, but directs the eyes and thoughts to what is most perfect in her; false art saves itself the trouble of direction, by removing or altering whatever it thinks objectionable. The evil results of which proceeding are twofold.

First. That beauty deprived of its proper foils and adjuncts ceases to be enjoyed as beauty, just as light deprived of all shadow ceases to be enjoyed as light. A white canvas cannot produce an effect of sunshine; the painter must darken it in some places before he can make it luminous in others; nor can an uninterrupted succession of beauty produce the true effect of beauty: it must be foiled by inferiority before its own power can be developed. Nature has for the most part mingled her inferior and nobler elements as she mingles sunshine with shade, giving due use and influence to both; and the painter who chooses to remove the shadow, perishes in the burning desert he has created. The truly high and beautiful art of Angelico is continually refreshed and strengthened by his frank portraiture of the most ordinary features of his brother monks, and of the recorded peculiarities of ungainly sanctity; but the modern German and Raphaelesque schools lose all honour and nobleness in barber-like admiration of handsome faces, and have, in fact, no real faith except in straight noses and curled hair. Paul Veronese opposes the dwarf to the soldier, and the negress to the queen; Shakespeare places Caliban beside Miranda, and Autolycus beside Perdita; but the vulgar idealist withdraws his beauty to the safety of the saloon, and his innocence to the seclusion of the cloister; he pretends that he does this in delicacy of choice and purity of sentiment, while in truth he has neither courage to front the monster, nor wit enough to furnish the knave.

It is only by the habit of representing faithfully all things, that we can truly learn what is beautiful, and what is not. The ugliest objects contain some element of beauty; and in all, it is an element peculiar to themselves, which cannot be separated from their ugliness, but must either be enjoyed together with it, or not at all. The more a painter accepts nature as he finds it, the more unexpected beauty he discovers in what he at first despised; but once let him arrogate the right of rejection, and he will gradually contract his circle of enjoyment, until what he supposed to be nobleness of selection ends in narrowness of perception. Dwelling perpetually upon one class of ideas, his art becomes at once monstrous and morbid; until at last he cannot faithfully represent even what he chooses to retain; his discrimination contracts into darkness, and his fastidiousness fades into fatuity.

The third characteristic of great art is *sincerity*. The artist should include the largest possible quantity of truth in the most perfect possible harmony. *All* the truths of nature cannot be given; hence a choice must be made of some facts which can be represented from amongst others which must be passed by in silence. 'The inferior artist chooses unimportant and scattered truths; the great artist chooses the most necessary first, and afterwards the most consistent with these, so as to obtain the greatest possible and most harmonious scene.' Thus, Rembrandt sacrifices all other effects to the representation of the exact force with which the light on the most illumined part of an object is opposed to its obscurer portions. Paul Veronese, on the contrary, endeavours to embrace all the great relations of visible objects; and this difference between him and Rembrandt as to light and shade is typical of the difference between great and inferior artists throughout the entire field of art. He is the greatest who conveys the largest sum of truth. And as the sum of truth can always be increased by delicacy of handling, it follows

that all great art must have this delicacy to the utmost possible degree. This rule is infallible and inflexible. All coarse work is the sign of low art. Only, it is to be remembered, that coarseness must be estimated by the distance from the eye; it being necessary to consult this distance, when great, by laying on touches which appear coarse when seen near; but which, so far from being coarse, are, in reality, more delicate in a master's work than the finest close handling, for they involve a calculation of result, and are laid on with a subtlety of sense precisely correspondent to that with which a good archer draws his bow; the spectator seeing in the action nothing but the strain of the strong arm, while there is, in reality, in the finger and eye, an *ineffably delicate estimate of distance, and touch on the arrow plume*.

The last characteristic of great art is *invention*. It must not only present grounds for noble emotion, but must furnish these grounds by imaginative power, i.e., by an inventive combination of distinctly known objects. Thus imaginative art includes the historical faculties, which simply represent observed facts, but renders these faculties subservient to a poetic purpose.

And now, finally, since this poetical power includes the historical, if we glance back to the other qualities required in great art, and put all together, we find that the sum of them is simply the sum of all the powers of man. For as (1) the choice of the high subject involves all conditions of right moral choice, and as (2) the love of beauty involves all conditions of right admiration, and as (3) the grasp of truth involves all strength of sense, evenness of judgement, and honesty of purpose, and as (4) the poetical power involves all swiftness of invention, and accuracy of historical memory, the sum of all these powers is the sum of the human soul. Hence we see why the word 'Great' is used of this art. It is literally great. It compasses and calls forth the entire human spirit, whereas any other kind of art, being more or less small or narrow, compasses and calls forth only *part* of the human spirit. Hence the idea of its magnitude is a literal and just one, the art being simply less or greater in proportion to the number of faculties it exercises and addresses. And this is the ultimate meaning of the definition I gave of it long ago, as containing the 'greatest number of the greatest ideas'.

We have next a discussion of the False Ideal, and first of all, in Religious Art. The want of realization in the early religious painters prevented their pictures from being more than suggestions to the feelings. They attempted to express, not the actual fact, but their own enthusiasm about the fact; they covered the Virgin's dress with gold, not with any idea of representing her as she ever was or will be seen, but with a burning desire to show their love for her. As art advanced in technical power and became more realistic, there arose a more pernicious falsity in the treatment of religious subjects; more pernicious, because it was more likely to be accepted as a representation of fact.

Take a very important instance. I suppose there is no event in the whole life of Christ to which, in hours of doubt or fear, men turn with more anxious thirst to know the close facts of it, or with more earnest and passionate dwelling upon every syllable of its recorded narrative, than Christ showing Himself to his disciples at the lake of Galilee. There is something pre-eminently open, natural, full fronting our disbelief in this manifestation. The others, recorded after the resurrection, were sudden, phantom-like, occurring to men in profound sorrow and wearied agitation of heart; not, it might seem, safe judges of what they saw. But the agitation was now over. They had gone back to their daily work, thinking still their business lay net-wards, unmeshed from the literal rope and drag. Simon Peter saith unto them, 'I go a fishing.' They say unto him, 'We also go with thee.' True words enough, and having far echo beyond those Galilean hills. That night they caught nothing; but when the morning came, in the clear light of it, behold, a figure stood on the shore. They were not thinking of anything but their fruitless hauls. They had no guess who it was. It asked them simply if they had caught anything. They said no. And it tells them to cast yet again. And John shades his eyes from the morning sun with his hand, to look who it is; and though the glinting of the sea, too, dazzles him, he makes out who it is, at last; and poor Simon, not to be outrun this time, tightens his fisher's coat about him, and dashes in, over the nets. One would have liked to see him swim those hundred yards, and stagger to his knees on the beach.

Well, the others get to the beach, too, in time, in such slow way as men in general do get, in this world, to its true shore, much impeded by that wonderful 'dragging the net with fishes'; but they get there—seven of them in all;—first the Denier, and then the slowest believer, and then the quickest believer, and then the two throne-seekers, and two more, we know not who.

They sit down on the shore face to face with Him, and eat their broiled fish as He bids. And then, to Peter, all dripping still, shivering, and amazed, staring at Christ in the sun, on the other side of the coal fire,—thinking a little, perhaps, of what happened by another coal fire, when it was colder, and having had no word once changed with him by his Master since that look of His,—to him, so amazed, comes the question, 'Simon, lovest thou me?' Try to feel that a little, and think of it till it is true to you; and then, take up that infinite monstrosity and hypocrisy—Raphael's cartoon of the Charge to Peter. Note, first, the bold fallacy—the putting *all* the Apostles there, a mere lie to serve the papal heresy of the Petric supremacy, by putting them all in the background while Peter receives the charge, and making them all witnesses to it. Note the handsomely curled hair and neatly tied sandals of the men who had been out all night in the sea-mists and on the slimy decks. Note their convenient dresses for going a-fishing, with trains that lie a yard along the ground, and goodly fringes,—all made to match, an apostolic fishing costume. Note how Peter especially (whose chief glory was in his wet coat *girt* about him and naked limbs) is enveloped in folds and fringes, so as to kneel and hold his keys with grace. No fire of coals at all, nor lonely mountain shore, but a pleasant Italian landscape, full of villas and churches, and a flock of sheep to be pointed at; and the whole group of Apostles, not round Christ, as they would have been naturally, but straggling away in a line, that they may all be shown.

The simple truth is, that the moment we look at the picture we feel our belief of the whole thing taken away. There is, visibly, no possibility of that group ever having existed, in any place, or on any occasion. It is all a mere mythic absurdity, and faded concoction of fringes, muscular arms, and curly heads of Greek philosophers.

Mr Ruskin glances rapidly at the False Ideal in profane art—the pursuit of mere physical beauty as a gratification to the idle senses; and then enters into an extended consideration of the True Ideal, distinguished by him into three branches. 1. Purist Idealism, which results from the unwillingness of pure and tender minds to contemplate evil, of which Angelico is the great example, among the early painters; and among the moderns, Stothard exhibits the same tendency in the treatment of worldly subjects. 2. Naturalist Idealism, which accepts the weaknesses, faults, and wrongnesses in all things that it sees, but so places them that they form a noble whole, in which the imperfection of each several part is not only harmless, but absolutely essential, and yet in which whatever is good in each several part shall be completely displayed. 3. The Grotesque Ideal, which is either playful, terrible, or symbolical. The essence of an admirable chapter on 'Finish' is, that all real finish is not mere polish, but *added truth*. Great artists finish not to show their skill, nor to produce a smooth piece of work, but to *render clearer the expression of knowledge*.

We resist the temptation to quote any of the very fine things Mr Ruskin says about the 'Use of Pictures', and pass on to the succeeding chapter, in which he enters on his special subject, namely, landscape painting. With that intense interest in landscape which is a peculiar characteristic of modern times, is associated the 'Pathetic Fallacy'—the transference to external objects of the spectator's own emotions, as when Kingsley says of the drowned maiden,—

> They rowed her in across the rolling foam—
> The *cruel, crawling foam*.*

The pleasure we derive from this fallacy is legitimate when the passion in which it originates is strong, and has an adequate cause. But the mental condition which admits of this fallacy is of a lower order than that in which, while the emotions are strong, the intellect is yet strong enough to assert its rule against them; and 'the whole man stands in an iron glow, white hot, perhaps, but still strong, and in nowise evaporating; even if he melts, losing none of his weight'. Thus the poets who delight in this fallacy are chiefly of the second order—the reflective and perceptive—such as Wordsworth, Keats, and Tennyson; while the creative poets, for example, Shakespeare, Homer, and Dante, use it sparingly.

Next follows one of the most delightful and suggestive chapters in the volume, on 'Classical Landscape', or the way in which the Greeks looked at external nature. Take a specimen on the details of the Homeric landscape:—

As far as I recollect, without a single exception, every Homeric landscape, intended to be beautiful, is composed of a fountain, a meadow, and a shady grove. This ideal is very interestingly marked, as intended for a perfect one, in the fifth book of the 'Odyssey'; when Mercury himself stops for a moment, though on a message, to look at a landscape, 'which even an immortal might be gladdened to behold'. This landscape consists of a cave covered with a running vine, all blooming into grapes, and surrounded by a grove of alder, poplar, and sweet-smelling cypress. Four fountains of white (foaming) water, springing *in succession* (mark the orderliness), and close to one another, flow away in different directions, through a meadow full of violets and parsley (parsley, to mark its moisture, being elsewhere called 'marsh-nourished', and associated with the lotus); the air is perfumed not only by these violets and by the sweet cypress, but by Calypso's fire of finely chopped cedar wood, which sends a smoke, as of incense, through the island; Calypso herself is singing; and finally, upon the trees are resting, or roosting, owls, hawks, and 'long-tongued sea-crows'. Whether these last are considered as a part of the ideal landscape, as marine singing-birds, I know not; but the approval of Mercury appears to be elicited chiefly by the fountains and violet meadow.

Now the notable things in this description are, first, the evident subservience of the whole landscape to human comfort, to the foot, the taste, or the smell; and secondly, that throughout the passage there is not a single figurative word expressive of the things being in any wise other than plain grass, fruit, or flower. I have used the term 'spring' of the fountains, because, without doubt, Homer means that they sprang forth brightly, having their source at the foot of the rocks (as copious fountains nearly always have); but Homer does not say 'spring', he says simply flow, and uses only one word for 'growing softly', or 'richly', of the tall trees, the vine, and the violets. There is, however, some expression of sympathy with the sea-birds; he speaks of them in precisely the same terms, as in other places of naval nations, saying they 'have care of the works of the sea'.

If we glance through the references to pleasant landscape which occur in other parts of the 'Odyssey', we shall always be struck by this quiet subjection of their every feature to human service, and by the excessive similarity in the scenes. Perhaps the spot intended, after this, to be most perfect, may be the garden of Alcinous, where the principal ideas are, still more definitely, order, symmetry, and fruitfulness; the beds being duly ranged between rows of vines, which, as well as the pear, apple, and figtrees, bear fruit continually, some grapes being yet sour, while others are getting black; there are plenty of '*orderly* square beds of herbs', chiefly leeks, and two fountains, one running through the garden, and one under the pavement of the palace to a reservoir for the citizens. Ulysses, pausing to contemplate this scene, is described nearly in the same terms as Mercury, pausing to contemplate the wilder meadow; and it is interesting to observe, that, in spite of all Homer's love of symmetry, the god's admiration is excited by the free fountains, wild violets, and wandering vine; but the mortal's, by the vines in rows, the leeks in beds, and the fountains in pipes.

The mediaeval feeling for landscape is less utilitarian than the Greek. Everything is pleasurable and horticultural—the knights and ladies sing and make love in pleasaunces and rose-gardens. There is a more sentimental enjoyment in external nature; but, added to this, there is a new respect for mountains, as places where a solemn presence is to be felt, and spiritual good obtained. As Homer is the grand authority for Greek landscape, so is Dante for the mediaeval; and Mr Ruskin gives an elaborate study of the landscape in the 'Divina Commedia'. To the love of brilliancy shown in mediaeval landscape, is contrasted the love of clouds in the modern, 'so that if a general and characteristic name were needed for modern landscape art, none better could be found than "the service of clouds" '. But here again Mr Ruskin seeks for the spirit of landscape first of all in literature; and he expects to surprise his readers by selecting Scott as the typical poet, and greatest literary man of his age. He, very justly, we think, places Creative literature such as Scott's, above Sentimental literature, even when this is of as high a character as in some passages of Byron or Tennyson.

To invent a story, or admirably and thoroughly tell any part of a story, it is necessary to grasp the entire mind of every personage concerned in it, and know precisely how they would be affected by what happens; which to do requires a colossal intellect; but to describe a separate emotion delicately, it is only needed that one should feel it oneself; and thousands of people are capable of feeling this or that noble emotion for one who is able to enter into all the feelings of somebody sitting on the other side of the table . . . I unhesitatingly receive as a greater manifestation of power the right invention of a few sentences spoken by Pleydell and Mannering across their supper-table, than the most tender and passionate melodies of the self-examining verse.

This appreciation of Scott's power puts us in such excellent humour, that we are not inclined to quarrel with Mr Ruskin about another judgement of his, to which we cannot see our way, in spite of the arguments he adduces. According to him Scott was eminently *sad*, sadder than Byron. On the other hand, he shows that this sadness did not lead Scott into the pathetic fallacy: the bird, the brook, the flower, and the cornfield, kept their gladsomeness for him, not withstanding his own melancholy. But the more we look into Mr Ruskin's volume, the more we want to quote or to question; so, remembering that we have other books to tell the reader about, we must shut this very seductive one, and content ourselves with merely mentioning the chapters on the 'Moral of Landscape', and on the 'Teachers of Turner', which occupy the remaining pages; the latter preparing the way for the special consideration of Turner, which is to follow in the fourth volume. If the matter of this book had arrested us less, we should, perhaps, have laid more stress

on the illustrations, some of which are very beautiful: for
example, a view of the Apennines by sunset, and a group
of leaves and grasses, from the author's own pencil.

The Natural History of German Life
(1856)

IT is an interesting branch of psychological observation to note the images that are habitually associated with abstract or collective terms—what may be called the picture-writing of the mind, which it carries on concurrently with the more subtle symbolism of language. Perhaps the fixity or variety of these associated images would furnish a tolerably fair test of the amount of concrete knowledge and experience which a given word represents, in the minds of two persons who use it with equal familiarity. The word *railways*, for example, will probably call up, in the mind of a man who is not highly locomotive, the image either of a 'Bradshaw',* or of the station with which he is most familiar, or of an indefinite length of tram-road; he will alternate between these three images, which represent his stock of concrete acquaintance with railways. But suppose a man to have had successively the experience of a 'navvy', an engineer, a traveller, a railway director and shareholder, and a landed proprietor in treaty with a railway company, and it is probable that the range of images which would by turns present themselves to his mind at the mention of the *word* 'railways', would include all the essential facts in the existence and relations of the *thing*. Now it is possible for the first-mentioned personage to entertain very expanded views as to the multiplication of railways in the abstract, and their ultimate function in civilization. He may talk of a vast network of railways stretching over the globe, of future 'lines' in Madagascar, and elegant refreshment-rooms in the Sandwich Islands, with none the less glibness because his distinct conceptions on the subject do not extend beyond his one station and his indefinite length of tram-road. But it is evident that if we want a railway to be made, or its affairs to be managed, this man of wide views and narrow observation will not serve our purpose.

Probably, if we could ascertain the images called up by the terms 'the people', 'the masses', 'the proletariat', 'the peasantry', by many who theorize on those bodies with eloquence, or who legislate for them without eloquence, we should find that they indicate almost as small an amount of concrete knowledge—that they are as far from completely representing the complex facts summed up in the collective term, as the railway images of our non-locomotive gentleman. How little the real characteristics of the working classes are known to those who are outside them, how little their natural history has been studied, is sufficiently disclosed by our Art as well as by our political and social theories. Where, in our picture exhibitions, shall we find a group of true peasantry? What English artist even attempts to rival in truthfulness such studies of popular life as the pictures of Teniers or the ragged boys of Murillo? Even one of the greatest painters of the pre-eminently realistic school, while, in his picture of 'The Hireling Shepherd', he gave us a landscape of marvellous truthfulness, placed a pair of peasants in the foreground who were not much more real than the idyllic swains and damsels of our chimney ornaments.* Only a total absence of acquaintance and sympathy with our peasantry, could give a moment's popularity to such a picture as 'Cross Purposes', where we have a peasant girl who looks as if she knew L. E. L.'s* poems by heart, and English rustics, whose costume seems to indicate that they are meant for ploughmen, with exotic features that remind us of a handsome *primo tenore*. Rather than such cockney sentimentality as this, as an education for the taste and sympathies, we prefer the most crapulous group of boors that Teniers ever painted. But even those among our painters who aim at giving the rustic type of features, who are far above the effeminate feebleness of the 'Keepsake' style, treat their subjects under the influence of traditions and prepossessions rather than of direct observation. The notion that peasants are joyous, that the typical moment to represent a man in a smock-frock is when he is cracking a joke and showing a row of sound teeth, that cottage matrons are usually buxom, and village children necessarily rosy and merry, are prejudices difficult to dislodge from the artistic mind, which looks for its subjects into literature instead of life. The painter is still under the influence of idyllic literature, which has always expressed the imagination of the cultivated and town-bred, rather than the truth of rustic life. Idyllic ploughmen are jocund when they drive their team afield; idyllic shepherds make bashful love under hawthorn bushes; idyllic villagers dance in the chequered shade and refresh themselves, not immoderately, with spicy nutbrown ale. But no one who has seen much of actual ploughmen thinks them jocund; no one who is well acquainted with the English peasantry can pronounce them merry. The slow gaze, in which no sense of beauty beams, no humour twinkles,—the slow utterance, and the heavy slouching walk, remind one rather of that melancholy animal the camel, than of the sturdy countryman, with striped stockings, red waistcoat, and hat aside, who represents the traditional English peasant. Observe a company of haymakers. When you see them at a distance, tossing up the forkfuls of hay in the golden light, while the wagon creeps slowly with its increasing burthen over the meadow, and the bright green space which tells of work done gets larger and larger, you pronounce the scene 'smiling', and you think these companions in labour must be as bright and cheerful as the picture to which they give animation. Approach nearer, and you will certainly find that haymaking time is a time for joking, especially if there are women among the labourers; but the coarse laugh that bursts out every now and then, and expresses the triumphant taunt, is as far as possible from your conception of idyllic merriment. That delicious effervescence of the mind which we call fun, has no equivalent for the northern peasant, except tipsy revelry; the only realm of fancy and imagination for the English clown exists at the bottom of the third quart pot.

The conventional countryman of the stage, who picks up pocket-books and never looks into them, and who is too simple even to know that honesty has its opposite, represents the still lingering mistake, that an unintelligible dialect is a guarantee for ingenuousness, and that slouching shoulders indicate an upright disposition. It is quite true that a thresher is likely to be innocent of any adroit arithmetical cheating, but he is not the less likely to carry home his master's corn in his shoes and pocket; a reaper is not given to writing begging-letters, but he is quite capable of cajoling the dairymaid into filling his small-beer bottle with ale. The selfish instincts are not subdued by the sight of buttercups, nor is integrity in the least established by that classic rural occupation, sheep-washing. To make men moral, something more is requisite than to turn them out to grass.

Opera peasants, whose unreality excites Mr Ruskin's indignation,* are surely too frank an idealization to be misleading; and since popular chorus is one of the most effective elements of the opera, we can hardly object to lyric rustics in elegant laced bodices and picturesque motley, unless we are prepared to advocate a chorus of colliers in their pit costume, or a ballet of char-women and stocking-weavers. But our social novels profess to represent the people as they are, and the unreality of their representations is a grave evil. The greatest benefit we owe to the artist, whether painter, poet, or novelist, is the extension of our sympathies. Appeals founded on generalizations and statistics require a sympathy ready-made, a moral sentiment already in activity; but a picture of human life such as a great artist can give, surprises even the trivial and the selfish into that attention to what is apart from themselves, which may be called the raw material of moral sentiment. When Scott takes us into Luckie Mucklebackit's cottage,* or tells the story of 'The Two Drovers',—when Wordsworth sings to us the reverie of 'Poor Susan',—when Kingsley shows us Alton Locke gazing yearningly over the gate which leads from the highway into the first wood he ever saw,—when Hornung paints a group of chimney-sweepers,—more is done towards linking the higher classes with the lower, towards obliterating the vulgarity of exclusiveness, than by hundreds of sermons and philosophical dissertations. Art is the nearest thing to life; it is a mode of amplifying experience and extending our contact with our fellow-men beyond the bounds of our personal lot. All the more sacred is the task of the artist when he undertakes to paint the life of the People. Falsification here is far more pernicious than in the more artificial aspects of life. It is not so very serious that we should have false ideas about evanescent fashions—about the manners and conversation of beaux and duchesses; but it *is* serious that our sympathy with the perennial joys and struggles, the toil, the tragedy, and the humour in the life of our more heavily-laden fellow-men, should be perverted, and turned towards a false object instead of the true one.

This perversion is not the less fatal because the misrepresentation which gives rise to it has what the artist considers a moral end. The thing for mankind to know is, not what are the motives and influences which the moralist thinks *ought* to act on the labourer or the artisan, but what are the motives and influences which *do* act on him. We want to be taught to feel, not for the heroic artisan or the sentimental peasant, but for the peasant in all his coarse apathy, and the artisan in all his suspicious selfishness.

We have one great novelist who is gifted with the utmost power of rendering the external traits of our town population; and if he could give us their psychological character—their conceptions of life, and their emotions—with the same truth as their idiom and manners, his books would be the greatest contribution Art has ever made to the awakening of social sympathies. But while he can copy Mrs Plornish's colloquial style* with the delicate accuracy of a sun-picture, while there is the same startling inspiration in his description of the gestures and phrases of 'Boots',* as in the speeches of Shakespeare's mobs or numbskulls, he scarcely ever passes from the humorous and external to the emotional and tragic, without becoming as transcendent in his unreality as he was a moment before in his artistic truthfulness. But for the precious salt of his humour, which compels him to reproduce external traits that serve, in some degree, as a corrective to his frequently false psychology, his preternaturally virtuous poor children and artisans, his melodramatic boatmen and courtesans, would be as noxious as Eugène

Sue's idealized proletaires* in encouraging the miserable fallacy that high morality and refined sentiment can grow out of harsh social relations, ignorance, and want; or that the working classes are in a condition to enter at once into a millennial state of *altruism*,* wherein everyone is caring for everyone else, and no one for himself.

If we need a true conception of the popular character to guide our sympathies rightly, we need it equally to check our theories, and direct us in their application. The tendency created by the splendid conquests of modern generalization, to believe that all social questions are merged in economical science, and that the relations of men to their neighbours may be settled by algebraic equations,—the dream that the uncultured classes are prepared for a condition which appeals principally to their moral sensibilities,—the aristocratic dilettantism which attempts to restore the 'good old times' by a sort of idyllic masquerading, and to grow feudal fidelity and veneration as we grow prize turnips, by an artificial system of culture,*—none of these diverging mistakes can co-exist with a real knowledge of the People, with a thorough study of their habits, their ideas, their motives. The landholder, the clergyman, the mill-owner, the mining-agent, have each an opportunity for making precious observations on different sections of the working classes, but unfortunately their experience is too often not registered at all, or its results are too scattered to be available as a source of information and stimulus to the public mind generally. If any man of sufficient moral and intellectual breadth, whose observations would not be vitiated by a foregone conclusion, or by a professional point of view, would devote himself to studying the natural history of our social classes, especially of the small shopkeepers, artisans, and peasantry,—the degree in which they are influenced by local conditions, their maxims and habits, the points of view from which they regard their religious teachers, and the degree in which they are influenced by religious doctrines, the interaction of the various classes on each other, and what are the tendencies in their positon towards disintegration or towards development,—and if, after all this study, he would give us the result of his observations in a book well-nourished with specific facts, his work would be a valuable aid to the social and political reformer.

What we are desiring for ourselves has been in some degree done for the Germans by Riehl, the author of the very remarkable books the titles of which are placed at the head of this article; and we wish to make these books known to our readers, not only for the sake of the interesting matter they contain and the important reflections they suggest, but also as a model for some future or actual student of our own people. By way of introducing Riehl to those who are unacquainted with his writings, we will give a rapid sketch from his picture of the German Peasantry, and perhaps this indication of the mode in which he treats a particular branch of his subject may prepare them to follow us with more interest when we enter on the general purpose and contents of his works.

In England, at present, when we speak of the peasantry, we mean scarcely more than the class of farm-servants and farm-labourers; and it is only in the most primitive districts, as in Wales, for example, that farmers are included under the term. In order to appreciate what Riehl says of the German peasantry, we must remember what the tenant-farmers and small proprietors were in England half a century ago, when the master helped to milk his own cows, and the daughters got up at one o'clock in the morning to brew,—when the family dined in the kitchen with the servants, and sat with them round the kitchen fire in the evening. In those days, the quarried parlour was innocent of a carpet, and its only specimens of art were a framed sampler and the best tea-board; the daughters even of substantial farmers had often no greater accomplishment in writing and spelling than they could procure at a dame-school; and, instead of carrying on sentimental correspondence, they were spinning their future table-linen, and looking after every saving in butter and eggs that might enable them to add to the little stock of plate and china which they were laying in against their marriage. In our own day, setting aside the superior order of farmers, whose style of living and mental culture are often equal to that of the professional class in provincial towns, we can hardly enter the least imposing farm-house without finding a bad piano in the 'drawing-room', and some old annuals, disposed with a symmetrical imitation of negligence, on the table; though the daughters may still drop their *h*'s, their vowels are studiously narrow; and it is only in very primitive regions that they will consent to sit in a covered vehicle without springs, which was once thought an advance in luxury on the pillion.

The condition of the tenant-farmers and small proprietors in Germany is, we imagine, about on a par, not, certainly, in material prosperity, but in mental culture and habits, with that of the English farmers who were beginning to be thought old-fashioned nearly fifty years ago, and if we add to these the farm servants and labourers, we shall have a class approximating in its characteristics to the *Bauernthum*, or peasantry, described by Riehl.

In Germany, perhaps more than in any other country, it is among the peasantry that we must look for the historical type of the national *physique*. In the towns this type has become so modified to express the personality of the individual, that even 'family likeness' is often but faintly marked. But the peasants may still be distinguished into groups by their physical peculiarities. In one part of the country we find a longer-legged, in another a broader-shouldered race, which has inherited these peculiarities for centuries. For example, in certain districts of Hesse are seen long faces, with high foreheads, long, straight noses, and small eyes with arched eyebrows and large eyelids. On comparing these physiognomies with the sculptures in the church of St Elizabeth, at Marburg, executed in the thirteenth century, it will be found that the same old Hessian type of face has subsisted unchanged, with this distinction only, that the sculptures represent princes and nobles, whose features then bore the stamp of their race, while that stamp is now to be found only among the peasants. A painter who wants to draw mediæval characters with historic truth, must seek his models among the peasantry. This explains why the old German painters gave the heads of their subjects a greater uniformity of type than the painters of our day: the race had not attained to a high degree of individualization in features and expression. It indicates, too, that the cultured man acts more as an individual; the peasant, more as one of a group. Hans drives the plough, lives, and thinks just as Kunz does; and it is this fact, that many thousands of men are as like each other in thoughts and habits as so many sheep or oysters, which constitutes the weight of the peasantry in the social and political scale.

In the cultivated world each individual has his style of speaking and writing. But among the peasantry it is the race, the district, the province, that has its style; namely, its dialect, its phraseology, its proverbs and its songs, which belong alike to the entire body of the people. This provincial style of the peasant is again, like his *physique*, a remnant of history to which he clings with the utmost tenacity. In certain parts of Hungary, there are still descendants of German colonists of the twelfth and thirteenth centuries, who go about the country as reapers, retaining their old Saxon songs and manners, while the more cultivated German emigrants in a very short time forget their own language, and speak Hungarian. Another remarkable case of the same kind is that of the Wends, a Slavonic race settled in Lusatia,* whose numbers amount to 200,000, living either scattered among the German population or in separate parishes. They have their own schools and churches, and are taught in the Slavonic tongue. The Catholics among them are rigid adherents of the Pope; the Protestants not less rigid adherents of Luther, or *Doctor* Luther, as they are particular in calling him—a custom which, a hundred years ago, was universal in Protestant Germany. The Wend clings tenaciously to the usages of his Church, and perhaps this may contribute not a little to the purity in which he maintains the specific characteristics of his race. German education, German law and government, service in the standing army, and many other agencies, are in antagonism to his national exclusiveness; but the *wives* and *mothers* here, as elsewhere, are a conservative influence, and the habits temporarily laid aside in the outer world are recovered by the fireside. The Wends form several stout regiments in the Saxon army; they are sought far and wide, as diligent and honest servants; and many a weakly Dresden or Leipzig child becomes thriving under the care of a Wendish nurse. In their villages they have the air and habits of genuine, sturdy peasants, and all their customs indicate that they have been, from the first, an agricultural people. For example, they have traditional modes of treating their domestic animals. Each cow has its own name, generally chosen carefully, so as to express the special qualities of the animal; and all important family events are narrated to the *bees*—a custom which is found also in Westphalia. Whether by the help of the bees or not, the Wend farming is especially prosperous; and when a poor Bohemian peasant has a son born to him, he binds him to the end of a long pole and turns his face towards Lusatia, that he may be as lucky as the Wends who live there.

The peculiarity of the peasant's language consists chiefly in his retention of historical peculiarities, which gradually disappear under the friction of cultivated circles. He prefers any proper name that may be given to a day in the calendar, rather than the abstract date, by which he very rarely reckons. In the baptismal names of his children he is guided by the old custom of the country, not at all by whim and fancy. Many old baptismal names, formerly common in Germany, would have become extinct but for their preservation among the peasantry, especially in North Germany; and so firmly have they adhered to local tradition in this matter, that it would be possible to give a sort of topographical statistic of proper names, and distinguish a district by its rustic names as we do by its Flora and Fauna. The continuous inheritance of certain favourite proper names in a family, in some districts, forces the peasant to adopt the princely custom of attaching a numeral to the name, and saying, when three generations are living at once, Hans I, II, and III; or—in the more antique fashion—Hans the elder, the middle, and the younger. In some of our English counties there is a similar adherence to a narrow range of proper names, and as a mode of distinguishing collateral branches in the same family, you will hear of Jonathan's Bess, Thomas's Bess, and Samuel's Bess—the three Bessies being cousins.*

The peasant's adherence to the traditional has much greater inconvenience than that entailed by a paucity of proper names. In the Black Forest and in Hüttenberg you will see him in the dog-days wearing a thick fur cap, because it is an historical fur cap—a cap worn by his grandfather. In the Wetterau, that peasant girl is considered the handsomest who wears the most petticoats. To go to field-labour in seven petticoats can be anything but convenient or agreeable; but it is the traditionally correct thing, and a German peasant girl would think herself as unfavourably conspicuous in an untraditional costume, as an English servant-girl would now think herself in a 'linsey-woolsey' apron or a thick muslin cap. In many districts no medical advice would induce the rustic to renounce the tight leather belt with which he injures his digestive functions; you could more easily persuade him to smile on a new communal system than on the unhistorical invention of braces. In the eighteenth century, in spite of the philanthropic preachers of potatoes, the peasant for years threw his potatoes to the pigs and the dogs, before he could be persuaded to put them on his own table. However, the unwillingness of the peasant to adopt innovations has a not unreasonable foundation in the fact, that for him experiments are practical, not theoretical, and must be made with expense of money instead of brains—a fact that is not, perhaps, sufficiently taken into account by agricultural theorists, who complain of the farmer's obstinacy. The peasant has the smallest possible faith in theoretic knowledge; he thinks it rather dangerous than otherwise, as is well indicated by a Lower Rhenish proverb—'One is never too old to learn, said an old woman; so she learned to be a witch.'

Between many villages an historical feud, once perhaps the occasion of much bloodshed, is still kept up under the milder form of an occasional round of cudgelling, and the launching of traditional nicknames. An historical feud of this kind still exists, for example, among many villages on the

Rhine and more inland places in the neighbourhood. *Rheinschnacke* (of which the equivalent is perhaps 'water-snake') is the standing term of ignominy for the inhabitant of the Rhine village, who repays it in kind by the epithet 'karst' (mattock) or 'kukuk' (cuckoo), according as the object of his hereditary hatred belongs to the field or the forest. If any Romeo among the 'mattocks' were to marry a Juliet among the 'water-snakes', there would be no lack of Tybalts and Mercutios to carry the conflict from words to blows, though neither side knows a reason for the enmity.

A droll instance of peasant conservatism is told of a village on the Taunus, whose inhabitants, from time immemorial, had been famous for impromptu cudgelling. For this historical offence the magistrates of the district had always inflicted the equally historical punishment of shutting up the most incorrigible offenders, not in prison, but in their own pig-sty. In recent times, however, the government, wishing to correct the rudeness of these peasants, appointed an 'enlightened' man as magistrate, who at once abolished the original penalty above-mentioned. But this relaxation of punishment was so far from being welcome to the villagers, that they presented a petition praying that a more energetic man might be given them as a magistrate, who would have the courage to punish according to law and justice, 'as had been beforetime'. And the magistrate who abolished incarceration in the pig-sty could never obtain the respect of the neighbourhood. This happened no longer ago than the beginning of the present century.

But it must not be supposed that the historical piety of the German peasant extends to anything not immediately connected with himself. He has the warmest piety towards the old tumbledown house which his grandfather built, and which nothing will induce him to improve, but towards the venerable ruins of the old castle that overlooks his village he has no piety at all, and carries off its stones to make a fence for his garden, or tears down the gothic carving of the old monastic church, which is 'nothing to him', to mark off a foot-path through his field. It is the same with historical traditions. The peasant has them fresh in his memory, so far as they relate to himself. In districts where the peasantry are unadulterated, you discern the remnants of the feudal relations in innumerable customs and phrases, but you will ask in vain for historical traditions concerning the empire, or even concerning the particular princely house to which the peasant is subject. He can tell you what 'half people and whole people' mean; in Hesse you will still hear of 'four horses making a whole peasant', or of 'four-day and three-day peasants'; but you will ask in vain about Charlemagne and Frederic Barbarossa.

Riehl well observes that the feudal system, which made the peasant the bondman of his lord, was an immense benefit in a country, the greater part of which had still to be colonized,—rescued the peasant from vagabondage, and laid the foundation of persistency and endurance in future generations. If a free German peasantry belongs only to modern times, it is to his ancestor who was a serf, and even, in the earliest times, a slave, that the peasant owes the foundation of his independence, namely, his capability of a settled existence,—nay, his unreasoning persistency, which has its important function in the development of the race.

Perhaps the very worst result of that unreasoning persistency is the peasant's inveterate habit of litigation. Every one remembers the immortal description of Dandie Dinmont's importunate application to Lawyer Pleydell to manage his 'bit lawsuit', till at length Pleydell consents to help him ruin himself, on the ground that Dandie may fall into worse hands.* It seems, this is a scene which has many parallels in Germany. The farmer's lawsuit is his point of honour; and he will carry it through, though he knows from the very first day that he shall get nothing by it. The litigious peasant piques himself, like Mr Saddletree,* on his knowledge of the law, and this vanity is the chief impulse to many a lawsuit. To the mind of the peasant, law presents itself as the 'custom of the country', and it is his pride to be versed in all customs. *Custom with him holds the place of sentiment, of theory, and in many cases of affection.* Riehl justly urges the importance of simplifying law proceedings, so as to cut off this vanity at its source, and also of encouraging, by every possible means, the practice of arbitration.

The peasant never begins his lawsuit in summer, for the same reason that he does not make love and marry in summer,—because he has no time for that sort of thing. Anything is easier to him than to move out of his habitual course, and he is attached even to his privations. Some years ago, a peasant youth, out of the poorest and remotest region of the Westerwald, was enlisted as a recruit, at Weilburg in Nassau. The lad, having never in his life slept in a bed, when he had to get into one for the first time began to cry like a child; and he deserted twice because he could not reconcile himself to sleeping in a bed, and to the 'fine' life of the barracks: he was homesick at the thought of his accustomed poverty and his thatched hut. A strong contrast, this, with the feeling of the poor in towns, who would be far enough from deserting because their condition was too much improved! The genuine peasant is never ashamed of his rank and calling; he is rather inclined to look down on every one who does not wear a smock-frock, and thinks a man who has the manners of the gentry is likely to be rather windy and unsubstantial. In some places, even in French districts, this feeling is strongly symbolized by the practice of the peasantry, on certain festival days, to dress the images of the saints in peasant's clothing. History tells us of all kinds of peasant insurrections, the object of which was to obtain relief for the peasants from some of their many oppressions; but of an effort on their part to step out of their hereditary rank and calling, to become gentry, to leave the plough and carry on the easier business of capitalists or government-functionaries, there is no example.

The German novelists who undertake to give pictures of peasant-life, fall into the same mistake as our English novelists; they transfer their own feelings to ploughmen and woodcutters, and give them both joys and sorrows of which they know nothing. The peasant never questions the obligation of family-ties—he questions *no custom*,—but tender affection, as it exists amongst the refined part of mankind, is almost as foreign to him as white hands and filbert-shaped nails. That the aged father who has given up his property to his children on condition of their maintaining him for the remainder of his life, is very far from meeting with delicate attentions, is indicated by the proverb current among the peasantry—'Don't take your clothes off before you go to bed.' Among rustic moral tales and parables, not one is more universal than the story of the ungrateful children, who made their greyheaded father, dependent on them for a maintenance, eat at a wooden trough, because he shook the food out of his trembling hands. Then these same ungrateful children observed one day that their own little boy was making a tiny wooden trough; and when they asked him what it was for, he answered—that his father and mother might eat out of it, when he was a man and had to keep them.

Marriage is a very prudential affair, especially among the peasants who have the largest share of property. Politic marriages are as common among them as among princes; and when a peasant-heiress in Westphalia marries, her husband adopts her name, and places his own after it with the prefix *geborner (né)*. The girls marry young, and the rapidity with which they get old and ugly is one among the many proofs that the early years of marriage are fuller of hardships than of conjugal tenderness. 'When our writers of village stories,' says Riehl, 'transferred their own emotional life to the peasant, they obliterated what is precisely his most predominant characteristic, namely, that with him general custom holds the place of individual feeling.'

We pay for greater emotional susceptibility too often by nervous diseases of which the peasant knows nothing. To him headache is the least of physical evils, because he thinks headwork the easiest and least indispensable of all labour. Happily, many of the younger sons in peasant families, by going to seek their living in the towns, carry their hardy nervous system to amalgamate with the overwrought nerves of our town population, and refresh them with a little rude vigour. And a return to the habits of peasant life is the best remedy for many moral as well as physical diseases induced by perverted civilization. Riehl points to colonization as presenting the true field for this regenerative process. On the other side of the ocean, a man will have the courage to begin life again as a peasant, while at home, perhaps, opportunity as well as courage will fail him. *Apropos* of this subject of emigration, he remarks the striking fact, that the native shrewdness and mother-wit of the German peasant seem to forsake him entirely when he has to apply them under new circumstances, and on relations foreign to his experience. Hence it is that the German peasant who emigrates, so constantly falls a victim to unprincipled adventurers in the preliminaries to emigration; but if once he gets his foot on the American soil, he exhibits all the first-rate qualities of an agricultural colonist; and among all German emigrants, the peasant class are the most successful.

But many disintegrating forces have been at work on the peasant character, and degeneration is unhappily going on at a greater pace than development. In the wine districts especially, the inability of the small proprietors to bear up under the vicissitudes of the market, or to ensure a high quality of wine by running the risks of a late vintage, and the competition of beer and cider with the inferior wines, have tended to produce that uncertainty of gain which, with the peasant, is the inevitable cause of demoralization. The small peasant proprietors are not a new class in Germany, but many of the evils of their position are new. They are more dependent on ready money than formerly; thus, where a peasant used to get his wood for building and firing from the common forest, he has now to pay for it with hard cash; he used to thatch his own house, with the help perhaps of a neighbour, but now he pays a man to do it for him; he used to pay taxes in kind, he now pays them in money. The chances of the market have to be discounted, and the peasant falls into the hands of money-lenders. Here is one of the cases in which social policy clashes with a purely economical policy.

Political vicissitudes have added their influence to that of economical changes in disturbing that dim instinct, that reverence for traditional custom, ·which is the peasant's principle of action. He is in the midst of novelties for which he knows no reason—changes in political geography, changes of the government to which he owes fealty, changes in bureaucratic management and police regulations. He finds himself in a new element before an apparatus for breathing in it is developed in him. His only knowledge of modern history is in some of its results—for instance, that he has to pay heavier taxes from year to year. His chief idea of a government is of a power that raises his taxes, opposes his harmless customs, and torments him with new formalities. The source of all this is the false system of 'enlightening' the peasant which has been adopted by the bureaucratic governments. A system which disregards the traditions and hereditary attachments of the peasant, and appeals only to a logical understanding which is not yet developed in him, is simply disintegrating and ruinous to the peasant character. The interference with the communal regulations has been of this fatal character. Instead of endeavouring to promote to the utmost the healthy life of the Commune, as an organism the conditions of which are bound up with the historical characteristics of the peasant, the bureaucratic plan of government is bent on improvement by its patent machinery of state-appointed functionaries and off-hand regulations in accordance with modern enlightenment. The spirit of communal exclusiveness—the resistance to the indiscriminate establishment of strangers, is an intense traditional feeling in the peasant. 'This gallows is for us and our children', is the typical motto of this spirit. But such exclusiveness is highly irrational and repugnant to modern liberalism; therefore a bureaucratic government at once opposes it, and encourages to the utmost the introduction of new inhabitants in the provincial communes. Instead of allowing the peasants to manage their own affairs, and, if they happen to believe that five and four make eleven, to unlearn the prejudice by their own experience in calculation, so that they may gradually understand processes, and not merely see results, bureaucracy comes with its 'Ready Reckoner' and works all the peasant's sums for him—the surest way of maintaining him in his stupidity, however it may shake his prejudice.

Another questionable plan for elevating the peasant, is the supposed elevation of the clerical character by preventing the clergyman from cultivating more than a trifling part of the land attached to his benefice; that he may be as much as possible of a scientific theologian, and as little as possible of a peasant. In this, Riehl observes, lies one great source of weakness to the Protestant Church as compared with the Catholic, which finds the great majority of its priests among the lower orders; and we have had the opportunity of making an analogous comparison in England, where many of us can remember country districts in which the great mass of the people were christianized by illiterate Methodist and Independent ministers, while the influence of the parish clergyman among the poor did not extend much beyond a few old women in scarlet cloaks, and a few exceptional church-going labourers.

Bearing in mind the general characteristics of the German peasant, it is easy to understand his relation to the revolutionary ideas and revolutionary movements of modern times. The peasant, in Germany as elsewhere, is a born grumbler. He has always plenty of grievances in his pocket, but he does not generalize those grievances; he does not complain of 'government' or 'society', probably because he has good reason to complain of the burgomaster. When a few sparks from the first French Revolution fell among the German peasantry, and in certain villages of Saxony the country people assembled together to write down their demands, there was no glimpse in their petition of the 'universal rights of man', but simply of their own particular affairs as Saxon peasants. Again, after the July revolution of 1830, there were many insignificant peasant insurrections; but the object of almost all was the removal of local grievances. Toll-houses were pulled down; stamped paper was destroyed; in some places there was a persecution of wild boars, in others, of that plentiful tame animal, the German *Rath*, or councillor who is never called into council. But in 1848, it seemed as if the movements of the peasants had taken a new character; in the small western states of Germany, it seemed as if the whole class of peasantry was in insurrection. But in fact, the peasant did not know the meaning of the part he was playing. He had heard that everything was being set right in the towns, and that wonderful things were happening there, so he tied up his bundle and set off. Without any distinct object or resolution, the country people presented themselves on the scene of commotion, and were warmly received by the party leaders. But, seen from the windows of ducal palaces and ministerial hotels, these swarms of peasants had quite another aspect, and it was imagined that they had a common plan of co-operation. This, however, the peasants have never had. Systematic co-operation implies general conceptions, and a provisional subordination of egoism, to which even the artisans of towns have rarely shown themselves equal, and which are as foreign to the mind of the peasant as logarithms or the doctrine of chemical proportions. And the revolutionary fervour of the peasant was soon cooled. The old mistrust of the towns was reawakened on the spot. The Tyrolese peasants saw no great good in the freedom of the press and the constitution, because these changes 'seemed to please the gentry so much'. Peasants who had given their voices stormily for a German parliament, asked afterwards, with a doubtful look, whether it were to consist of infantry or cavalry. When royal domains were declared the property of the State, the peasants in some small principalities rejoiced over this, because they interpreted it to mean that every one would have his share in them, after the manner of the old common and forest rights.

The very practical views of the peasants, with regard to the demands of the people, were in amusing contrast with the abstract theorizing of the educated townsmen. The peasant continually withheld all State payments until he saw how matters would turn out, and was disposed to reckon up the solid benefit, in the form of land or money, that might come to him from the changes obtained. While the townsman was heating his brains about representation on the broadest basis, the peasant asked if the relation between tenant and landlord would continue as before, and whether the removal of the 'feudal obligations' meant that the farmer should become owner of the land?

It is in the same naïve way that Communism is interpreted by the German peasantry. The wide spread among them of communistic doctrines, the eagerness with which they listened to a plan for the partition of property, seemed to countenance the notion, that it was a delusion to suppose the peasant would be secured from this intoxication by his love of secure possession and peaceful earnings. But, in fact, the peasant contemplated 'partition' by the light of an historical reminiscence rather than of novel theory. The golden age, in the imagination of the peasant, was the time when every member of the commune had a right to as much wood from the forest as would enable him to sell some, after using what he wanted in firing,—in which the communal possessions were so profitable that, instead of his having to pay rates at the end of the year, each member of the commune was something in pocket. Hence the peasants in general understood by 'partition', that the State lands, especially the forests, would be divided among the communes, and that, by some political legerdemain or other, everybody would have free fire-wood, free grazing for his cattle, and over and above that, a piece of gold without working for it. That he should give up a single clod of his own to further the general 'partition', had never entered the mind of the peasant Communist; and the perception that this was an essential preliminary to 'partition', was often a sufficient cure for his Communism.

In villages lying in the neighbourhood of large towns, however, where the circumstances of the peasantry are very different, quite another interpretation of Communism is prevalent. Here the peasant is generally sunk to the position of the proletaire, living from hand to mouth; he has nothing to lose, but everything to gain by 'partition'. The coarse nature of the peasant has here been corrupted into bestiality by the disturbance of his instincts, while he is as yet incapable of principles; and in this type of the degenerate peasant is seen the worst example of ignorance intoxicated by theory.

A significant hint as to the interpretation the peasants put on revolutionary theories, may be drawn from the way they employed the few weeks in which their movements were unchecked. They felled the forest trees and shot the game; they withheld taxes; they shook off the imaginary or real burdens imposed on them by their mediatized princes, by presenting their 'demands' in a very rough way before the ducal or princely 'Schloss'; they set their faces against the bureaucratic management of the communes, deposed the government functionaries who had been placed over them as burgomasters and magistrates, and abolished the whole bureaucratic system of procedure, simply by taking no notice of its regulations, and recurring to some tradition—some old order or disorder of things. In all this it is clear that they were animated not in the least by the spirit of modern revolution, but by a purely narrow and personal impulse towards reaction.

The idea of constitutional government lies quite beyond the range of the German peasant's conceptions. His only notion of representation is that of a representation of ranks—of classes; his only notion of a deputy is of one who takes care, not of the national welfare, but of the interests of his own order. Herein lay the great mistake of the democratic party, in common with the bureaucratic governments, that they entirely omitted the peculiar character of the peasant from their political calculations. They talked of the 'people', and forgot that the peasants were included in the term. Only a baseless misconception of the peasant's character could induce the supposition that he would feel the slightest enthusiasm about the principles involved in the reconstitution of the Empire, or even about that reconstitution itself. He has no zeal for a written law, as such, but only so far as it takes the form of a living law—a tradition. It was the external authority which the revolutionary party had won in Baden that attracted the peasants into a participation in the struggle.

Such, Riehl tells us, are the general characteristics of the German peasantry—characteristics which subsist amidst a wide variety of circumstances. In Mecklenburg, Pomerania, and Brandenburg, the peasant lives on extensive estates; in Westphalia he lives in large isolated homesteads; in the

Westerwald and in Sauerland, in little groups of villages and hamlets; on the Rhine, land is for the most part parcelled out among small proprietors, who live together in large villages. Then, of course, the diversified physical geography of Germany gives rise to equally diversified methods of land-culture; and out of these various circumstances grow numerous specific differences in manner and character. But the generic character of the German peasant is everywhere the same: in the clean mountain hamlet and in the dirty fishing village on the coast; in the plains of North Germany and in the backwoods of America. 'Everywhere he has the same historical character—everywhere custom is his supreme law. Where religion and patriotism are still a naïve instinct—are still a sacred *custom*, there begins the class of the German Peasantry.'

Our readers will perhaps already have gathered from the foregoing portrait of the German peasant, that Riehl is not a man who looks at objects through the spectacles either of the doctrinaire or the dreamer; and they will be ready to believe what he tells us in his Preface, namely, that years ago he began his wanderings over the hills and plains of Germany for the sake of obtaining, in immediate intercourse with the people, that completion of his historical, political, and economical studies which he was unable to find in books. He began his investigations with no party prepossessions, and his present views were evolved entirely from his own gradually amassed observations. He was, first of all, a pedestrian, and only in the second place a political author. The views at which he has arrived by this inductive process, he sums up in the term—*social-political-conservatism*; but his conservatism is, we conceive, of a thoroughly philosophical kind. He sees in European society *incarnate history*, and any attempt to disengage it from its historical elements must, he believes, be simply destructive of social vitality.[1] What has grown up historically can only die out historically, by the gradual operation of necessary laws. The external

---

[1] Throughout this article, in our statement of Riehl's opinions, we must be understood not as quoting Riehl, but as interpreting and illustrating him.

conditions which society has inherited from the past are but the manifestation of inherited internal conditions in the human beings who compose it; the internal conditions and the external are related to each other as the organism and its medium, and development can take place only by the gradual consentaneous development of both. Take the familiar example of attempts to abolish titles, which have been about as effective as the process of cutting off poppy-heads in a corn-field. *Jedem Menschen*, says Riehl, *ist sein Zopf angeboren, warum soll denn der sociale Sprachgebrauch nicht auch seinen Zopf haben?*—which we may render—'As long as snobbism runs in the blood, why should it not run in our speech?' As a necessary preliminary to a purely rational society, you must obtain purely rational men, free from the sweet and bitter prejudices of hereditary affection and antipathy; which is as easy as to get running streams without springs, or the leafy shade of the forest without the secular growth of trunk and branch.

The historical conditions of society may be compared with those of language. It must be admitted that the language of cultivated nations is in anything but a rational state; the great sections of the civilized world are only approximatively intelligible to each other, and even that, only at the cost of long study; one word stands for many things, and many words for one thing; the subtle shades of meaning, and still subtler echoes of association, make language an instrument which scarcely anything short of genius can wield with definiteness and certainty. Suppose, then, that the effort which has been again and again made to construct a universal language on a rational basis has at length succeeded, and that you have a language which has no uncertainty, no whims of idiom, no cumbrous forms, no fitful shimmer of many-hued significance, no hoary archaisms 'familiar with forgotten years'* a patent deodorized and nonresonant language, which effects the purpose of communication as perfectly and rapidly as algebraic signs. Your language may be a perfect medium of expression to science, but will never express *life*, which is a great deal more than science. With the anomalies and inconveniences of historical language, you will have parted with its music and its passion, with its vital qualities as an expression of individual character, with its subtle capabilities of wit, with everything that gives it power over the imagination; and the next step in simplification will be the invention of a talking watch, which will achieve the utmost facility and dispatch in the communication of ideas by a graduated adjustment of ticks, to be represented in writing by a corresponding arrangement of dots. A melancholy 'language of the future'! The sensory and motor nerves that run in the same sheath, are scarcely bound together by a more necessary and delicate union than that which binds men's affections, imagination, wit, and humour, with the subtle ramifications of historical language. Language must be left to grow in precision, completeness, and unity, as minds grow in clearness, comprehensiveness, and sympathy. And there is an analogous relation between the moral tendencies of men and the social conditions they have inherited. The nature of European men has its roots intertwined with the past, and can only be developed by allowing those roots to remain undisturbed while the process of development is going on, until that perfect ripeness of the seed which carries with it a life independent of the root. This vital connexion with the past is much more vividly felt on the Continent than in England, where we have to recall it by an effort of memory and reflection; for though our English life is in its core intensely traditional, Protestantism and commerce have modernized the face of the land and the aspects of society in a far greater degree than in any continental country:—

'Abroad,' says Ruskin, 'a building of the eighth or tenth century stands ruinous in the open street; the children play round it, the peasants heap their corn in it, the buildings of yesterday nestle about it, and fit their new stones in its rents, and tremble in sympathy as it trembles. No one wonders at it, or thinks of it as separate, and of another time; we feel the ancient world to be a real thing, and one with the new; antiquity is no dream; it is rather the children playing about the old stones that are the dream. But all is continuous; and the words "from generation to generation" understandable here.'

This conception of European society as incarnate history, is the fundamental idea of Riehl's books. After the notable failure of revolutionary attempts conducted from the point of view of abstract democratic and socialistic theories, after the practical demonstration of the evils resulting from a bureaucratic system which governs by an undiscriminating, dead mechanism, Riehl wishes to urge on the consideration of his countrymen, a social policy founded on the special study of the people as they are—on the natural history of the various social ranks. He thinks it wise to pause a little from theorizing, and see what is the material actually present for theory to work upon. It is the glory of the Socialists—in contrast with the democratic doctrinaires who have been too much occupied with the general idea of 'the people' to inquire particularly into the actual life of the people—that they have thrown themselves with enthusiastic zeal into the study at least of one social group, namely, the factory operatives; and here lies the secret of their partial success. But unfortunately, they have made this special study of a single fragment of society the basis of a theory which quietly substitutes for the small group of Parisian proletaires or English factory-workers, the society of all Europe—nay, of the whole world. And in this way they have lost the best fruit of their investigations. For, says Riehl, the more deeply we penetrate into the knowledge of society in its details, the more thoroughly we shall be convinced that *a universal social policy has no validity except on paper*, and can never be carried into successful practice. The conditions of German society are altogether different from those of French, of English, or of Italian society; and to apply the same social theory to these nations indiscriminately, is about as wise a procedure as Triptolemus Yellowley's application of the agricultural directions in Virgil's 'Georgies' to his farm in the Shetland Isles.*

It is the clear and strong light in which Riehl places this important position, that in our opinion constitutes the suggestive value of his books for foreign as well as German readers. It has not been sufficiently insisted on, that in the various branches of Social Science there is an advance from the general to the special, from the simple to the complex, analogous with that which is found in the series of the sciences, from Mathematics to Biology.* To the laws of quantity comprised in Mathematics and Physics are super-added, in Chemistry, laws of quality; to these again are added, in Biology, laws of life; and lastly, the conditions of life in general, branch out into its special conditions, or Natural History, on the one hand, and into its abnormal conditions, or Pathology, on the other. And in this series or ramification of the sciences, the more general science will not suffice to solve the problems of the more special. Chemistry embraces phenomena which are not explicable by Physics; Biology embraces phenomena which are not explicable by Chemistry; and no biological generalization will enable us to predict the infinite specialities produced by the complexity of vital conditions. So Social Science, while it has departments which in their fundamental generality correspond to mathematics and physics, namely, those grand and simple generalizations which trace out the inevitable march of the human race as a whole, and, as a ramification of these, the laws of economical science, has also, in the departments of government and jurisprudence, which embrace the conditions of social life in all their complexity, what may be called its Biology, carrying us on to innumerable special phenomena which outlie the sphere of science, and belong to Natural History. And just as the most thorough acquaintance with physics, or chemistry, or general physiology will not enable you at once to establish the balance of life in your private vivarium, so that your particular society of zoophytes, molluscs, and echinoderms may feel themselves, as the Germans say, at ease in their skin; so the most complete equipment of theory will not enable a statesman or a political and social reformer to adjust his measures wisely, in the absence of a special acquaintance with the section of society for which he legislates, with the peculiar characteristics of the nation, the province, the class whose well-being he has to consult. In other words, a wise social policy must be based not simply on abstract social science, but on the Natural History of social bodies.

Riehl's books are not dedicated merely to the argumentative maintenance of this or of any other position; they are
intended chiefly as a contribution to that knowledge of the
German people on the importance of which he insists. He
is less occupied with urging his own conclusions than with
impressing on his readers the facts which have led him to
those conclusions. In the volume entitled *Land und Leute*,
which, though published last, is properly an introduction to
the volume entitled *Die Bürgerliche Gesellschaft*, he considers
the German people in their physical-geographical relations;
he compares the natural divisions of the race, as determined
by land and climate, and social traditions, with the artificial
divisions which are based on diplomacy; and he traces the
genesis and influences of what we may call the ecclesiastical
geography of Germany—its partition between Catholicism
and Protestantism. He shows that the ordinary antithesis of
North and South Germany represents no real ethnographical
distinction, and that the natural divisions of Germany,
founded on its physical geography, are threefold; namely,
the low plains, the middle mountain region, and the high
mountain region, or Lower, Middle, and Upper Germany;
and on this primary natural division all the other broad
ethnographical distinctions of Germany will be found to
rest. The plains of North or Lower Germany include all
the seaboard the nation possesses; and this, together with
the fact that they are traversed to the depth of 600 miles
by navigable rivers, makes them the natural seat of a trading
race. Quite different is the geographical character of Middle
Germany. While the northern plains are marked off into
great divisions, by such rivers as the Lower Rhine, the
Weser, and the Oder, running almost in parallel lines, this
central region is cut up like a mosaic by the capricious lines
of valleys and rivers. Here is the region in which you find
those famous roofs from which the rain-water runs towards
two different seas, and the mountain-tops from which you
may look into eight or ten German States. The abundance
of water-power and the presence of extensive coal-mines
allow of a very diversified industrial development in Middle
Germany. In Upper Germany, or the high mountain region,

we find the same symmetry in the lines of the rivers as in the north; almost all the great Alpine streams flow parallel with the Danube. But the majority of these rivers are neither navigable nor available for industrial objects, and instead of serving for communication, they shut off one great tract from another. The slow development, the simple peasant life of many districts is here determined by the mountain and the river. In the south-east, however, industrial activity spreads through Bohemia towards Austria, and forms a sort of balance to the industrial districts of the Lower Rhine. Of course, the boundaries of these three regions cannot be very strictly defined; but an approximation to the limits of Middle Germany may be obtained by regarding it as a triangle, of which one angle lies in Silesia, another in Aix-la-Chapelle, and a third at Lake Constance.

This triple division corresponds with the broad distinctions of climate. In the northern plains the atmosphere is damp and heavy; in the southern mountain region it is dry and rare, and there are abrupt changes of temperature, sharp contrasts between the seasons, and devastating storms; but in both these zones men are hardened by conflict with the roughnesses of the climate. In Middle Germany, on the contrary, there is little of this struggle; the seasons are more equable, and the mild, soft air of the valleys tends to make the inhabitants luxurious and sensitive to hardships. It is only in exceptional mountain districts that one is here reminded of the rough, bracing air on the heights of Southern Germany. It is a curious fact that, as the air becomes gradually lighter and rarer from the North German coast towards Upper Germany, the average of suicides regularly decreases. Mecklenburg has the highest number, then Prussia, while the fewest suicides occur in Bavaria and Austria.

Both the northern and southern regions have still a large extent of waste lands, downs, morasses, and heaths; and to these are added, in the south, abundance of snow-fields and naked rock; while in Middle Germany culture has almost overspread the face of the land, and there are no large tracts of waste. There is the same proportion in the distribution of forests. Again, in the north we see a monotonous continuity of wheat-fields, potato-grounds, meadow lands, and vast heaths, and there is the same uniformity of culture over large surfaces in the southern table-lands and the Alpine pastures. In Middle Germany, on the contrary, there is a perpetual variety of crops within a short space; the diversity of land surface and the corresponding variety in the species of plants are an invitation to the splitting up of estates, and this again encourages to the utmost the motley character of the cultivation.

According to this threefold division, it appears that there are certain features common to North and South Germany in which they differ from Central Germany, and the nature of this difference Riehl indicates by distinguishing the former as *Centralized Land* and the latter as *Individualized Land*; a distinction which is well symbolized by the fact that North and South Germany possess the great lines of railway which are the medium for the traffic of the world, while Middle Germany is far richer in lines for local communication, and possesses the greatest length of railway within the smallest space. Disregarding superficialities, the East Frieslanders, the Schleswig-Holsteiners, the Mecklenburghers, and the Pomeranians are much more nearly allied to the old Bavarians, the Tyrolese, and the Styrians, than any of these are allied to the Saxons, the Thuringians, or the Rhinelanders. Both in North and South Germany original races are still found in large masses, and popular dialects are spoken; you still find there thoroughly peasant districts, thorough villages, and also, at great intervals, thorough cities; you still find there a sense of rank. In Middle Germany, on the contrary, the original races are fused together or sprinkled hither and thither; the peculiarities of the popular dialects are worn down or confused; there is no very strict line of demarcation between the country and the town population, hundreds of small towns and large villages being hardly distinguishable in their characteristics; and the sense of rank, as part of the organic structure of society, is almost extinguished. Again, both in the north and south there is still a strong ecclesiastical spirit in the people, and the Pomeranian sees Anti-christ in the Pope as clearly as the Tyrolese sees him in Doctor Luther; while in Middle Germany the confessions are mingled, they exist peaceably side by side in very narrow space, and tolerance or indifference has spread itself widely even in the popular mind. And the analogy, or rather the causal relation, between the physical geography of the three regions and the development of the population goes still further:

'For,' observes Riehl, 'the striking connexion which has been pointed out between the local geological formations in Germany and the revolutionary disposition of the people has more than a metaphorical significance. Where the primæval physical revolutions of the globe have been the wildest in their effects, and the most multiform strata have been tossed together or thrown one upon the other, it is a very intelligible consequence that on a land surface thus broken up, the population should sooner develop itself into small communities, and that the more intense life generated in these smaller communities, should become the most favourable nidus for the reception of modern culture, and with this a susceptibility for its revolutionary ideas; while a people settled in a region where its groups are spread over a large space will persist much more obstinately in the retention of its original character. The people of Middle Germany have none of that exclusive one-sidedness which determines the peculiar genius of great national groups, just as this one-sidedness or uniformity is wanting to the geological and geographical character of their land.'

This ethnographical outline Riehl fills up with special and typical descriptions, and then makes it the starting-point for a criticism of the actual political condition of Germany. The volume is full of vivid pictures, as well as penetrating glances into the maladies and tendencies of modern society. It would be fascinating as literature, if it were not important for its facts and philosophy. But we can only commend it to our readers, and pass on to the volume entitled *Die Bürgerliche Gesellschaft*, from which we have drawn our sketch of the German peasantry. Here Riehl gives us a series of studies in that natural history of the people, which he regards as the proper basis of social policy. He holds that, in European society, there are *three natural ranks* or *estates*: the hereditary landed aristocracy, the citizens or commercial class, and the peasantry or agricultural class. By *natural ranks* he means ranks which have their roots deep in the historical structure of society, and are still, in the present, showing vitality above ground; he means those great social groups which are not only distinguished externally by their vocation, but essentially by their mental character, their habits, their mode of life,—by the principle they represent in the historical development of society. In his conception of the 'Fourth Estate' he differs from the usual interpretation, according to which it is simply equivalent to the proletariat, or those who are dependent on daily wages, whose only capital is their skill or bodily strength—factory-operatives, artisans, agricultural labourers, to whom might be added, especially in Germany, the day-labourers with the quill, the literary proletariat. This, Riehl observes, is a valid basis of economical classification, but not of social classification. In his view, the Fourth Estate is a stratum produced by the perpetual abrasion of the other great social groups; it is the sign and result of the decomposition which is commencing in the organic constitution of society. Its elements are derived alike from the aristocracy, the bourgeoisie, and the peasantry. It assembles under its banner the deserters of historical society, and forms them into a terrible army, which is only just awaking to the consciousness of its corporate power. The tendency of this Fourth Estate, by the very process of its formation, is to do away with the distinctive historical character of the other estates, and to resolve their peculiar rank and vocation into a uniform social relation founded on an abstract conception of society. According to Riehl's classification, the day-labourers, whom the political economist designates as the Fourth Estate, belong partly to the peasantry or agricultural class, and partly to the citizens or commercial class.

Riehl considers, in the first place, the peasantry and aristocracy as the 'forces of social persistence', and, in the second, the bourgeoisie and the 'Fourth Estate' as the 'forces of social movement'.

The aristocracy, he observes, is the only one among these four groups which is denied by others besides Socialists to have any natural basis as a separate rank. It is admitted that there was once an aristocracy which had an intrinsic ground of existence, but now, it is alleged, this is an historical fossil, an antiquarian relic, venerable because grey with age. In what, it is asked, can consist the peculiar vocation of the aristocracy, since it has no longer the monopoly of the land, of the higher military functions, and of government offices, and since the service of the court has no longer any political importance? To this Riehl replies that in great revolutionary crises, the 'men of progress' have more than once 'abolished' the aristocracy. But remarkably enough, the aristocracy has always reappeared. This measure of abolition showed that the nobility were no longer regarded as a real class, for to abolish a real class would be an absurdity. It is quite possible to contemplate a voluntary breaking up of the peasant or citizen class in the socialistic sense, but no man in his senses would think of straightway 'abolishing' citizens and peasants. The aristocracy, then, was regarded as a sort of cancer, or excrescence of society. Nevertheless, not only has it been found impossible to annihilate an hereditary nobility by decree; but also, the aristocracy of the eighteenth century outlived even the self-destructive acts of its own perversity. A life which was entirely without object, entirely destitute of functions, would not, says Riehl, be so persistent. He has an acute criticism of those who conduct a polemic against the idea of an hereditary aristocracy while they are proposing an 'aristocracy of talent', which after all is based on the principle of inheritance. The Socialists are, therefore, only consistent in declaring against an aristocracy of talent. 'But when they have turned the world into a great Foundling Hospital, they will still be unable to eradicate the "privileges of birth".' We must not follow him in his criticism, however; nor can we afford to do more than mention hastily his interesting sketch of the mediæval aristocracy, and his admonition to the German aristocracy of the present day, that the vitality of their class is not to be sustained by romantic attempts to revive mediæval forms and sentiments, but only by the exercise of functions as real and salutary for actual society as those of the mediæval aristocracy were for the feudal age. 'In modern society the divisions of rank indicate *division of labour*, according to that distribution of functions in the social organism which the historical constitution of society has determined. In this way the principle of differentiation and the principle of unity are identical.'

The elaborate study of the German bourgeoisie, which forms the next division of the volume, must be passed over, but we may pause a moment to note Riehl's definition of the social *Philister* (Philistine), an epithet for which we have no equivalent, not at all, however, for want of the object it represents. Most people, who read a little German, know that the epithet *Philister* originated in the *Burschen-leben*, or Student-life, of Germany, and that the antithesis of *Bursch* and *Philister* was equivalent to the antithesis of 'gown' and 'town'; but since the word has passed into ordinary language, it has assumed several shades of significance which have not yet been merged in a single, absolute meaning; and one of the questions which an English visitor in Germany will probably take an opportunity of asking is, 'What is the strict meaning of the word *Philister*?' Riehl's answer is, that the *Philister* is one who is indifferent to all social interests, all public life, as distinguished from selfish and private interests; he has no sympathy with political and social events except as they affect his own comfort and prosperity, as they offer him material for amusement or opportunity for gratifying his vanity. He has no social or political creed, but is always of the opinion which is most convenient for the moment. He is always in the majority, and is the main element of unreason and stupidity in the judgement of a 'discerning public'. It seems presumptuous in us to dispute Riehl's interpretation of a German word, but we must think that, in literature, the epithet *Philister* has usually a wider meaning than this—includes his definition and something more. We imagine the *Philister* is the personification of the spirit which judges everything from a lower point of view than the subject demands—which judges the affairs of the parish from the egotistic or purely personal point of view— which judges the affairs of the nation from the parochial point of view, and does not hesitate to measure the merits of the universe from the human point of view. At least, this must surely be the spirit to which Goethe alludes in a passage cited by Riehl himself, where he says that the Germans need not be ashamed of erecting a monument to him as well as to Blücher; for if Blücher had freed them from the French, he (Goethe) had freed them from the nets of the *Philister*:—

> Ihr mögt mir immer ungescheut
> Gleich Blüchern Denkmal setzen!
> Von Franzosen hat er euch befreit,
> Ich von Philister-netzen.*

Goethe could hardly claim to be the apostle of public spirit; but he is eminently the man who helps us to rise to a lofty point of observation, so that we may see things in their relative proportions.

The most interesting chapters in the description of the Fourth Estate, which concludes the volume, are those on the 'Aristocratic Proletariat' and the 'Intellectual Proletariat'. The Fourth Estate in Germany, says Riehl, has its centre of gravity not, as in England and France, in the day-labourers and factory-operatives, and still less in the degenerate peasantry. In Germany, the *educated* proletariat is the leaven that sets the mass in fermentation; the dangerous classes there go about, not in blouses, but in frock-coats; they begin with the impoverished prince and end in the hungriest *littérateur*. The custom that all the sons of a nobleman shall inherit their father's title, necessarily goes on multiplying that class of aristocrats who are not only without function but without adequate provision, and who shrink from entering the ranks of the citizens by adopting some honest calling. The younger son of a prince, says Riehl, is usually obliged to remain without any vocation; and however zealously he may study music, painting, literature, or science, he can never be a regular musician, painter, or man of science; his pursuit will be called a 'passion', not a 'calling', and to the end of his days he remains a dilettante. 'But the ardent pursuit of a fixed practical calling can alone satisfy the active man.' Direct legislation cannot remedy this evil. The inheritance of titles by younger sons is the universal custom, and custom is stronger than law. But if all government preference for the 'aristocratic proletariat' were withdrawn, the sensible men among them would prefer emigration, or the pursuit of some profession, to the hungry distinction of a title without rents.

The intellectual proletaires Riehl calls the 'church militant' of the Fourth Estate in Germany. In no other country are they so numerous; in no other country is the trade in material and industrial capital so far exceeded by the wholesale and retail trade, the traffic and the usury, in the intellectual capital of the nation. *Germany yields more intellectual produce than it can use and pay for.*

This over-production, which is not transient but permanent, nay, is constantly on the increase, evidences a diseased state of the national industry, a perverted application of industrial powers, and is a far more pungent satire on the national condition than all the poverty of operatives and peasants . . . Other nations need not envy us the preponderance of the intellectual proletariat over the proletaires of manual labour. For man more easily becomes diseased from over-study than from the labour of the hands; and it is precisely in the intellectual proletariat that there are the most dangerous seeds of disease. This is the group in which the opposition between earnings and wants, between the ideal social position and the real, is the most hopelessly irreconcilable.

We must unwillingly leave our readers to make acquaintance for themselves with the graphic details with which Riehl follows up this general statement; but before quitting these admirable volumes, let us say, lest our inevitable omissions should have left room for a different conclusion, that Riehl's conservatism is not in the least tinged with the partisanship of a class, with a poetic fanaticism for the past, or with the prejudice of a mind incapable of discerning the grander evolution of things to which all social forms are but temporarily subservient. It is the conservatism of a clear-eyed, practical, but withal large-minded man—a little caustic, perhaps, now and then in his epigrams on democratic doctrinaires who have their nostrum for all political and social diseases, and on communistic theories which he regards as 'the despair of the individual in his own manhood, reduced to a system', but nevertheless able and willing to do justice to the elements of fact and reason in every shade of opinion and every form of effort. He is as far as possible from the folly of supposing that the sun will go backward on the dial, because we put the hands of our clock backward; he only contends against the opposite folly of decreeing that it shall be mid-day, while in fact the sun is only just touching the mountain-tops, and all along the valley men are stumbling in the twilight.

Silly Novels by Lady Novelists (1856)

SILLY novels by Lady Novelists are a genus with many species, determined by the particular quality of silliness that predominates in them—the frothy, the prosy, the pious, or the pedantic. But it is a mixture of all these—a composite order of feminine fatuity, that produces the largest class of such novels, which we shall distinguish as the *mind-and-millinery* species. The heroine is usually an heiress, probably a peeress in her own right, with perhaps a vicious baronet, an amiable duke, and an irresistible younger son of a marquis as lovers in the foreground, a clergyman and a poet sighing for her in the middle distance, and a crowd of undefined adorers dimly indicated beyond. Her eyes and her wit are both dazzling; her nose and her morals are alike free from any tendency to irregularity; she has a superb *contralto* and a superb intellect; she is perfectly well-dressed and perfectly religious; she dances like a sylph, and reads the Bible in the original tongues. Or it may be that the heroine is not an heiress—that rank and wealth are the only things in which she is deficient; but she infallibly gets into high society, she has the triumph of refusing many matches and securing the best, and she wears some family jewels or other as a sort of crown of righteousness at the end. Rakish men either bite their lips in impotent confusion at her repartees, or are touched to penitence by her reproofs, which, on appropriate occasions, rise to a lofty strain of rhetoric; indeed, there is a general propensity in her to make speeches, and to rhapsodize at some length when she retires to her bedroom. In her recorded conversations she is amazingly eloquent, and in her unrecorded conversations, amazingly witty. She is understood to have a depth of insight that looks through and through the shallow theories of philosophers, and her superior instincts are a sort of dial by which men have only to set their clocks and watches, and all will go well. The men play a very subordinate part by her side.

You are consoled now and then by a hint that they have affairs, which keeps you in mind that the working-day business of the world is somehow being carried on, but ostensibly the final cause of their existence is that they may accompany the heroine on her 'starring' expedition through life. They see her at a ball, and are dazzled; at a flower-show, and they are fascinated; on a riding excursion, and they are witched by her noble horsemanship; at church, and they are awed by the sweet solemnity of her demeanour. She is the ideal woman in feelings, faculties, and flounces. For all this, she as often as not marries the wrong person to begin with, and she suffers terribly from the plots and intrigues of the vicious baronet; but even death has a soft place in his heart for such a paragon, and remedies all mistakes for her just at the right moment. The vicious baronet is sure to be killed in a duel, and the tedious husband dies in his bed, requesting his wife, as a particular favour to him, to marry the man she loves best, and having already dispatched a note to the lover informing him of the comfortable arrangement. Before matters arrive at this desirable issue our feelings are tried by seeing the noble, lovely, and gifted heroine pass through many *mauvais moments*, but we have the satisfaction of knowing that her sorrows are wept into embroidered pocket-handker-chiefs, that her fainting form reclines on the very best upholstery, and that whatever vicissitudes she may undergo, from being dashed out of her carriage to having her head shaved in a fever, she comes out of them all with a complexion more blooming and locks more redundant than ever.

We may remark, by the way, that we have been relieved from a serious scruple by discovering that silly novels by lady novelists rarely introduce us into any other than very lofty and fashionable society. We had imagined that destitute women turned novelists, as they turned governesses, because they had no other 'lady-like' means of getting their bread. On this supposition, vacillating syntax and improbable incident had a certain pathos for us, like the extremely supererogatory pincushions and ill-devised nightcaps that are offered for sale by a blind man. We felt the commodity to be a nuisance, but we were glad to think that the money went to relieve the necessitous, and we pictured to ourselves lonely women struggling for a maintenance, or wives and daughters devoting themselves to the production of 'copy' out of pure heroism,—perhaps to pay their husband's debts, or to purchase luxuries for a sick father. Under these impressions we shrank from criticizing a lady's novel: her English might be faulty, but, we said to ourselves, her motives are irreproachable; her imagination may be uninventive, but her patience is untiring. Empty writing was excused by an empty stomach, and twaddle was consecrated by tears. But no! This theory of ours, like many other pretty theories, has had to give way before observation. Women's silly novels, we are now convinced, are written under totally different circumstances. The fair writers have evidently never talked to a tradesman except from a carriage window; they have no notion of the working classes except as 'dependants'; they think five hundred pounds a year a miserable pittance; Belgravia and 'baronial halls' are their primary truths; and they have no idea of feeling interest in any man who is not at least a great landed proprietor, if not a prime minister. It is clear that they write in elegant boudoirs, with voilet-coloured ink and a ruby pen; that they must be entirely indifferent to publishers' accounts, and inexperienced in every form of poverty except poverty of brains. It is true that we are constantly struck with the want of verisimilitude in their representations of the high society in which they seem to live; but then they betray no closer acquaintance with any other form of life. If their peers and peeresses are improbable, their literary men, tradespeople, and cottagers are impossible; and their intellect seems to have the peculiar impartiality of reproducing both what they *have* seen and heard, and what they have *not* seen and heard, with equal unfaithfulness.

There are few women, we suppose, who have not seen something of children under five years of age, yet in 'Compensation',* a recent novel of the mind-and-millinery species, which calls itself a 'story of real life', we have a

child of four and a half years old talking in this Ossianic*
fashion—

'Oh, I am so happy, dear gran'mamma;—I have seen,—I have seen
such a delightful person: he is like everything beautiful,—like the
smell of sweet flowers, and the view from Ben Lomond;—or no,
better than that—he is like what I think of and see when I am
very, very happy; and he is really like mamma, too, when she
sings; and his forehead is like *that distant sea*,' she continued,
pointing to the blue Mediterranean; 'there seems no end—no end;
or like the clusters of stars I like best to look at on a warm fine
night . . . Don't look so . . . your forehead is like Loch Lomond,
when the wind is blowing and the sun is gone in; I like the sunshine
best when the lake is smooth . . . So now—I like it better than ever
. . . it is more beautiful still from the dark cloud that has gone over
it, *when the sun suddenly lights up all the colours of the forests and
shining purple rocks, and it is all reflected in the waters below.*'

We are not surprised to learn that the mother of this infant
phenomenon, who exhibits symptoms so alarmingly like
those of adolescence repressed by gin, is herself a phoenix.
We are assured, again and again, that she had a remarkably
original mind, that she was a genius, and 'conscious of her
originality', and she was fortunate enough to have a lover
who was also a genius, and a man of 'most original mind'.

This lover, we read, though 'wonderfully similar' to
her 'in powers and capacity', was 'infinitely superior to her
in faith and development', and she saw in him the
' "Agapé"*—so rare to find—of which she had read and
admired the meaning in her Greek Testament; having, *from
her great facility in learning languages*, read the Scriptures in
their original *tongues*.' Of course! Greek and Hebrew are mere
play to a heroine; Sanscrit is no more than *a b c* to her; and
she can talk with perfect correctness in any language except
English. She is a polking polyglot, a Creuzer* in crinoline.
Poor men! There are so few of you who know even Hebrew;
you think it something to boast of if, like Bolingbroke, you
only 'understand that sort of learning, and what is writ about
it'; and you are perhaps adoring women who can think
slightingly of you in all the Semitic languages successively.
But, then, as we are almost invariably told, that a heroine

has a 'beautifully small head', and as her intellect has probably been early invigorated by an attention to costume and deportment, we may conclude that she can pick up the Oriental tongues, to say nothing of their dialects, with the same aerial facility that the butterfly sips nectar. Besides, there can be no difficulty in conceiving the depth of the heroine's erudition, when that of the authoress is so evident.

In 'Laura Gay',* another novel of the same school, the heroine seems less at home in Greek and Hebrew, but she makes up for the deficiency by a quite playful familiarity with the Latin classics—with the 'dear old Virgil', 'the graceful Horace, the humane Cicero, and the pleasant Livy'; indeed, it is such a matter of course with her to quote Latin, that she does it at a picnic in a very mixed company of ladies and gentlemen, having, we are told, 'no conception that the nobler sex were capable of jealousy on this subject. And if, indeed,' continues the biographer of Laura Gay, 'the wisest and noblest portion of that sex were in the majority, no such sentiment would exist; but while Miss Wyndhams and Mr Redfords abound, great sacrifices must be made to their existence.' Such sacrifices, we presume, as abstaining from Latin quotations, of extremely moderate interest and applicability, which the wise and noble minority of the other sex would be quite as willing to dispense with as the foolish and ignoble majority. It is as little the custom of well-bred men as of well-bred women to quote Latin in mixed parties; they can contain their familiarity with 'the humane Cicero' without allowing it to boil over in ordinary conversation, and even references to 'the pleasant Livy' are not absolutely irrepressible. But Ciceronian Latin is the mildest form of Miss Gay's conversational power. Being on the Palatine with a party of sightseers, she falls into the following vein of well-rounded remark:—

Truth can only be pure objectively, for even in the creeds where it predominates, being subjective, and parcelled out into portions, each of these necessarily receives a hue of idiosyncrasy, that is, a taint of superstition more or less strong; while in such creeds as the Roman Catholic, ignorance, interest, the bias of ancient idolatries, and the force of authority, have gradually accumulated on the pure truth, and transformed it, at last, into a mass of super-stition for the majority of its votaries; and how few are there, alas! whose zeal, courage, and intellectual energy are equal to the analysis of this accumulation, and to the discovery of the pearl of great price which lies hidden beneath this heap of rubbish.

We have often met with women much more novel and profound in their observations than Laura Gay, but rarely with any so inopportunely long-winded. A clerical lord, who is half in love with her, is alarmed by the daring remarks just quoted, and begins to suspect that she is inclined to free-thinking. But he is mistaken; when in a moment of sorrow he delicately begs leave to 'recall to her memory, a *dépôt* of strength and consolation under affliction, which, until we are hard pressed by the trials of life, we are too apt to forget', we learn that she really has 'recurrence to that sacred *dépôt*', together with the tea-pot. There is a certain flavour of orthodoxy mixed with the parade of fortunes and fine carriages in 'Laura Gay', but it is an orthodoxy mitigated by study of 'the humane Cicero', and by an 'intellectual disposition to analyse'.

'Compensation' is much more heavily dosed with doctrine, but then it has a treble amount of snobbish worldliness and absurd incident to tickle the palate of pious frivolity. Linda, the heroine, is still more speculative and spiritual than Laura Gay, but she has been 'presented', and has more, and far grander, lovers; very wicked and fascinating women are introduced—even a French *lionne*; and no expense is spared to get up as exciting a story as you will find in the most immoral novels. In fact, it is a wonderful *pot pourri* of Almack's, Scotch second-sight, Mr Rogers's breakfasts,* Italian brigands, death-bed conversions, superior autho-resses, Italian mistresses, and attempts at poisoning old ladies, the whole served up with a garnish of talk about 'faith and development', and 'most original minds'. Even Miss Susan Barton, the superior authoress, whose pen moves in a 'quick decided manner when she is composing', declines the finest opportunities of marriage; and though old enough to be Linda's mother (since we are told that she refused Linda's father), has her hand sought by a young earl, the heroine's rejected lover. Of course, genius and morality must be backed by eligible offers, or they would seem rather a dull affair; and piety, like other things, in order to be *comme il faut*, must be in 'society', and have admittance to the best circles.

'Rank and Beauty'* is a more frothy and less religious variety of the mind-and-millinery species. The heroine, we are told, 'if she inherited her father's pride of birth and her mother's beauty of person, had in herself a tone of enthusiastic feeling that perhaps belongs to her age even in the lowly born, but which is refined into the high spirit of wild romance only in the far descended, who feel that it is their best inheritance'. This enthusiastic young lady, by dint of reading the newspaper to her father, falls in love with the *prime minister*, who, through the medium of leading articles and 'the *resumé* of the debates', shines upon her imagination as a bright particular star, which has no parallax for her, living in the country as simple Miss Wyndham. But she forthwith becomes Baroness Umfraville in her own right, astonishes the world with her beauty and accomplishments when she bursts upon it from her mansion in Spring Gardens, and, as you foresee, will presently come into contact with the unseen *objet aimé*. Perhaps the words 'prime minister' suggest to you a wrinkled or obese sexagenarian; but pray dismiss the image. Lord Rupert Conway has been 'called while still almost a youth to the first situation which a subject can hold in the *universe*', and even leading articles and a *resumé* of the debates have not conjured up a dream that surpasses the fact.

The door opened again, and Lord Rupert Conway entered. Evelyn gave one glance. It was enough; she was not disappointed. It seemed as if a picture on which she had long gazed was suddenly instinct with life, and had stepped from its frame before her. His tall figure, the distinguished simplicity of his air—it was a living Vandyke, a cavalier, one of his noble cavalier ancestors, or one to whom her fancy had always likened him, who long of yore had, with an Umfraville, fought the Paynim far beyond sea. Was this reality?

Very little like it, certainly.

By and by, it becomes evident that the ministerial heart is touched. Lady Umfraville is on a visit to the Queen at Windsor, and,—

The last evening of her stay, when they returned from riding, Mr Wyndham took her and a large party to the top of the Keep, to see the view. She was leaning on the battlements, gazing from that 'stately height' at the prospect beneath her, when Lord Rupert was by her side. 'What an unrivalled view!' exclaimed she.

'Yes, it would have been wrong to go without having been up here. You are pleased with your visit?'

'Enchanted! "A Queen to live and die under", to live and die for!'

'Ha!' cried he, with sudden emotion, and with a *eureka* expression of countenance, as if he had *indeed found a heart in unison with his own.*

The '*eureka* expression of countenance', you see at once to be prophetic of marriage at the end of the third volume; but before that desirable consummation, there are very complicated misunderstandings, arising chiefly from the vindictive plotting of Sir Luttrell Wycherley, who is a genius, a poet, and in every way a most remarkable character indeed. He is not only a romantic poet, but a hardened rake and a cynical wit; yet his deep passion for Lady Umfraville has so impoverished his epigrammatic talent, that he cuts an extremely poor figure in conversation. When she rejects him, he rushes into the shrubbery, and rolls himself in the dirt; and on recovering, devotes himself to the most diabolical and laborious schemes of vengeance, in the course of which he disguises himself as a quack physician, and enters into general practice, foreseeing that Evelyn will fall ill, and that he shall be called in to attend her. At last, when all his schemes are frustrated, he takes leave of her in a long letter, written, as you will perceive from the following passage, entirely in the style of an eminent literary man:—

Oh, lady, nursed in pomp and pleasure, will you ever cast one thought upon the miserable being who addresses you? Will you ever, as your gilded galley is floating down the unruffled stream of prosperity, will you ever, while lulled by the sweetest music—

thine own praises,—hear the far-off sigh from that world to which I am going?

On the whole, however, frothy as it is, we rather prefer 'Rank and Beauty' to the two other novels we have mentioned. The dialogue is more natural and spirited; there is some frank ignorance, and no pedantry; and you are allowed to take the heroine's astounding intellect upon trust, without being called on to read her conversational refutations of sceptics and philosophers, or her rhetorical solutions of the mysteries of the universe.

Writers of the mind-and-millinery school are remarkably unanimous in their choice of diction. In their novels, there is usually a lady or gentleman who is more or less of a up-as tree: the lover has a manly breast; minds are redolent of various things; hearts are hollow; events are utilized; friends are consigned to the tomb; infancy is an engaging period; the sun is a luminary that goes to his western couch, or gathers the rain-drops into his refulgent bosom; life is a melancholy boon; Albion and Scotia are conversational epithets. There is a striking resemblance, too, in the character of their moral comments, such, for instance, as that 'It is a fact, no less true than melancholy, that all people, more or less, richer or poorer, are swayed by bad example'; that 'Books, however trivial, contain some subjects from which useful information may be drawn'; that 'Vice can too often borrow the language of virtue'; that 'Merit and nobility of nature must exist, to be accepted, for clamour and pretension cannot impose upon those too well read in human nature to be easily deceived'; and that, 'In order to forgive, we must have been injured'. There is, doubtless, a class of readers to whom these remarks appear peculiarly pointed and pungent; for we often find them doubly and trebly scored with the pencil, and delicate hands giving in their determined adhesion to these hardy novelties by a distinct *très vrai*, emphasized by many notes of exclamation. The colloquial style of these novels is often marked by much ingenious inversion, and a careful avoidance of such cheap phraseology as can be heard every day. Angry young gentlemen exclaim—' 'Tis ever thus, methinks'; and in the half hour before dinner a young lady informs her next neighbour that the first day she read Shakespeare she 'stole away into the park, and beneath the shadow of the green-wood tree, devoured with rapture the inspired page of the great magician'. But the most remarkable efforts of the mind-and-millinery writers lie in their philosophic reflections. The authoress of 'Laura Gay', for example, having married her hero and heroine, improves the event by observing that 'if those sceptics, whose eyes have so long gazed on matter that they can no longer see aught else in man, could once enter with heart and soul into such bliss as this, they would come to say that the soul of man and the polypus are not of common origin, or of the same texture'. Lady novelists, it appears, can see something else besides matter; they are not limited to phenomena, but can relieve their eyesight by occasional glimpses of the *noumenon*, and are, therefore, naturally better able than any one else to confound sceptics, even of that remarkable, but to us unknown school, which maintains that the soul of man is of the same texture as the polypus.

The most pitiable of all silly novels by lady novelists are what we may call the *oracular* species—novels intended to expound the writer's religious, philosophical, or moral theories. There seems to be a notion abroad among women, rather akin to the superstition that the speech and actions of idiots are inspired, and that the human being most entirely exhausted of common sense is the fittest vehicle of revelation. To judge from their writings, there are certain ladies who think that an amazing ignorance, both of science and of life, is the best possible qualification for forming an opinion on the knottiest moral and speculative questions. Apparently, their recipe for solving all such difficulties is something like this:—Take a woman's head, stuff it with a smattering of philosophy and literature chopped small, and with false notions of society baked hard, let it hang over a desk a few hours every day, and serve up hot in feeble English, when not required. You will rarely meet with a lady novelist of the oracular class who is diffident of her ability to decide on theological questions,—who has any suspicion that she is not capable of discriminating with the nicest accuracy between the good and evil in all church parties,—who does not see precisely how it is that men have gone wrong hitherto,—and pity philosophers in general that they have not had the opportunity of consulting her. Great writers, who have modestly contented themselves with putting their experience into fiction, and have thought it quite a sufficient task to exhibit men and things as they are, she sighs over as deplorably deficient in the application of their powers. 'They have solved no great questions'—and she is ready to remedy their omission by setting before you a complete theory of life and manual of divinity, in a love story, where ladies and gentlemen of good family go through genteel vicissitudes, to the utter confusion of Deists, Puseyites, and ultra-Protestants, and to the perfect establishment of that particular view of Christianity which either condenses itself into a sentence of small caps, or explodes into a cluster of stars on the three hundred and thirtieth page. It is true, the ladies and gentlemen will probably seem to you remarkably little like any you have had the fortune or misfortune to meet with, for, as a general rule, the ability of a lady novelist to describe actual life and her fellow-men, is in inverse proportion to her confident eloquence about God and the other world, and the means by which she usually chooses to conduct you to true ideas of the invisible is a totally false picture of the visible.

As typical a novel of the oracular kind as we can hope to meet with, is 'The Enigma: a Leaf from the Chronicles of the Wolchorley House'.* The 'enigma' which this novel is to solve, is certainly one that demands powers no less gigantic than those of a lady novelist, being neither more nor less than the existence of evil. The problem is stated, and the answer dimly foreshadowed on the very first page. The spirited young lady, with raven hair, says, 'All life is an inextricable confusion'; and the meek young lady, with auburn hair, looks at the picture of the Madonna which she is copying, and—'*There* seemed the solution of that mighty enigma.' The style of this novel is quite as lofty as its purpose; indeed, some passages on which we have spent much patient study are quite beyond our reach, in spite of the illustrative aid of italics and small caps; and we must await further 'development' in order to understand them. Of Ernest, the model young clergyman, who sets every one right on all occasions, we read, that 'he held not of marriage in the marketable kind, after a social desecration'; that, on one eventful night, 'sleep had not visited his divided heart, where tumultuated, in varied type and combination, the aggregate feelings of grief and joy'; and that, 'for the *marketable* human article he had no toleration, be it of what sort, or set for what value it might, whether for worship or class, his upright soul abhorred it, whose ultimatum, the self-deceiver, was to him THE *great spiritual lie*, "living in a vain show, deceiving and being deceived"; since he did not suppose the phylactery and enlarged border on the garment to be *merely* a social trick.' (The italics and small caps are the author's, and we hope they assist the reader's comprehension.) Of Sir Lionel, the model old gentleman, we are told that 'the simple ideal of the middle age, apart from its anarchy and decadence, in him most truly seemed to live again, when the ties which knit men together were of heroic cast. The first-born colours of pristine faith and truth engraven on the common soul of man, and blent into the wide arch of brotherhood, where the primaeval law of *order* grew and multiplied, each perfect after his kind, and mutually interdependent.' You see clearly, of course, how colours are first engraven on a soul, and then blent into a wide arch, on which arch of colours—apparently a rainbow—the law of order grew and multiplied, each—apparently the arch and the law—perfect after his kind? If, after this, you can possibly want any further aid towards knowing what Sir Lionel was, we can tell you, that in his soul 'the scientific combinations of thought could educe no fuller harmonies of the good and the true, than lay in the primaeval pulses which floated as an atmosphere around it!' and that, when he was sealing a letter, 'Lo! the responsive throb in that good man's bosom echoed back in simple truth the honest witness of a heart that condemned him not, as his eye, bedewed with love, rested, too, with something of ancestral pride, on the undimmed motto of the family—*Loiauté.*'

The slightest matters have their vulgarity fumigated out of them by the same elevated style. Commonplace people would say that a copy of Shakespeare lay on a drawing-room table; but the authoress of 'The Enigma', bent on edifying periphrasis, tells you that there lay on the table, 'that fund of human thought and feeling, which teaches the heart through the little name, "Shakespeare"'. A watchman sees a light burning in an upper window rather longer than usual, and thinks that people are foolish to sit up late when they have an opportunity of going to bed; but, lest this fact should seem too low and common, it is presented to us in the following striking and metaphysical manner: 'He marvelled—as man *will* think for others in a necessarily separate personality, consequently (though disallowing it) in false mental premise,—how differently *he* should act, how gladly *he* should prize the rest so lightly held of within.' A footman—an ordinary Jeames, with large calves and aspirated vowels—answers the door-bell, and the opportunity is seized to tell you that he was a 'type of the large class of pampered menials, who follow the curse of Cain—"vagabonds" on the face of the earth, and whose estimate of the human class varies in the graduated scale of money and expenditure . . . These, and such as these, O England, be the false lights of thy morbid civilization!' We have heard of various 'false lights', from Dr Cumming to Robert Owen, from Dr Pusey to the Spirit-rappers,* but we never before heard of the false light that emanates from plush and powder.

In the same way very ordinary events of civilized life are exalted into the most awful crises, and ladies in full skirts and *manches à la Chinoise*, conduct themselves not unlike the heroines of sanguinary melodramas. Mrs Percy, a shallow woman of the world, wishes her son Horace to marry the auburn-haired Grace, she being an heiress; but he, after the manner of sons, falls in love with the raven-haired Kate, the heiress's portionless cousin; and, moreover, Grace herself shows every symptom of perfect indifference to Horace. In such cases, sons are often sulky or fiery, mothers are alternately manœuvring and waspish, and the portionless young lady often lies awake at night and cries a good deal. We are getting used to these things now, just as we are used to eclipses of the moon, which no longer set us howling and beating tin kettles. We never heard of a lady in a fashionable 'front' behaving like Mrs Percy under these circumstances. Happening one day to see Horace talking to Grace at a window, without in the least knowing what they are talking about, or having the least reason to believe that Grace, who is mistress of the house and a person of dignity, would accept her son if he were to offer himself, she suddenly rushes up to them and clasps them both, saying, 'with a flushed countenance and in an excited manner'—'This is indeed happiness; for, may I not call you so, Grace?—my Grace—my Horace's Grace!—my dear children!' Her son tells her she is mistaken, and that he is engaged to Kate, whereupon we have the following scene and tableau:—

Gathering herself up to an unprecedented height, (!) her eyes lightning forth the fire of her anger:—

'Wretched boy!' she said, hoarsely and scornfully, and clenching her hand. 'Take then the doom of your own choice! Bow down your miserable head and let a mother's—'

'Curse not!' spake a deep low voice from behind, and Mrs Percy started, scared, as though she had seen a heavenly visitant appear, to break upon her in the midst of her sin.

Meantime, Horace had fallen on his knees at her feet, and hid his face in his hands.

Who, then, is she—who! Truly his 'guardian spirit' hath stepped between him and the fearful words, which, however unmerited, must have hung as a pall over his future existence;—a spell which could not be unbound—which could not be unsaid.

Of an earthly paleness, but calm with the still, iron-bound calmness of death—the only calm one there,—Katherine stood; and her words smote on the ear in tones whose appallingly slow and separate intonation rung on the heart like the chill, isolated tolling of some fatal knell.

'He would have plighted me his faith, but I did not accept it; you cannot, therefore—you *dare* not curse him. And here,' she continued, raising her hand to heaven, whither her large dark eyes also rose with a chastened glow, which, for the first time, *suffering* had lighted in those passionate orbs,—'here I promise, come weal, come woe, that Horace Wolchorley and I do never interchange vows without his mother's sanction—without his mother's blessing!'

Here, and throughout the story, we see that confusion of purpose which is so characteristic of silly novels written by women. It is a story of quite modern drawing-room society—a society in which polkas are played and Puseyism discussed; yet we have characters, and incidents, and traits of manner introduced, which are mere shreds from the most heterogeneous romances. We have a blind Irish harper 'relic of the picturesque bards of yore', startling us at a Sunday-school festival of tea and cake in an English village; we have a crazy gypsy, in a scarlet cloak, singing snatches of romantic song, and revealing a secret on her death-bed which, with the testimony of a dwarfish miserly merchant, who salutes strangers with a curse and a devilish laugh, goes to prove that Ernest, the model young clergyman, is Kate's brother; and we have an ultra-virtuous Irish Barney, discovering that a document is forged, by comparing the date of the paper with the date of the alleged signature, although the same document has passed through a court of law, and occasioned a fatal decision. The 'Hall' in which Sir Lionel lives is the venerable country-seat of an old family, and this, we suppose, sets the imagination of the authoress flying to donjons and battlements, where 'lo! the warder blows his horn'; for, as the inhabitants are in their bedrooms on a night certainly within the recollection of Pleaceman X.,* and a breeze springs up, which we are at first told was faint, and then that it made the old cedars bow their branches to the greensward, she falls into this mediaeval vein of description (the italics are ours): 'The banner *unfurled it* at the sound, and shook its guardian wing above, while the startled owl *flapped her* in the ivy; the firmament looking down through her "argus eyes"—

Ministers of heaven's mute melodies.

And lo! two strokes tolled from out the warder tower, and "Two o'clock" re-echoed its interpreter below.'

Such stories as this of 'The Enigma' remind us of the pictures clever children sometimes draw 'out of their own head', where you will see a modern villa on the right, two knights in helmets fighting in the foreground, and a tiger grinning in a jungle on the left, the several objects being brought together because the artist thinks each pretty, and perhaps still more because he remembers seeing them in other pictures.

But we like the authoress much better on her mediaeval stilts than on her oracular ones,—when she talks of the *Ich* and of 'subjective' and 'objective', and lays down the exact line of Christian verity, between 'right-hand excesses and left-hand declensions'. Persons who deviate from this line are introduced with a patronizing air of charity. Of a certain Miss Inshquine she informs us, with all the lucidity of italics and small caps, that '*function*, not *form*, *as the inevitable outer expression of the spirit in this tabernacled age*, weakly engrossed her'. And *à propos* of Miss Mayjar, an evangelical lady who is a little too apt to talk of her visits to sick women and the state of their souls, we are told that the model clergyman is 'not one to disallow, through the *super* crust, the undercurrent towards good in the *subject*, or the positive benefits, nevertheless, to the *object*'. We imagine the double-refined accent and protrusion of chin which are feebly represented by the italics in this lady's sentences. We abstain from quoting any of her oracular doctrinal passages, because they refer to matters too serious for our pages just now.

The epithet 'silly' may seem impertinent, applied to a novel which indicates so much reading and intellectual activity as 'The Enigma'; but we use this epithet advisedly. If, as the world has long agreed, a very great amount of instruction will not make a wise man, still less will a very mediocre amount of instruction make a wise woman. And the most mischievous form of feminine silliness is the literary form, because it tends to confirm the popular prejudice against the more solid education of women. When men see girls wasting their time in consultations about bonnets and ball dresses, and in giggling or sentimental love-confidences, or middle-aged women mismanaging their children, and solacing themselves with acrid gossip, they can hardly help saying, 'For Heaven's sake, let girls be better educated; let them have some better objects of thought—some more solid occupations.' But after a few hours' conversation with an oracular literary woman, or a few hours' reading of her books, they are likely enough to say, 'After all, when a woman gets some knowledge, see what use she makes of it! Her knowledge remains acquisition, instead of passing into culture; instead of being subdued into modesty and simplicity by a larger acquaintance with thought and fact, she has a feverish consciousness of her attainments; she keeps a sort of mental pocket-mirror, and is continually looking in it at her own 'intellectuality'; she spoils the taste of one's muffin by questions of metaphysics; 'puts down' men at a dinner-table with her superior information; and seizes the opportunity of a *soirée* to catechize us on the vital question of the relation between mind and matter. And then, look at her writings! She mistakes vagueness for depth, bombast for eloquence, and affectation for originality; she struts on one page, rolls her eyes on another, grimaces in a third, and is hysterical in a fourth. She may have read many writings of great men, and a few writings of great women; but she is as unable to discern the difference between her own style and theirs as a Yorkshireman is to discern the difference between his own English and a Londoner's: rhodomontade is the native accent of her intellect. No—the average nature of women is too shallow and feeble a soil to bear much tillage; it is only fit for the very lightest crops.'

It is true that the men who come to such a decision on such very superficial and imperfect observation may not be among the wisest in the world; but we have not now to contest their opinion—we are only pointing out how it is unconsciously encouraged by many women who have volunteered themselves as representatives of the feminine intellect. We do not believe that a man was ever strengthened in such an opinion by associating with a woman of true culture, whose mind had absorbed her knowledge instead of being absorbed by it. A really cultured woman, like a really cultured man, is all the simpler and the less obtrusive for her knowledge; it has made her see herself and her opinions in something like just proportions; she does not make it a pedestal from which she flatters herself that she commands a complete view of men and things, but makes it a point of observation from which to form a right estimate of herself. She neither spouts poetry nor quotes Cicero on slight provocation; not because she thinks that a sacrifice must be made to the prejudices of men, but because that mode of exhibiting her memory and Latinity does not present itself to her as edifying or graceful. She does not write books to confound philosophers, perhaps because she is able to write books that delight them. In conversation she is the least formidable of women, because she understands you, without wanting to make you aware that you *can't* understand her. She does not give you information, which is the raw material of culture,—she gives you sympathy, which is its subtlest essence.

A more numerous class of silly novels than the oracular, (which are generally inspired by some form of High Church, or transcendental Christianity,) is what we may call the *white neck-cloth* species, which represent the tone of thought and feeling in the Evangelical party. This species is a kind of genteel tract on a large scale, intended as a sort of medicinal sweetmeat for Low Church young ladies; an Evangelical substitute for the fashionable novel, as the May Meetings* are a substitute for the Opera. Even Quaker children, one would think, can hardly have been denied the indulgence of a doll; but it must be a doll dressed in a drab gown and a coal-scuttle bonnet—not a worldly doll, in gauze and spangles. And there are no young ladies, we imagine,—unless they belong to the Church of the United Brethren, in which people are married without any love-making—who can dispense with love stories. Thus, for Evangelical young ladies there are Evangelical love stories, in which the vicissitudes of the tender passion are sanctified by saving views of Regeneration and the Atonement. These novels differ from the oracular ones, as a Low Churchwoman often differs from a High Churchwoman: they are a little less supercilious, and a great deal more ignorant, a little less correct in their syntax, and a great deal more vulgar.

The Orlando* of Evangelical literature is the young curate, looked at from the point of view of the middle class, where cambric bands are understood to have as thrilling an effect on the hearts of young ladies as epaulettes have in the classes above and below it. In the ordinary type of these novels, the hero is almost sure to be a young curate, frowned upon, perhaps, by worldly mammas, but carrying captive the hearts of their daughters, who can 'never forget *that* sermon'; tender glances are seized from the pulpit stairs instead of the opera-box; *tête-à-têtes* are seasoned with quotations from Scripture, instead of quotations from the poets; and questions as to the state of the heroine's affections are mingled with anxieties as to the state of her soul. The young curate always has a background of well-dressed and wealthy, if not fashionable society;—for Evangelical silliness is as snobbish as any other kind of silliness; and the Evangelical lady novelist, while she explains to you the type of the scapegoat on one page, is ambitious on another to represent the manners and conversation of aristocratic people. Her pictures of fashionable society are often curious studies considered as efforts of the Evangelical imagination; but in one particular the novels of the White Neck-cloth School are meritoriously realistic,—their favourite hero, the Evangelical young curate, is always rather an insipid personage.

The most recent novel of this species that we happen to have before us, is 'The Old Grey Church'.* It is utterly tame and feeble; there is no one set of objects on which the writer seems to have a stronger grasp than on any other; and we should be entirely at a loss to conjecture among what phases of life her experience has been gained, but for certain vulgarisms of style which sufficiently indicate that she has had the advantage, though she has been unable to use it, of mingling chiefly with men and women whose manners and characters have not had all their bosses and angles rubbed down by refined conventionalism. It is less excusable in an Evangelical novelist, than in any other, gratuitously to seek her subjects among titles and carriages. The real drama of Evangelicalism—and it has abundance of fine drama for any one who has genius enough to discern and reproduce it—lies among the middle and lower classes; and are not Evangelical opinions understood to give an especial interest in the weak things of the earth, rather than in the mighty? Why then, cannot our Evangelical lady novelists show us the operation of their religious views among people (there really are many such in the world) who keep no carriage, 'not so much as a brass-bound gig', who even manage to eat their dinner without a silver fork, and in whose mouths the authoress's questionable English would be strictly consistent? Why can we not have pictures of religious life among the industrial classes in England, as interesting as Mrs Stowe's pictures of religious life among the negroes?* Instead of this, pious ladies nauseate us with novels which remind us of what we sometimes see in a worldly woman recently 'converted';—she is as fond of a fine dinner table as before, but she invites clergymen instead of beaux; she thinks as much of her dress as before, but she adopts a more sober choice of colours and patterns; her conversation is as trivial as before, but the triviality is flavoured with Gospel instead of gossip. In 'The Old Grey Church', we have the same sort of Evangelical travesty of the fashionable novel, and of course the vicious, intriguing baronet is not wanting. It is worth while to give a sample of the style of conversation attributed to this high-born rake—a style that in its profuse italics and palpable innuendoes, is worthy of Miss Squeers.* In an evening visit to the ruins of the Colosseum, Eustace, the young clergyman, has been withdrawing the heroine, Miss Lushington, from the rest of the party, for the sake of a *tête-à-tête*. The baronet is jealous, and vents his pique in this way:—

There they are, and Miss Lushington, no doubt, quite safe; for she is under the holy guidance of Pope Eustace the First, who has, of course, been delivering to her an edifying homily on the wickedness of the heathens of yore, who, as tradition tells us, in this very place let loose the wild *beasties* on poor Saint Paul!—Oh, no! by the bye, I believe I am wrong, and betraying my want of clergy, and that it was not at all Saint Paul, nor was it here. But no matter, it would equally serve as a text to preach from, and from which to diverge to the degenerate *heathen* Christians of the present day, and all their naughty practices, and so end with an exhortation to 'come out from among them, and be separate';—and I am sure, Miss Lushington, you have most scrupulously conformed to that injunction this evening, for we have seen nothing of you since our arrival. But every one seems agreed it has been a *charming party of pleasure*, and I am sure we all feel *much indebted* to Mr Grey for having *suggested* it; and as he seems so capital a cicerone, I hope he will think of something else equally agreeable to *all*.

This drivelling kind of dialogue, and equally drivelling narrative, which, like a bad drawing, represents nothing, and barely indicates what is meant to be represented, runs through the book; and we have no doubt is considered by the amiable authoress to constitute an improving novel, which Christian mothers will do well to put into the hands of their daughters. But everything is relative; we have met with American vegetarians whose normal diet was dry meal, and who, when their appetite wanted stimulating, tickled it with *wet* meal; and so, we can imagine that there are Evangelical circles in which 'The Old Grey Church' is devoured as a powerful and interesting fiction.

But, perhaps, the least readable of silly women's novels, are the *modern-antique* species, which unfold to us the domestic life of Jannes and Jambres, the private love affairs of Sennacherib, or the mental struggles and ultimate conversion of Demetrius the silversmith.* From most silly novels we can at least extract a laugh; but those of the modern-antique school have a ponderous, a leaden kind of fatuity, under which we groan. What can be more demonstrative of the inability of literary women to measure their own powers, than their frequent assumption of a task which can only be justified by the rarest concurrence of acquirement with genius? The finest effort to reanimate the past is of course only approximative—is always more or less an infusion of the modern spirit into the ancient form,—

Was ihr den Geist der Zeiten heisst,
Das ist im Grund der Herren eigner Geist,
In dem die Zeiten sich bespiegeln.*

Admitting that genius which has familiarized itself with all the relics of an ancient period can sometimes, by the force of its sympathetic divination, restore the missing notes in the 'music of humanity', and reconstruct the fragments into a whole which will really bring the remote past nearer to us, and interpret it to our duller apprehension,—this form of imaginative power must always be among the very rarest, because it demands as much accurate and minute knowledge as creative vigour. Yet we find ladies constantly choosing to make their mental mediocrity more conspicuous, by clothing it in a masquerade of ancient names; by putting their feeble sentimentality into the mouths of Roman vestals or Egyptian princesses, and attributing their rhetorical arguments to Jewish high-priests and Greek philosophers. A recent example of this heavy imbecility is 'Adonijah, a Tale of the Jewish Dispersion',* which forms part of a series, 'uniting,' we are told, 'taste, humour, and sound principles'. *Adonijah*, we presume, exemplifies the tale of 'sound principles'; the taste and humour are to be found in other members of the series. We are told on the cover, that the incidents of this tale are 'fraught with unusual interest', and the preface winds up thus: 'To those who feel interested in the dispersed of Israel and Judea, these pages may afford, perhaps, information on an important subject, as well as amusement'. Since the 'important subject' on which this book is to afford information is not specified, it may possibly lie in some esoteric meaning to which we have no key; but if it has relation to the dispersed of Israel and Judea at any period of their history, we believe a tolerably well-informed school-girl already knows much more of it than she will find in this 'Tale of the Jewish Dispersion'. 'Adonijah' is simply the feeblest kind of love story, supposed to be instructive, we presume, because the hero is a Jewish captive, and the heroine a Roman vestal; because they and their friends are converted to Christianity after the shortest and easiest method approved by the 'Society for Promoting the Conversion of the Jews'; and because, instead of being written in plain language, it is adorned with that peculiar style of grandiloquence which is held by some lady novelists to give an antique colouring; and which we recognize at once in such phrases as these:—'the splendid regnal talents undoubtedly possessed by the Emperor Nero'—'the expiring scion of a lofty stem'—'the virtuous partner of his couch'—'ah, by Vesta!'—and 'I tell thee, Roman'. Among the quotations which serve at once for instruction and ornament on the cover of this volume, there is one from Miss Sinclair,* which informs us that 'Works of imagination are *avowedly* read by men of science, wisdom, and piety'; from which we suppose the reader is to gather the cheering inference that Dr Daubeny, Mr Mill, or Mr Maurice,* may openly indulge himself with the perusal of 'Adonijah', without being obliged to secrete it among the sofa cushions, or read it by snatches under the dinner-table.

'Be not a baker if your head be made of butter,' says a homely proverb, which, being interpreted, may mean, let no woman rush into print who is not prepared for the consequences. We are aware that our remarks are in a very different tone from that of the reviewers who, with a perennial recurrence of precisely similar emotions, only paralleled, we imagine, in the experience of monthly nurses, tell one lady novelist after another that they 'hail' her productions 'with delight'. We are aware that the ladies at whom our criticism is pointed are accustomed to be told, in the choicest phraseology of puffery, that their pictures of life are brilliant, their characters well-drawn, their style fascinating, and their sentiments lofty. But if they are inclined to resent our plainness of speech, we ask them to reflect for a moment on the chary praise, and often captious blame, which their panegyrists give to writers whose works are on the way to become classics. No sooner does a woman show that she has genius or effective talent, than she receives the tribute of being moderately praised and severely criticized. By a peculiar thermometric adjustment, when a woman's talent is at zero, journalistic approbation is at the boiling pitch; when she attains mediocrity, it is already at no more than summer heat; and if ever she reaches excellence, critical enthusiasm drops to the freezing point. Harriet Martineau, Currer Bell, and Mrs Gaskell have been treated as cavalierly as if they had been men. And every critic who forms a high estimate of the share women may ultimately take in literature, will, on principle, abstain from any exceptional indulgence towards the productions of literary women. For it must be plain to every one who looks impartially and extensively into feminine literature, that its greatest deficiencies are due hardly more to the want of intellectual power than to the want of those moral qualities that contribute to literary excellence—patient diligence, a sense of the responsibility involved in publication, and an appreciation of the sacredness of the writer's art. In the majority of women's books you see that kind of facility which springs from the absence of any high standard; that fertility in imbecile combination or feeble imitation which a little self-criticism would check and reduce to barrenness; just as with a total want of musical ear people will sing out of tune, while a degree more melodic sensibility would suffice to render them silent. The foolish vanity of wishing to appear in print, instead of being counterbalanced by any consciousness of the intellectual or moral derogation implied in futile authorship, seems to be encouraged by the extremely false impression that to write *at all* is a proof of superiority in a woman. On this ground, we believe that the average intellect of women is unfairly represented by the mass of feminine literature, and that while the few women who write well are very far above the ordinary intellectual level of their sex, the many women who write ill are very far below it. So that, after all, the severer critics are fulfilling a chivalrous duty in depriving the mere fact of feminine authorship of any false prestige which may give it a delusive attraction, and in recommending women of mediocre faculties—as at least a negative service they can render their sex—to abstain from writing.

The standing apology for women who become writers
without any special qualification is, that society shuts them
out from other spheres of occupation. Society is a very
culpable entity, and has to answer for the manufacture of
many unwholesome commodities, from bad pickles to bad
poetry. But society, like 'matter', and Her Majesty's Government, and other lofty abstractions, has its share of excessive blame as well as excessive praise. Where there is one
woman who writes from necessity, we believe there are three
women who write from vanity; and, besides, there is something so antiseptic in the mere healthy fact of working for
one's bread, that the most trashy and rotten kind of feminine
literature is not likely to have been produced under such
circumstances. 'In all labour there is profit'; but ladies' silly
novels, we imagine, are less the result of labour than of busy
idleness.

Happily, we are not dependent on argument to prove that
Fiction is a department of literature in which women can,
after their kind, fully equal men. A cluster of great names,
both living and dead, rush to our memories in evidence that
women can produce novels not only fine, but among the
very finest;—novels, too, that have a precious speciality,
lying quite apart from masculine aptitudes and experience.
No educational restrictions can shut women out from the
materials of fiction, and there is no species of art which is
so free from rigid requirements. Like crystalline masses, it
may take any form, and yet be beautiful; we have only to
pour in the right elements—genuine observation, humour,
and passion. But it is precisely this absence of rigid require-
ment which constitutes the fatal seduction of novel-writing
to incompetent women. Ladies are not wont to be very
grossly deceived as to their power of playing on the piano;
here certain positive difficulties of execution have to be
conquered, and incompetence inevitably breaks down. Every
art which has its absolute *technique* is, to a certain extent,
guarded from the instrusions of mere left-handed imbecility.
But in novel-writing there are no barriers for incapacity to
stumble against, no external criteria to prevent a writer from
mistaking foolish facility for mastery. And so we have again

and again the old story of La Fontaine's ass, who puts his nose to the flute, and, finding that he elicits some sound, exclaims, 'Moi, aussi, je joue de la flute';—a fable which we commend, at parting, to the consideration of any feminine reader who is in danger of adding to the number of 'silly novels by lady novelists'.

How I Came To Write Fiction (1857)

SEPTEMBER 1856 made a new era in my life, for it was then I began to write Fiction. It had always been a vague dream of mine that some time or other I might write a novel, and my shadowy conception of what the novel was to be, varied, of course, from one epoch of my life to another. But I never went farther towards the actual writing of the novel than an introductory chapter describing a Staffordshire village and the life of the neighbouring farm houses, and as the years passed on I lost any hope that I should ever be able to write a novel, just as I desponded about everything else in my future life. I always thought I was deficient in dramatic power, both of construction and dialogue, but I felt I should be at my ease in the descriptive parts of a novel. My 'introductory chapter' was pure description though there were good materials in it for dramatic presentation. It happened to be among the papers I had with me in Germany and one evening at Berlin, something led me to read it to George. He was struck with it as a bit of concrete description, and it suggested to him the possibility of my being able to write a novel, though he distrusted—indeed disbelieved in, my possession of any dramatic power. Still, he began to think that I might as well try, some time, what I could do in fiction, and by and bye when we came back to England and I had greater success than he had ever expected in other kinds of writing, his impression that it was worth while to see how far my mental power would go towards the production of a novel, was strengthened. He began to say very positively, 'You must try and write a story,' and when we were at Tenby* he urged me to begin at once. I deferred it, however, after my usual fashion, with work that does not present itself as an absolute duty. But one morning as I was lying in bed, thinking what should be the subject of my first story, my thoughts merged themselves into a dreamy doze, and I imagined myself writing a story of which the title was—'The Sad Fortunes of the Reverend Amos Barton'. I was soon wide awake again, and told G. He said, 'O what a capital title!' and from that time I had settled in my mind that this should be my first story. George used to say, 'It may be a failure—it may be that you are unable to write fiction. Or perhaps, it may be just good enough to warrant your trying again.' Again, 'You may write a chef-d'œuvre at once—there's no telling.' But his prevalent impression was that though I could hardly write a *poor* novel, my effort would want the highest quality of fiction—dramatic presentation. He used to say, 'You have wit, description and philosophy—those go a good way towards the production of a novel. It is worth while for you to try the experiment.'

We determined that if my story turned out good enough, we would send it to Blackwood, but G. thought the more probable result was, that I should have to lay it aside and try again.

But when we returned to Richmond I had to write my article on Silly Novels and my review of Contemporary Literature for the Westminster; so that I did not begin my story till September 22.* After I had begun it, as we were walking in the Park, I mentioned to G. that I had thought of the plan of writing a series of stories containing sketches drawn from my own observation of the Clergy, and calling them 'Scenes from Clerical Life' opening with 'Amos Barton'. He at once accepted the notion as a good one—fresh and striking; and about a week afterwards when I read him the early part of 'Amos,' he had no longer any doubt about my ability to carry out the plan. The scene at Cross Farm, he said, satisfied him that I had the very element he had been doubtful about—it was clear I could write good dialogue. There still remained the question whether I could command any pathos, and that was to be decided by the mode in which I treated Milly's death. One night G. went to town on purpose to leave me a quiet evening for writing it. I wrote the chapter from the news brought by the shepherd to Mrs Hackit, to the moment when Amos is dragged from the bedside and I read it to G. when he came home. We both cried over it, and then he came up to me and kissed me, saying 'I think your pathos is better than your fun.'

So when the story was finished G. sent it to Blackwood, who wrote in reply, that he thought the 'Clerical reminiscences would do', congratulated the author on being 'worthy the honours of print and pay', but would like to see more of the series before he undertook to print. However, when G. wrote that the author was discouraged by this editorial caution, Blackwood disclaimed any distrust and agreed to print the story at once.* The first part appeared in the January number 1857. Before the appearance of the Magazine—on sending me the proof, Blackwood already expressed himself with much greater warmth of admiration, and when the first part had appeared, he sent me a charming letter with a cheque for fifty guineas, and a proposal about republication of the series. When the story was concluded he wrote me word* how Albert Smith had sent him a letter saying he had never read anything that affected him more than Milly's death, and, added Blackwood, 'the men at the club seem to have mingled their tears and their tumblers together. It will be curious if you should be a member and be hearing your own praises!' There was clearly no suspicion that I was a woman. It is interesting, as an indication of the value there is in such conjectural criticism generally, to remember that when G. read the first part of 'Amos' to a party at Helps's, they were all sure I was a clergyman—a Cambridge man. Agnes* thought I was the father of a family—was sure I was a man who had seen a great deal of society etc. etc. Blackwood seemed curious about the author, and when I signed my letter 'George Eliot' hunted up some old letters from Eliot Warburton's brother, to compare the handwritings, though, he said, 'Amos seems to me not in the least like what that good artillery man would write.'

Several pleasant bits of admiration came about that time:—a letter from the Rev. Mr Swaine, saying that 'Amos,' in its charming tenderness, reminded him of the 'Vicar of Wakefield', is the only one I remember just now. The adverse critics mentioned by Blackwood were Colonel Hamley and Prof. Aytoun. Professor Aytoun came round afterwards, said he had been quite mistaken in his estimate of the powers of the author of 'Amos Barton', and expressed great admiration of 'Mr Gilfil's Love Story' *—or rather at the conclusion of it. Colonel Hamley said I was 'a man of science, but not a practised writer.' Blackwood was eager for the second story, and much delighted with the two first parts of 'Mr Gilfil's Love Story', which I sent him together. I wrote the fourth part at Scilly—the epilogue, sitting on the Fortification Hill, one sunshiny morning.* Blackwood himself wrote in entire admiration of it, and in the same letter told us that Thackeray 'thought highly of the series'. When we were at Jersey, he was in London, and wrote from thence that he heard nothing but approval of 'Mr Gilfil's Love Story'. Lord Stanley, among other people, had spoken to him about the 'Clerical Scenes' at Bulwer's,* and was astonished to find Blackwood in the dark as to the author.

I began 'Janet's Repentance'* at Scilly and sent off the first Part from Jersey, G. declaring it to be admirable, almost better than the other stories. But to my disappointment, Blackwood did not like it so well, seemed to misunderstand the characters, and be doubtful about the treatment of clerical matters. I wrote at once to beg him to give up printing the story if he felt uncomfortable about it, and he immediately sent a very anxious, cordial letter, saying the thought of putting a stop to the series 'gave him quite a turn'—'he didn't meet with George Eliots every day'—and so on.

One of the pleasantest little incidents at Jersey was a letter from Archer Gurney to the unknown author of 'Mr Gilfil's Love Story', expressing simply but warmly his admiration of the truth and originality he found in the Clerical Scenes. Dear G. came upstairs to me with the letter in his hands, his face bright with gladness, saying, 'Her fame's beginning already!'

I had meant to carry on the series beyond 'Janet's Repentance', and especially I longed to tell the story of the Clerical Tutor, but my annoyance at Blackwood's want of sympathy* in the first two parts of 'Janet', (although he came round to admiration at the third part) determined me to close the series and republish them in two volumes.

The first volume is printed, and the advertisements greet our eyes every week, but we are still wondering how the public will behave to my first book.

'The Sad Fortunes of the Reverend Amos Barton', Chapter 5 (1858)

THE Rev. Amos Barton, whose sad fortunes I have undertaken to relate, was, you perceive, in no respect an ideal or exceptional character; and perhaps I am doing a bold thing to bespeak your sympathy on behalf of a man who was so very far from remarkable,—a man whose virtues were not heroic, and who had no undetected crime within his breast; who had not the slightest mystery hanging about him, but was palpably and unmistakably commonplace; who was not even in love, but had had that complaint favourably many years ago. 'An utterly uninteresting character!' I think I hear a lady reader exclaim—Mrs Farthingale, for example, who prefers the ideal in fiction; to whom tragedy means ermine tippets, adultery, and murder; and comedy, the adventures of some personage who is quite a 'character'.*

But, my dear madam, it is so very large a majority of your fellow-countrymen that are of this insignificant stamp. At least eighty out of a hundred of your adult male fellow-Britons returned in the last census are neither extraordinarily silly, nor extraordinarily wicked, nor extraordinarily wise; their eyes are neither deep and liquid with sentiment, nor sparkling with suppressed witticisms; they have probably had no hairbreadth escapes or thrilling adventures; their brains are certainly not pregnant with genius, and their passions have not manifested themselves at all after the fashion of a volcano. They are simply men of complexions more or less muddy, whose conversation is more or less bald and disjointed. Yet these commonplace people—many of them—bear a conscience, and have felt the sublime prompting to do the painful right; they have their unspoken sorrows, and their sacred joys; their hearts have perhaps gone out towards their first-born, and they have mourned over the irreclaimable dead. Nay, is there not a pathos in their very insignificance—in our comparison of their dim and narrow existence with the glorious possibilities of that human nature which they share?

Depend upon it, you would gain unspeakably if you would learn with me to see some of the poetry and the pathos, the tragedy and the comedy, lying in the experience of a human soul that looks out through dull grey eyes, and that speaks in a voice of quite ordinary tones.* In that case, I should have no fear of your not caring to know what farther befell the Rev. Amos Barton, or of your thinking the homely details I have to tell at all beneath your attention. As it is, you can, if you please, decline to pursue my story farther; and you will easily find reading more to your taste, since I learn from the newspapers that many remarkable novels, full of striking situations, thrilling incidents, and eloquent writing, have appeared only within the last season.

Adam Bede, Book II, Chapter 17 (1859)

'THIS Rector of Broxton is little better than a pagan!' I hear one of my readers exclaim. 'How much more edifying it would have been if you had made him give Arthur some truly spiritual advice! You might have put into his mouth the most beautiful things—quite as good as reading a sermon.'

Certainly I could, if I held it the highest vocation of the novelist to represent things as they never have been and never will be. Then, of course, I might refashion life and character entirely after my own liking; I might select the most unexceptionable type of clergyman and put my own admirable opinions into his mouth on all occasions. But it happens, on the contrary, that my strongest effort is to avoid any such arbitrary picture, and to give a faithful account of men and things as they have mirrored themselves in my mind. The mirror is doubtless defective; the outlines will sometimes be disturbed, the reflection faint or confused; but I feel as much bound to tell you as precisely as I can what that reflection is, as if I were in the witness-box, narrating my experience on oath.

Sixty years ago—it is a long time, so no wonder things have changed—all clergymen were not zealous; indeed, there is reason to believe that the number of zealous clergymen was small, and it is probable that if one among the small minority had owned the livings of Broxton and Hayslope in the year 1799, you would have liked him no better than you like Mr Irwine. Ten to one, you would have thought him a tasteless, indiscreet, methodistical man. It is so very rarely that facts hit that nice medium required by our own enlightened opinions and refined taste! Perhaps you will say, 'Do improve the facts a little, then; make them more accordant with those correct views which it is our privilege to possess. The world is not just what we like; do touch it up with a tasteful pencil, and make believe it is not quite such a mixed entangled affair. Let all people who hold unexceptionable opinions act unexceptionally. Let your most faulty characters always be on the wrong side, and your virtuous ones on the right. Then we shall see at a glance whom we are to condemn and whom we are to approve. Then we shall be able to admire, without the slightest disturbance of our prepossessions: we shall hate and despise with that true ruminant relish which belongs to undoubting confidence.'

But, my good friend, what will you do then with your fellow-parishioner who opposes your husband in the vestry? With your newly appointed vicar, whose style of preaching you find painfully below that of his regretted predecessor? With the honest servant who worries your soul with her one failing? With your neighbour, Mrs Green, who was really kind to you in your last illness, but has said several ill-natured things about you since your convalescence? Nay, with your excellent husband himself, who has other irritating habits besides that of not wiping his shoes? These fellow-mortals, every one, must be accepted as they are: you can neither straighten their noses, nor brighten their wit, nor rectify their dispositions; and it is these people— amongst whom your life is passed—that it is needful you should tolerate, pity, and love: it is these more or less ugly, stupid, inconsistent people whose movements of goodness you should be able to admire—for whom you should cherish all possible hopes, all possible patience. And I would not, even if I had the choice, be the clever novelist who could create a world so much better than this, in which we get up in the morning to do our daily work, that you would be likely to turn a harder, colder eye on the dusty streets and the common green fields—on the real breathing men and women, who can be chilled by your indifference or injured by your prejudice; who can be cheered and helped onward by your fellow-feeling, your forbearance, your outspoken, brave justice.

So I am content to tell my simple story, without trying to make things seem better than they were; dreading nothing, indeed, but falsity, which, in spite of one's best efforts, there is reason to dread. Falsehood is so easy, truth so difficult. The pencil is conscious of a delightful facility in drawing a griffin—the longer the claws, and the larger the wings, the better; but that marvellous facility which we mistook for genius is apt to forsake us when we want to draw a real unexaggerated lion. Examine your words well, and you will find that even when you have no motive to be false, it is a very hard thing to say the exact truth, even about your own immediate feelings—much harder than to say something fine about them which is *not* the exact truth.

It is for this rare, precious quality of truthfulness that I delight in many Dutch paintings, which lofty-minded people despise. I find a source of delicious sympathy in these faithful pictures of a monotonous homely existence, which has been the fate of so many more among my fellow-mortals than a life of pomp or of absolute indigence, of tragic suffering or of world-stirring actions. I turn, without shrinking, from cloud-borne angels, from prophets, sibyls, and heroic warriors, to an old woman bending over her flower-pot, or eating her solitary dinner, while the noonday light, softened perhaps by a screen of leaves, falls on her mob-cap, and just touches the rim of her spinning-wheel, and her stone jug, and all those cheap common things which are the precious necessaries of life to her—or I turn to that village wedding, kept between four brown walls, where an awkward bridegroom opens the dance with a high-shouldered, broad-faced bride, while elderly and middle-aged friends look on, with very irregular noses and lips, and probably with quart-pots in their hands, but with an expression of unmistakable contentment and goodwill. 'Foh!' says my idealistic friend, 'what vulgar details! What good is there in taking all these pains to give an exact likeness of old women and clowns? What a low phase of life! What clumsy, ugly people!'

But bless us, things may be lovable that are not altogether handsome, I hope? I am not at all sure that the majority of the human race have not been ugly, and even among those 'lords of their kind', the British, squat figures, ill-shapen nostrils, and dingy complexions are not startling exceptions. Yet there is a great deal of family love amongst us. I have a friend or two whose class of features is such that the Apollo curl on the summit of their brows would be decidedly trying; yet to my certain knowledge tender hearts have beaten for them, and their miniatures—flattering, but still not lovely—are kissed in secret by motherly lips. I have seen many an excellent matron, who could have never in her best days have been handsome, and yet she had a packet of yellow love-letters in a private drawer, and sweet children showered kisses on her sallow cheeks. And I believe there have been plenty of young heroes, of middle stature and feeble beards, who have felt quite sure they could never love anything more insignificant than a Diana, and yet have found themselves in middle life happily settled with a wife who waddles. Yes! Thank God; human feeling is like the mighty rivers that bless the earth: it does not wait for beauty—it flows with resistless force and brings beauty with it.

All honour and reverence to the divine beauty of form! Let us cultivate it to the utmost in men, women, and children—in our gardens and in our houses. But let us love that other beauty too, which lies in no secret of proportion, but in the secret of deep human sympathy. Paint us an angel, if you can, with a floating violet robe, and a face paled by the celestial light; paint us yet oftener a Madonna, turning her mild face upward and opening her arms to welcome the divine glory; but do not impose on us any æsthetic rules which shall banish from the region of Art those old women scraping carrots with their work-worn hands, those heavy clowns taking holiday in a dingy pot-house, those rounded backs and stupid weather-beaten faces that have bent over the spade and done the rough work of the world—those homes with their tin pans, their brown pitchers, their rough curs, and their clusters of onions. In this world there are so many of these common coarse people, who have no picturesque sentimental wretchedness! It is so needful we should remember their existence, else we may happen to leave them quite out of our religion and philosophy and frame lofty theories which only fit a world of extremes. Therefore, let Art always remind us of them; therefore let us always have men ready to give the loving pains of a life to the faithful representing of commonplace things—men who see beauty in these commonplace things, and delight in showing how kindly the light of heaven falls on them. There are few prophets in the world; few sublimely beautiful women; few heroes. I can't afford to give all my love and reverence to such rarities: I want a great deal of those feelings for my everyday fellow-men, especially for the few in the foreground of the great multitude, whose faces I know, whose hands I touch, for whom I have to make way with kindly courtesy. Neither are picturesque lazzaroni or romantic criminals half so frequent as your common labourer, who gets his own bread and eats it vulgarly but creditably with his own pocket-knife. It is more needful that I should have a fibre of sympathy* connecting me with that vulgar citizen who weighs out my sugar in a vilely assorted cravat and waistcoat, than with the handsomest rascal in red scarf and green feathers—more needful that my heart should swell with loving admiration at some trait of gentle goodness in the faulty people who sit at the same hearth with me, or in the clergyman of my own parish, who is perhaps rather too corpulent and in other respects is not an Oberlin or a Tillotson,* than at the deeds of heroes whom I shall never know except by hearsay, or at the sublimest abstract of all clerical graces that was ever conceived by an able novelist.

And so I come back to Mr Irwine, with whom I desire you to be in perfect charity, far as he may be from satisfying your demands on the clerical character.

A Word for the Germans (1865)

JOHN BULL is open to instruction; slowly, by gentle degrees, he revises his opinions, his habits, and his laws. It is not to be expected that he will ever cease to regard himself as the supreme type of manhood, or to think that the most unmixed truth may always be known by the mark 'British,' which prevents imposture. But he does modify his opinions about other nations. It is no longer his belief that a Frenchman is invariably of the dancing-master type, demanding nothing from existence, but 'his girl, his fiddle, and his frisk',* and that if he has a soul at all it is really of too light a quality to be worth saving. The Italian of John Bull's imagination is no longer exclusively that dangerous jesuitical personage, with dark hair and darker intentions, who avails himself of momentary privacy to feel the edge of his stiletto; a personage adorned now with a false title, but in his earlier years nothing better than a small vagrant, who went about exhibiting his white mice and white teeth for casual halfpence.*

Having shown himself thus ready to abandon those favourite old portable notions of Frenchmen and Italians, it is a pity he should obstinately retain certain worn-out phrases about the Germans, which hardly imply a more comprehensive estimate. In these days when the excellent Bull is ethnological, and feels himself at home with the widest-grinning 'natives'—nay, shows an eager anxiety as to the personal habits of the gorilla, it might be wished that he would conceive the typical German under some more average aspect than that of 'the cloudy metaphysician'. We venture to suggest that this phrase is quite insufficient to express the *differentia* of the German people. In the first place, only a small proportion of them are metaphysicians; quite as many are bakers, making excellent bread—not inferior, perhaps, to the British in any quality except heaviness. Secondly, the most eminent of German metaphysicians, Kant, is cloudy in no other sense than that in which a mathematician is cloudy to one ignorant of mathematics. What book more nebulous than *Euclid* to a reader acquainted neither with the subject-matter nor with the terminology? What more Laputan* and unpractical than algebraic formulæ to one who has never studied algebra? Kant was a rigorous thinker, who, like all other rigorous thinkers, felt the need of terms undefaced by a long currency, free from confusing associations. The recipe for understanding Kant is first to get brains capable of following his argument, and next to master his terminology. Observing this recipe, the *Critique of Pure Reason* is not indeed easy reading, but it is not in the least cloudy. It is not fit for the club table. Some gentleman there, turning over the pages and seeing such terms as *synthetic judgments, antinomies*, and the like, would be conscious of superior clearness of head, and say: 'Bosh! what dreamers these Germans are!' But possibly, if that clear-headed clubman were imperatively called upon to declare the meaning of *co-efficient and hypothenuse* and assured that no smiling would be accepted as legal tender for knowledge, he would discover that these terms also are painfully cloudy. It is one of the interesting weaknesses common to us men to suppose that clearness ends where our own vision fails. The sound British thinker kicks a stone to prove that matter exists,* and so confound the metaphysicians; concluding that their arguments are necessarily shallow because he can't see far into them.

Thirdly, we object to 'cloudy metaphysician' as the accepted periphrasis for a German, because it has begotten another habit of speech which the most constant familiarity could not endear to us. Views are set aside by saying that 'they are German.' Doubtless there is a peculiarly German view of things as there is an English view, a French view, a Hindu view, and so on, down to a Patagonian view, perhaps the least metaphysical of all. The English view may be the soundest, and all but born Englishmen may be comparatively pitiable. But the human race has not been educated on a plan of uniformity, and it is precisely that partition of mankind into races and nations, resulting in various national points of view or varieties of national genius, which has been the means of enriching and rendering more and more complete man's knowledge of the inner and outer world. The Seventy who translated the Hebrew Scriptures into Greek* are said to have been placed in separate confinement that each might produce his independent version, and their versions, when afterwards compared, were found to be identical. This agreement as to the meaning of a text was highly satisfactory, and some inconvenience might have been saved if subsequent interpretations had been equally harmonious. But it would have been a dreary issue for mankind, if the division into nations had ended in such an identity of mental products, even though the standard had been English. And no one who has an acquaintance worth mentioning with the productions of the German mind in any one department, is unaware that the peculiarities of that mind, its characteristic qualities, have been the source of pre-eminently important contributions to the sum of our mental wealth.

The German mind possesses in a high degree two tendencies which are often represented as opposed to each other: namely, largeness of theoretic conception, and thoroughness in the investigation of facts. So undeniable is it that the typical German has these tendencies, that their excess is the very vice he is reproached with by those who know him and don't like him. Your German, it is said, can not write about the drama without going back to the Egyptian mysteries; he sees that everything is related to everything else, and is determined to exhaust you and the subject; his doctrine is all-embracing, and so is his detail. Quite true. No man is less disposed than our German to accept a too slight induction, to let pass an inaccuracy of statement, or to report a conclusion from imperfect observation or experiment; on the other hand, no man is more likely to be contemptuous towards desultory labours which are not *wissenschaftlich* (scientific)—*i.e.* not bound together by a rational doctrine, or conducted in the full sense of a need for such a doctrine. If he is an experimentor, he will be thorough in his experiments; if he is a scholar, he will be thorough in his researches. Accordingly no one in this day really studies any subject without having recourse to German books, or else wishing he knew their language that he might have recourse to them; and the footnotes of every good French or English book that appears, whether in scholarship, history, or natural science, are filled with references to German authors. Without them, historical criticism would have been simply nowhere;* take away the Germans, with their patience, their thoroughness, their need for a doctrine which refers all transient and material manifestations to subtler and more permanent causes, and all that we most value in our appreciation of early history would have been wanting to us.

It is true the German rarely writes well, rarely arranges his matter well, or manages it with economy, and therefore seldom produces a good book in the fullest sense of the word. From the necessity his mind is under of looking at a subject in every one of its facets, he is prone to pile one modifying consideration on another, and so perpetually to disappoint a reader who is in a hurry for a conclusion. The German is never in a hurry: for him, art is long, and life, expanded by the absence of adventitious needs, is not so short as for Englishmen making haste to be rich. His writing will sometimes seem to be all stairs and landingplaces without any floors. Then the structure of his language lends itself to the formation of involved sentences, like coiled serpents, showing neither head nor tail. Nevertheless, the proportionate badness of German books is much exaggerated. The cumbrousness of the language apart, there is not perhaps a much larger proportion of poor books in German than in French or English; it would be nearer the truth to say that there are more books in German of which the matter is valuable, and the style bad, than in any other tongue. Our own literature does not positively swarm with good writers. The difference lies chiefly in this, that when a German author is a blockhead, he is, as Heine says, *kein oberflächlicher Narr**—no superficial blockhead: his sentences and his book do not come to an end so soon as if he were an Englishman or a Frenchman. He has a great deal more straw to chop, and he chops it slowly. Still, a blockhead is never exhilarating, though he may have learned to write in epigrams, and to give stupidity the most dapper air of neatness. His sentences may each have a paragraph to itself, and his book may be half white paper, but we decline it as resolutely as if it were covered with German print without a break from beginning to end. It is as short work *not* to read one book as another.

In fact, if anyone in the present day can be called cultivated who dispenses with a knowledge of German, it is because the two other greatest literatures of the world are now impregnated with the results of German labour and German genius. Let those who know this have the piety to acknowledge it. Let those who do not know it abstain from portraying the typical German until they have made his acquaintance. We have no objection to caricatures; each nation should be content to lend itself to the humour of the world in this passive way. But a caricature to be good, must come from close observation.

Address to Working Men, by Felix Holt

FELLOW-WORKMEN,—I am not going to take up your time by complimenting you. It has been the fashion to compliment kings and other authorities when they have come into power, and to tell them that, under their wise and beneficent rule, happiness would certainly overflow the land. But the end has not always corresponded to that beginning. If it were true that we who work for wages had more of the wisdom and virtue necessary to the right use of power than has been shown by the aristocratic and mercantile classes, we should not glory much in that fact, or consider that it carried with it any near approach to infallibility.

In my opinion, there has been too much complimenting of that sort; and whenever a speaker, whether he is one of ourselves or not, wastes our time in boasting or flattery, I say, let us hiss him. If we have the beginning of wisdom, which is, to know a little truth about ourselves, we know that as a body we are neither very wise nor very virtuous. And to prove this, I will not point specially to our own habits and doings, but to the general state of the country. Any nation that had within it a majority of men—and we are the majority—possessed of much wisdom and virtue, would not tolerate the bad practices, the commercial lying and swindling, the poisonous adulteration of goods, the retail cheating, and the political bribery which are carried on boldly in the midst of us. A majority has the power of creating a public opinion. We could groan and hiss before we had the franchise: if we had groaned and hissed in the right place, if we had discerned better between good and evil, if the multitude of us artisans, and factory hands, and miners, and labourers of all sorts, had been skilful, faithful, well-judging, industrious, sober—and I don't see how there can be wisdom and virtue anywhere without those qualities—we should have made an audience that would have shamed the other classes out of their share in the national vices. We should have had better members of Parliament, better religious teachers, honester tradesmen, fewer foolish demagogues, less impudence in infamous and brutal men; and we should not have had among us the abomination of men calling themselves religious while living in splendour on ill-gotten gains. I say, it is not possible for any society in which there is a very large body of wise and virtuous men to be as vicious as our society is—to have as low a standard of right and wrong, to have so much belief in falsehood, or to have so degrading, barbarous a notion of what pleasure is, or of what justly raises a man above his fellows. Therefore, let us have done with this nonsense about our being much better than the rest of our countrymen, or the pretence that that was a reason why we ought to have such an extension of the franchise as has been given to us. The reason for our having the franchise, as I want presently to show, lies somewhere else than in our personal good qualities, and does not in the least lie in any high betting chance that a delegate is a better man than a duke, or that a Sheffield grinder is a better man than any one of the firm he works for.

However, we have got our franchise now. We have been sarcastically called in the House of Commons the future masters of the country;* and if that sarcasm contains any truth, it seems to me that the first thing we had better think of is, our heavy responsibility; that is to say, the terrible risk we run of working mischief and missing good, as others have done before us. Suppose certain men, discontented with the irrigation of a country which depended for all its prosperity on the right direction being given to the waters of a great river, had got the management of the irrigation before they were quite sure how exactly it could be altered for the better, or whether they could command the necessary agency for such an alteration. Those men would have a difficult and dangerous business on their hands; and the more sense, feeling, and knowledge they had, the more they would be likely to tremble rather than to triumph. Our situation is not altogether unlike theirs. For general prosperity and well-being is a vast crop, that like the corn in Egypt can be come at, not at all by hurried snatching, but only by a well-judged patient process; and whether our political power will be any good to us now we have got it, must depend entirely on the means and materials—the knowledge, ability, and honesty, we have at command. These three things are the only conditions on which we can get any lasting benefit, as every clever workman among us knows: he knows that for an article to be worth much there must be a good invention or plan to go upon, there must be well-prepared material, and there must be skilful and honest work in carrying out the plan. And by this test we may try those who want to be our leaders. Have they anything to offer us besides indignant talk? When they tell us we ought to have this, that, or the other thing, can they explain to us any reasonable, fair, safe way of getting it? Can they argue in favour of a particular change by showing us pretty closely how the change is likely to work? I don't want to decry a just indignation; on the contrary, I should like it to be more thorough and general. A wise man, more than two thousand years ago, when he was asked what would most tend to lessen injustice in the world, said, 'If every bystander felt as indignant at a wrong as if he himself were the sufferer'. Let us cherish such indignation. But the long-growing evils of a great nation are a tangled business, asking for a good deal more than indignation in order to be got rid of. Indignation is a fine war-horse, but the war-horse must be ridden by a man: it must be ridden by rationality, skill, courage, armed with the right weapons, and taking definite aim.

We have reason to be discontented with many things, and, looking back either through the history of England to much earlier generations or to the legislation and administrations of later times, we are justified in saying that many of the evils under which our country now suffers are the consequences of folly, ignorance, neglect, or self-seeking in those who, at different times have wielded the powers of rank, office, and money. But the more bitterly we feel this, the more loudly we utter it, the stronger is the obligation we

lay on ourselves to beware, lest we also, by a too hasty
wresting of measures which seem to promise an immediate
partial relief, make a worse time of it for our own generation, and leave a bad inheritance to our children. The
deepest curse of wrong doing, whether of the foolish, or
wicked sort, is that its effects are difficult to be undone. I
suppose there is hardly anything more to be shuddered at
than that part of the history of disease which shows how,
when a man injures his constitution by a life of vicious
excess, his children and grandchildren inherit diseased
bodies and minds, and how the effects of that unhappy
inheritance continue to spread beyond our calculation. This
is only one example of the law by which human lives are
linked together; another example of what we complain of
when we point to our pauperism, to the brutal ignorance
of multitudes among our fellow countrymen, to the weight
of taxation laid on us by blamable wars, to the wasteful
channels made for the public money, to the expense and
trouble of getting justice, and call these the effects of bad
rule. This is the law that we all bear the yoke of, the law
of no man's making, and which no man can undo. Everybody now sees an example of it in the case of Ireland. We
who are living now are sufferers by the wrong-doing of those
who lived before us; we are sufferers by each other's wrong
doing; and the children who come after us are and will be
sufferers from the same causes. Will any man say he doesn't
care for that law—it is nothing to him—what he wants is
to better himself? With what face then will he complain of
any injury? If he says that in politics or in any sort of social
action he will not care to know what are likely to be the
consequences to others besides himself, he is defending the
very worst doings that have brought about his discontent.
He might as well say that there is no better rule needful
for men than that each should tug and rive for what will
please him, without caring how that tugging will act on the
fine widespread network of society in which he is fast
meshed. If any man taught that as a doctrine, we should
know him for a fool. But there are men who act upon it;
every scoundrel, for example, whether he is a rich religious

scoundrel who lies and cheats on a large scale, and will perhaps come and ask you to send him to Parliament, or a poor pocket-picking scoundrel, who will steal your loose pence while you are listening round the platform. None of us are so ignorant as not to know that a society, a nation is held together by just the opposite doctrine and action—by the dependence of men on each other and the sense they have of a common interest in preventing injury. And we working men are, I think, of all classes the last that can afford to forget this; for if we did we should be much like sailors cutting away the timbers of our own ship to warm our grog with. For what else is the meaning of our Trades-unions? What else is the meaning of every flag we carry, every procession we make, every crowd we collect for the sake of making some protest on behalf of our body as receivers of wages, if not this: that it is our interest to stand by each other, and that this being the common interest, no one of us will try to make a good bargain for himself without considering what will be good for his fellows? And every member of a union believes that the wider he can spread his union, the stronger and surer will be the effect of it. So I think I shall be borne out in saying that a working man who can put two and two together, or take three from four and see what will be the remainder, can understand that a society, to be well off, must be made up chiefly of men who consider the general good as well as their own.

Well, but taking the world as it is—and this is one way we must take it when we want to find out how it can be improved—no society is made up of a single class: society stands before us like that wonderful piece of life, the human body, with all its various parts depending on one another, and with a terrible liability to get wrong because of that delicate dependence. We all know how many diseases the human body is apt to suffer from, and how difficult it is even for the doctors to find out exactly where the seat or beginning of the disorder is. That is because the body is made up of so many various parts, all related to each other, or likely all to feel the effect if any of them goes wrong. It is somewhat the same with our old nations or societies. No society ever stood long in the world without getting to be composed of different classes. Now, it is all pretence to say that there is no such thing as Class Interest. It is clear that if any particular number of men get a particular benefit from any existing institution, they are likely to band together, in order to keep up that benefit and increase it, until it is perceived to be unfair and injurious to another large number, who get knowledge and strength enough to set up a resistance. And this, again, has been part of the history of every great society since history began. But the simple reason for this being, that any large body of men is likely to have more of stupidity, narrowness, and greed than of farsightedness and generosity, it is plain that the number who resist unfairness and injury are in danger of becoming injurious in their turn. And in this way a justifiable resistance has become a damaging convulsion, making everything worse instead of better. This has been seen so often that we ought to profit a little by the experience. So long as there is selfishness in men; so long as they have not found out for themselves institutions which express and carry into practice the truth, that the highest interest of mankind must at last be a common and not a divided interest; so long as the gradual operation of steady causes has not made that truth a part of every man's knowledge and feeling, just as we now not only know that it is good for our health to be cleanly, but feel that cleanliness is only another word for comfort, which is the under-side or lining of all pleasure; so long, I say as men wink at their own knowingness, or hold their heads high, because they have got an advantage over their fellows; so long Class Interest will be in danger of making itself felt injuriously. No set of men will get any sort of power without being in danger of wanting more than their right share. But, on the other hand, it is just as certain that no set of men will get angry at having less than their right share, and set up a claim on that ground, without falling into just the same danger of exacting too much, and exacting it in wrong ways. It's human nature we have got to work with all round, and nothing else. That seems like saying something very commonplace—nay, obvious; as if one should say that where there are hands there are mouths. Yet, to hear a good deal of the speechifying and to see a good deal of the action that goes forward, one might suppose it was forgotten.

But I come back to this: that, in our old society, there are old institutions, and among them the various distinctions and inherited advantages of classes, which have shaped themselves along with all the wonderful slow-growing system of things made up of our laws, our commerce, and our stores of all sorts, whether in material objects, such as buildings and machinery, or in knowledge, such as scientific thought and professional skill. Just as in that case I spoke of before, the irrigation of a country, which must absolutely have its water distributed or it will bear no crop; there are the old channels, the old banks, and the old pumps, which must be used as they are until new and better have been prepared, or the structure of the old has been gradually altered. But it would be fool's work to batter down a pump only because a better might be made, when you had no machinery ready for a new one: it would be wicked work, if villages lost their crops by it. Now the only safe way by which society can be steadily improved and our worst evils reduced, is not by any attempt to do away directly with the actually existing class distinctions and advantages, as if everybody could have the same sort of work, or lead the same sort of life (which none of my hearers are stupid enough to suppose), but by the turning of Class Interests into Class Functions or duties.* What I mean is, that each class should be urged by the surrounding conditions to perform its particular work under the strong pressure of responsibility to the nation at large; that our public affairs should be got into a state in which there should be no impunity for foolish or faithless conduct. In this way, the public judgment would sift out incapability and dishonesty from posts of high charge, and even personal ambition would necessarily become of a worthier sort, since the desires of the most selfish men must be a good deal shaped by the opinions of those around them; and for one person to put on a cap and bells, or to go about dishonest or paltry ways of getting rich that he may spend a vast sum of money in having more finery than his neighbours, he must be pretty sure of a crowd who will applaud him. Now changes can only be good in proportion as they help to bring about this sort of result: in proportion as they put knowledge in the place of ignorance, and fellow-feeling in the place of selfishness. In the course of that substitution class distinctions must inevitably change their character; and represent the varying Duties of men, not their varying Interests. But this end will not come by impatience. 'Day will not break the sooner because we get up before the twilight.' Still less will it come by mere undoing, or change merely as change. And moreover, if we believed that it would be unconditionally hastened by our getting the franchise, we should be what I call superstitious men, believing in magic, or the production of a result by hocus-pocus. Our getting the franchise will greatly hasten that good end in proportion only as every one of us has the knowledge, the foresight, the conscience, that will make him well-judging and scrupulous in the use of it. The nature of things in this world has been determined for us beforehand, and in such a way that no ship can be expected to sail well on a difficult voyage, and reach the right port, unless it is well manned: the nature of the winds and the waves, of the timbers, the sails and the cordage, will not accommodate itself to drunken, mutinous sailors.

You will not suspect me of wanting to preach any cant to you, or of joining in the pretence that everything is in a fine way, and need not be made better. What I am striving to keep in our minds is the care, the precaution, with which we should go about making things better, so that the public order may not be destroyed, so that no fatal shock may be given to this society of ours, this living body in which our lives are bound up. After the Reform Bill of 1832 I was in an election riot,* which showed me clearly, on a small scale, what public disorder must always be; and I have never forgotten that the riot was brought about chiefly by the agency of dishonest men who professed to be on the people's side. Now, the danger hanging over change is great, just in proportion as it tends to produce such disorder by giving any large number of ignorant men, whose notions of what is good are of a low and brutal sort, the belief that they have got power into their hands, and may do pretty much as they like. If any one can look round us and say that he sees no signs of any such danger now, and that our national condition is running along like a clear broadening stream, safe not to get choked with mud, I call him a cheerful man: perhaps he does his own gardening, and seldom takes exercise far away from home. To us who have no gardens, and often walk abroad, it is plain that we can never get into a bit of a crowd but we must rub clothes with a set of Roughs, who have the worst vices of the worst rich—who are gamblers, sots, libertines, knaves, or else mere sensual simpletons and victims. They are the ugly crop that has sprung up while the stewards have been sleeping; they are the multiplying brood begotten by parents who have been left without all teaching save that of a too craving body, without all wellbeing save the fading delusions of drugged beer and gin. They are the hideous margin of society, at one edge drawing towards it the undesigning ignorant poor, at the other darkening imperceptibly into the lowest criminal class. Here is one of the evils which cannot be got rid of quickly, and against which any of us who have got sense, decency, and instruction have need to watch. That these degraded fellow-men could really get the mastery in a persistent disobedience to the laws and in a struggle to subvert order, I do not believe; but wretched calamities would come from the very beginning of such a struggle, and the continuance of it would be a civil war, in which the inspiration on both sides might soon cease to be even a false notion of good, and might become the direct savage impulse of ferocity. We have all to see to it that we do not help to rouse what I may call the savage beast in the breasts of our generation— that we do not help to poison the nation's blood, and make richer provision for bestiality to come. We know well enough that oppressors have sinned in this way—that oppression has notoriously made men mad; and we are determined to resist oppression. But let us, if possible, show that we can keep sane in our resistance, and shape our means more and more reasonably towards the least harmful, and therefore the speediest, attainment of our end. Let us, I say, show that our spirits are too strong to be driven mad, but can keep that sober determination which alone gives mastery over the adaptation of means. And a first guarantee of this sanity will be to act as if we understood that the fundamental duty of a government is to preserve order, to enforce obedience of the laws. It has been held hitherto that a man can be depended on as a guardian of order only when he has much money and comfort to lose. But a better state of things would be, that men who had little money and not much comfort should still be guardians of order, because they had sense to see that disorder would do no good, and had a heart of justice, pity, and fortitude, to keep them from making more misery only because they felt some misery themselves. There are thousands of artisans who have already shown this fine spirit, and have endured much with patient heroism. If such a spirit spread, and penetrated us all, we should soon become the masters of the country in the best sense and to the best ends. For, the public order being preserved, there can be no government in future that will not be determined by our insistance on our fair and practicable demands. It is only by disorder that our demands will be choked, that we shall find ourselves lost amongst a brutal rabble, with all the intelligence of the country opposed to us, and see government in the shape of guns that will sweep us down in the ignoble martyrdom of fools.

It has been a too common notion that to insist much on the preservation of order is the part of a selfish aristocracy and a selfish commercial class, because among these, in the nature of things, have been found the opponents of change. I am a Radical; and, what is more, I am not a Radical with a title, or a French cook, or even an entrance into fine society. I expect great changes, and I desire them. But I don't expect them to come in a hurry, by mere inconsiderate sweeping. A Hercules with a big besom is a fine thing for filthy stable,* but not for weeding a seed-bed, where his besom would soon make a barren floor.

That is old-fashioned talk, some one may say. We know all that.

Yes, when things are put in an extreme way, most people think they know them; but, after all, they are comparatively few who see the small degrees by which those extremes are arrived at, or have the resolution and self-control to resist the little impulses by which they creep on surely towards a fatal end. Does anybody set out meaning to ruin himself, or to drink himself to death, or to waste his life so that he becomes a despicable old man, a superannuated nuisance, like a fly in winter? Yet there are plenty, of whose lot this is the pitiable story. Well now, supposing us all to have the best intentions, we working men, as a body, run some risk of bringing evil on the nation in that unconscious manner—half-hurrying, half-pushed in a jostling march towards an end we are not thinking of. For just as there are many things which we know better and feel much more strongly than the richer, softer-handed classes can know or feel them; so there are many things—many precious benefits—which we, by the very fact of our privations, our lack of leisure and instruction, are not so likely to be aware of and take into our account. Those precious benefits form a chief part of what I may call the common estate of society: a wealth over and above buildings, machinery, produce, shipping, and so on, though closely connected with these; a wealth of a more delicate kind, that we may more unconsciously bring into danger, doing harm and not knowing that we do it. I mean that treasure of knowledge, science, poetry, refinement of thought, feeling, and manners, great memories and the interpretation of great records, which is carried on from the minds of one generation to the minds of another. This is something distinct from the indulgences of luxury and the pursuit of vain finery; and one of the hardships in the lot of working men is that they have been for the most part shut out from sharing in this treasure. It can make a man's life very great, very full of delight, though he has no smart furniture and no horses: it also yields a great deal of discovery that corrects error, and of invention that lessens bodily pain, and must at last make life easier for all.

Now the security of this treasure demands, not only the preservation of order, but a certain patience on our part with many institutions and facts of various kinds, especially touching the accumulation of wealth, which from the light we stand in, we are more likely to discern the evil than the good of. It is constantly the task of practical wisdom not to say, 'This is good, and I will have it', but to say, 'This is the less of two unavoidable evils, and I will bear it'. And this treasure of knowledge, which consists in the fine activity, the exalted vision of many minds, is bound up at present with conditions which have much evil in them. Just as in the case of material wealth and its distribution we are obliged to take the selfishness and weaknesses of human nature into account, and however we insist that men might act better, are forced, unless we are fanatical simpletons, to consider how they are likely to act; so in this matter of the wealth that is carried in men's minds, we have to reflect that the too absolute predominance of a class whose wants have been of a common sort, who are chiefly struggling to get better and more food, clothing, shelter, and bodily recreation, may lead to hasty measures for the sake of having things more fairly shared, which, even if they did not fail of their object, would at last debase the life of the nation. Do anything which will throw the classes who hold the treasures of knowledge—nay, I may say, the treasure of refined needs—into the background, cause them to withdraw from public affairs, stop too suddenly any of the sources by which their leisure and ease are furnished, rob them of the chances by which they may be influential and pre-eminent, and you do something as shortsighted as the acts of France and Spain when in jealousy and wrath, not altogether unprovoked, they drove from among them races and classes that held the traditions of handicraft and agriculture. You injure your own inheritance and the inheritance of your children. You may truly say that this which I call the common estate of society has been anything but common to you; but the same may be said, by many of us, of the sunlight and the air, of the sky and the fields, of parks and holiday games. Nevertheless, that these blessings exist makes life worthier to us, and urges us the more to energetic, likely means of getting our share in them; and I say, let us watch carefully, lest we do anything to lessen this treasure which is held in the minds of men, while we exert ourselves first of all, and to the very utmost, that we and our children may share in all its benefits. Yes; exert ourselves to the utmost, to break the yoke of ignorance. If we demand more leisure, more ease in our lives, let us show that we don't deserve the reproach of wanting to shirk that industry which, in some form or other, every man, whether rich or poor, should feel himself as much bound to as he is bound to decency. Let us show that we want to have some time and strength left to us, that we may use it, not for brutal indulgence, but for the rational exercise of the faculties which make us men. Without this no political measures can benefit us. No political institution will alter the nature of Ignorance, or hinder it from producing vice and misery. Let Ignorance start how it will, it must run the same round of low appetites, poverty, slavery, and superstition. Some of us know this well—nay, I will say, feel it; for knowledge of this kind cuts deep; and to us it is one of the most painful facts belonging to our condition that there are numbers of our fellow-workmen who are so far from feeling in the same way, that they never use the imperfect opportunities already offered them for giving their children some schooling, but turn their little ones of tender age into bread-winners, often at cruel tasks, exposed to the horrible infection of childish vice. Of course, the causes of these hideous things go a long way back. Parents' misery has made parents' wickedness. But we, who are still blessed with the hearts of fathers and the consciences of men—we who have some knowledge of the curse entailed on broods of creatures in human shape, whose enfeebled bodies and dull perverted minds are mere centres of uneasiness, in whom even appetite is feeble and joy impossible—I say we are bound to use all the means at our command to help in putting a stop to this horror. Here, it seems to me, is a way in which we may use extended co-operation among us to the most momentous of all purposes, and make conditions of enrolment that would strengthen all educational measures. It is true enough that there is a low sense of parental duties in the nation at large, and that numbers who have no excuse in bodily hardship seem to think it a light thing to beget children, to bring human beings with all their tremendous possibilities into this difficult world, and then take little heed how they are disciplined and furnished for the perilous journey they are sent on without any asking of their own. This is a sin shared in more or less by all classes; but there are sins which, like taxation, fall the heaviest on the poorest, and none have such galling reasons as we working-men to try and rouse to the utmost the feeling of responsibility in fathers and mothers. We have been urged into co-operation by the pressure of common demands. In war men need each other more; and where a given point has to be defended, fighters inevitably find themselves shoulder to shoulder. So fellowship grows, so grow the rules of fellowship, which gradually shape themselves to thoroughness as the idea of a common good becomes more complete. We feel a right to say, If you will be one of us, you must make such and such a contribution—you must renounce such and such a separate advantage—you must set your face against such and such an infringement. If we have any false ideas about our common good, our rules will be wrong, and we shall be co-operating to damage each other. But now, here is a part of our good, without which everything else we strive for will be worthless—I mean, the rescue of our children. Let us demand from the members of our Unions that they fulfil their duty as parents in this definite matter, which rules can reach. Let us demand that they send their children to school, so as not to go on recklessly breeding a moral pestilence among us, just as strictly as we demand that they pay their contributions to a common fund, understood to be for a common benefit. While we watch our public men, let us watch one another as to this duty, which is also public, and more momentous even than obedience to sanitary regulations. Whilst we resolutely declare against the wickedness in high places, let us set ourselves also against the wickedness in low places, not quarrelling which came first, or which is the worse of the two—not trying to settle the miserable precedence of plague or famine, but insisting unflinchingly on remedies once ascertained, and summoning those who hold the treasure of knowledge to remember that they hold it in trust, and that with them lies the task of searching for new remedies, and finding the right methods of applying them.

To find right remedies and right methods. Here is the great function of knowledge: here the life of one man may make a fresh era straight away, in which a sort of suffering that has existed shall exist no more. For the thousands of years down to the middle of the sixteenth century that human limbs had been hacked and amputated, nobody knew how to stop the bleeding except by searing the ends of the vessels with red hot iron. But then came a man named Ambrose Paré,* and said, 'Tie up the arteries!' That was a fine word to utter. It contained the statement of a method—a plan by which a particular evil was for ever assuaged. Let us try to discern the men whose words carry that sort of kernel, and choose such men to be our guides and representatives—not choose platform swaggerers, who bring us nothing but the ocean to make our broth with.

To get the chief power into the hands of the wisest, which means to get our life regulated according to the truest principles mankind is in possession of, is a problem as old as the very notion of wisdom. The solution comes slowly, because men collectively can only be made to embrace principles, and to act on them, by the slow stupendous teaching of the world's events. Men will go on planting potatoes, and nothing else but potatoes, till a potato-disease comes and forces them to find out the advantage of a varied crop. Selfishness, stupidity, sloth, persist in trying to adapt the world to their desires, till a time comes when the world manifests itself as too decidedly inconvenient to them. Wisdom stands outside of man and urges itself upon him, like the marks of the changing seasons, before it finds a home within him, directs his actions, and from the precious effects of obedience begets a corresponding love.

But while still outside of us, wisdom often looks terrible, and wears strange forms, wrapped in the changing conditions of a struggling world. It wears now the form of wants and just demands in a great multitude of British men: wants and demands urged into existence by the forces of a maturing world. And it is in virtue of this—in virtue of this presence of wisdom on our side as a mighty fact, physical, and moral, which must enter into and shape the thoughts and actions of mankind—that we working men have obtained the suffrage. Not because we are an excellent multitude, but because we are a needy multitude.

But now, for our own part, we have seriously to consider this outside wisdom which lies in the supreme unalterable nature of things, and watch to give it a home within us and obey it. If the claims of the unendowed multitude of working men hold within them principles which must shape the future, it is not less true that the endowed classes, in their inheritance from the past, hold the precious material without which no worthy, noble future can be moulded. Many of the highest uses of life are in their keeping; and if privilege has often been abused, it also has been the nurse of excellence.* Here again we have to submit ourselves to the great law of inheritance. If we quarrel with the way in which the labours and earnings of the past have been preserved and handed down, we are just as bigoted, just as narrow, just as wanting in that religion which keeps an open ear and an obedient mind to the teachings of fact, as we accuse those of being, who quarrel with the new truths and new needs which are disclosed in the present. The deeper insight we get into the causes of human trouble, and the ways by which men are made better and happier, the less we shall be inclined to the unprofitable spirit and practice of reproaching classes as such in a wholesale fashion. Not all the evils of our condition are such as we can justly blame others for; and, I repeat, many of them are such as no changes of institutions can quickly remedy. To discern between the evils that energy can remove and the evils that patience must bear, makes the difference between manliness and childishness, between good sense and folly. And more than that, without such discernment, seeing that we have grave duties towards our own body and the country at large, we can hardly escape acts of fatal rashness and injustice.

I am addressing a mixed assembly of workmen, and some of you may be as well or better fitted than I am to take up this office. But they will not think it amiss in me that I have tried to bring together the considerations most likely to be of service to us in preparing ourselves for the use of our new opportunities. I have avoided touching on special questions. The best help towards judging well on these is to approach them in the right temper without vain expectation, and with a resolution which is mixed with temperance.

Notes on Form in Art (1868)

ABSTRACT words and phrases which have an excellent genealogy are apt to live a little too much on their reputation and even to sink into dangerous impostors that should be made to show how they get their living. For this reason it is often good to consider an old subject as if nothing had yet been said about it; to suspend one's attention even to revered authorities and simply ask what in the present state of our knowledge are the facts which can with any congruity be tied together and labelled by a given abstraction.

For example, to any but those who are under the dire necessity of using the word and cannot afford to wait for a meaning, it must be more fruitful to ask, what relations of things can be properly included under the word 'Form' as applied to artistic composition, than to decide without any such previous inquiry that a particular work is wanting in form, or to take it for granted that the works of any one period or people are the examples of all that is admissible in artistic form.

Plain people, though indisposed to metaphysical subtleties, can yet understand that Form, as an element of human experience, must begin with the perception of separateness, derived principally from touch of which the other senses are modifications; and that things must be recognized as separate wholes before they can be recognized as wholes composed of parts, or before these wholes again can be regarded as relatively parts of a larger whole.

Form, then, as distinguished from merely massive impression, must first depend on the discrimination of wholes and then on the discrimination of parts. Fundamentally, form is unlikeness, as is seen in the philosophic use of the word 'Form' in distinction from 'Matter'; and in consistency with this fundamental meaning, every difference is Form. Thus, sweetness is a form of sensibility, rage is a form of passion, green is a form both of light and of sensibility. But with this fundamental discrimination is born in necessary antithesis the sense of wholeness or unbroken connexion in space and time: a flash of light is a whole compared with the darkness which precedes and follows it; the taste of sourness is a whole and includes parts or degrees as it subsides. And as knowledge continues to grow by its alternating processes of distinction and combination, seeing smaller and smaller unlikenesses and grouping or associating these under a common likeness, it arrives at the conception of wholes composed of parts more and more multiplied and highly differenced, yet more and more absolutely bound together by various conditions of common likeness or mutual dependence. And the fullest example of such a whole is the highest example of Form: in other words, the relation of multiplex interdependent parts to a whole which is itself in the most varied and therefore the fullest relation to other wholes. Thus, the human organism comprises things as diverse as the finger-nails and tooth-ache, as the nervous stimulus of muscle manifested in a shout, and the discernment of a red spot on a field of snow; but all its different elements or parts of experience are bound together in a more necessary wholeness or more inseparable group of common conditions than can be found in any other existence known to us. The highest Form, then, is the highest organism, that is to say, the most varied group of relations bound together in a wholeness which again has the most varied relations with all other phenomena.*

It is only in this fundamental sense that the word 'Form' can be applied to Art in general. Boundary or outline and visual appearance are modes of Form which in music and poetry can only have a metaphorical presence. Even in the plastic arts Form obviously, in its general application, means something else than mere imitation of outline, more or less correctness of drawing or modelling—just as, with reference to descriptive poetry, it means something more than the bare delineation of landscape or figures. Even those who use the phrase with a very dim understanding, always have a sense that it refers to structure or composition, that is, to the impression from a work considered as a whole. And what is a structure but a set of relations selected and combined in accordance with the sequence of mental states in the constructor, or with the preconception of a whole which he has inwardly evolved? Artistic form, as distinguished from mere imitation, begins in sculpture and painting with composition or the selection of attitudes and the formation of groups, let the objects be of what order they may. In music it begins with the adjustment of tones and rhythm to a climax, apart from any direct imitation. But my concern is here chiefly with poetry which I take in its wider sense as including all literary production of which it is the prerogative and not the reproach that the choice and sequence of images and ideas—that is, of relations and groups of relations—are more or less not only determined by emotion but intended to express it. I say more or less; for even the ravings of madness include multitudinous groups and sequences which are parts of common experience; and in the range of poetry we see wide distances of degree in the combination of emotive force with sequences that are not arbitrary and individual but true and universal, just as the guiding emotion varies from an idiosyncrasy only short of madness to a profoundly human passion which is or must come to be the heritage of all mankind. Sometimes the wider signification of poetry is taken to be fiction or invention as opposed to ascertained external fact or discovery. But what is fiction other than an arrangement of events or feigned correspondences according to predominant feeling? We find what destiny pleases; we make what pleases us—or what we think will please others.

Even taken in its derivative meaning of outline, what is Form but the limit of that difference by which we discriminate one object from another?—a limit determined partly by the intrinsic relations or composition of the object, and partly by the extrinsic action of other bodies upon it. This is true whether the object is a rock or a man; but in the case of the inorganic body, outline is the result of a nearly equal struggle between inner constitution and the outer play of forces; while in the human organism the outline is mainly determined by the intrinsic relation of its parts, and what is called fitness, beauty, or harmony in its outline and movements is dependent on the inward balance. The muscular strength which hurls, the muscular grace which gives a rhythmic movement to half a dozen balls, show a moving outline of which the chief factors are relations within the body; but the line with which a rock cuts the sky, or the shape of a boulder, may be more due to outer forces than to inner constitution. In ordinary language, the form of a stone is accidental. But the true expression of the difference is, that the wholeness of the stone depends simply on likeness of crystallization and is merely a wholeness of mass which may be broken up into other wholes; whereas the outline defining the wholeness of the human body is due to a consensus or constant interchange of effects among its parts. It is wholeness not merely of mass but of strict and manifold dependence. The word 'consensus' expresses that fact in a complex organism by which no part can suffer increase or diminution without a participation of all other parts in the effect produced and a consequent modification of the organism as a whole.

By this light, forms of art can be called higher or lower only on the same principle as that on which we apply these words to organisms; viz. in proportion to the complexity of the parts bound up into an indissoluble whole. In Poetry—which has this superiority over all the other arts, that its medium, language, is the least imitative, and is in the most complex relation with what it expresses—Form begins in the choice of rhythms and images as signs of a mental state, for this is a process of grouping or association of a less spontaneous and more conscious order than the grouping or association which constitutes the very growth and natural history of mind. *Poetry* begins when passion weds thought by finding expression in an image; but *Poetic Form* begins with a choice of elements, however meagre, as the accordant expression of emotional states. The most monotonous burthen chanted by an Arab boatman on the Nile is still a beginning of poetic form.

Poetic Form was not begotten by thinking it out or framing it as a shell which should hold emotional expression, any more than the shell of an animal arises before the living creature; but emotion, by its tendency to repetition, i.e., rhythmic persistence in proportion as diversifying thought is absent, creates a form by the recurrence of its elements in adjustment with certain given conditions of sound, language, action, or environment. Just as the beautiful expanding curves of a bivalve shell are not first made for the reception of the unstable inhabitant, but grow and are limited by the simple rhythmic conditions of its growing life.*

It is a stale observation that the earliest poetic forms arose in the same spontaneous unreflecting way—that the rhythmic shouts with clash of metal accompanying the huntsman's or conqueror's course were probably the nucleus of the ballad epic; that the funeral or marriage sing-song, wailing or glad, with more or less violent muscular movement and resonance of wood or metal made the rude beginnings of lyric poetry. But it is still worth emphasis that this spontaneous origin is the most completely demonstrated in relation to a form of art which ultimately came to be treated more reflectively than any other—the tragic and comic drama.

A Form being once started must by and by cease to be purely spontaneous: the form itself becomes the object and material of emotion, and is sought after, amplified and elaborated by discrimination of its elements till at last by the abuse of its refinement it preoccupies the room of emotional thinking; and poetry, from being the fullest expression of the human soul, is starved into an ingenious pattern-work, in which tricks with vocables take the place of living words fed with the blood of relevant meaning, and made musical by the continual intercommunication of sensibility and thought.

The old phrases should not give way to scientific explanation, for speech is to a great extent like sculpture, expressing observed phenomena and remaining true in spite of Harvey and Bichat.* In the later development of poetic fable the ἀναγνώρισις tends to consist in the discernment of a previously unrecognized *character*, and this may also form the περιπέτεια, according to Aristotle's notion that in the highest form the two coincide.*

EXPLANATORY NOTES

From the Translation of Strauss's The Life of Jesus (1846), Introduction

David Friedrich Strauss's *Das Leben Jesu, kritisch bearbeitet* (1835–6; fourth edition 1840), was translated anonymously by Mary Ann Evans, 3 vols. (London, 1846). The last part of the Introduction is reprinted here.

5 *Thus, one gospel . . . into prison*: cf. Mark 1: 14, 'Now after that John was put in prison, Jesus came into Galilee', and John 3: 22–4, 'After these things came Jesus and his disciples into the land of Judaea . . . For John was not yet cast into prison.'

argumentum ex silentio: argument from silence.

6–7 *prophecy of Balaam . . . command of Pharaoh*: cf. Numbers 24: 17 and Exodus 1: 15–22. Strauss is referring also to the Gospel according to St Matthew 2: 1–18.

7 *Josephus*: Flavius Josephus (*c*.37–*c*.95), Jewish historian, author of *The Jewish Antiquities*, a history of the Jews from the creation of the world to the outbreak of the war with Rome.

Letter to Charles Bray, 21 October 1846

George Eliot to Charles Bray, 21 Oct. 1846, *The George Eliot Letters*, ed. Gordon S. Haight, 9 vols. (New Haven, Conn., 1954–5, 1978; subsequently referred to as *GEL*), viii. 12–15.

11 *Cara*: Cara Bray (née Hennell), Charles Bray's wife.

Mary: Mary Sibree, friend of the Brays.

Professor Bücherwurm, Moderig University: 'Professor Bookworm of Musty University', an obvious imitation of Carlyle's fictional Germans, Diogenes Teufelsdröckh (Devil's Dung) in *Sartor Resartus* (1836) and Professor Sauerteig (Sour Dough) in *Chartism* (1839). Lewes also adopted a Carlylean joke German in this early essays—Professor Wolfgang von Bibundtücker (see *Bentley's Miscellany*, VI (1839), 599). Professor Bücherwurm is an early version of the ageing pedant in George Eliot's writings, of whom Mr Casaubon in *Middlemarch* is the most famous example.

Emperor Julian: Julian, Emperor of Rome, AD 361–3.

12 *book of Tobit*: one of the books of the Old Testament Apocrypha.

Greek Digamma: sixth letter of original Greek alphabet, later disused, but important in philology from correspondences with cognate languages.

Cheops: the king who built the Great Pyramid in Egypt.

our divine Schiller . . . the age to come: words spoken by the Marquis of Posa in *Don Carlos* (1787), III. x ('Das Jahrhundert/Ist meinem Ideal nicht reif. Ich lebe/ Ein Bürger derer, welche kommen werden', 'The age is not ready for my ideal. I live a citizen of those ages which are yet to come.').

13 *but a younger brother's revenue*: *As You Like It*, III. ii. 351–2.

tocher: dowry (Scots).

14 *Sara*: Sara Hennell, Cara Bray's sister.

J. A. Froude's The Nemesis of Faith

This review of J. A. Froude's *The Nemesis of Faith* appeared in the *Coventry Herald and Observer*, 16 Mar. 1849.

15 *bright particular star*: *All's Well that Ends Well*, I. i. 80.

'*son of the morning*': Isaiah 14: 12, 'How art thou fallen from heaven, | O day star, son of the morning'.

16–17 quotations from *The Nemesis of Faith*, with some minor inaccuracies. See *The Nemesis of Faith* (London, 1849, repr. 1988), 6–7, 8–9, 42, 43.

R. W. Mackay's The Progress of the Intellect

This review of R. W. Mackay's *The Progress of the Intellect, as Exemplified in the Religious Development of the Greeks and Hebrews*, 2 vols. (1850), appeared in the *Westminster Review*, liv (Jan. 1851), 353–68.

18 *Auguste Comte*: French social philosopher (1798–1857), founder of Positivism, a theory of stages of culture from the theological (classical and medieval times) via the metaphysical (eighteenth-century Enlightenment) to the positive or scientific (nineteenth century).

awful eye: Milton, 'On the Morning of Christ's Nativity', l. 59.

19   *idola theatri*: idols of the theatre, one of the idols (or entrenched habits) of mind identified by Francis Bacon in *The Advancement of Learning* (1605).

20   *'antithetically mixt'*: Byron, *Childe Harold's Pilgrimage*, III. 36.

   Cudworth: Ralph Cudworth (1617–88), Anglican divine, one of the Cambridge Platonists.

   biblical criticism: George Eliot has Strauss's *Life of Jesus* particularly in mind.

22   *theory of practice and duty*: should read 'theory and practice of duty' (Mackay, i. 10).

   sensibility: should read 'insensibility' (Mackay, i. 10).

   natural: 'notional' in Mackay (i. 10).

23   *ascensio mentis . . . creaturum rerum*: the ascent of the mind towards God by the ladder of created things.

   external: 'substantial' in Mackay (i. 38).

24   *opposite extreme of incredulity*: 'opposite irrational extreme of incredulity' in Mackay (i. 39).

26   *Bryant*: Jacob Bryant (1715–1804), author of *A New System; or, an Analysis of Ancient Mythology* (1774–6). In *Middlemarch*, ch. 22, Will Ladislaw tells Dorothea that Mr Casaubon is ignorant of recent German scholarship in the field, 'crawling a little way after men of the last century—men like Bryant'.

   O. Müller: Karl Otfried Müller, *Prolegomena zu einer wissenschaftlichen Mythologie* (*Prolegomena to a Scientific Mythology*, 1825).

27   *Creuzer*: Georg Friedrich Creuzer, historian of religion, author of *Symbolik und Mythologie der alten Völker, besonders der Griechen* (*Symbolism and Mythology of the Ancient Peoples, particularly the Greeks*, 1810–12).

29   *High instincts . . . like a guilty thing surprised*: slightly misquoted from Wordsworth, 'Ode, Intimations of Mortality from Recollections of Early Childhood', ll. 150–1.

30   *rerum naturâ*: in the natural order.

   Philo . . . Origen: Philo, Jewish philosopher of Alexandria (*c*.30 BC–AD 45); Origen, theologian of Alexandria (*c*.185–*c*.254).

Jacob . . . Joshua: Genesis 27: 18 ff. and Joshua 8: 1–29.

31 *Pharaoh and Abimelech*: Genesis 12: 10–20 and Genesis 20.

    eat of the prey . . . blood of the slain: Numbers 23: 24.

33 παρρησία: plain-speaking.

Woman in France: Madame de Sablé

George Eliot reviewed Victor Cousin's *Madame de Sablé: Études sur les femmes illustres et la société du dix-septième siècle* (Paris, 1854), for the *Westminster Review*, lxii (Oct. 1854), 448–73. The article nominally reviews also Charles Augustin Sainte-Beuve's *Portraits de femmes* (Paris, 1844) and Jules Michelet's *Les femmes de la révolution* (Paris, 1854).

37 *Richardson's Lady G.*: Charlotte, Lady Grandison, in Samuel Richardson's *Sir Charles Grandison* (1754).

39 *Madame de Sévigné*: famous for her letters to her daughter, published after her death, in 1725.

    Madame Dacier: classical scholar (*c.*1654–1720), translator of the *Iliad* and the *Odyssey*, and of plays by Terence and Plautus.

    Madame de Staël: novelist and critic (1766–1817), most famous in England for her *De l'Allemagne* (1810).

    Madame Roland: she held a salon frequented by the Girondins, a group of deputies in the Legislative Assembly of 1791–3.

    George Sand: pseudonym of Amandine Aurore-Lucille Dupin, Mme Dudevant (1804–76), novelist and free liver of great influence and notoriety. George Eliot admired her, see *GEL*, i. 277–8.

    Jean Jacques: Jean-Jacques Rousseau (1712–78), philosopher, novelist, forerunner of Romanticism. George Eliot writes of her admiration for Rousseau in the same letter of 1846 in which she praises George Sand, *GEL*, i. 277.

41 *'die of a rose'*: Pope, *Essay on Man*, Epistle I. l. 200.

43 *Précieuses Ridicules and Les Femmes Savantes*: satirical comedies by Molière.

    Madelon and Cathos . . . Mademoiselle Scudéry: Madelon and Cathos (the *Westminster* misprints the name as Caltros) are the précieuses ridicules; Mlle Scudéry, blue-stocking and satirical writer (1607–1701).

44 *bouts rimés*: set rhymes.

47 '*un heureux mélange . . . et de bonté*': a happy mixture of reason, wit, charm, and kindness.

tons criards: gaudy colours.

49 *lèse-amitié*: injured friendship.

'*galimatias*': nonsense.

50 *Malheureuse . . . le savoir*: 'Ignorance is unfortunate, and knowledge even more so', Jean Bertaut (1552–1611), court poet to Henri III and Henri IV.

53 *Reine de Mionie*: i.e. Reine de Misne.

54 *Port Royalists*: community of intellectuals established in 1633 in the ancient Cistercian abbey at Port Royal des Champs, near Versailles.

'*En vérité . . . me saigner*': Truly, I do not think I could do better than to give it all up and go there. But what would become of those fears of having no doctors to choose from, and no surgeon to bleed me?

friandise: delicacies.

bonnes bouches: tasty morsels.

'*Je vous demande . . . scrupule*': I beg you in God's name not to prepare any special dish for me. Above all, don't give me a feast. In God's name let there be nothing but what one can eat, for you know it is useless for me; moreover, I have scruples about it.

55 *Jansenism*: reforming movement within the Catholic Church against Cardinal Richelieu and Louis XIV, taking its name from Cornelius Jansen (1585–1638).

56 *La non pareille . . . très fine*: the peerless Bois-Dauphine, finest pearl among ladies.

57 *frondeurs*: members of the Fronde, the party opposed to the French court during the minority of Louis XIV. Hence a general term for critics of the establishment or malcontents.

58 '*vaquer enfin . . . sa santé*': at last attend at her ease to her salvation and her health.

'*Vous savez . . . du coeur*': You know that I believe that you alone are to be trusted on certain chapters, and especially about the secrets of the heart.

59 *Je crois . . . madame, votre, etc.*: I believe I am the only person capable of doing so well exactly the opposite of what I mean to do, for it is true that there is nobody whom I honour more than you, yet I have acted in a way you will hardly believe. It was not enough to persuade you of my being unworthy of your good graces and remembrance that I failed for so long to write to you; I had to delay yet another fortnight before allowing myself the honour of replying to your letter. Truly, madame, this makes me look so culpable that if it were anyone else than you I would rather actually be culpable than undertake the hard task of justifying myself. But I feel so innocent in my heart, and I have such esteem, such respect, for you that it seems to me you must recognize it a hundred miles away, without my saying a single word about it. That is what gives me courage to write to you now, but not what has hindered me for so long from doing so. I began to fail perforce, having had many troubles, and since then it has been through shame, and I swear to you that if I had not now the confidence you have given me by your reassurance, and the confidence I draw from my own feelings for you, I would never try to make you remember me; but I am sure that you will forget everything when I assure you that I will never again allow myself to be hardened in my faults, and that I remain inviolably, madame, yours etc.

61 '*L'envie . . . le rhume*': the desire to make maxims spreads like the common cold.

62 '*Voilà tout . . . ragoût de mouton*': Here are all the maxims I have; but as I give nothing for nothing, I demand of you a carrot soup and a mutton stew.

63 '*On ne pourroit faire . . . mon libérateur*': One could not give a more proper instruction to a catechumen to convert his mind and will to God . . . If there were nothing in the world but this piece of writing and the Gospel, I would still want to be a Christian. The one would teach me how to know my sorrows, and the other how to pray to my saviour.

64 '*Je vous envoie . . . ce dictum*': I send you what I have been able to wring from my brain for putting in the *Journal des Savants*. I have put in the passage about which you are so

sensitive so that you can overcome the self-consciousness which made you print the preface without cutting anything out, and I have not been afraid of putting it in because I am sure you will not have it printed, however much the rest may please you. I assure you, too, that I will be more obliged to you if you use it as if it were yours to correct or to throw on the fire. We great authors are too rich to fear losing any of our productions. Let me know how you like this dictum.

67 *I one day asked . . . count them*: from Sainte-Beuve's *Portraits de femmes* (*1844*).

From the Translation of Feuerbach's The Essence of Christianity (1854)

Ludwig Feuerbach's *Das Wesen des Christenthums* (1841), trans. Marian Evans (London, 1854). The Concluding Application is reprinted here, with the exception of the final two pages of rhapsody on the natural benefits of baptism.

69 *In the contradiction . . . exhibited*: ch. 26, 'The Contradiction of Faith and Love', in which Feuerbach argues that Faith, whether Jewish or Christian, is exclusive and negative, requiring that non-believers be anathematized, and is therefore in opposition to Love, which unifies and liberates. Men do good for God's sake (and out of fear of God's punishment) rather than for man's sake and out of love of goodness itself. Compare George Eliot's similar view as expressed in 'Evangelical Teaching: Dr Cumming' (included in this volume): 'with the conception of God which his teaching presents, the love of man for God's sake involves, as his writings abundantly show, a strong principle of hatred'.

From the Translation of Spinoza's Ethics (1854–5)

Benedict de Spinoza's *Ethica* (1677), was translated by Marian Evans in 1854–5. (Published in the series Salzburg Studies in English Literature, edited by Thomas Deegan (Salzburg, 1981).) Reprinted here is the opening of Part 5, 'On the Power of the Intellect, or, on Human Liberty'.

75 *the other part of Ethics*: Spinoza has dealt in the preceding section with 'Human Servitude, or, the Strength of the Emotions'. He now considers how we can strive to control our passions by reason.

76 *treatise on the Passions*: René Descartes, *Passions de l'âme* (Paris, 1649). Spinoza refers to the Latin edition *Passiones animae* (1650).

80 *united with true ideas*: the Spinozan idea of reflecting on our emotions until we form a clear idea of them which, in turn, enables us to turn them into positive rather than negative forces is most graphically illustrated in George Eliot's own work by Dorothea in *Middlemarch*, ch. 80: 'She began now to live through that yesterday morning deliberately again, forcing herself to dwell on every detail and its possible meaning. Was she alone in that scene? Was it her event only? She forced herself to think of it as bound up with another woman's life—a woman towards whom she had set out with a longing to carry some clearness and comfort into her beclouded youth . . . She yearned towards the perfect Right, that it might make a throne within her, and rule her errant will. "What should I do—how should I act now, this very day if I could clutch my own pain, and compel it to silence, and think of those three!" It had taken long for her to come to that question, and there was light piercing into the room.'

Liszt, Wagner, and Weimar (1855)

This article is reprinted from *Fraser's Magazine*, lii (July 1855), 48–62.

82 *'blazed the comet of a season'*: Byron, 'Churchill's Grave', ll. 1–2.

falsity of this conception: George Eliot and Lewes met Liszt frequently in Weimar society; he was Kapellmeister to the Duke of Weimar's court. George Eliot took courage from the similarity of Liszt's domestic situation to her own. He was living with a married woman, Princess Carolyne von Sayn-Wittgenstein. As she noted in letters home to England, such relationships were tolerated at the Court of Weimar, see letter to Charles Bray, 16 Aug. 1854, *GEL*, ii. 171.

Ary Scheffer: Dutch portraitist, who did a portrait of Liszt in 1838.

83 *laudatores temporis acti*: from Horace, 'laudator temporis acti se puero' (he who sings the praises of his boyhood's days).

'one crowded hour of glorious life': Walter Scott, *Old Mortality* (1816), ch. 33.

84 '*music of the future*': Wagner's own term, 'Das Kunstwerk der Zukunft', often used by critics to mock him. Wagner had spent three months performing concerts in London just before this article was written, and had been ridiculed by the London music critics.

an Owenite parallelogram: communal building suggested by the social idealist Robert Owen in 1817 as part of his idea for improving the lot of the poor.

Overbeck: Johann Friedrich Overbeck (1789–1869), founder of the 'Nazarene' school of German painters in Rome devoted to reviving Christian art. George Eliot has Will Ladislaw consort with the Nazarenes in Rome, *Middlemarch*, ch. 19.

86 *Alice and Marcel*: in *Robert le Diable* and *Les Huguenots* respectively.

Kind: Friedrich Kind, librettist of Weber's *Der Freischütz* (1821). George Eliot heard the opera in Weimar in 1854.

Wagner's theory of the opera: George Eliot is relying on Liszt's article on the history of opera in his *Neue Zeitschrift für Musik* (June 1854) for much of this discussion.

87 *Lohengrin*: George Eliot and Lewes heard the opera in Weimar on 22 Oct. 1854, but found it tedious, see Haight, *George Eliot: A Biography* (subsequently referred to as *GE*), 156.

Stabreim: alliteration.

'*in the morning of the times*': Tennyson, 'The Day-Dream, L'Envoie', l. 20.

88 *set the teeth of all hearers on edge*: Rousseau, *Confessions* (1781), part i, bk 4.

92 *Ich sei's . . . das Heil erreichen!*: Let it be me who liberates you by my faithfulness! May God's angel reveal me to you; through me you shall attain salvation!

Er sucht . . . zu grunde gehn!: He is seeking me; I must see him; I must be lost with him!

93 *Wohl kenn ich . . . bis zum Tod!*: I well know woman's sacred duties; therefore be comforted, unhappy man! Let Fate pass judgement on her who can defy his judgement! I know the high command of loyalty; the man to whom I dedicate my loyalty shall be given loyalty till death!

96 *Sterblich . . . nach schmerzen!*: Ah, I have remained mortal, and your love is too great for me. Whereas a god can enjoy

forever, I am subject to change. Pleasure alone is not enough for me; I yearn for pain amidst all this joy!

98 *Dem ziemt . . . Liebe*: Man gets pleasure from gratifying his desires, and in pleasure only do I know love.

Armsel'ge . . . der Venus ein!: You poor wretches who have never enjoyed love, come, come to the mountain of Venus!

103 *Leb wohl . . . wenn ich noch bleib!*: Farewell, farewell, farewell, my sweet wife! Farewell, the Grail will be angry with me if I stay longer!

106 *by torchlight*: the episode is described in Lewes's *Life of Goethe* (1855), bk iv, ch. 5 ('Private Theatricals').

107 *Prince Pückler Muskau*: German adventurer-prince whose *Briefe eines Verstorbenen* (1831) was translated in 1832 by Sarah Austin as *Tour in England, Ireland, and France . . . by a German Prince*.

Jacobi's Woldemar: Goethe nailed this sentimental novel (1779) by his admirer Friedrich Heinrich Jacobi (1743–1819) to a beech tree in the park at Ettersburg.

108 *the giant Cormoran*: in 'Jack the Giant Killer'.

109 *Ueber allen Gipfeln . . . Ruhest du auch*: 'There is peace over all the peaks; in all the treetops you sense hardly a breath. The little birds in the wood are silent. Only wait, soon you too will be at peace.' This is the most famous of Goethe's simple lyric poems in praise of nature.

Charley Kingsley's Westward Ho!

This review appeared in 'Belles Lettres', *Westminster Review*, lxiv (July 1855), 288–94.

110 *O Mary! . . . sands of Dee*: Kingsley, 'The Sands of Dee' (1849).

'*carpet consideration*': *Twelfth Night*, III. iv. 225–6. The term is used to describe a knighting at court rather than on the battlefield.

Kiss's Amazon: the German sculptor August Kiss exhibited his sculpture 'Mounted Amazon Attacked by a Tiger' at the Great Exhibition of 1851.

111 '*to the manner born*': *Hamlet*, I. iv. 15.

112   *Boanerges' vein*: name given to the disciples James and John, who threatened to call down fire from Heaven when the Samaritans refused to receive Christ, see Luke 9: 54.

     Teufelsdröckh: the learned German philosopher in Carlyle's *Sartor Resartus* (1836).

     all heterodoxy: Kingsley had defended himself in 1851 in a letter to the *Guardian* against an attack on his novel *Yeast*, claiming to believe 'all the doctrines of the Catholic and Apostolic Church of England'.

115   '*will hear . . . forbear*': Ezekiel 2: 5, 2: 7, 3: 11.

116   '*builded better than they knew*': Ralph Waldo Emerson, 'The Problem', l. 23.

117   *Humboldt*: Alexander von Humboldt (1769–1859), German scientist and explorer.

Geraldine Jewsbury's Constance Herbert

This review appeared in 'Belles Lettres', *Westminster Review*, lxiv (July 1855), 294–6.

122   *Miss Grace Lee*: heroine of the novel of that name by Julia Kavanagh (1855).

     a melancholy Viola: in *Twelfth Night*.

Lord Brougham's Literature

This review of Lord Brougham's *Lives of Men of Letters and Science, Who Flourished in the Time of George III*, 2 vols. (1845–6, reprinted 1855), appeared in the *Leader*, vi (7 July 1855), 652–3.

123   *Hoby*: George Hoby's bootmaker's shop in St James's St.

     Crispin: patron saint of shoemakers.

125   *To blunt a moral and to spoil a tale*: pastiche of Samuel Johnson's line 'To point a moral, or adorn a tale', *The Vanity of Human Wishes* (1749), l. 222.

126   *Scotch 'wut'*: 'Their only idea of wit . . . is laughing immoderately at stated intervals', *A Memoir of the Rev. Sydney Smith, by his Daughter, Lady Holland*, 2 vols. (1855), i. 25.

     Dr Cumming . . . Robert Owen: for George Eliot's views on Dr Cumming's religion, see her essay on him in this volume. Robert Owen was the utopian socialist who set up his model community at New Lanark.

127 *Christo et Musis . . . Edinenses*: the citizens of Edinburgh have dedicated this temple to Christ and the Muses.

The Morality of Wilhelm Meister

This article appeared in the *Leader*, vi (21 July 1855), 703. Ostensibly a review of R. Dillon Boylan's recent translation of *Wilhelm Meister's Apprenticeship*, this is really a plea, ahead of publication of Lewes's *Life of Goethe* in Nov. 1855, for tolerance of Goethe's seeming immorality as a novelist.

129 *passionless Mejnour*: a character in Bulwer-Lytton's novel *Zanoni* (1842).

130 *crushed by a railway train*: George Eliot may have had in mind the death of Mr Carker in Dickens's *Dombey and Son* (1848).

132 *insupportables justes . . . l'humanité*: insufferable righteous ones who from the height of their golden seats look down on the sufferings of humanity.

Lothario: compare George Eliot's defence of the novel with that of Lewes in the *Life of Goethe* (bk vi, ch. 2). Lewes writes of the 'marvellous art with which the characters unfold themselves . . . They are never described, they exhibit themselves.' '*Wilhelm Meister* is not a moral story—that is to say, not a story written with the express purpose of illustrating some obvious maxim . . . the Artist has been content to paint scenes of life, *without comment*.'

The Future of German Philosophy

This review of Otto Friedrich Gruppe's *Gegenwart und Zukunft der Philosophie in Deutschland* (*Present and Future of Philosophy in Germany*, 1855) appeared in the *Leader* vi (28 July 1855), 723–4. George Eliot had met Gruppe in Berlin in 1855, see *GEL*, ii. 192–3.

133 *German system-mongers*: particularly Hegel, on whose philosophy of the identity of contraries Lewes had poured scorn in his *Biographical History of Philosophy*, 2 vols. (1845–6).

134 *imperfect attention*: a reference to John Stuart Mill's celebrated *System of Logic* (1843).

135 *dizziness and delusion are the consequence*: the paragraph is a statement of the empirical school of philosophy's main objection to the idealist school. Though Kant in his *Critique of*

Pure Reason (1781) carefully steered a middle path between empiricism and idealism (by means of the 'critical method'), he was often taken for an out-and-out idealist, or believer in the existence of, and the possibility of access to, universal truths.

Evangelical Teaching: Dr Cumming

A review of several works by Dr John Cumming, minister of the Scottish National Church in Covent Garden and writer of popular interpretations of Biblical prophecy, reprinted from the *Westminster Review*, lxiv (Oct. 1855), 436–62. It was this article which convinced Lewes of George Eliot's genius, according to John Cross, *George Eliot's Life as Related in Her Letters and Journals*, 3 vols. (1885), i. 384.

138 *Goshen*: the region of Egypt occupied by the Israelites before the exodus.

139 *'horn' . . . 'spirits'*: Daniel 7: 8 and Revelation 16: 13. *locusts whose sting is in their tail*: Revelation 9: 10.

Amphitryon: host, from Plautus's comedy of the same name.

141 *Puseyites*: after Edward Pusey (1800–82), a leading member of the Oxford Movement of High Anglicans in the 1830s.

Dr Chalmers and Mr Wilberforce: Thomas Chalmers (1780–1847), first Moderator of the Free Church of Scotland, and William Wilberforce (1759–1833), the famous Evangelical and abolitionist.

142 *Robert Hall . . . Isaac Taylor*: Evangelical preachers. Hall and Foster were Baptists.

143 *'clouts o' cauld parritch'*: Walter Scott, *Rob Roy* (1817), a description of the 'cold porridge' of degenerate preaching.

144 *little horn . . . seven vials*: Daniel 7: 8 and Revelation 21: 9.

Christianitatem, quocunque modo, Christianitatem: Christianity, by whatever means, Christianity.

146 *professor of Padua*: Francesco Sizi, Florentine astronomer who attacked Galileo with this argument in his *Dianoia astronomia* (1610).

148 *Though gay companions . . . I quit the scene*: these four verses actually come from three different Byron poems (none of them written when he was, or thought he was, dying). The first verse comes from 'One Struggle More, and I Am Free' (1811), ll. 21–4, the second and third from 'Euthanasia'

(1811), ll. 29–36, and the fourth from 'To a Youthful Friend' (1808), ll. 45–8. Cumming presumably ran the verses together to intensify the impression of Byron's 'infidelity'.

149 *Leland*: probably a mistake for Charles Leslie, *A Short and Easie Method with the Deists* (1698).

151 *bachelors of Salamanca*: *Don Quixote*, Part II, ch. 33.

152 *sunt quibus . . . pignus*: there are those for whom it is an honour not to have believed, and their unbelief is a guarantee of future faith.

'*perplext in faith but pure in deeds*': Tennyson, *In Memoriam*, xcvi. l. 9.

154 *Si Dieu . . . l'inventer*: if God did not exist, it would be necessary to invent him.

Voltaire's death: the story that he died in terror and despair.

155 *the author of the Vestiges*: Robert Chambers (1802–71), anonymous author of the popular evolutionary work *Vestiges of the Natural History of Creation* (1844).

160 *Cardinal Wiseman*: Nicholas Wiseman (1802–65), appointed Cardinal in 1850 on the establishment of a Roman Catholic hierarchy in England.

161 '*Whether we live . . . unto the Lord*': Romans 14: 8.

A closer walk . . . heavenly frame: William Cowper, 'Walking with God', *Olney Hymns* (1779), 1–2.

162 '*cathedrize here . . . temple of God*': Matthew 26: 36. The Authorized Version reads: 'Sit ye here, while I go and pray yonder'.

170 *Let knowledge . . . but vaster*: Tennyson, Prologue to *In Memorian*, 25–9.

Tennyson's Maud

This review appeared in 'Belles Lettres', *Westminster Review*, lxiv (Oct. 1855), 596–601.

171 *Aus Morgenduft . . . Wahrheit*: 'from the hand of truth poetry's veil spun from morning fragrance and the sun's clarity', Goethe, 'Zueignung' (1784), 95–6.

172 *Apollo Belvedere*: statue of Apollo in the Belvedere gallery in the Vatican.

generous seed . . . thought and deed: Tennyson, 'The Two Voices' (1842), 143–4.

173 *'with horrible discord and jarring sound'*: 'With impetuous recoil and jarring sound', Milton, *Paradise Lost*, Bk 11, l. 880.

174 *modern Conrad*: in Byron's *Corsair* (1814), i, l. 223.

176 *Mr Bright*: John Bright (1811–89), politician and advocate of free trade.

Would love the gleams . . . veil his eyes: Tennyson, 'Love Thou Thy Land' (1842), ll. 89–90.

Thekla's song: in *Die Piccolomini*, the second part of Schiller's *Wallenstein* trilogy, III. vii: 'Ich habe genossen das irdische Glück, | Ich habe gelebt und geliebet' (I have enjoyed earthly happiness; I have lived and loved).

178 *Summer Chace*: Tennyson, 'The Talking Oak' (1842), l. 30. The line actually reads 'Broad Oak of Sumner-chace'.

Margaret Fuller and Mary Wollstonecraft

This review of Margaret Fuller Ossoli's *Woman in the Nineteenth Century, and Kindred Papers relating to the Sphere, Condition, and Duties of Woman* (1855) appeared in the *Leader*, vi (13 Oct. 1855), 988–9. Margaret Fuller Ossoli (1810–50) was an American critic, feminist, and friend of Emerson.

180 *Parasitic forms . . . distinctive womanhood*: Tennyson, *The Princess* (1847), vii. ll. 253–8.

Rights of Woman: Mary Wollstonecraft (1759–97), *A Vindication of the Rights of Woman* (1792).

183 *Mrs Malaprop*: in Sheridan's *The Rivals* (1775).

184 *Fourier*: Charles Fourier (1772–1837), French social theorist, advocate of communal living.

186 *If she be small . . . men grow?*: Tennyson, *The Princess*, vii. ll. 249–50.

Thomas Carlyle

This review of Thomas Ballantyne's *Passages selected from the Writings of Thomas Carlyle* (1855) appeared in the *Leader*, vi (27 Oct. 1855), 1034–5.

188 *Sartor Resartus . . . history of their minds*: George Eliot wrote to a friend in 1841 shortly after reading Carlyle's *Sartor*

Resartus, 'His soul is a shrine of the brightest and purest philanthropy, kindled by the live coal of gratitude and devotion to the Author of all things. I should observe that he is not "orthodox" ', *GEL*, i. 123.

190 *On the whole . . . the question of questions*: from Carlyle, *On Heroes, Hero-Worship and the Heroic in History* (1841), Lecture II ('The Hero as Prophet').

What we call 'Formulas' . . . in this world: from *On Heroes*, Lecture V ('The Hero as Man of Letters').

192 *Perhaps few narratives . . . in our day*: from Carlyle, *Past and Present* (1843), ch. 3 ('Gospel of Dilettantism').

German Wit: Heinrich Heine

This is the longest of four articles on Heine which George Eliot wrote in 1855–6. The others appeared in the *Leader*, Sept. 1855 and Aug. 1856, and the *Saturday Review*, Apr. 1856. 'German Wit: Heinrich Heine', *Westminster Review*, lxv (Jan. 1856), 1–33.

193 *'Nothing', says Goethe . . . laughable'*: Goethe, *Die Wahlverwandtschaften* (*Elective Affinities*, 1809), Part ii, ch. 4 ('From Ottilie's Diary').

194 *Chamfort*: Sebastien Roch Nicolas Chamfort (1741–94), French man of letters.

amiable-looking pre-Adamite amphibia . . . their kindred: Richard Owen (1804–92), naturalist and friend of Lewes, supervised the construction in 1854 of models of prehistoric creatures for Crystal Palace Park in south London. They are still there.

195 *Reineke Fuchs*: Goethe's version (1794) of the medieval beast epic *Reynard the Fox*.

196 *Micromégas*: Voltaire's imitation of *Gulliver's Travels* published in 1752.

197 *Jean Paul*: Johann Paul Friedrich Richter (1763–1825), known as Jean Paul, German satirist and rhapsodist, a favourite of Carlyle's.

198 *Barclay's treble X*: strong beer brewed by Barclay, Perkins & Co.

Shakespearian wit: The Two Gentlemen of Verona, I. i. 108.

Hamburgische Dramaturgie: by Gotthold Ephraim Lessing (1729–81), German dramatist and critic.

200 *Phidian statue*: Phidias (*c*.500 –*c*.430 BC), Greek sculptor.

201 *Talents*: Matthew 25: 14–30.

  1799: actually 1797.

204 *Wie mächtig . . . langgesuchte Liebe*: 'No matter how strongly my proud spirit puffs itself up, a humble hesitation often grips me when in your sweet familiar presence' (first extract). 'And ever I wandered after love, ever after love, but I never found love, and I turned round for home, ill and sad. Then you came towards me, and oh, what swam in your eye was the sweet, long-sought after love' (second extract).

206 *Varnhagen*: Karl August Varnhagen von Ense (1785–1858), German diplomat and writer, whom Lewes and George Eliot knew.

207 '*Paris vaut bien une messe . . . Berlin vaut bien une prêche*': Paris is worth a mass; Berlin is worth a sermon.

209 *Johnson's advice to Hannah More*: in Hester Thrale Piozzi, *Anecdotes of Samuel Johnson* (1786).

212 *his book on Börne*: Heine's biography of his rival satirist Ludwig Börne (1786–1837).

215 *Spontini, or Kalkbrenner*: contemporary composers.

226 *Short swallow flights . . . skim away*: Tennyson, *In Memoriam*, xlviii. ll. 15–16.

227 *She dwelt alone . . . The difference to me*: slightly misquoted from Wordsworth, 'She dwelt among the untrodden ways' (1800), ll. 9–12, beginning 'She lived unknown . . . '

228 *Kennst du die Hölle . . . verdammen*: Know'st thou not Dante's Hell, the terrible *terze rime*? Whomever the poet has imprisoned within those no God can save. No God, no saviour will ever free him from these singing flames! Take care that we don't condemn you too to such a hell.

229 'no end in wandering mazes lost': *Paradise Lost*, II. l. 561.

233 *Countess Hahn-Hahn*: Ida, Countess Hahn-Hahn (1805–80), prolific novelist.

Robert Browning's *Men and Women*

This review of Robert Browning's *Men and Women* was published in 'Belles Lettres', *Westminster Review*, lxv (Jan. 1856), 290–6.

234 *Heinsius*: Daniel Heinsius (1580–1655), Dutch classicist, editor of Aristotle's works.

235 *He stood . . . expect as much*: Browning, 'How It Strikes a Contemporary' (1855), ll. 23–35.

236 *Dogberrys*: from the foolish constable in *Much Ado About Nothing*.

242 *My perfect wife . . . rocks obstruct*: from 'By the Fireside' (1855), stanzas 21–2, 25–6.

The Antigone and Its Moral

This essay was published in the *Leader*, vii (29 Mar. 1856), 306.

243 *the Parthenon to Strasburg Cathedral*: A. W. Schlegel, *A Course of Lectures on Dramatic Art and Literature*, trans. John Black (London, 1815; reprinted 1861), 23. Schlegel actually compares the Pantheon to Westminster Abbey or St Stephen's, Vienna. In his notes for a lecture on Shakespeare, probably written in 1813, Coleridge 'borrowed' Schlegel's comparison of Sophocles and Shakespeare to the Pantheon and Westminster Abbey, adding York Minster for good measure, see *Coleridge on Shakespeare*, ed. Terence Hawkes (Harmondsworth, 1969), 109.

Hermanns and Böckhs: rival German philologists.

E'en in their ashes live their wonted fires: Gray's 'Elegy written in a Country Churchyard' (1751), l. 92.

244 Οὐ γάρ . . . 'φάνη *from Antigone*, ll. 456–7 (Not now, nor yesterday's, they always live, and no one knows their origin in time).

John Ruskin's Modern Painters, Vol. III

George Eliot reviewed John Ruskin's *Modern Painters*, vol. III, for 'Art and Belles Lettres', *Westminster Review*, lxv (Apr. 1856), 628–33.

255 *They rowed her in . . . crawling foam*: from Kingsley's *Alton Locke* (1850), ch. 26.

The Natural History of German Life

This review of Wilhelm Heinrich von Riehl's books on German cultural history was published in the *Westminster Review*, lxvi (July 1856), 51–79.

260 *a 'Bradshaw'*: railway guide, after George Bradshaw's monthly railway guides.

261 *Even one of the greatest painters . . . ornaments*: William Hol-
man Hunt (1827–1910) exhibited this painting at the Royal
Academy in 1852.

L. E. L.: Letitia Elizabeth Landon (1802–38), magazine poet.

263 *Opera peasants . . . indignation*: Ruskin, *Modern Painters*, vol.
IV (1856), part v, ch. 19.

Luckie Mucklebackit's cottage: in Scott's *The Antiquary* (1816).

264 *Mrs Plornish's colloquial style*: in Dickens's *Little Dorrit*,
being published in monthly parts from Dec. 1855 to June
1857.

'Boots': probably Cobb, the bootblack in Dickens's Christmas
story 'The Holly-Tree Inn' (1855).

265 *Eugène Sue's idealized proletaires*: Eugène Sue's best
known novel of Parisian low life was *Les Mystères de Paris*
(1842–3).

altruism: word coined by Auguste Comte and introduced into
English usage by Lewes in his *Comte's Philosophy of the
Sciences* (1853).

artificial system of culture: a reference to the Young England
group of Tories led by Disraeli.

268 *Lusatia*: area around Dresden.

270 *the three Bessies*: cf. Chad's Bess and Timothy's Bess in *Adam
Bede*.

272 *worse hands*: in Scott's *Guy Mannering* (1815). Cf. Mr Tulliver's litigious behaviour in *The Mill on the Floss*.

Mr Saddletree: in Scott's *Heart of Midlothian* (1818).

282 *'familiar with forgotten years'*: Wordsworth, *The Excursion*
(1814), bk i. l. 276.

284 *Shetland Isles*: in Scott's *The Pirate* (1821).

285 *from Mathematics to Biology*: this analysis of the sciences is
close to Comte's and to Lewes's exposition of Comte in
Comte's Philosophy of the Sciences (1853).

293 *Ihr mögt . . . Philister-netzen*: 'You may unashamedly set up
a monument to me like the one to Blücher! He freed you
from the French; I freed you from the nets of Philistines',
Goethe, 'Sprüche' (*c*.1832), No. 112.

Silly Novels by Lady Novelists

This article was finished by 12 Sept. 1856 and was published in the *Westminster Review*, lxvi (Oct. 1856), 442–61. On 23 Sept. George Eliot began 'The Sad Fortunes of the Reverend Amos Barton', see Haight, *GE*, 210.

298 *'Compensation'*: novel by Lady Chatterton (1856).

299 *Ossianic*: after Ossian, legendary Gaelic bard whose poetry was 'discovered' and published in 1762 by James Macpherson.

   'Agapé': non-sexual love.

   Creuzer: Friedrich Creuzer (1771–1858), German philologist.

300 *'Laura Gay'*: anonymous novel (1856).

301 *Almacks . . . breakfasts*: Almacks was a suite of assembly rooms in St James's. Samuel Rogers (1763–1855) was famous for his breakfasts, attended by the rich and famous.

302 *'Rank and Beauty'*: anonymous novel (1856).

306 *'The Enigma . . . Wolchorley House'*: anonymous novel (1856).

308 *Spirit-rappers*: Spirit-rapping and table-tapping had become a craze following the visit to England in 1855 of Daniel Home, the American spiritualist.

310 *Pleaceman X*: unidentified.

313 *May Meetings*: annual meetings of the Church of England Missionary Society at Exeter Hall.

314 *Orlando*: in love with Rosalind in *As You Like It*.

   'The Old Grey Church': novel by Lady Scott (1856).

315 *life among the negroes?*: George Eliot reviewed Harriet Beecher Stowe's *Dred* in the same issue of the *Westminster Review*.

   Miss Squeers: in Dickens's *Nicholas Nickleby* (1838–9).

316 *Jannes and Jambres . . . Demetrius the silversmith*: 2 Timothy 3: 8 and Acts 19: 24ff.

317 *Was ihr den Geist . . . sich bespiegeln*: from Goethe's *Faust*, part i, 'Nacht', ll. 577–9 (What you call the spirit of the age is at bottom the gentlemen's own spirit, in which the age is mirrored).

   'Adonijah . . . Jewish Dispersion': novel by Jane Margaret Strickland (1856).

318 *Miss Sinclair*: Catherine Sinclair, popular novelist.

Dr Daubeny, Mr Mill, or Mr Maurice: Charles Giles Daubeny (1795–1867), novelist and writer on social affairs; John Stuart Mill (1800–73), philosopher; and Frederick Denison Maurice (1805–72), professor of theology at King's College London.

How I Came to Write Fiction

This is an extract from George Eliot's Journal, 6 Dec. 1857, *GEL*, ii. 406–10.

322 *at Tenby*: George Eliot and Lewes were at Tenby in July and August 1856. Lewes was zoologizing for *Sea-Side Studies* (1858), first published as a series of articles in *Blackwood's Magazine*, 1856–7 (where it more than once appeared adjacent to the anonymous 'Scenes of Clerical Life').

323 *September 22*: probably 23 September, see *GEL*, ii. 407 note.

324 *to print the story at once*: Blackwood wrote to Lewes on 12 Nov. 1856, 'I am happy to say that I think your friend's reminiscences of Clerical Life will do', but asked to see more before he would agree to publish. Lewes replied that his friend was 'discouraged' (15 Nov.), at which Blackwood waived his objection and agreed to publish 'Amos Barton' without seeing the rest of the series (18 Nov.). On 30 Jan. 1857 Blackwood told George Eliot that he had met Thackeray and told him he had 'lighted upon a new Author, who is uncommonly like a first class passenger', *GEL*, ii. 272, 273, 275, 291.

wrote me word: see Blackwood to George Eliot, 10 Feb. 1857, *GEL*, II. 293.

Agnes: Agnes Jervis Lewes, Lewes's wife, whom he continued to visit for his children's sake.

'*Mr Gilfil's Love Story*': the second of the *Scenes of Clerical Life*.

325 *one sunshiny morning*: 8 Apr. 1857, see *GEL*, ii. 409 note.

at Bulwer's: Bulwer-Lytton (1803–73), fashionable novelist and acquaintance of Lewes's.

'*Janet's Repentance*': the third (and last) of *Scenes of Clerical Life*.

Blackwood's want of sympathy: Blackwood wrote that he was 'rather puzzled' by the first part of the story, which was 'exceedingly clever', but not pleasant (a reference to the frank depiction of the drunken behaviour of Janet's husband Dempster), Blackwood to George Eliot, 8 June 1857, *GEL*, ii. 344.

The Sad Fortunes of the Reverend Amos Barton, Chapter 5

The opening part of ch. 5 of 'The Sad Fortunes of the Reverend Amos Barton', *Scenes of Clerical Life* (1858), first published in parts in *Blackwood's Magazine*, Jan.–Feb. 1857, is reproduced here.

326 *Mrs Farthingale . . . quite a 'character'*: i.e., the kinds of novel George Eliot had just attacked in 'Silly Novels by Lady Novelists'.

327 *quite ordinary tones*: cf. George Eliot's argument in her essay 'The Natural History of German Life'.

Adam Bede, Book II, Chapter 17

This is George Eliot's most famous utterance in favour of realism in art: *Adam Bede* (1859), bk ii, ch. 17 ('In Which the Story Pauses a Little'). The argument here is similar to that in her most recent critical writings, particularly her review of Ruskin's *Modern Painters*, vol. III, and her essay 'The Natural History of German Life'.

332 *fibre of sympathy*: see Introduction and the extracts from George Eliot's translations for the influence of Spinoza and Feuerbach on her view of ethics.

an Oberlin or a Tillotson: Jean Frédéric Oberlin (1740–1826), German Protestant pastor and philanthropist; John Tillotson (1630–94), Dean of St Paul's, famous for his sermons.

A Word for the Germans

This article was published in the *Pall Mall Gazette*, i (7 Mar. 1865), 201.

333 *'his girl, his fiddle, and his frisk'*: William Cowper, 'Table Talk' (1782), l. 237.

a small vagrant . . . casual halfpence: in *Middlemarch*, ch. 50, Mrs Cadwallader likens Will Ladislaw to 'an Italian with white mice'.

334 *Laputan*: a reference to part III of *Gulliver's Travels* (1736), 'A Voyage to Laputa', an island in the air where learned men are engaged in futile researches.

the sound British thinker . . . exists: Samuel Johnson, who, according to Boswell, kicked a stone to prove wrong Bishop Berkeley's idealistic philosophy of the non-existence of matter, saying, 'I refute it *thus*', James Boswell, *Life of Johnson* (1791, repr. 1969, ed. R. W. Chapman), 333.

335 *The Seventy . . . Greek*: the septuagint, the Greek version of the Old Testament and Apocrypha, was made *c*.270 BC by seventy-two translators.

336 *Without them . . . nowhere*: George Eliot is thinking of Strauss and Feuerbach, and of Strauss's predecessors in the eighteenth century, among them Reimarus and Eichhorn.

kein oberflächlicher Narr: Heine, *Die Romantische Schule* (1836), bk 1.

Address to Working Men by Felix Holt

The 'Address to Working Men, by Felix Holt' was published in *Blackwood's Magazine*, ciii (Jan. 1868), 1–11.

339 *future masters of the country*: when Disraeli's Reform Bill was passed in 1867, Robert Lowe announced that it would be necessary to 'compel our future masters to learn their letters', Arthur Patchett Martin, *Life and Letters of the Rt. Hon. Robert Lowe, Viscount Sherbrooke*, 2 vols. (London, 1893), ii. 323. George Eliot also believed, though in no such sneering spirit, that education was the key to the proper implementing of democracy, see her argument here and Introduction.

344 *duties*: the argument here is a culmination of George Eliot's ethical views, as informed by the thinking of Spinoza, Feuerbach, and Comte. What holds good for the individual—the moralizing of the affections, the acting out of sympathy for others who share our humanity—is applicable to social classes too.

345 *I was in an election riot*: the plot of *Felix Holt, the Radical* (1866) involves Felix getting caught up in a riot, trying to lead the rioters away to safety, and being wrongly accused of inciting them to riot.

347 *Hercules . . . filthy stable*: reference to the stables of Augeas which Hercules cleansed by turning the river Alpheus through them.

352 *Ambrose Paré*: Ambroise Paré (1510–90), French surgeon.

353 *Many of the highest uses . . . excellence*: George Eliot's portrait of the English aristocracy in *Daniel Deronda* (1876) is more critical than her argument here. In the novel she represents the English nobility as vicious and trivial.

Notes on Form in Art

'Notes on Form in Art' (1868), in a George Eliot notebook in Yale University Library, was first published in Thomas Pinney's edition of *Essays of George Eliot* (1963).

356 *The highest Form . . . all other phenomena*: the argument shows George Eliot's keen interest in the scientific work of her contemporaries, not least Lewes, whose physiological experiments were concerned with questions of form and function.

359 *Poetic Form . . . its growing life*: George Eliot here reformulates, in specifically scientific terms, the Romantic view, as expressed by Wordsworth, Coleridge, and German Romantic critics like the brothers Schlegel, of literature as organic form.

Harvey and Bichat: William Harvey (1578–1657), who first demonstrated the circulation of the blood; Marie François Xavier Bichat (1771–1802), French anatomist, admired by Comte and mentioned in *Middlemarch* as Lydgate's inspiration (ch. 15).

Aristotle's notion . . . coincide: in the *Poetics*. The Greek terms are anagnorisis (recognition) and peripeteia (reversal), and Aristotle's example of a play in which the two elements coincide is Sophocles' *Oedipus*.

THE WORLD'S CLASSICS

A Select List

MARY SHELLEY: Frankenstein
Edited by M. K. Joseph

PERCY BYSSHE SHELLEY:
Zastrozzi *and* St. Irvyne
Edited by Stephen Behrendt

SIR PHILIP SIDNEY:
The Countess of Pembroke's Arcadia (The Old Arcadia)
Edited by Katherine Duncan-Jones

CHARLOTTE SMITH: The Old Manor House
Edited by Anne Henry Ehrenpreis

TOBIAS SMOLLETT: The Expedition of Humphry Clinker
Edited by Lewis M. Knapp
Revised by Paul-Gabriel Boucé

Peregrine Pickle
Edited by James L. Clifford
Revised by Paul-Gabriel Boucé

ROBERT LOUIS STEVENSON: Kidnapped and Catriona
Edited by Emma Letley

Treasure Island
Edited by Emma Letley

BRAM STOKER: Dracula
Edited by A. N. Wilson

R. S. SURTEES: Mr. Façey Romford's Hounds
Edited by Jeremy Lewis

Mr. Sponge's Sporting Tour
Introduction by Joyce Cary

JONATHAN SWIFT: Gulliver's Travels
Edited by Paul Turner

IZAAK WALTON and CHARLES COTTON:
The Compleat Angler
Edited by John Buxton
Introduction by John Buchan

MRS HUMPHREY WARD: Robert Elsmere
Edited by Rosemary Ashton

OSCAR WILDE: Complete Shorter Fiction
Edited by Isobel Murray

The Picture of Dorian Gray
Edited by Isobel Murray

MARY WOLLSTONECRAFT:
Mary *and* The Wrongs of Woman
Edited by Gary Kelly

ÉMILE ZOLA:
The Attack on the Mill and other stories
Translated by Douglas Parmeé